ALSO BY LARRY LEHMER

The Day the Music Died: The Last Tour of Buddy Holly, the Big Bopper, and Ritchie Valens

BANDSTANDLAND

HOW DANCING TEENAGERS TOOK OVER AMERICA AND DICK CLARK TOOK OVER ROCK & ROLL

LARRY LEHMER

Mechanicsburg, PA USA

Published by Sunbury Press, Inc.
Mechanicsburg, Pennsylvania

www.sunburypress.com

Copyright © 2019 by Larry Lehmer.
Cover Copyright © 2019 by Sunbury Press, Inc.

Sunbury Press supports copyright. Copyright fuels creativity, encourages diverse voices, promotes free speech, and creates a vibrant culture. Thank you for buying an authorized edition of this book and for complying with copyright laws. Except for the quotation of short passages for the purpose of criticism and review, no part of this publication may be reproduced, scanned, or distributed in any form without permission. You are supporting writers and allowing Sunbury Press to continue to publish books for every reader. For information contact Sunbury Press, Inc., Subsidiary Rights Dept., PO Box 548, Boiling Springs, PA 17007 USA or legal@sunburypress.com.

For information about special discounts for bulk purchases, please contact Sunbury Press Orders Dept. at (855) 338-8359 or orders@sunburypress.com.

To request one of our authors for speaking engagements or book signings, please contact Sunbury Press Publicity Dept. at publicity@sunburypress.com.

ISBN: 978-1-62006-013-1 (Trade paperback)

Library of Congress Control Number: 2019937717

FIRST SUNBURY PRESS EDITION: March 2019

Product of the United States of America
0 1 1 2 3 5 8 13 21 34 55

Set in Bookman Old Style
Designed by Crystal Devine
Cover by Terry Kennedy
Edited by Lawrence Knorr

Continue the Enlightenment!

This book is dedicated to
Tony Mammarella,
the longtime producer of
Bandstand and *American Bandstand*,
the creative force behind the scenes
whose patience and expertise
were critical to the show's success.

CONTENTS

Acknowledgments ix

Introduction xiii

Chapter 1: Bunny's Story 1

Chapter 2: WFIL's Folly 3

Chapter 3: The "Beehive of Juvenile Jive" 19

Chapter 4: The Fall 32

Chapter 5: The New Guy 39

Chapter 6: It's My Show Now 50

Chapter 7: Branching Out 66

Chapter 8: The Philly Scene 85

Chapter 9: A Time of Reckoning 109

Chapter 10: Whatever It Is . . . He's Got It 122

Chapter 11: The Regulars 144

Chapter 12: New Directions 168

Chapter 13: Paying the Piper 207

Chapter 14: Payola 241

Chapter 15: Landing on His Feet 278

Chapter 16: Flying Solo 292

Chapter 17: Farewell to Bandstandland 310

Epilogue 326

Bibliography 358

About the Author 365

ACKNOWLEDGMENTS

"That book isn't going to write itself, mister!"

My mother didn't actually say that to me, but I could certainly imagine those words of "encouragement" from her every time I took a break from this project. And there were plenty of breaks in my pursuit of the story that resulted in *Bandstandland*. However, I've since learned that my writing rhythms are not that unusual for nonfiction writers: work intensely for a few months then clean house, mow the lawn, bake pies and play Sudoku for a few months.

Consider that the first interview for this book was done in March 1999. The last was done in June 2017. It's impossible to determine how much actual work on this book was done in that 18-year span, but I'm sure it was considerable, if intermittent. And, although it's my name on the cover, this book was truly a team effort.

From my first trip to Philadelphia in 1997 to the time I sent the completed manuscript to my Pennsylvania publisher, I was privileged to meet and engage with many of the people most intimately connected to *American Bandstand* in its Philadelphia years, including WFIL-TV staffers, people who performed or danced on the show and fans from around the country.

Davey Frees was the first person to help shape this book. He spent several hours with me around his kitchen table and in his "Bandstand room," sharing stories from his decades-long role as founder of the American Bandstand Fan Club. Davey put me in touch with Bunny Gibson, one of the more popular regular dancers on the show in the early 1960s. Bunny, one of the kindest souls on the planet, also shared behind-the-scene *Bandstand* stories when she wasn't delivering sandwiches to the homeless or sharing her passion for dance with young Southern California children.

Bunny, in turn, put me in touch with Pam Mammarella, the daughter of longtime *Bandstand* producer Tony Mammarella. This book is dedicated to Tony Mammarella who really was the glue that held the show together from its inception under Bob Horn through Dick Clark and right up to the payola years, when he left the show. Mammarella was working on a book about his years on the show, provocatively titled *Bandstand Off My Back*, at the time of his death. I am profoundly grateful to the Mammarella family for allowing me to use portions of his unpublished manuscript in this book.

I am also grateful for assistance from the family of original *Bandstand* host Bob Horn. Bob Horn's son, Peter, provided much helpful biographical information and grandson Rob Graham provided photographs.

Many co-workers of Bob Horn and Dick Clark at WFIL-TV shared stories with me, including Walter Beaulieu, Marvin Brooks, John Butterworth, John Carlton, Ralph DiCocco, Eleanor Faragalli, Tom Foley, Shelly Gross, George Koehler, Hank Latven, Marie K. Pantarelli, Bill Russell, Max E. Solomon, Allen Stone, Bill Webber, Marge Weiting and Ed Yates.

I learned much about the Philadelphia music scene from rock pioneer Charlie Gracie, radio legend Ed Hurst (whose show provided inspiration for the original *Bandstand*), record promotion man Al Kelly, Bill Haley & His Comets bass player Marshall Lytle, the family of *Bandstand* photographer Edgar Brinker, Philadelphia ad man Les Waas and Baton records owner Sol Rabinowitz.

Stories (and photos) from the dance floor came from Mary Ann (Colella) Baker, Dorothy (Bradley) Boring, Frank Brancaccio, Earle Drake, Jack Fisher, Rick Fisher, Bunny Gibson, Myrna Horowitz, Diane Iaquinto Celotto, Ron Joseph, Ed Kelly, Stan Marks, Bob Tharp, Barbara (Marcen) Wilston and Chuck Zamal.

Among fans sharing their stories were Bruce Aydelotte, Pamela Beasley, Marian Driscoll, Charlie Heffernan, Robert Nash, Ray Otto, Kathryn Sacchetti and Linda Zimmerman.

Thanks to Steven M. Bob of The Enterprise Center and Paul W. Hermannsfeldt of *Architectural Record* for historical details about the WFIL-TV facility.

INTRODUCTION

Despite the efforts of all the people previously mentioned, there wouldn't be a book if it weren't for the helpful folks at Sunbury Press—Lawrence Knorr, Terry Kennedy and Crystal Devine.

Thanks, also, to my wife, Linda, whose patience is finally rewarded now that *Bandstandland* has advanced from project to a proper book.

Larry Lehmer
March 2019

INTRODUCTION

The fall of 1957 was a transition time for me.

For starters, I was changing schools. After seven years with pretty much the same kids at my elementary school, I was joining kids from five other schools for our junior high years.

Although the big transition to girls, Friday night dances and high school sporting events were a couple of years in our futures, I could already feel the tides turning.

Baseball, the mainstay of my youth to date, was fading fast. It was becoming obvious as I matured that my batting prowess, fielding range and lack of arm strength doomed me to years of bench duty should I continue. On the other hand, the music I was hearing was pretty cool.

My station of choice (and that of most of my friends) was KOIL in Omaha, "the mighty 1290." One afternoon each week was devoted to KOIL's Top 50 countdown. Not content to follow the national trend to Top 40 radio (which originated in Omaha), KOIL went 10 tunes better, and I eagerly awaited the weekly countdown to learn how my favorite tunes were faring.

KOIL was pretty much the fuel that was driving my move from baseball to music appreciation that fall of 1957 but, unbeknownst to me, another potent force was on the horizon.

Omaha, long promised a new TV station to compete with our CBS and NBC stations, was finally getting one. On Sept. 17, 1957, KETV, Channel 7, finally hit the airwaves, forcing adjustments to rabbit ears and hoity-toity rooftop antennas across the Omaha-Council Bluffs metroplex as the American Broadcasting Company finally arrived.

As a young boy, I was eager for the steady diet of westerns that ABC promised, shows like *Maverick, Wyatt Earp, Tombstone Territory,* and *Zorro. Ozzie and Harriet* and *The Real McCoys* would be welcomed as well.

We were much less interested in the ABC daytime schedule, which, for all practical purposes didn't really exist. We quickly outgrew *The Mickey Mouse Club* and the half-hour of reruns of kids shows that followed, before giving way to dinnertime news.

Most of us did arrive home in time, however, to catch the tail end of something that looked to be promising, a show called *American Bandstand*. It had a likable young host, featured dancing teenagers that looked a lot like those I saw in my neighborhood and school and, most of all, played the music I really liked.

The network thought enough of the show to launch its daytime schedule with it. Unlike the other networks, ABC had zilch on its schedule before *American Bandstand* came on at 3 P.M. Eastern Time. That was an hour earlier for us in the Midwest, when we were still in school. Still, we caught enough of the show to know we liked it. So, apparently, did others. It became one of ABC's top attractions, holding its own financially even against the prime-time offerings.

As much as I liked *American Bandstand* as a youngster, it's not the reason I wrote this book.

I didn't watch *American Bandstand* for the dancing, although the moves I saw on that black and white TV screen in my family living room were far superior to almost anything I saw in my admittedly limited exposure to actual live rock & roll dancing in my community.

I watched *American Bandstand* (and Clark's follow-up *Saturday Night Show*) for the music and to actually see the artists that were performing it. Sure, I was disappointed that the singers were lip-syncing instead of actually singing, but at least I got to see them. That was a relative rarity in those days.

But, as my musical tastes evolved, I found myself less interested in what I was seeing on *American Bandstand* and more interested in what I was hearing on non-Top 40 radio. More to the point, I couldn't figure out why a disc jockey like Alan Freed (who was connected to more of the music I liked) got tossed because of the federal government's payola hearings and why a bland TV disc jockey like Dick Clark seemed to come out of the same hearings unscathed, indeed, seemed to grow even more popular.

INTRODUCTION

That was the basic question I sought to answer.

To answer that question, I started looking into the history of *American Bandstand* and its predecessor, the local Philadelphia show *Bandstand*. I learned a lot through my research and interviews —surprising facts, some shocking details but all leading to what was ultimately a simple answer to my basic question.

As Philadelphia record veteran Harold Lipsius put it, Alan Freed was the street hustler and Dick Clark was the altar boy. But, as the title of this book suggests, there's much more to how Dick Clark created a safe public space for teenagers while realizing his own personal business ambitions.

Bandstandland is not an actual place. It's more a state of mind. Dick Clark did not create the show that became *American Bandstand*, but he did create Bandstandland. He took a popular Philadelphia TV dance program, scrubbed it up a bit and sold it to a national audience.

The two words that best describe *American Bandstand*'s Philadelphia years are "squeaky clean." Clark set the tone with his neatly pressed dark suits, perfectly combed hair, Pepsodent smile and "Aw shucks" style of speaking. The kids who danced on the show mirrored the genial host's conservative dress and displayed the same decorum one might expect at a Sunday morning church service.

Bandstandland was a safe haven, a place where good friends could gather and have a good time, free of school rules and parental interference. It all seemed so natural.

But Bandstandland was far from natural. It existed only within the walls of WFIL-TV's Studio B—and in millions of living rooms across the land—for an hour or so every weekday afternoon. Bandstandland was, in reality, a contrivance, an alternate universe created and cultivated by Dick Clark.

That's not to minimize its importance. From its humble beginnings to its last gasps, the show ran for more than 35 years, a tribute to Dick Clark's business acumen, stubbornness, and resilience. Even though it's been gone from the airwaves for nearly as long as it was on, it still has a dedicated core of followers and fans. That's impressive.

So, here it is, the results of thousands of hours of reading and research and hundreds of hours of conversations and interviews. Welcome to Bandstandland.

CHAPTER 1

BUNNY'S STORY

The bus was late.

The wind was picking up, swirling leaves along the sidewalk and tugging at the hem of the woolen skirt that marked its wearer as a Holy Cross girl.

She barely noticed as she checked the time, again and again. Where is it, she wondered. I'll be late. For Bunny Gibson, that would be catastrophic. A nation was waiting.

But here she was, standing on a New Jersey street corner, cradling the hatbox-shaped luggage that contained the trappings of her alternate world and facing straight into the wind, anxiously searching for the bus that would whisk her from the drudgery of her everyday world.

She jammed her hands into the waistband of her skirt, hiding them from passersby. A few days earlier, her trademark long fingernails were the envy of classmates. When a typing teacher suggested her work might improve if she got rid of them, she balked. As nuns dragged her down the hall by her hair, she protested. When the pinking shears reduced them to nubs, she was devastated.

Why me, she complained.

She was a decent student, one of the top spellers in her class. She was one of the top candy sellers in the school's fund-raising drive. She never caused trouble at school, at least not intentionally. Still, she couldn't please the nuns.

Her sweaters were too tight. She was boy crazy. A brazen brat.

She *did* like Elvis, but who didn't? She loved wearing her mother's jewelry and probably wore too much makeup, but that was no reason for kids to snicker and make cruel remarks about her.

And she loved to dance.

She imagined herself on the dance floor as she boarded the bus for Philadelphia.

After settling in at the back, she opened her luggage and began her daily ritual.

She carefully wriggled out of her Holy Cross uniform and slipped into a more fashionable skirt and blouse. She teased her hair into a towering bouffant, alternately backcombing and spraying. She applied makeup as best she could as the bus bounced down city streets.

The driver did a double take as she left the bus and scrambled onto the train for the final leg of her journey.

By the time the train pulled back into the daylight a block or two from its West Philadelphia destination, she was nervous in anticipation. She glanced down at the tan brick building and saw a long line stretching at least a block, boys on one side, girls on the other. She allowed herself a smile. She was almost there.

Bouncing down the stairs from the elevated station, familiar voices called out.

"Hey Bunny."

Her joy was evident as she bounced right past the line of teenaged boys.

"How's it going, Bunny?"

"Bunny, save a dance for me."

She was beaming as she reached the head of the line and flashed a card at a guard.

Barely glancing at the card, he pushed open the big green door.

"Nice to see you, Bunny. Come on in."

She catches her breath and steps into the building, where some of her friends have already gathered.

"I thought you'd never make it," Eddie Kelly says as he greets her. They work their way toward the rows of bleachers and a dance floor flooded with light.

"I'd never miss this," she says.

She's home, on *American Bandstand*.

CHAPTER 2

WFIL'S FOLLY

American Bandstand was really cool in 1960. Bunny Gibson knew that.

But what she and millions of avid *Bandstand* fans around the nation didn't know was that the show was a broadcasting fluke. Teenagers of the early 1950s were very different from Gibson's peers, yet it was teens of that earlier era that set the stage for the most successful music program in television history, rescuing a floundering Philadelphia TV station in the process.

Despite general manager Roger Clipp's best efforts, WFIL-TV was lagging badly behind the competition in Philadelphia in 1952. But dealing with problems came with the territory, Clipp knew, and who better to solve them than himself.

His no-nonsense approach had propelled him up the ranks in his two decades in broadcasting. As general manager of WFIL radio and television, the TV station was already turning a profit, even though it had been on the air for less than five years.

Clipp, a former banker and accountant, had been with the station from the beginning, ever since Walter Annenberg obtained a license for the 13th television station in the United States. Annenberg was intent on adding to his Triangle Publications media empire, which already included WFIL radio and the *Philadelphia*

Inquirer newspaper. Annenberg was building on the business started by his father, Moe.

Moses L. "Moe" Annenberg started his career working for newspaper tycoon William Randolph Hearst in Chicago.

"The Annenbergs were very skillful circulation people," said Temple University historian Mark Haller. "(They knew) how to write a headline, how to scoop the other paper, but (they were) also very skillful at the street war. They hired gunmen. They hired sluggers to ride on their trucks to threaten newsboys with getting beaten if they didn't push the Hearst papers."[1]

Slate columnist Jack Shafer described Moe Annenberg as a "congenital criminal." A reported 27 news dealers died in the Chicago circulation wars and Moe Annenberg is said to have hired Lucky Luciano to help him when he moved to New York City.

In the early 1920s, Moe Annenberg bought the *Racing Form* and became a major owner of the General News Bureau, a move that allowed him to monopolize the nation's race wire and effectively made him a partner of the nation's bookies.

Moe Annenberg made millions off his race wire, enough to buy the *Philadelphia Inquirer* newspaper for $15 million in 1936. When Moe Annenberg was sent to prison in 1940 for tax evasion, his 32-year-old son, Walter, took over as editor and publisher of the *Inquirer*.

Moe Annenberg became ill in prison and he was paroled two years into his three-year sentence. He died at age 64 in June 1942 from a brain tumor just 39 days after his release.

Thrust into the role of leader of his father's media empire, Walter Annenberg began what would be a life-long campaign to rehabilitate the family name.

In 1944, he established the first magazine aimed at teenagers, *Seventeen*. In 1946, he paid $1.9 million to buy WFIL radio. In 1947, he combined his family's business assets into a new corporation, Triangle Publications.

Walter Annenberg was also interested in expanding into the mostly experimental world of television. Despite advice to the contrary, Annenberg applied for a television license for Philadelphia and in 1947 he got it.

Annenberg plunged into the television business full force, ordering the construction of the first building in America to be used

---

1. *Philadelphia Inquirer*, January 7, 1990.

specifically for television. The wily Annenberg had the WFIL-TV studios built in West Philadelphia, next door to the Philadelphia Arena, a property he had snatched up in June 1947, giving the station ready access to the area's major sporting events, formerly the province of rival WPTZ.

He ordered state-of-the-art equipment. Electrical outlets offered 110 or 220 volts every few feet and scenery could be hung from the wood framework that made up the interior walls of the tan brick building that sat at the foot of the 46th and Market stop of the Market-Frankfort el and the bus lines of the Philadelphia Transit Company.

The building took nearly two years to complete, but Clipp didn't wait, putting together a hodge-podge of a schedule to accommodate the station's status as the first independently owned affiliate of the fledgling ABC-TV network. The station hit the air part-time on Sept. 13, 1947, from the engineer's office of WFIL radio on the 18th floor of the Widener Building in downtown Philadelphia. The strength of the WFIL signal interfered with that of WPTZ, just a few blocks away, forcing owners of Philadelphia's 10,000 television sets to repeatedly readjust their finicky new entertainment devices.

Bright 5,000-watt lights were installed, creating an instant studio. Broadcasters struggled to keep from being blinded by the lights as sweat dripped down their noses in the 120-degree heat.

After a short time, the studio was moved to a mailroom on the 11th floor. Although the new studio was larger, it presented its own problems. Mail equipment had to be removed each day and cameras were forced into the hall to provide wide shots, causing complaints from other businesses on the floor.

Although WFIL-TV had to operate from the makeshift Widener Building facility for about a year, the station started showing a profit after just six months under Clipp's direction. Clipp persuaded the Democratic Party to move its 1948 national convention to Philadelphia from San Francisco because of the television exposure. The Republican Party soon jumped on board, too.

By the time WFIL-TV made the move into its new studio in early 1949, Clipp's programming was coming together. He persuaded Temple University professor John Roberts to do newscasts. The new studio included a kitchen where the accident-prone Mary Durante entertained family cooks. *The Philadelphia Catholic Hour* was the first religious program to be regularly televised in the

United States. *Phil and the Three Cheers* was a studio show pretending to originate from a neighborhood soda fountain.

WFIL veteran Jack Steck was assigned the task of producing the *TV Teen Club*, hosted by Paul "Pop" Whiteman from an Armory at Broad and Calla Hill streets. There kids could dance and vote on the *TV Jury* segment.

The husband and wife team of Howard and Mary Jones hosted the *Farmer Jones Program* at 6 A.M. daily from Wiffletree Farm (named from WFIL), their farm in rural Montgomery County.

Still, Clipp's station was dead last among the three Philadelphia television stations in the ratings for the coveted late afternoon audience. Clipp knew the sparse audience was weary of the British movies holding that spot. In 1951, he replaced them with *Parade of Stars*, a program built around video music films hosted by the station's sports director, Tom Moorehead. Moorehead was replaced by popular radio disc jockey Bob Horn in the summer of 1952.

Bob Horn's Bandstand was a popular late-night program on WFIL radio, but that popularity didn't transfer to television

Working from a bare-bones set made up to resemble a living room for *Parade of Stars*, Horn sat in a comfortable-looking chair across from a guest in a similar chair and chatted with them before having them lip-sync to their latest record. Horn proudly boasted that WFIL was a "45 station" at a time when many stations hadn't yet made the transition from 78 rpm discs. Interspersed among the interviews and lip syncing were music clips.

Horn's musical expertise allowed for some lively banter with guests, which was the highlight of the show, but the bulk of the show was filled with the musical clips called Snaders.

Snaders were produced specifically for television, but they proved to be unpopular with viewers. What few advertisers WFIL had corralled were fleeing to the other Philadelphia TV stations, WCAU and WPTZ, and ratings were plummeting even further.

Station owner Annenberg was growing impatient with the slipping ratings. "Something has to be done," he told Clipp.

How about a televised version of that 950 Club show over at WPEN radio? That seems to be pulling in some big numbers.

Indeed, the *950 Club* had been Philadelphia's top-rated radio program almost from the day it first aired in 1946 from the 22nd floor of a downtown office building, hosted by the curious combination of Joe Grady and Ed Hurst.

The paternal Grady frequently took to playing the organ or reciting poetry while the more youthful Hurst was a wise-cracking sidekick. The show was especially popular with teenagers, who initially filled the halls outside the studio and eventually were invited in, where they started dancing.

They also loved joy-riding the elevators and clogging the building's mail chutes, which eventually got Grady and Hurst kicked out of the building, a fortuitous move as it turned out.

WPEN's owner, the Sun Ray Drug Company, secured space behind a popular luncheonette and constructed an auditorium studio to accommodate the popular radio duo.

Between songs, teens were interviewed on air. A roll call feature was added, allowing youngsters to proudly proclaim their high school affiliation to classmates listening at home or in their cars. Some of the regular attendees received *950 Club* membership cards, guaranteeing admittance. Anyone could buy "950 sockaroos," which were the perfect footwear for dancing on the show.

Celebrity guests like Frankie Laine, Tony Bennett, and Eddie Fisher dropped by to lip-sync their songs and to be interviewed. When Johnnie Ray popped into town to promote his weepy *Cry,* a crowd estimated at 3,500 jammed into the studio.

The younger Hurst saw the potential television held for their show. WPEN had allowed the duo to briefly take their dance show format to WPTZ-TV in 1950 as a means of promoting the radio show.

Clipp gave Hurst a call.

"Can you and Grady be in my office at 8:45 on Monday morning? I think I have an interesting proposition for you."

Grady and Hurst showed up at WFIL for the meeting, right on time. Clipp got right to the point.

"You're going to do a simulcast. It starts in two weeks. Name your salary demands and call me back."

The 26-year-old Hurst was elated at the opportunity to break into television, but Grady had a glum look on his face.

"What's your problem?" Hurst asked.

"You don't think 'PEN's gonna let us out, do you?" said Grady, aware that the duo had recently signed a new contract to continue the *950 Club* on WPEN

"Are you kidding?" said the dumbfounded Hurst. "Would they stand in the way of our progress?"

"I'll tell you what. I'll let you go in and tell management we want to leave," responded Grady.

Hurst did exactly that, walking into the station manager's office and giving him their two weeks' notice. We'll get back to you, the manager said.

That evening, an angry WPEN general manager Bill Sylk called Annenberg.

If you attempt to raid our talent, we'll take a million dollars of Sun Ray Drug billings from the Inquirer and put them in the Philadelphia Bulletin.

Grady and Hurst received a telephone call from Clipp the next morning.

"We find that this is not the propitious time to bring you boys over here," Clipp said. "We'll have to start our own."

With Grady and Hurst unavailable, Clipp and station manager George Koehler considered their options. Fortunately, there were plenty. The demanding Clipp earlier had assigned Koehler the task of recruiting a diverse, young staff of college graduates who looked good enough to make the transition to television, in case that part of the operation continued to grow.

Koehler and his wife had first sorted through applications strewn about their bedroom floor. Then Koehler conducted telephone interviews, eventually inviting the more promising candidates in for personal interviews. A handful of the invitees joined the staff.

Clipp and Koehler considered them all for the new show—including Dick Clark, Joe Novenson, Jim McCann and Jim Gallant. In the end, though, they settled on a more senior staff announcer, Bob Horn.

In many ways, Horn was an odd choice to front a television show aimed at teenagers. He was a pudgy, 36-year-old married father of three whose musical tastes leaned heavily to jazz. But he also had nearly two decades of radio experience, most of it in Philadelphia, he was well-connected within the music business and he had proven popular with the younger set in his two years at WFIL.

It was blind luck that first put Horn in front of a microphone.

Born Donald Loyd Horn in Pine Grove, Pennsylvania, Horn disliked his first name so much that he went by Robert Horn while attending Reading High School. Horn was a poor student, dropped out of school and took a job as a delivery boy for a laundry.

WFIL'S FOLLY

Horn got his first experience behind a mike when he stepped in for a friend who developed stage fright at WRAW radio in Reading. That improbable debut led to a staff position at WRAW and in 1935 Horn married his childhood sweetheart, Jeanette Castor.

In 1939, Horn moved to WCAM in Camden, N.J., followed by a move to WIP in Philadelphia, where he was "Bob Adams," the popular host of the late-night *C'Mon 'n' Dance Show* which was the most popular late evening program in Philadelphia according to a 1944 survey.[2]

For years, Horn deejayed skate parties at roller rinks and developed a taste for jazz. In 1945, he teamed with Nat Segall, owner of the Downbeat Club, to promote jazz programs, including one at the Philadelphia Academy of Music that featured a young Sarah Vaughan and South Philadelphian "Dizzy" Gillespie.

Horn's after-hours jazz lifestyle put a strain on his marriage. He and Jeanette divorced in 1945 and Jeanette returned to Reading with their children, Peter and Claudia.

In 1946, Horn met dancer Ann Davidow, who had recently returned from a South Pacific USO tour with Carl Reiner. Impatient with his slow career path in Philadelphia, Horn accepted a job with KMPC radio in Beverly Hills, California. En route to California Horn and Davidow took a detour and were married in Rosarita, Mexico.

Horn's California radio career was brief. He resigned in 1947 after what he called "the station's interference with newsroom activities." Horn later testified at an FCC hearing that KMPC owner G.A. Richards ordered him which items to include on the morning newscast and how they were to be played. That included playing up Jewish-sounding names in a story about black marketing convictions and leaving out comments unfavorable to the Ku Klux Klan.

Horn and his wife settled into a rented brownstone in South Philadelphia as he worked as a free-lance disc jockey on WPEN and WIP. Night club owner Frank Palumbo installed radio lines in his Ciro's club in the summer of 1947 to allow Horn to do remote broadcasts on WIP from the lounge on Saturday nights. Ads for WIP in trade publications described Horn as an "Ace Philly Spinner."

Horn and Segall formed the Keystone Amusement Agency just weeks before Ann Davidow Horn gave birth to a daughter,

---
2. *Pulse of New York* survey taken by Dr. Sydney Rostow, 1944.

Marianne, on Christmas Day 1947. The Horn family relocated to Beverly, N.J.

On April 12, 1948, Horn again walked away from a program because of outside interference. He quit WIP's late-night *Danceland* program when sponsor Adams Clothes insisted on selecting the records to be played each night. By January 1949 Horn had been added to the WPEN staff, with a nightly 9 to 11 P.M. show called *Bandstand*. Horn made his first venture into television that spring, as host for the short-lived *Laugh, Grin & Giggle* on WCAU-TV.

In August 1950, Roger Clipp lured Horn to WFIL with a late-night radio show sponsored by Esslinger Beer. The presence of the 34-year-old Horn gave WFIL some star power to go with the young staff TV station manager George Koehler was putting together. With the success of the *Bob Horn Bandstand* every weeknight from 11 P.M. to midnight, Clipp added Horn to the 11 P.M. to midnight slot on Saturday nights as well with *Valley Forge Stardust Time*.

Horn's TV duties included occasional slots during the day. In 1952, Clipp moved Horn into the 3–4 P.M. *Parade of Stars* slot, replacing Moorehead, and added a 15-minute music clip spot called *Hollywood Varieties* at 2:15 P.M.

Around the same time, the late-night *Bob Horn Bandstand* radio program was moved to the late afternoon. This created a logistical problem for Horn since the television studios were in West Philadelphia and the radio studios were still downtown. After Horn concluded his television duties at 46th and Market, he had to dash downtown to do his radio program. This earned him the nickname "Rapid Robert."

Horn allowed himself 2 minutes and 35 seconds to cover the 75 yards from the WFIL-TV studios to the el steps and up the platform. During the 10-minute ride to 13th Street, he studied his radio script. He raced up the escalator, through Wanamaker's Department Store to the Widener Building and caught an elevator to the 18th-floor radio studios, usually arriving just a minute or two before air time.[3]

Horn's popularity led to the formation of the Bob Horn Fan Club, some 400 members of which honored the WFIL DJ with a picnic at Woodside Park on August 2, 1952.

---

3. *TV Digest*, August 9, 1952.

WFIL'S FOLLY

Woodside had linked with WFIL in the summer of 1952, with personalities Leroy Miller, Chief Halftown and Marge Weiting appearing at various events, including the sixth annual WFIL Day on June 21. Although more than 100,000 discounted tickets had been distributed for WFIL Day, Horn's August picnic was even more special. It was the climax to Bob Horn Week, which marked his 18 years in radio. His fan club presented him with a gold record to mark the occasion.

Despite Horn's radio popularity, WFIL-TV remained a dismal last in the ratings during his afternoon slot. With rumors of changes spinning through the office grapevine, Horn prepared for the worst when he was summoned to a meeting with Clipp and Koehler on a sultry late summer day in 1952.

* * *

Hey Bob. How's it going?
Not bad. What's up?
We've got a proposition for you. Instead of showing those lousy film clips every afternoon, how about a dance show for kids? Like that radio show up the street.
Sounds great. When do we start?
In a few weeks. Oh yeah, one more thing. Lee Stewart will be your partner. It's going to be a two-man show.
Um, uh. Lee?
Yep. It's a done deal. He's bringing a sponsor.
I see. (Oh great).

* * *

In the nearly two decades Horn had been in the broadcast business he'd never had a partner. Now, the WFIL-TV brass were telling him, he'd be tethered to a cohort on the air at least two hours every day. Lee Stewart, no less.

Stewart had become a local celebrity with his manic on-air sales pitches for Muntz television sets.

Earl "Madman" Muntz, a former used car salesman, high school dropout and self-taught engineer, turned to making television sets in the post-war era. His $99.95 specials were engineered to work within eyesight of the transmitters, which he figured was just fine for his urban markets. The flamboyant Muntz sold TVs the way he sold cars—loud and fast.

"I'd love to give these away, friends, but my wife won't let me," he'd deadpan to the camera. "So I buy 'em retail, and sell 'em wholesale."

Stewart, a 41-year-old with a big nose and thick, horned-rim glasses, followed Muntz's lead, delivering a frantic line of patter. He was a comical, and successful, salesman in Philadelphia. Madman Muntz was the sponsor Stewart would bring to the show.

WFIL staffer Shelley Gross, a distant relative of Stewart's, minced no words in describing the diminutive, bespectacled pitchman. "He was a strange little guy," he said.

WFIL intended Horn and Stewart to be the televised version of Grady and Hurst, with Horn playing the straight man to the hopefully comedic Stewart. The station began touting the duo through local newspapers and on-air plugs. Staff member Nat Elkitz started building a set for the program, which would originate from the station's new Studio B, a 3,100-square-foot addition that was the crown jewel of the station's recent expansion, which also brought the radio studios to the West Philadelphia location.

Elkitz and his crew constructed a stage for Horn and Stewart that would let cameras shoot over the heads of the dancing teens that were expected to fill the studio. A canvas backdrop painted to resemble the interior of a record store was resurrected from the Paul Whiteman show and the name *Bandstand* was added to a faux window. Pennants of local high schools were attached to curtains flanking the stage and a lectern resembling a store counter was built, with space in front to list the top 10 tunes of the week. Collapsible bleachers were installed on one side of the studio, giving it the appearance of a high school gymnasium.

Horn also worked to develop a memorable opening to the show.

"He went out and bought a toy," said production staffer Ed Yates. "It was maybe 3½ feet wide by 5 feet long and it had figures in it and the arms were moving and they were hitting drums and seemed to be blowing horns."

Tony Mammarella, a native South Philadelphian who had produced Horn's ill-fated Snaders show, was named producer of the show.

Horn spent the weeks before the first show booking guests, selecting records and looking for ways to fill dead time between records. The entire Snaders library was placed at his disposal, but Horn looked to innovations used on Grady & Hurst's radio show instead.

The first show was scheduled to air from 3:30 to 4:45 P.M. on Monday, October 13, 1952.

Teenagers would be admitted free of charge, with most of the audience expected to come from three schools that were within walking distance of the studio. West Catholic School for Girls was just around the corner, the West Catholic School for Boys was two blocks to the west and West Philadelphia High School was a mere six blocks away.

As the show's debut approached, Horn got nervous.

What if no kids show up?

The record promotion men with whom Horn regularly did business offered to fill the studio with kids. No, Horn said. If the kids want to come, they'll come.

* * *

Not everyone was convinced that WFIL-TV's new venture would be a hit. Indeed, some referred to the launching of *Bandstand* as "FIL's Folly."

Station manager George Koehler described the show as "a time eater," a generous description according to other staffers.

"The people in the studio thought this was a waste of time," said Yates, one of the show's directors. "What are you gonna do with a bunch of kids dancing? So what? The directors didn't care much for the thing and I know the engineers thought it was stupid. . . . It was a pain in the neck to them."

Cameraman Bill Russell shared Yates' opinion.

"Someone asked me what I thought of the show," Russell said. "I said it might last three weeks."

Russell's perspective was as good as anyone's in the still-evolving TV business. A former motion picture operator for Goldman Theaters in Philadelphia, Russell moved into television when WFIL hired him as a dolly pusher for the bulky two-man Fearless Crane camera.

"They'd hire you if you were breathing," Russell says of those early days.

WFIL-TV was definitely a fly-by-the-seat-of-your-pants operation in the early days.

"We would say, well let's give this a shot and see what happens," Russell said. "We didn't know. Nobody knew. There wasn't anybody in television who could tell you. They never did it before. It was a lot of trial and a lot of error, but really, when you think about it, not too many errors."

WFIL staff announcer Bill Webber said many of the errors came at the most inopportune times, during sponsor-paid commercials.

During pitches showing the ease of operation of storm windows, the windows would refuse to budge. During one vacuum cleaner commercial, a white powder was sprinkled over a dark rug and sucked up by the powerful machine, only to have the bag inside the vacuum burst, filling the studio with a white cloud. Lee Stewart's Kissling sauerkraut-in-a-bag demonstration was a disaster when the contents exploded all over the studio when punctured with a fork.

Just lighting a set proved to be an adventure.

"We used to say that they could have a very small staff because the lighting was so imperfect that you looked different each time you went on," said staff announcer Shelly Gross.

It was decided early on that *Bandstand* would be a three-camera show—two working from the flanks of the dance floor and the Fearless Crane in the center, cranked to its full height to allow clear views of Horn and Stewart over the dancers that were between them and the control room. Above the control room windows, was another row of windows where sponsors could watch the show. To the side of the sponsors' booth was an area for station executives.

Audiences entered the studio through a door near the control room. Monitors were hidden to keep the kids from watching themselves on camera. A band of 2-inch-wide tape on the floor separated the dancers from the camera crew. The building's air conditioning was cranked up to help offset the tremendous heat generated by the studio's lights.

Cameraman Marvin Brooks recalls a factory worker who entered the building wearing a plastic security badge. "The badge melted under the lighting," he said.

The WFIL crew's work was further complicated by having to set up for *Bandstand* at the same time they were working on programs from other studios. While half the crew worked the smaller studios, the other half was preparing Studio B.

Just before 3:30 P.M. on Monday, October 13, 1952, the WFIL crew took its positions and Mammarella began choreographing a brand-new television show. The director and engineer gently turned dials and whispered commands from the control booth at the rear of the studio as Horn and Stewart took the *Bandstand* stage for the first time, staring into the stark emptiness of Studio B, sweat beading on their foreheads from the dozen or so man-made suns suspended from the rafters of WFIL's center ring.

Air time. No kids.

Hi, I'm Bob Horn and welcome to Bandstand, something new for television.

A quick explanation. Introductions. Come on in kids. Cut to commercial.

Welcome back to Bandstand. The only show of its kind in the Delaware Valley, where you can be the star. Speaking of stars, here's one of the biggest.

Roll one of those damn Snaders. Cue up another. Hold it! What's this? A couple of kids in the back of the studio? And look. Some more are right behind them. Hallelujah!

One of the things we'll be doing on Bandstand is introducing you to some of the fine teenagers in the Philadelphia area. Here's a young girl who was just entertaining us with her dancing during the last number. Your name is? . . . Blanche McCleary. Nice to meet you, Blanche . . .

As more kids climbed the bleachers and spilled onto the dance floor, the director switched between shots of kids chatting in the bleachers to dancers jitterbugging in front of a delighted Horn and Stewart. By the time the show wrapped up for the first day, about 50 kids had shown up, most of them girls.

Not bad for the first show, but no indication of things to come.

Within three days, the show's executives were faced with the daunting challenge of accommodating 1,000 kids who wanted into a studio that could accommodate just 250 of them.

"We had kids lined up around the building, waiting to come in," said Marie K. Pantarelli of the WFIL traffic department.

"The kids loved it," said Koehler.

Within a week, WFIL issued a press release, noting that Horn was being rewarded with the new title of director of recorded music for WFIL and WFIL-TV.

Although the WFIL hierarchy was ecstatic over the show's immediate popularity, Horn advised caution. Let's let the show evolve, he said. Let's listen to the kids.

It was obvious from the start that Horn and Stewart weren't the stars of the shows. Nor were the guest stars. It was the dancing kids that viewers wanted to see. The girls who walked out of their West Catholic High School classrooms, stopping to plop their books on a car fender while they put on makeup and rolled up their skirts before standing in line to get on the show. The boys who looked so suave and cool in their six-button Bennies.

Also obvious was the fact that they simply couldn't handle 1,000 kids a day. Some rules would have to be established.

Mammarella suggested that they admit the kids to the studio in two shifts, in effect doubling the studio audience. Security guards were also added to the entrance to control the flow of kids into the building. To get an even gender balance for the show, two lines were formed—one for boys and one for girls. A dress code was instituted—no dungarees, pedal pushers or open sport shirts

Within a month, Horn decided to put together a committee of regulars to lend a hand in the studio when the show was on the air. These regulars would help enforce the rules and guaranteed an audience each day. Horn and Mammarella carefully observed the dancers for several weeks before hand-picking the first committee of 12 teenagers.

As the show grew in popularity, things got even more hectic for the WFIL production crew.

"We had a skeleton crew that did it all," said Pantarelli, who worked in the station's traffic department. "We doubled up on a lot of jobs."

The fledgling ABC television network relied heavily on its Philadelphia affiliate for programming and technical support.

"They sent a lot of talent to use the WFIL studios," recalled Pantarelli, who spent many hours typing up program logs and running off copies on a ditto machine.

Sports programming from the adjacent Arena filled a good chunk of the WFIL schedule. Wednesday night fights went to the other ABC affiliates each week and the station broadcast the Eastern Hockey League home games of the Philadelphia Ramblers.

For veteran ad salesman Max E. Solomon, the growing popularity of *Bandstand* made his job easier. As the No. 3 station in the Philadelphia market, Solomon and the rest of the ad salesmen faced stiff challenges daily.

"Everything was a hard sell in those days," said Solomon, whose career with WFIL dated to 1929, when it was just a part-time radio station. "We had to sell price. We gave you more time for the same amount of money."

WFIL'S FOLLY

In its first few weeks, *Bandstand* was kept on the air by Solomon's shrewd selling.

"We sold packages of advertising and we included spots in *Bandstand*," Solomon said. "*Bandstand* wasn't selling so fast. We didn't have enough advertisers to warrant us carrying the show. We had to stuff *Bandstand* into packages so that we'd have a reason to have the program."

But *Bandstand* soon started pulling its own weight with its unique programming. Although demographics had yet to become part of the advertisers' lingo, prospective sponsors recognized the sales potential of all those teenagers who settled in front of a television screen every weekday afternoon.

One by one, they added their names to the WFIL client list for *Bandstand*. Kissling Sauerkraut. Lem Pudding. Coca Cola. Cheerios. Tastykakes. Bosco Chocolate Flavored Syrup.

WFIL was soon airing two minutes of commercials after every two dance numbers to accommodate all the sponsors. Some of the show's more popular elements—the roll call, guest spots, interviews, and special promotions—were squeezed in, giving the show a rapid pace that only added to its excitement.

Bandstand's popularity extended anywhere the WFIL signal could be picked up. Soon, kids from as far away as Pottstown, Pennsylvania, Wilmington, Del., and Trenton, N.J., were writing to request tickets to *Bandstand*.

A ticket policy was established, where committee members were guaranteed admittance, but others were granted either by mail or were handed out in the studio for a later date. A few tickets each day were held back for out-of-towners, who frequently arrived by school bus.

"We could have had 20 busloads a day," Mammarella said of the heavy demand.[4]

Horn and Mammarella diplomatically fended off suggestions for improving the show from the station's inner circle.

Triangle owner Walter Annenberg's wife suggested the kids wear tuxedos and party dresses and that maybe station officials could get rid of those unsightly bleachers and replace them with some nice cocktail tables. A former *Paul Whiteman Show* director suggested that a Glenn Miller tune every day would be a good idea. Another suggestion was to cover those teenage blemishes with some strategically applied makeup.

---

4. *Bandstand Off My Back*, unpublished manuscript by Tony Mammarella.

Sponsors were always ready to have the teens try their products on the show as well.

"All the things that kids are not, they wanted the kids to be," Mammarella said.[5]

Fortunately, station officials adopted a hands-off attitude and let the show develop and mature from within. As ratings soared and sponsors climbed aboard, the show took the next obvious step. On January 19, 1953, it expanded by 30 minutes, with an air time from 3 P.M. to 4:45 each weekday.

John Carlton, a staff announcer who hosted WFIL's *Movietime USA* show that filled the time slot immediately before *Bandstand*, reaped an unexpected benefit from the show's success.

"Every bartender in Philadelphia knew me," Carlton said. "Not because I'd been to every bar, but they'd turn on the last 10–15 minutes of the movie so they wouldn't miss all the pretty little girls on *Bandstand*."

Nobody was talking about Snaders anymore.

---

5. Ibid.

CHAPTER 3

THE "BEEHIVE OF JUVENILE JIVE"

Ed Hurst was livid.

Within weeks after his employer, WPEN, had told him that he and partner Joe Grady couldn't be the hosts of *Bandstand*, he had to watch from the sidelines as Bob Horn took the show into the same living rooms every day where Grady & Hurst had reigned for years with their *950 Club*.

"The whole idea was swiped from us," Hurst said

Horn, at least, recognized Hurst's value. To dump partner Stewart, Horn called Hurst and offered him the sidekick position. Hurst, aware that WPEN would not allow such a move, called his partner, Grady.

"Listen, if you don't get off your ass and do some television, I'm going to work with Horn," Hurst told Grady.

WPEN would eventually relent—after *Bandstand* was established— allowing Grady and Hurst do a televised popular music dance show, but only between 11 A.M. and noon on Saturdays on WPTZ, channel 3.

The introduction of Grady & Hurst to the televised Philadelphia musical scene was of little concern to Horn, who by then was firmly entrenched atop the ratings in the late afternoon weekday slot.

Television sets were still considered a luxury in 1953, so many viewers huddled around sets in firehouses, department stores, and record stores every afternoon to watch the kids on *Bandstand*.

Horn had taken the *950 Club* radio format and given it the "sight value" coveted by viewers and sponsors. He gave the show a few touches of his own, too. He allowed kids in the studio to interview singers in other cities by telephone. He started a Rate-a-Record segment where kids would evaluate new records. When introducing the live musical guests, Horn would loudly let the audience know "We've got company!" He frequently tossed Tastykakes to his audience, asking, "Is everybody ready?"

Tony Mammarella, the show's producer, also enjoyed a connection with the kids as he roamed the studio, pockets stuffed with safety pins and paper clips to fix a broken belt or mend a bra strap and small change for a kid's bus fare home.

For the musical guests, *Bandstand* was *the* place to plug their latest recordings. Joni James once missed a train from Atlantic City and paid $34 to take a cab to Philadelphia in order not to miss the show.[1]

When bandleader Ray Anthony's recording of "Bunny Hop" first broke on the West Coast in early 1953, he made a quick trip to Philadelphia where Horn used the song in a *Bandstand* dance contest.

It was the opportunity of a lifetime for young Harvey Sheldon.

Sheldon, a 15-year-old with show business aspirations, left his final-period study hall at Lincoln High and hopped on the el to dance on the first *Bandstand* show. Young Sheldon began dressing like Horn—wearing flat-front pants, button-down shirts, a tie and a vest to the show. He and his dancing partner, Dimples (Irma Eininger), were sensations when they started bunny hopping through Studio B.

A reporter and photographer from the *Philadelphia Inquirer* did a lengthy feature on Harvey and Dimples and the dance craze they had helped foster. Anthony took the couple to New York, where they demonstrated the dance to enthusiastic crowds, earning a cover story in *Parade* magazine in the process.

The *Philadelphia Bulletin* reported that "5,000 high school kids now have membership cards which admit them on two specific

---

1. *Philadelphia Bulletin*, January 16, 1953

afternoons each week." There was talk of network interest in the show's format.

Philadelphia Bulletin writer Rex Polier described the show as "the city's beehive of juvenile jive." Some kids were reported to have even dropped out of school to attend the show.

Horn stayed on top of the popular music scene to ensure he got the most popular recording artists on his show. When a group from nearby Chester, Bill Haley & His Comets, broke out nationally with their up-tempo "Rock This Joint," Horn booked them on *Bandstand*.

WFIL tacked another 15 minutes to the show in the spring of 1953, moving the starting time to 2:45 P.M., giving it a full two hours on the air each day.

The sales department no longer had to pack *Bandstand* commercials into packages of ads built around other shows. Indeed, a "10 spot package" that guaranteed five *Bandstand* commercials and five others on other programs of the station's choosing, was a hot seller since *Bandstand* was typically oversold and now enjoyed a waiting list of potential sponsors.

Horn proved to be a tireless promoter of the show.

From his small office, Horn's booming voice could frequently be heard in the announcers' lounge, which was just a thin partition away.

"It got very colorful at times," said staff announcer John Carlton. "You weren't sure who he was talking to but when he'd yell and scream at somebody and say, 'All right, Doris,' you had an inkling that it might be Doris Day. It wasn't unusual to see a famous recording star walking down the hall."

Horn entertained a steadily growing parade of song pluggers, bearing gifts to persuade Horn to play their label's songs on *Bandstand*. Besides his office, Horn also conducted business at a tiny pub just down the street, the Brown Jug.

"A tremendous amount of business was done there," said WFIL staff announcer Bill Webber.

In May 1953, less than eight months after taking to the air, *Bandstand* gave plaques to winners of the first WFIL *Bandstand* Poll. Frankie Laine showed up in person to pick up his most popular male vocalist award.

TV Guide, the newest publication in Walter Annenberg's Triangle Publications empire, was barely a month old when it described *Bandstand* as the place where "Teenagers let loose" in its sixth issue on May 8, 1953.

Recalling the success of the Bob Horn Fan Club picnic the previous summer, Horn decided to take *Bandstand* back to Woodside Park for a remote broadcast in the summer of 1953.

Woodside Park, once a prime entertainment center for Philadelphians, was on the decline in the 1950s. WFIL clinched the deal by guaranteeing 1,000 admissions, twice the average for a normal Tuesday, with the station handling all promotion and ticket sales.

For $2, a person got into the park for the entire day and received tickets to five rides and a box lunch containing a ham and cheese sandwich, Tastykake, soft drink, and apple. All proceeds went to the Philadelphia Children's Heart Hospital.

At least 1,000 tickets were sold in the studio alone; another 7,000 were sold by mail. The park's concessionaire ran out of food and soft drinks within an hour after the park's opening. A second supply of food and drinks was gone by 1 P.M. as over 12,000 people brought the park to life, a sight not seen since its heyday decades earlier.

Before *Bandstand's* afternoon broadcast from Sylvan Hall, people amused themselves with volleyball, potato races, and a celebrity softball game.

In the evening, Horn took *Bandstand* into the Arena adjacent to the WFIL studio for a special evening performance, aimed more at parents than kids. They ran out of food there, too, as a larger-than-expected crowd turned out.

With the expansion of his *Bandstand* television duties in the first hectic months of its successful start, Horn was ready to let something go. It would be the *Bandstand* radio show, he decided.

Horn was only a part-time presence on the show, anyway. From the start of the television show, after WFIL finally consolidated its radio and television operations into the 46th and Market facility, the bulk of the *Bandstand* radio show was handled by Dick Clark, one of the young staff announcers George Koehler had hired.

Although Clark was the primary host on radio's *Bandstand*, Horn started and closed the show, using the first few minutes each day to hype his television show. The intrusion was a major annoyance to young Clark, who clearly wanted to establish his own identity with the station.

In late summer 1953, Clark got his wish. WFIL announced that Horn would soon give up the radio show and Clark would take over. Horn moved into the 11 A.M.-1 P.M. radio slot at WFIL, which gave him ample time to prepare for each afternoon's show.

While the kids were lining up along Market Street, Horn would be finalizing the list of records he would play each day. If he needed to have a disc pulled from the station's 40,000 record library, he would consult with record librarian George Smith.

Just before air time, Horn and Mammarella would have a quick meeting in the control room with director Ed Yates to go over last-minute details. Horn would deliver his records and playlist and review the day's schedule of commercials as a projectionist lined up films and slides to make for a smooth operation.

* * *

Bandstand celebrated its first birthday in a big way on October 12, 1953.

The audience lined up for a piece of birthday cake and an autographed record. Horn's musical guests included pop singers Eileen Barton and Georgia Gibbs and a couple of local boys, Mike Pedicin and Bill Haley.

Bandstand had been expanded again, to 135 minutes each day (2:45–5 P.M.), and spawned copycat shows around the country, many hosted by disc jockeys who visited Horn's show to see what made it so popular.

The show's influence on record sales was incredibly strong.

After spawning a national craze with the bunny hop, Horn tried to do the same with Sammy Kaye's "Dance of Mexico." The disc sold well in Philadelphia, some 65,000 copies, but stiffed everywhere else.

The kids dancing on the show also became well-known to viewers. Several of the regulars had fan clubs of their own and Horn started delivering fan mail to the young stars during the show.

Nevertheless, the popularity of the young dancers could be a problem.

"They begin to think the show can't go on without them," Horn told Harry Harris of the *Evening Bulletin*. "Then we have to clamp down by taking away their membership cards for a while."

Barbara Marcen, who was a *Bandstand* regular from late 1953 through late 1958 and won a jitterbug contest, agreed that being a card-carrying member of "the Committee" had its perks.

"You didn't have to wait in line. You could just walk right in," Marcen said. And, even though the show was split into two sessions with lines as long as two blocks for each session, "the ones in the Committee could stay for the whole session."

Marcen, who was taught how to dance by the show's other regulars, learned something else from the other Committee members—how to jockey for position before the cameras.

"When you'd see the little red light [on the camera], you'd know which camera was on."

Cameraman Marvin Brooks said that the teen dancers were a challenge for the crew.

"They fought constantly," Brooks said. "Not fist fighting. They would push and shove a little bit. . . . The director would say 'Look, I'm getting tired of seeing so and so.' But the kids learned how the tally lights worked on the cameras so they would be able to know which camera was on the air. . . . If we would punch a camera on one side, they would drift over and get in front of that camera."

Marcen, who attended Southern High School—the same school that Fabian, Frankie Avalon, and Mario Lanza attended—also attended many dances in the Philadelphia area, at churches and public venues like the Carman Roller Skating Rink, where Horn held weekly hops. Her celebrity as a *Bandstand* dancer even led to opportunities outside of Philadelphia, some organized by Horn.

"They would drive us over to Atlantic City to dance there," Marcen recalled. Other teens "would ask for autographs. They sort of looked on us as celebrities."

Mary Ann Colella, another regular in the early *Bandstand* era, said Horn made sure that Committee members had rides to and from dances.

"He wanted us to enjoy ourselves and we did," Colella said, adding that Horn expected the Committee to help him keep things orderly on the show.

"We had rules and regulations. You couldn't get into trouble. No fighting. I had a girl come up there, I think she went to my school that started a fight. She ripped the blouse I had on. . . . I got suspended. I had to beg Bob Horn to let me back in."

* * *

After a solid year devoted to building up *Bandstand*, Horn wanted a break.

THE "BEEHIVE OF JUVENILE JIVE"

Shortly after the show passed the one-year milestone, Horn took a three-week vacation to Canada. Wary of leaving the show in the hands of co-host Stewart, Horn came up with an alternative.

Tony Mammarella had been WFIL's substitute host for just about every show in the station's lineup and had recently been assigned full-time hosting duties of the *Hopalong Cassidy* program that immediately followed *Bandstand*. For the three weeks that Horn would be gone, Mammarella would select the records, interview the guests and kids and read the commercials while Stewart would continue in his second banana role.

To not lose contact altogether with his young audience, Horn arranged to phone Mammarella each day and file a vacation update.

The arrangement didn't sit well with Stewart, a longtime acquaintance of Mammarella. The relationship between Stewart and Horn was more strained than ever on Horn's return.

Roger Clipp and George Koehler summoned Mammarella to the front office.

You're the producer, Tony. What can we do about these guys? Why can't they get along?

Stewart isn't funny, Mammarella explained. Plus, he's a drag to the entire operation. He and Horn can't agree on which records to play or which guests to invite.

Maybe we ought to replace him. There are lots of good, young staff announcers who would jump at the chance. Bill Webber. Jim Gallant. Johnny Carlton. Dick Clark. Maybe we should make a switch.

I don't think so, Mammarella said. The show doesn't need two hosts. Bob already has the regulars who are there every day. That's enough co-hosts.

OK, Tony. Thanks. We'll work this out.

Mammarella left the meeting fully expecting that a replacement would soon be named for Stewart. Indeed, Stewart was soon gone, shuffled off to a morning show called *Lee Stewart's Coffeetime*, where Stewart could proffer his comic skills unfettered by an uncooperative sidekick.

Still, Horn was concerned. He told Mammarella he feared that the station might try "to force Dick Clark down his throat" as his co-host.

"Bob figured they would try to get Dick on the show," Mammarella recalled. "For a while, Dick would play it cool as No. 2

boy until he felt he knew enough to run the show by himself. Then they could bounce Bob out completely and it would become Dick Clark's *Bandstand*. That thought haunted Bob Horn and he stayed awake nights thinking of ways to prevent Clark from horning in on *Bandstand*."[2]

Within a few months, however, Stewart and *Coffeetime* were gone and Horn was still working alone.

* * *

After 20 years in broadcasting, Bob Horn was a star. He was ready to live like one.

That meant finding a nice place where he could settle in with wife Ann and their three young daughters. A place that provided all the modern comforts of 1950s life without the noise, clatter and clutter of the city, a place where young girls could breathe sweet air, run through lush green fields, walk safely to school and mature into fine young women.

He found his paradise just 20 miles away, in Levittown.

Levittown was unlike any other community in Pennsylvania. In fact, the only other place in all of America that came close was the *other* Levittown, in Long Island, N.Y.

It was in New York that brothers Alfred and William Levitt refined their vision of the perfect planned community. Philadelphians eager to flee the city joined the lines around the Levitt's model homes, some people waiting hours for just a glimpse.

The Levitts finished a house every 12 minutes, as their crews combined the construction techniques Bill Levitt learned as a U.S. Navy Seabee with the assembly line techniques pioneered by Henry Ford.

Levittown included schools, churches, and shopping areas. Streets were designed so that the heaviest traffic went around each section, rather than through it. No child ever had to cross a major road to get to a school in Levittown.

It was an idyllic life in Levittown, where as many as 10 bread and milk companies offered porch-side delivery and Fuller brush salesmen were greeted as benevolent visitors. It was a community of one-car families, stay-at-home moms, babysitting clubs and where young girls got demerits in gym class for having dirty sneakers.

---

2. *Bandstand Off My Back*, unpublished manuscript by Tony Mammarella.

THE "BEEHIVE OF JUVENILE JIVE"

It was here that Horn moved his family, to 66 Sweetgum Road in the relatively ritzy Snowball Gate section of Levittown.

Horn bought his wife a station wagon so she would fit into the suburban lifestyle. The kids were entertained by Rin, the boxer who was the family's pet. Horn mowed his own lawn, while the girls entertained themselves with their own swing set in the backyard.

Horn allowed himself a few indulgences, too. His Cadillac was prominently parked in the WFIL parking lot most afternoons. He bought a 42-foot Richardson cabin cruiser, which he appropriately dubbed *Bandstand*. The boat was moored at Stone Harbor, N.J., where the Horns had a summer home. Horn loved to fish and spent many a weekend patrolling the Chesapeake Bay with his good friend, Ray Jackson, owner of the Carman Roller Skating Rink. He also found time to pursue his passion of hunting each fall and described himself as a "better-than-fair" marksman.

* * *

As *Bandstand's* popularity grew, it went through the growing pains of success.

For Hank Latven, it meant new duties.

Latven was a relative newcomer to the WFIL-TV staff in 1953. The ex-Marine had returned to his native city after attending college in Alabama and was lucky enough to land a job in the WFIL mailroom.

But the station added a new line to Latven's job description, that of station doorman. With throngs of kids wrapping around the block every weekday afternoon, someone needed to regulate the flow into the building, so Latven left the mailroom every afternoon and assumed his position.

Two other mailroom employees were also drafted into security duty, Marvin Brooks and Bob Hopkins. The husky Hopkins was physically well-suited for the role. Another of his many duties at the station was donning a gorilla suit for countless skits. Brooks, who later became a cameraman for *Bandstand*, was much smaller, weighing in at around 140 pounds.

"The girls from West Catholic High School got out early and were the first in line," Brooks said. "When I opened that door, they ran right over me. So I had to open the door and step out of the way, fast."

Bandstand policy dictated roughly equal numbers of girls and boys in the studio, but the girls' line was much longer than the boys' every day. The regulars flashed their passes for easy entry, but the remaining crowd needed to be screened to make certain they measured up to the show's standards.

Horn and Mammarella early on adopted a policy that boys must wear sports coats and ties to gain admission. Gum chewing was not allowed in the studio and dancers were expected to behave like ladies and gentlemen.

Once the studio was filled, the security crew patrolled inside.

Although Studio B had been constructed to handle *Bandstand*-sized crowds of up to 250, the rest of the building had difficulties handling twice that many teenagers for the split shifts of Horn's show.

"The building wasn't designed for something as big as that," said Marie K. Pantarelli, who could hear the throngs of youngsters from her office. "They were chirping outside like magpies. You could hear them all the time."

Video engineer Walt Beaulieu remembers the girls congregating around the drinking fountain.

"They were something else," Beaulieu said. "The four-letter words would jump out . . . They weren't using 'Goddam', it was 'fuck this' and 'fuck that'."

Station facilities manager John Scheuer barred the youngsters from the building's basement, saying in a memo "they have defaced the men's room down there and other parts of the building."

Horn, learning of the edict, fired off his own memo:

> I also learned that getting a drink of water was forbidden. In view of your 'no toilet' edict, I can see your thinking on the 'no water' rule.

Bandstand was formally recognized as the best music show in Philadelphia on March 3, 1954, by *TV Guide*. Of the 14 awards given, WFIL-TV picked up just one other, Shelly Gross as the best commercial announcer.

Horn was invited to take his show to a network. But, after a weekend trip to New York City to discuss the matter, Horn rejected the offer, saying the New York studio simply wasn't big enough to handle his show.

By the summer of 1954, another 15 minutes had been tacked on to the show, which now ran from 2:30 to 5 P.M., five days a week. That summer also brought a shift in the kind of music Horn was playing on his show.

The music business was changing rapidly. In the five years following World War II, the number of radio stations in the U.S. more than doubled and with recording restrictions that were in place for some of the war years no longer in effect, the market for recorded music grew exponentially.

Because the national networks were shifting their focus from radio to television, many radio stations were forced into filling airtime themselves. Records were the answer. Independent radio stations for the first time could select from a diverse range of tunes that made it possible to target audiences that were previously ignored.

The rise of independent record labels paralleled the rise of independent radio stations, a trend that clearly bothered major labels like RCA Victor and Columbia, who had previously enjoyed what amounted to a monopoly.

Record company executives were no longer able to dictate which songs or which artists would dominate sales. That role was increasingly shifting to the men on the radio who played the discs. Whether known as platter pilots, wax whirlers or disc jockeys, these men behind the mikes were becoming the power brokers of the music industry.

The major labels responded by having their artists record new versions of songs that were selling well on independent labels, then sending out legions of promotion men to radio stations to encourage them to play their records.

This was often successful, but many disc jockeys weren't biting on these "cover" versions. Horn was among those who preferred the originals.

Horn's transition coincided with a 1954 hit song called "Sh-Boom." The version recorded by a black group called the Chords was a national rhythm and blues hit. But a white Canadian group known as the Crew Cuts was topping the pop charts with their cover version of the song, a song that Horn was preparing to play on *Bandstand*.

But Horn had wisely engaged the services of a young teenager, Jerry Blavat, to serve as something of an ombudsman for the kids who danced on the show.

Young Blavat was one of *Bandstand's* earliest stars, gaining a following with the dance skills that allowed him to win just about every dance contest he entered until Horn pulled the plug. But Horn saw Blavat's value to the show and hired him at $15 a week to oversee the Committee and offer advice from the teenagers' point of view, like on which records to play. It was Blavat who steered Horn to the Chords' version of "Sh-Boom."

In August 1954, Horn booked Woodside Park for his third annual picnic. This time, however, the gates opened an hour earlier and concessionaires were better prepared for the 7,500 (including more than 30 busloads of fans from Pennsylvania, Delaware, and New Jersey) who crowded through the gates, despite gray skies and occasional rain.

For the first time in the park's history, it was closed to the general public. Bill Haley & His Comets headlined a program that included evening radio and television programs in addition to the remote broadcast of *Bandstand*. Horn used the proceeds to buy a mobile X-ray unit for Eagleville Sanatorium in nearby Montgomery County.

The *Bandstand* host seemed to be popping up everywhere.

On the show's second anniversary, Gene E. Stout, Philadelphia editor of *TV Guide*, dropped by to present Horn with a cake. Horn showed up at the festival at St. Christopher's Hospital for Children and Police Commissioner Thomas J. Gibbons honored Horn for his support of the department's drive to recruit policewomen. *Bandstand* fans contributed $500 to the March of Dimes to combat infantile paralysis and "O Dem Golden Slippers" was the theme on New Year's Day as a special Mummers' float saluted *Bandstand*.

But, as big as Horn and *Bandstand* were in Philadelphia, they hadn't made that big of a stir nationally.

Billboard magazine published an in-depth article about TV disc jockey programs that hinted that Chicago was the epicenter of such programming.

While acknowledging that *Paul Dixon's Song Shop* was the first of the genre, launching in 1950 from Cincinnati, the *Billboard* article went on to say that four DJs from Chicago—Dave Garroway, Howard Miller, Ray Rayner, and Jim Lounsbury—were the most successful.

Horn wasn't totally ignored by the article. His name appeared almost as a footnote, lumped in with eight other DJs called "successful" in the last paragraph.

In January 1955, Horn took a week off the show, again turning hosting duties over to Mammarella. On one program, a bunch of buddies enlisted in the Air Force together and headed to Lackland Air Force Base in Texas where they went through basic training as "the *Bandstand* flight."

Horn capped his fourth annual picnic at Woodside Park on July 28, 1955, with a half-hour live *Bandstand from Woodside* program that evening and turned over the day's proceeds to the Philadelphia Chapter of the Pennsylvania Association for Retarded Children.

In the first three years of *Bandstand*, it was estimated that 250,000 teens had appeared on the show. Joe Grady and Ed Hurst, who had continued at WPEN with their *950 Club* as Horn's popularity soared with a show they had inadvertently helped create, had had enough. Not satisfied with their weekly dance party at WPTZ, the duo bought out their contract with WPEN and negotiated a deal with WPFH-TV in Wilmington, Del., that gave them a daily dance show that went head-to-head with Horn's *Bandstand*.

As they contacted local record distributors to line up talent for their October 3, 1955, premiere, Horn called the same distributors, "urging" them to send their stars his way as his show planned a third anniversary special the same day. Most of the distributors saw things Horn's way, making for a rocky debut for the *Grady & Hurst Show*.

Horn and Mammarella persuaded WFIL-TV brass to try a New Year's Eve broadcast of *Bandstand* to ring out 1955. The regular *Bandstand* set was set aside for the occasion and replaced by a more formal setting. Tables were grouped around the dance floor for the semi-formal affair and each girl was given a corsage as she arrived in a taxicab provided by the station. The regulars danced to Billy Butterfield's Orchestra and Horn revealed the winners of *Bandstand* awards for top song of 1955. the top group and top male and female singers.

Not surprisingly, Horn was named the Krakauer Beneficial Association's "man of the year" for 1955.

The year 1956, would not turn out nearly as well.

CHAPTER 4

THE FALL

"Want to buy a lion cub?"

Bob Horn paused just slightly to consider the question before responding.

"That's a helluva idea. I wonder what one costs?"

Tony Mammarella was half-kidding with the question, prompted by an ad placed in *Billboard* magazine by a Louisiana snake farm. His boss' response sent him scurrying to a phone.

Yes, we do, indeed, sell lion cubs, he was told. They cost $75, but you'll have to wait. The cub won't be born for a day or two and it will be at least two weeks before we can ship it to you.

Horn bought the cub.

The plan was simple. Horn and Mammarella would take care of the lion at the station, feeding it and playing with it on the air. Before they would turn the lion over to the Philadelphia Zoo when it was 5 months old, they would conduct a contest, inviting viewers to mail in suggested names for the lion.

Set man Nat Elkitz built a cage and tucked it into a corner of Studio B. During the day, the lion roamed free in Horn's office before it was taken to the studio for the show. It was locked in the prop room overnight.

The lion was an immediate hit. Horn and Mammarella fed the lion, variously referred to as Baby and Whatchamacallum, on-air.

Although the lion was treated well when Horn was around, the same could not be said at night.

"The crew would tease the lion and they would say 'We have company,' which was Bob Horn's phrase for a guest shot," recalled staff announcer John Carlton. "They would tease the lion and repeat that phrase. Finally, they brought the lion in loose one day and it just happened to be before a guest shot. Horn said, 'We've got company.' The lion almost ate him."

Horn routinely took the lion home on weekends. It was kept in a utility room where Horn's daughters and the family dog could play with it. The lion grew quickly on its diet of round steak, vitamins, milk, and water and was the size of a German shepherd by the time the contest was over in June.

The contest drew 70,000 entries and Frankford High School senior Joan Denniston claimed the top prize of a Chevrolet for naming the lion "Prince Bandi."

Horn was on a roll.

He and Mammarella created a *Bandstand Yearbook* that sold more than 50,000 copies. He was the highest-paid personality at the station and pulled down extra cash from his many appearances at record hops. He was part owner in the Teen and Sound record labels with longtime associate Nat Segall and Bernie Lowe, a local pianist.

And the kids on the show loved him.

Bobbie Young, who started dancing on the show in 1954 and joined the Committee in 1956, said Horn often treated Committee members to dinner out when traveling to dances out of town. Another Committee member, Mary Ann Colella called the years she danced on *Bob Horn's Bandstand* "happy, happy years." Horn took her fishing on his boat and to his house in Levittown. "He was very fatherly," she said.

Colella, whose parents were divorced, found comfort on *Bandstand*, from the cakes she got on her birthday to the postcards she received from record promoter Johnny Arthur, redeemable for Ship & Shore blouses. Four Coins manager Danny Kessler sent her records in hopes she'd tell Horn, who would play the record on Rate-a-Record and put her on to rate it.

"Of course, they always got a 98," she said.

Horn's public persona was one of a hep-talking, smooth operator who knew his way around a studio and who could hold his own with the pushy, eccentric people of the music business that he encountered daily.

It wasn't that simple.

"He was a nervous guy," Hank Latven said. "He liked to smoke all the time." Bill Russell says Horn may have smoked as much as five packs a day.

Marge Weiting shared a tiny WFIL office with Horn in his pre-*Bandstand* days. Weiting's popular *Street of Dreams* radio program immediately followed Horn's *Bandstand* radio program each night at midnight.

"He had a desk and I had a desk, but I never used mine because he always had all these people in there. I always worked out of the record room because I didn't want to sit there and chat all night. Then they'd go in the studio and sit with him while he did a show. He couldn't stand to be alone. I never saw him alone, he always had a group of guys. Record pluggers, mostly"

The record pluggers were Horn's lifeline, his connection to the music business. Although payola wasn't a well-known term in 1956, the practice was very much in vogue, especially for someone in Horn's position.

"Everybody in television was a god in those days," Marvin Brooks said. "People would do anything to get on television."

Horn was the biggest beneficiary of the record companies' largesse, pocketing cash, jewelry and even a silver candelabra for his home.

Station manager George Koehler, whose second-floor office overlooked the dance area of Studio B, gave Horn plenty of leeway as he built the most successful show on the station. That included ignoring the increasingly heavy stream of record pushers trying to catch the ears of Horn.

"They're the ones who delivered the stars," Koehler explained. "They were happy and the people who made the records were happy for the exposure. I'm sure these people came around and asked for the moon, but I don't know that there was any trouble with them."

Besides, the rest of the staff benefited from the popularity of Horn's show.

"We were all disc jockeys as well, so they'd try to get us to play the songs, too," Bill Webber said of the song pluggers.

"They'd bring in records if they had an artist appearing [in town]," said John Carlton. "They would give us tickets or urge us to go see them wherever they happened to be, even make arrangements for dinner."

THE FALL

Jerry Blavat, the teenage Committee leader who helped Horn pick records for *Bandstand*, also was well-acquainted with the record pluggers and often accompanied Horn to dinners with them. Blavat became increasingly important to Horn, helping him with dances at the Starlight Ballroom in Wildwood, N.J., serving as a cabin boy on Horn's boat and even spending weekends at Horn's home.

As Blavat grew closer to Horn, he became increasingly aware of Horn's indulgence in imported beer and Old Granddad whiskey.

"Once in a while, he would combine the two by drinking a 'boilermaker,' otherwise known as 'a shot and a beer'," Blavat wrote in his 2011 book, *You Only Rock Once*. "At times like that, his fondness for booze was something to keep an eye on, and by the time I was 15, I started to do just that."

On those occasions, the underage Blavat would frequently drink the shots himself, often leaving Horn in a confused haze.

On June 20, 1956, Blavat was with Horn at his regular Wednesday night teen dance at the Carman Roller Skating Rink in North Philadelphia. After the dance ended around 9 P.M., Horn and Blavat went to Funzie's, a bar near the rink. Horn was to meet up with his son, Peter, who was stationed with the Air Force at Dover Air Force Base in Delaware. Blavat left the bar before Peter Horn's arrival, which was sometime after midnight.

As Horn and his son drove toward Levittown in Horn's green 1955 El Dorado, Horn drove through a red light, narrowly missing a police car, When the police overtook Horn and prepared to issue him a citation for running a red light, Horn reportedly turned boisterous.

Suspecting that Horn had been drinking, the officers took him to a nearby street station where a police surgeon pronounced him drunk at 2:30 A.M. and made a call to Koehler.

Koehler had dealt with many contentious station issues since joining WFIL immediately following Army Air Corps service in World War II.

It was Koehler who was assigned the task of finding a home for the infamous Snaders that Roger Clipp had saddled the company with. On a business trip to Los Angeles on another occasion, he received a frantic call from Clipp, who told Koehler that the entire sales staff had quit after Clipp "raised a big rumpus." Koehler caught the red-eye back to Philadelphia just in time to salvage most of the staff and confront Clipp in what was "not a warm and cozy meeting."

For the most part, however, *Bandstand* was not a major concern. Horn and Mammarella ran a tight ship.

But this was trouble Horn didn't see coming. After Horn told Koehler that he had gotten a "bum rap," Koehler called Jack Steck.

"He [Steck] knew a lot of policemen, so I asked Jack to go to the arraignment and try to keep it quiet," Koehler said. The Philadelphia Police Department was in the midst of a month-long crackdown on drunk drivers, a campaign Walter Annenberg's *Inquirer* heartily endorsed.

"Well, there was no keeping it quiet," Koehler said. "So, we called Horn and sent him on vacation for three weeks. We just felt that booze and drunk driving didn't go with a guy that was running a pure kids' show. We took him off until we could somehow overcome it, but we never had to do that because the next mix-up made it impossible. We found out that he had gotten into deeper trouble."

The deeper trouble was a massive tri-state vice investigation that was just a month old but had already implicated Horn. It would be another four months before Horn would be formally charged, but Koehler learned that one of the charges would be statutory rape of a 13-year-old girl.

While Koehler may have only learned of Horn's transgressions on June 21, 1956, other WFIL-TV staffers were well aware of his most un-*Bandstand*ish behavior.

Even office worker Marie K. Pantarelli was aware of Horn's carrying on.

"Of course, everybody knew it . . . everybody knew what was going on," she said.

Steve Cohen, an employee at WFIL at the time, wrote in 2002 on the web site TotalTheater.com about what he observed:

> "I used to see Horn with the girl when she accompanied him to the station for his 11-to-midnight radio show. She was an attractive brunette who sat with Bob at a table in a small studio while engineers observed their behavior from behind the glass. Horn almost always brought an entourage of men, and sometimes additional girls. Horn's male guests sat on chairs against the walls of the studio and the girls sometimes knelt in front of them, satisfying the men while Horn laughed."

"Bob was a very nice guy as far as I was concerned," staff announcer Shelley Gross said. "But he used to have prostitutes hanging around, drinking . . . it was a very bad image for that show."

Says John Carlton: "I knew there were girls around. What they did for a living, I never knew. I'll tell you, none of them were homely."

Walter Beaulieu was a night supervisor when Horn had a radio show in Studio D.

"One night I'm in master control and over the loudspeaker system, 'Walt Beaulieu. Walt Beaulieu, report to Studio D immediately.' Jesus, I thought, what the hell's going on? So I run down the hall and I open the door and here they've got two prostitutes in there. And there's a bunch of DJs and some of the guys from the station. I got out of there quickly."

It would later be alleged that Horn kept a small apartment in the area for his trysts.

"I think it was called the whore of the month club, something like that," Beaulieu said. "I remember a few of the guys from the station, who will go nameless, they used to talk about the whore of the month club and I think it was that apartment. . . . there were other people who patronized the thing."

Many staffers were familiar with the young girl, too, though she was not a *Bandstand* regular. She did appear, however, on *Paul Whiteman's TV Teen Club*, when Beaulieu was technical director.

"She was cute as hell, she held up a sign when we would go to a commercial," Beaulieu said. "She'd be in a short dress, holding up this sign. They'd take a shot of her and then they'd go to commercial.

"She hung around the station an awful lot. . . . One day I'm going down to the Brown Jug for lunch and all these song pluggers are there and Horn is walking behind with her. I caught her later and I said to her 'Look, you're getting into a lot of trouble when you hang around with these guys, who are not pussycats.' So, she eventually got into trouble. I don't take any credit for it, but if she had listened to me, she wouldn't have gotten involved."

John Carlton also knew the girl.

"The expression around the station was, if he ever got charged with anything, no judge in the world would convict him after they saw this girl. She was gorgeous and did not look whatever age she was at the time."

George Koehler knew enough on the morning of June 21, 1956, that the future of *Bandstand* would not include Bob Horn.

But the show was too important to dump. Fortunately, Tony Mammarella was there to fill the void pending a more permanent change.

Earlier, Jack Steck had made the case for a young staffer in a memo to Roger Clipp. In the memo, Steck recommended that Dick Clark be hired for WFIL-TV. "Voice excellent, appearance angelic, despite his college education, this kid is smart. . . . hire him."

Eleanor Faragalli was in the office that day when they brought Clark in.

"I thought, 'Uh oh. He probably is the new host of the show," Faragalli recalled. "I just knew that he had it, that he would be the new host."

She was right.

CHAPTER 5

THE NEW GUY

In the weeks following Horn's arrest, WFIL executives wrestled with every decision related to *Bandstand*. Two things were clear, however—Horn was out and the show would go on.

Despite Horn's skills as a hit-maker and his authoritative on-air persona, he was far from a beloved figure.

Record pluggers were disdainful of his demands, saying he was the greediest of all Philadelphia disc jockeys. While most were happy with an occasional bottle of whiskey, Horn demanded full cases of liquor, and only the good stuff. His boat was reputed to have been provided by a record company, which also allegedly provided women for his pleasure.

Nor was Horn popular with everyone on the WFIL staff.

"Horn was not a popular man with the crew or anybody else there," John Carlton said.

But getting rid of Horn was not a simple proposition. Management had recently signed him to a three-year contract to host *Bandstand*. The contract included a morals clause, but Horn was extremely popular with the kids who appeared on the show and those who watched it. Finding a replacement that would be acceptable to the kids was mandatory. Fortunately, there were plenty of options.

Carlton, who had been on staff for two years and did 5th Avenue candy bar commercials on *Bandstand*, was one of the frontrunners.

"They hired people who could step into these key roles," Carlton explained. "And they didn't just necessarily hire one, they'd usually hire a couple . . . We were all about the same age. We were all youthful in appearance. I don't know if they had that in mind when they hired us, but we were there."

Bill Webber, another top contender to succeed Horn, agreed.

"Anybody could have done *Bandstand*, I think, any one of 20 people," Webber said.

The most obvious choice, though, was Tony Mammarella, a longtime WFIL employee who had been with the show from the beginning and had experience as Horn's vacation replacement. Even after being banished from the show, Horn pushed for Mammarella to succeed him.

Many staffers favored Carlton for the position, but it was evident that station executives were leaning toward Dick Clark, a clean-cut 26-year-old who had been at the station for four years and once filled in for Horn on *Bandstand* in late 1955 when Mammarella was unavailable.

Horn had been suspicious of Clark for years, fearing that the young New York transplant was positioning himself to eventually take the show from him.

Indeed, on the day of his dismissal, Horn met with Mammarella at the Brown Jug following Mammarella's hosting duties on *Bandstand*.

"Tony, I don't really know Dick Clark and I have nothing against him," Horn told Mammarella. "I'm not asking you to do anything to hurt Clark, but if he turns out not to be a nice guy, don't do anything to help him."[1]

Clark's squeaky-clean image suggested that he was, indeed, a nice guy.

Born in Bronxville, N.Y., Clark was the second son born to a cosmetic salesman, Richard A. Clark, and his wife, Julia. He spent his younger years in the upscale Park Lane Apartments in Mount Vernon, N.Y., on grounds that once formed the estate of circus magnate James A. Bailey. Among his neighbors were Arthur and Kathryn Murray, who hosted a nationally televised

---

1. *Bandstand Off My Back*, unpublished manuscript by Tony Mammarella.

dance instruction program. The Murrays sometimes babysat "Young Dickie" and his older brother, Brad.

As a child, Clark liked to build tree huts and craft tunnels in the woods behind his house. He and a cousin once got the attention of Rome, N.Y., police after making weird noises and scaring passersby while hidden on the porch of his grandparents' home.

From an early age, Clark showed an entrepreneurial spirit. At the age of 5, he published a neighborhood gossip sheet. By the age of 6, he was selling peanut butter sandwiches from the sidewalk and hawked old magazines and gum at a backyard carnival he had created.

"As a kid, I was always scrambling around," Clark said. "I ran a restaurant in the living room, sold two different magazines on two different days of the week, shined shoes."[2]

Clark shared a bedroom with brother Brad, who was five years older. Brad was athletic and a star football player at A.B. Davis High School before his graduation in 1943. Rather than waiting to be drafted into action for World War II, Brad Clark volunteered for flight training school. While a fighter pilot stationed in Europe, Brad Clark was killed in a plane crash on December 23, 1944. Dick Clark was shattered.

Though slight of build and painfully shy because of a skin disease, the younger Clark tried to follow his brother's path. He tried football, track and swimming without success before joining the less formal Punching Bag Club, where he finally could vent some of his grief.

"I was painfully self-conscious," Clark said. "I brooded about being homely and underweight and having a bad complexion. I found myself staring in the mirror all the time, hoping for improvement."[3]

Clark developed a serious nail-biting habit. His parents had him wear gloves, but he continued to nibble. When his dad tried applying a salve, Clark developed a fondness for the salve. Finally, they limited his nail-biting to certain times of the day.

"Here I was, growing into manhood, and all I could think about was, "Hooray, at eight o'clock, I'll be able to bite my nails!" Clark said.[4] But within 10 days, the habit was broken.

---

2. *Philadelphia Inquirer*, October 29, 1981.
3. *Philadelphia Daily News*, November 6, 1985.
4. *Look* magazine, November 24, 1959.

Clark started developing self-confidence when he got into school politics and joined the school's drama club. Speech-making and appearing on stage started turning things around for Clark.

When he wasn't listening to big band music on a wind-up Victrola posted in the hallway outside his parents' bedroom, Clark was listening to the Philco radio in his bedroom. While he enjoyed music programs like Martin Block's *Make Believe Ballroom* and Art Ford's *Milkman Matinee*, it was the voices—Dave Garroway, Steve Allen, Garry Moore and especially Arthur Godfrey—that most fascinated him.

After his mother took Clark in 1943 to see *The Camel Comedy Caravan* starring Jimmy Durante and Garry Moore at Radio City Music Hall in New York City, Clark decided that radio was the career for him. The once-shy teen blossomed into what he described as a "determined extrovert." He claims to have set a school record for pushups and was voted by his peers as the "Man Most Likely to Sell the Brooklyn Bridge." He also was a member of the National Thespians and served on his school's Dance Committee.

Socially, Clark was much more confident leaving high school than he was when he entered. He and his best friend, Andy Grass, shared a 15-year-old sedan they dubbed "The Green Hornet."

He also had a steady girlfriend, cheerleader Barbara Mallery.

Although Clark met Mallery, better known as Bobbie, in her freshman year, literally bumping into her and spilling her books, it wasn't until later that they got together for a double date. Although Mallery was Grass' date on that night, Clark soon started dating Mallery and they were steadies until his graduation in 1947.

Just before Clark's graduation, his uncle Bradley Barnard, owner of the *Sentinel* newspaper in Rome, N.Y., called his dad with a job proposition. Barnard was expanding into radio with a new station in Utica, Would the elder Clark be interested in leading the sales team at the new WRUN?

The answer was yes and the Clark family moved to Utica in the summer of 1947. Dick Clark, whose application for admission to Yale had been turned down, applied at nearby Syracuse University and was accepted. Before starting classes, young Clark was doing odd jobs around his uncle's station. He started by running the mimeograph machine, sorting and delivering mail and running errands for the staff. In July, he got his big break—delivering weather reports on the Rural Radio Network from WRUN-FM. He often joked that his WRUN audience consisted of "three farmers and two geese."

Before the summer was done, Clark had advanced to doing commercials and delivering news on the AM outlet. Then it was time to head to Syracuse, where he majored in advertising and minored in radio. While at Syracuse, Clark was on the staff of campus radio station WAER-FM.

Bobbie Mallery graduated from A.B. Davis High School in 1948, but her family moved that summer to Salisbury, Md., where she planned to attend a state teachers' college. Clark and Mallery mostly kept in touch by mail, but Clark occasionally made the 17-hour drive from Syracuse, in a 1934 Ford convertible that lacked a heater. He worked a variety of odd jobs to pay for the car and gas—bed-maker at a fraternity house, "pot and pan man" at a hash house, cornhusker, 52-cent-an-hour boxer in a chicken factory and brush salesman.

The arrangement lasted until Clark's senior year, when Mallery's mother allowed her to transfer to Oswego State College in New York, just a few miles from Syracuse. Clark and Mallery were a steady couple with Clark presenting her first with his Delta Kappa Epsilon fraternity pin and, eventually, an engagement ring he bought wholesale from the father of a friend. They decided to put off marriage for a year after Clark's graduation, giving him time to establish a foothold on a radio career while she completed her senior year of college.

Before his graduation in January 1951, Clark began looking for work. He found it, working weekends on Syracuse radio station WOLF. Within a month, Clark was working full-time, hosting a country music show, *The WOLF Buckaroos*, at a salary of $1 an hour.

Clark stayed with WOLF until a couple months after receiving his Bachelors of Science in Business Administration, gaining valuable experience and learning one very important lesson—pay attention to your listeners.

WOLF owner Sherman Marshall had created a very popular late-night show called *Sandman Serenade*. The show ran four hours each night and featured songs requested by the station's listeners, who started calling in requests in the early morning. WOLF staff compiled a playlist based on the requests.

In July 1951, Clark moved back to Utica as a summer replacement announcer at WRUN, where his dad was now station manager. Since both men were known as Dick Clark, the younger Clark adopted the on-air name of Dick Clay to avoid confusion. In his biography, Clark acknowledged that he "hated being Dick Clay."

Nevertheless, that was the name Clark used on his next job—at WKTV, Channel 13, Utica's only television station in 1951. It wouldn't be the only name Clark used at WKTV, a small station where he wore many hats for $52.50 a week after being hired by Michael Fusco, a friend of Clark's father.

Besides writing commercials and moving scenery, Clark assumed the title role in a country show, *Cactus Dick and the Santa Fe Riders*. Clark also took over as the lead newscaster, replacing the departing Bob Earle.

Clark was in awe of Earle, who appeared to go flawlessly through an entire newscast while barely glancing at a script. After observing this for several days, Clark approached Earle and asked how he did it.

"Meet Elmer, my helper," said Earle, ushering Clark behind the anchor desk and pointing to a small tape recorder that sat at his feet.

Earle explained that he recorded the entire 15-minute newscast on tape before going on air, then listened to himself through an earpiece delicately wound beneath his clothing and up the back of his neck before emerging unobtrusively to his ear, making it virtually invisible in a front camera view.

The impressed Clark immediately purchased his own small Webcor recorder with foot controller and earpiece and began practicing the technique himself. Soon, he was delivering the news, flawlessly most nights—thanks to his own "Elmer."

Other broadcasters noticed. Gordon Alderman, general manager of WHEN-TV in Syracuse, was the first to come calling, offering Clark a position with a hefty raise, to $75. When Fusco got wind of the offer, he called Alderman and told him to back off, boosting Clark's pay to $75 himself.

After six months, though, Clark was itching to move to a bigger market. A Schenectady television station made an offer, which Clark discussed with his father. His dad suggested that maybe the younger Clark would be interested in a job in a bigger city, instead. He could call a man he knew in Philadelphia, Roger Clipp, who ran WFIL radio and television if Clark was interested.

For Clipp, who required that new hires be college graduates, young Dick Clark was worth a look. Within days, the senior Clark had arranged a tryout for his son with Jack Steck, program director of WFIL-TV.

Clark showed up for his tryout accompanied by a good friend—Elmer.

After a formal interview, Clark was left alone for a few minutes with a stack of copy so he could prepare for an audition newscast. As Clark and Elmer prepared, WFIL staffers curiously awaited the audition. Several were hanging around the station lounge when word of Clark's unique technique reached them.

"Someone said, 'Jesus, there's a kid doing a 15-minute newscast ad-lib'," Shelley Gross said. "So we all ran to master control to watch. And, sure enough, he was doing that. . . . He had recorded the entire 15-minute newscast."

Koehler, who was tasked with screening potential young hires for Clipp, was also impressed.

"Dick, of them all, was far and away the best. There was no question. Absolutely none," Koehler said.

Steck thought Clark would be a good hire for his TV operation, but he had no openings at the time. How about radio, he asked Clark? We'll be needing some summer replacements later.

Clark took a few days before making his decision—television in Schenectady or radio in Philadelphia? With one eye on New York City, Clark opted for Philadelphia, rationalizing that the Big Apple was just around the corner.

Clark's first day at WFIL was May 13, 1952; Bobbie Mallery was to graduate from college in early June. The pair decided to get married in Salisbury, Md., on June 28.

While Bobbie worked out the wedding details, including buying her own wedding ring, Clark took up residence in a $1.65 a day room at the downtown Philadelphia YMCA, just a few blocks from the WFIL radio studios in the Widener Building. It was also down the street from a Horn & Hardart automat, where Clark took most of his meals in the six weeks before his marriage.

Following the wedding, the Clarks took up residence in a $35 a month apartment in suburban Drexel Hills. Clark spent much of his professional career in the first six months doing station breaks, commercials, and newscasts, with an occasional role in a local drama program.

As summer 1952 wound down, WFIL consolidated its radio and television operations into the recently expanded studios at 46th and Market Streets. Clark was also rewarded with his first radio program, *Dick Clark's Caravan of Music*, which aired from 1:45 to 6 P.M. beginning in August 1952.

Clark supplemented his radio income by doing commercials on WFIL-TV.

"They would post a thing in the announcers' lounge saying we're looking for someone to do a beer commercial. Show up at 3 o'clock.' And we'd show up at 3 o'clock and do it," said Bill Webber, adding that everybody on staff had to memorize their lines—except Clark.

Putting Elmer to work, Clark was hard to top in the auditions.

"Three minutes after he got a piece of copy, he was ready to do the spot," Webber said. "He did that for years."

Shelly Gross found the situation to be frustrating.

"I used to have to audition against him," Gross recalled. "While I was trying to remember the words, he was repeating them. . . . I never lost an ad-lib audition until Dick Clark came along. He was the golden boy."

If there was a downside to Clark's early career arc, it was the same thing that would earn him adulation years later—he just looked too young.

John Butterworth, an engineer at WFIL-TV, said Clark "was very, very, very frustrated" by his youthful appearance. "He used to come back very downhearted and dejected because the clients all said the same thing: 'He's too young, he's too young, he's too young'."

It's possible that Clark's youthful appearance may have kept him from an early move to his dream city, New York City.

One of Clark's more lucrative accounts was with Schaefer Beer, one of the nation's oldest breweries. Besides doing Schaefer commercials in Philadelphia, Clark commuted each week to New York City where he did Schaefer commercials for a wrestling telecast—until owner Rudy Schaefer caught Clark on-air one night.

Stunned by Clark's youthful appearance, Schaefer ordered that Clark be replaced since he didn't look old enough to be drinking beer.

No such controversy followed Clark, however, when he did Tastykake commercials on WFIL-TV between innings of Athletics and Phillies games at Connie Mack Stadium, even though Clark later acknowledged in his biography that he spent his non-air time in the stands reading the newspaper and listening to music on a portable radio.

THE NEW GUY

"I was probably the only commercial announcer they ever had who hated baseball," Clark wrote in *Rock, Roll and Remember* in 1976.

In the fall of 1952, Clark landed another plum job—that of Tootsie Roll spokesman on Paul Whiteman's *TV Teen Club*. The show was one of WFIL's biggest hits and Whiteman was a bona fide star with a large national following.

The roots of the show went to 1945 when orchestra leader Whiteman led a drive to build a youth center in Lambertville, N.J. Juvenile delinquency was a growing youth problem when four young Lambertville men were killed in an alcohol-related traffic accident. Whiteman, a major radio star at the time, suggested the town hold weekly dances for area teens at a local center. When the dances proved successful and juvenile delinquency was falling, film producer Justin B. Herman began filming what would be *The Lambertville Story* for Paramount Pictures.

As the film was readied for its May 1949 premiere, Whiteman, announced the formation of a national club for teens, which would offer dances across the country. In conjunction with the new club, a new television show would be broadcast on the ABC network, originating from WFIL-TV.

To assemble the first-rate band Whiteman felt the show deserved, he called on Bernie Lowenthal, a 32-year-old Juilliard graduate who was a respected jazz pianist and composer. Joining Lowenthal's quartet was bassist Artie Singer, a well-known Philadelphia vocal coach. Both would later be key figures in Dick Clark's rise to prominence.

Whiteman's show was a mix of young contestants plus a core of talented teen singers and dancers who appeared as regular fixtures. One of the regulars was Eddie Fisher; among the contestants were trumpet player Frankie Avalon and singers Leslie Uggams, Carol Diann Johnson (later known as Diahann Carroll) and Robert Ridarelli (later known as Bobby Rydell).

The show was first sponsored by Griffin Shoe Polish but Tootsie Roll took over sponsorship for show's fourth and final season, which began on November 22, 1952. It was during the Tootsie Roll spots that Clark made his national network TV debut with his radio show moving to the 11 A.M.-1 P.M. slot.

When the Whiteman show ended just six months later, Clark was given a shot at his own TV show. Clark was paired with another Whiteman alum, the 19-year-old singer and piano player

Nancy Lewis, in a show appropriately titled *Lewis & Clark*. Lewis & Clark was soon dropped but Clark found himself briefly hosting a 15-minute local show called *Quick Movie Quiz*.

In the fall of 1953, Clark first entered the orbit of WFIL's huge afternoon TV hit, *Bandstand,* not long after *Dick Clark's Caravan of Music* returned to the afternoon radio lineup. Now that the radio and TV operations were together in the same building, why not do some cross promotions, station executives asked?

Why not, indeed. With TV's *Bandstand* barely a year old, Clark's radio program was renamed *Bandstand* as well and Horn was instructed to open and close the show, giving him ample opportunity to plug the TV show. For the first few minutes of the radio show, Horn would spin a few records before excusing himself to head over to the TV studio, inviting radio listeners to follow him on the tube. Similarly, Horn would show up for the final minutes of the radio show, tell listeners what they had missed on the TV and remind them to tune in tomorrow.

The arrangement rankled both men, who saw it as an unwarranted imposition on their respective turfs. Clark addressed the situation in his 1976 autobiography, *Rock, Roll & Remember:*

> [Horn] was minimally polite to me. He put up with me," Clark wrote, adding, "The more I worked with Horn the less I liked him.

Station executives were not satisfied with Clark's radio ratings, which failed to take off despite the new *Bandstand* name. When Clark protested that he was stymied by station edicts that his music be taken from the WFIL pop music library while Horn was given free rein on what he could play on TV, WFIL management responded by sending Clark to Pittsburgh for a week to see how a successful disc jockey can get it done in the afternoons.

Again, Clark protested that it was the type of music he was forced to play that limited his audience, not his announcing skills. He tried other methods to boost his audience: a month-long contest for listeners voting on Philadelphia's favorite recording artist and a stint spinning records in the lobby of the Tower Theater in Upper Darby in the hopes teens would drop by to watch and, maybe, even dance. Few did.

While Horn was riding the wave of unprecedented popularity with the success of TV's *Bandstand,* Clark was marking time in the 12-by-20-foot WFIL-AM cubicle down the hall. He had managed to replace his old Studebaker after staffers complained about constantly having to push it to get it started, but he was still waiting for that big break.

In late 1955, he got a whiff of the rarefied *Bandstand* atmosphere when Horn was on vacation and his regular substitute, Tony Mammarella, was unable to make it to the studio. Clark was pressed into the host role. With one day of *Bandstand* duty under his belt, Clark felt he was justified in describing himself as Horn's substitute.

He made a call to WEWS-TV in Cleveland and made a pitch to do a *Bandstand*-like show for them but was bluntly rejected.[5]

Even though Clark was unable to create the big break he so earnestly sought, his nemesis, Bob Horn, as it turned out, provided it himself when he ran that red light in the early morning hours of June 21, 1956.

Two weeks later, George Koehler gave Clark a call at home. Could he come in to discuss an important matter?

---

5. *Rock, Roll & Remember*, p. 46.

CHAPTER 6

IT'S MY SHOW NOW

When Clark arrived at WFIL in mid-afternoon on Monday, July 9, 1956, he was greeted by a throng of teenage picketers carrying signs in support of Bob Horn. The protest was organized by the head of Horn's Committee of regulars, Jerry Blavat, who reasoned "No dancers; no show."

Inside the building, Koehler delivered the news to Clark. Horn is gone and you're the new host of *Bandstand*, starting this afternoon. Tony Mammarella will continue as producer.

But what about the kids, Clark asked?

Koehler and Clark went outside and invited Blavat inside where they tried to appease the young teen. "What if we double your salary to $30 a week?"

"No dice," replied Blavat. "It's not about the money. We want Bob Horn back."

"That's not going to happen, Koehler told the young protester. Dick Clark is taking over the show and that's that."

Blavat returned to the sidewalk where, minutes later, he was arrested by Philadelphia police and shuffled off to the 55th and Pine Street station, but not before rallying his fellow protestors. "Keep picketing," he said.[1]

---

1. Jerry Blavat, *You Only Rock Once*, pp. 60–61

IT'S MY SHOW NOW

A half hour later, Blavat was released and back at the WFIL building, but the picketers were gone, their signs leaning against the building. Clark had persuaded the teens to end their protest by explaining that, while he was not Bob Horn, he'd do his best to give them a show they'd like.

"A lot of my friends said don't go in there. We're picketing because Bob Horn was fired," recalls former Committee member Barbara Marcen. "So I didn't go in. A few of us went in front of the *Inquirer* building. We picketed there, on Broad Street. A lot of us didn't go to the show again for a few weeks because we all wanted Bob Horn back."

But many of the protestors relented and did enter the studio as the potential crisis subsided.

Clark took it slowly at first. As a practical matter, there was no reason to tinker with the success that had landed *Bandstand* in the top spot among Philadelphia daytime television shows. The same crew operated from the same set and the show retained the familiar Rate-a-Record, Spotlight Dance and Roll Call segments.

One big change—for Clark, at least—came in the music. Clark's personal tastes didn't include the rock & roll that was throwing the music business on its head in 1956. *Billboard* magazine called rock & roll "the most important artist and repertoire trend during 1956." *Melody Maker* called it the "influence of the year."

But, since his radio playlist had been limited to the pop standards in the WFIL record library, Clark was unfamiliar with the music he would now be spinning for three hours on television each afternoon.

Jerry Ross, who joined WFIL as a disc jockey soon after Clark took over *Bandstand*, put it succinctly: Clark "didn't know Chuck Berry from a huckleberry."[2]

Fortunately, Clark had Tony Mammarella. Mammarella, who was involved in virtually every aspect of *Bandstand* from the show's beginning, also had his pulse on the lives of the teens that attended the show.

For the first few weeks that Clark hosted *Bandstand*, Mammarella picked the music. Just keeping up with the music scene was a laborious process for Clark and Mammarella. Fortunately,

---

2. John A. Jackson, *American Bandstand: Dick Clark and the Making of a Rock 'N' Roll Empire*, p. 40.

Philadelphia had a flourishing radio market they could tap into, especially R&B stations WDAS and WHAT.

WDAS employed two of the most popular disc jockeys in Philadelphia—Georgie Woods and Douglas "Jocko" Henderson.

Henderson had arrived in Philadelphia about the same time *Bandstand* debuted. It was in Philadelphia that he adopted the name Jocko and began shaping his "Rocketship Commander" persona. His bouncy, rhyming patter between songs is often credited for inspiring rap music decades later:

> Here's the ace from outer space. And way up here in the stratosphere we got to holler mighty loud and clear. Daddy-o! Mommy-o! This is Jocko, engineer, aboard the big Rocket Ship Show saying greetings, salutations, oo-pappa-doo and how do you do?

Woods began his Philadelphia career at WHAT in 1953 for $25 a week. Earning the nickname "The Man With the Goods," Woods soon became one of Philadelphia's most influential hit makers. Besides his radio show, he promoted concerts featuring black artists, ringing his signature cowbell to introduce acts at the Uptown Theater.

Woods and Clark eventually developed a long-lasting friendship and the connection was immensely helpful in those early years as Clark learned the ins and outs of the music business. That included learning how to handle the steady stream of record promotion men—and Philadelphia drew some of the most influential and colorful figures around.

One of those figures was Martin A. "Red" Schwartz, a high school classmate of Tony Mammarella's. Schwartz sold cars before starting in radio in 1949 as "Red Martin." As "Red Top" he was the only white deejay at WDAS before moving into record promotion for Main Line Distributing, pushing discs from independent labels Vee Jay and Roulette.

The rise of the independents created the need for aggregate distributors like Main Line to manage the sales and promotions for multiple, smaller labels.

Another of those distributors was Cosnat, which had moved into Philadelphia from its New York base in 1954. Its sales manager in 1956 was Harry Chipetz. Clark would go on to have long professional relationships with Schwartz and Chipetz.

Ed Cohn of Lesco Distributing, who knew Clark from his radio days, was another regular, as were the Rosen brothers—David and Harry. David Rosen handled the jukeboxes and pinball machines for David Rosen, Inc., the most established of the Philadelphia distributors, while his brother, Harry, oversaw the record operation. Harry was well-known throughout the Delaware Valley with his felt fedora and red Cadillac convertible. He threw lavish promotional parties around the city and was known to camp out in a disc jockey's office until he agreed to play Rosen's records.

As colorful as Harry Rosen was, he was a piker compared to his ace promo man, Matty "The Humdinger" Singer, sometimes described as "Philly's feistiest, most colorful record promotion man."[3]

Singer practically lived out of his car, its big trunk stuffed with records, often visiting secondary markets outside of the city. "If I saw a radio tower, I went in," Singer said. "The big joke was that I even serviced police radio."[4]

Singer was also a great storyteller and often regaled his audience with an off-color story or two. Besides leaving behind the record he was promoting, Singer tossed in a Snickers bar or two and a "thought for today."

Even at his funeral, Singer left attendees with smiles on their faces. In a taped message, he said: "I even had the funeral director put me in this casket face down so every one of you can file by and kiss my ass."[5]

A dubious business decision by David Rosen in 1955 paved the way for a new power broker in town. Mercury Records had asked Rosen to drop all other labels he was representing so his promotion men could concentrate on Mercury discs. When Rosen agreed, the dropped labels went to new homes.

Two of them—Chess and ABC Paramount—ended up with the relatively new Universal Record Distributing Corporation, a company that was formed by brothers Paul and David Miller expressly to cater to the new independent labels of the emerging rock & roll scene.

The Millers were pioneers in the post-war recording industry, recording black vocal groups, gospel groups, and Philadelphia string bands before breaking out with singer Al Martino and a country and western group from nearby Chester, Bill Haley & the Saddlemen. By 1952, their recording empire also included a

---
3. *Philadelphia Daily News*, October 26, 1982.
4. Ibid.
5. *Philadelphia Inquirer*, April 19, 1993.

record pressing plant and its own distribution network and Bill Haley & the Saddlemen had become Bill Haley & His Comets.

As the Millers hustled to set up Universal Distributing, they enlisted two Philadelphia music pros with strong connections—Harry Finfer and Harold Lipsius.

Finfer, who started his career working with Ivin Ballen at Gotham Records, had started Guyden Records in 1954. Lipsius was a Philadelphia lawyer who drew up the papers to incorporate Universal. In lieu of direct payment for his services, Lipsius accepted 10 percent ownership in the company.

When the Millers found themselves overextended with their various enterprises, Lipsius brought in a client, Allen Sussell, who was looking for a new business venture to supplement his successful mail order dental supply business.

With Sussell's fresh influx of cash, Finfer's technical knowledge of distribution (plus the experience of being a label owner), and Lipsius handling legal matters, Universal was in capable hands.

With Guyden Records virtually indistinguishable from Universal under this arrangement, Finfer, Lipsius, and Sussell launched another record label in early 1956, Jamie, named after Sussell's daughter.

Sussell soon got cold feet, however, and backed out of Universal, leaving Lipsius and Finfer to assemble what amounted to a dream team of promotion men. The team met regularly, mapping strategies to put the right records in the hands of the right jocks at the right time.

That meant that salesmen like Gunter Hauer and Joe Beiderman could fill the trunks of their cars with records and head out to the 50–60 stations they had targeted in their eastern Pennsylvania-Delaware market. They hit record hops, too, often towing along artists, ginning up interest wherever they could.

They couldn't hit every place they wanted so they also sent records by mail. When word reached Universal salesman Tom Kennedy that some jockeys were passing the packages along to their kids unopened, he started inserting a Tootsie Roll pop, just the right size to fit in a 45-record's hole. The packages started being opened.

The traffic of promotion men became so heavy around the WFIL studios that Mammarella and Clark soon designated Tuesday as record promotion day. As many as 10–12 promotion men would crowd into the small meeting room at the rear of the Brown Jug every Tuesday to talk shop and swap stories.

"Next to the Brill Building in New York, more music deals were made in that back room than anywhere else at the time," Clark said.[6]

While Clark spent a good deal of his time working on the nuts and bolts of producing Philadelphia's top-rated daytime television show, he also worked on introducing himself to the kids who made the show so popular.

He doubled the number of regulars on the Committee and worked to win over those Philadelphia teens who remained loyal to Horn and were skeptical of Clark.

Clark kept in place a number of rules Horn had established early on:
1. Boys were required to wear a suit jacket, shirt, and necktie.
2. Girls could not wear tight sweaters, low-necked dresses or pants.
3. No gum allowed.
4. No smoking in the building
5. Obscene or profane language would not be tolerated.
6. Coats, hats, pocketbooks and school books must be checked at the door.
7. No one under age 14 or older than 18 is to be admitted.

For Clark's part, he was always seen in a dark suit with perfectly arranged hair and a perfect smile. He spoke in soft tones and chose his words carefully, avoiding controversial terms like "going steady," as he gently deflected attention to performers and the kids who populated the dance floor.

Clark, too, proved to be a tireless promoter of the show. He continued to work record hops, sometimes traveling as far as Pottstown or Atlantic City. He designated special days for big names on the emerging rock & roll scene—like Elvis Presley, Fats Domino, Bill Haley, and Pat Boone. Elvis was named *Bandstand's* top male vocalist for 1956; Patti Page was top female vocalist.

Clark also provided a springboard for many Philadelphia-area artists, like Eddie Dano, who was *Bandstand's* most promising vocalist of 1956. Other local acts getting valuable airplay included

---

6. Dick Clark & Richard Robinson, *Rock, Roll & Remember*, p. 64.

Sunny Gale, the Jodimars (a spinoff of Bill Haley's Comets), the DeJohn Sisters from Chester and Lillian Briggs of Allentown.

On October 13, 1956, Walter Tillman of *TV Guide* showed up on *Bandstand* with a cake for Clark to mark the fourth anniversary of the show although Clark had been the show's host for just three months. That was long enough, though, for President Dwight D. Eisenhower to invite Clark and seven other U.S. disc jockeys to the White House for a conference in December to discuss fighting juvenile delinquency.

Clark also continued the show's popular dance contests. The first prize in the 1956 fast dance contest—a pair of Italian Lambretta motor scooters—went to regulars Elaine Biaselli and Joe Cramatula.

As 1956 wound down, *Bandstand's* Christmas special turned into a family affair, with Dick Clark Sr. and a very pregnant Barbara Clark among the honored guests. Also making a token appearance was the Clark family dog, a dachshund named Looie.

On January 9, 1957, Richard A. Clark II was born at University Hospital, weighing in at 5 pounds 6 ounces.

As *Bandstand* continued to grow in popularity, the demand for Clark's appearances at record hops grew as well. Working with good friend Eddie McAdam, Clark zipped from hop to hop carrying rolls of quarters and an empty 45-rpm record box. McAdam would take dollar bills from kids at the door to cover the 75-cent admission fee, give them back a quarter and stuff the dollar bills into the record case.

"[Eddie] used to sweat profusely. Literally, he would perspire all the time," said Clark. "By the end of the night, the sweat would drip off the end of his tie and into the box with all the money, which was coming in hand over fist.

"We'd take the boxes of money and stick them in a spare bedroom. Two or three weeks would go by and then my wife and I would try to straighten out all these crumpled, sweaty one-dollar bills."[7]

Clark, wary of potential tax problems, claims he reported that income, which amounted to as much as $50,000 some years. That concern led to the creation of his first business, Click Corporation.

Click—a contraction of "Cl"ark and D"ick"—was incorporated on March 8, 1957. Clark would later tell government investigators

---

7. Joe Smith, *Off the Record*, pp. 103–105.

that he formed the company to go into the music publishing business and to handle the record hop income. Clark and his wife were named as directors of the company and Clark's manager, Marvin Josephson, was listed as vice president.

While Clark would later estimate that some 8,000 musical acts appeared on his television shows, two of the biggest stars of the 1950s never appeared on *Bandstand*—Ricky Nelson and Elvis Presley.

Nelson's absence is understandable since his televised musical appearances were limited to the family show, *The Adventures of Ozzie & Harriet*. Presley, however, rarely passed on an opportunity to appear on TV in the early years of his career. While phone calls to Presley were prominently aired several times on *Bandstand* over the years, he never performed on the show, an oversight Clark usually attributed to Presley's manager, Colonel Tom Parker, who refused to let Elvis perform for union scale.

Nevertheless, it appears Clark let a golden opportunity slip by when Presley did four shows at the Arena, right next to the WFIL studios, on April 5–6, 1957.

The Philadelphia concerts—Elvis' first in the city—were noteworthy in several ways.

First, the *Philadelphia Daily News* reported that its reporters had uncovered and foiled a plot by 15 University of Pennsylvania students (10 of them male) to overtake Presley and shave his head and sideburns while in Philadelphia.

Instead of popping in next door to *Bandstand* on the afternoon of Friday, April 5, Elvis met with a dozen teen journalists backstage at the Arena, where he fielded questions on the future of rock & roll, its role in juvenile delinquency and his high school grades.

Despite the publicity, none of Elvis' shows sold out at the Arena and the first one drew just 2,300, barely one-third of capacity. Although Elvis didn't generate much news with his music on that visit, his last show managed to capture headlines when a group of four Villanova students pelted him with eggs during *All Shook Up*.

The closest an egg came to Elvis landed three feet away, smashing on Scotty Moore's guitar, prompting Elvis to quip to the crowd, "Whoever threw that will never make the Yankees."[8]

Although Clark struck out with Elvis, he connected with the Philadelphia Boys' Apparel Guild, which gave him its Achievement

---

8. *Philadelphia Sunday Bulletin*, April 7, 1957.

Award on April 17, 1957, "for consistent encouragement of the principles of right dress."[9]

Things were still going smoothly for *Bandstand* in May. It was still the top-rated daytime show in Philadelphia, but Clark was concerned. Where does he go from here?

Bandstand was one of the most copied shows in television history. It was a rare month that some station or another didn't send someone to Philadelphia to check the show out. Even the National Broadcasting Company had sent someone six months earlier. After considering *Bandstand* for a network spot, NBC executives eventually passed on the opportunity.

Now, Clark and Mammarella heard rumblings that ABC was revamping its daytime lineup, possibly putting *Bandstand* itself in jeopardy. Clark decided to take a proactive approach. He called ABC director of programs Ted Fetter in New York and offered to provide a kinescope of *Bandstand* for his consideration.

Although Fetter's response was lukewarm at best, he knew something Clark didn't: ABC executives already had some kinescopes of the show, thanks to Ollie Treyz.

Treyz was a savvy veteran of the TV business whose roots included WFIL's Roger Clipp—who had first hired him at ABC in 1948—and Leonard Goldenson, who had brokered the deal to take over ABC from Life Saver candy magnate Ed Noble in 1953.

Although Treyz had left ABC in 1954 to become president of the Television Bureau of Advertising, Goldenson lured him back in November 1956 as vice president of the network.

The 38-year-old Treyz was a devout student of ratings and market research and a firm believer in catering to the emerging teenage demographic and its estimated $30 billion annual purchasing power.

When Treyz returned to ABC-TV, the network was stumbling with its daytime programming. Goldenson's business relationship with Walt Disney had proved profitable, but the Disney influence at the network was waning.

One of the conditions of ABC's $500,000 loan to Disney for construction of Disneyland was that the network would receive Disney programming. *Disneyland* went on the air in 1954 and *The Mickey Mouse Club* followed in 1955.

While *The Mickey Mouse Club* did well its first year, ratings were slipping in its second season. Disney, which had also ventured

---

9. From plaque on Bandstand set.

into the live action movie business, found its facilities stretched beyond its means and had already decided to trim *Mickey Mouse* from an hour to 30 minutes so it could concentrate on one of Walt Disney's pet projects, *Zorro*, which would debut in the fall of 1957.

Treyz noticed that the ratings for *Bandstand* were exceedingly strong in the time slot preceding *The Mickey Mouse Club*, but that Philadelphia viewers were abandoning the Disney show at 5 P.M. Why is that, Treyz asked?

He called his old friend Roger Clipp and asked for kinescopes of Clark's show, which George Koehler quickly dispatched to New York. Treyz soon saw the difference in the two shows.

Bandstand was high energy in a spacious environment. Viewers could watch the kids having a good time doing the latest dance steps, something they could emulate in their own living room. It also had a smooth, youthful host who had a brotherly rapport with the kids onscreen.

By contrast, the kids dancing on *The Mickey Mouse Club* were stuck in the swing era, performing highly choreographed group routines that were impossible for viewers to replicate. And host Jimmie Dodd seemed preachy in contrast to Clark, more like a father than a friend.

Although Treyz saw little in common between the two shows, he also saw something else: Why should the network keep subsidizing a fading show like *The Mickey Mouse Club* when a highly popular show like *Bandstand* could be available at a fraction of the cost?

While Treyz, vice president in charge of programming James Aubrey and manager of program development Daniel Melnick considered whether to add *Bandstand* to the ABC lineup, Fetter dashed off a "don't call us, we'll call you" letter to Clark dated June 18, 1957.

Clark learned of the letter while visiting his parents in Utica, N.Y., and took Fetter's closing "If you are ever in New York, why don't you drop in and say hello" as an invitation.

He interrupted his family vacation to fly to New York and make his case personally to Fetter. In July, Fetter led an entourage from New York to check out the show for themselves.

Despite some concerns, Fetter soon made an offer to Clark: a four-week trial beginning on August 5, a $1,500 weekly budget (the same as the cost of a one-minute commercial on the show) and some help with a new set and lighting. Clark would receive a few minutes of advertising he could sell himself and he could sell *Bandstand* yearbooks and keep half for himself. Oh, and the show would henceforth be called *American Bandstand*.

Clark said yes.

* * *

For Irvin "Shorty" Yeaworth, the summer of 1957 was certain to be his springboard to cinematic glory. For eight years he'd been turning out religious films through his Good News Productions. But now, Yeaworth was excitedly working on his first secular film, a science fiction opus tentatively titled *The Molten Meteor*. For the new production, Yeaworth had created Valley Forge Films, Inc. The entire film would be shot in Chester County, within 30 miles of Philadelphia.

Yeaworth had secured $100,000 in financing and worked with a handful of writers to come up with a script that told the story of a group of teenagers fighting to protect their town from an amorphous, all-consuming, jelly-like creature of dubious origin.

The film would feature an up-and-coming 27-year-old actor named Steve McQueen. The inanimate star of the film was an amalgamation of several types of silicone, colorized by a smattering of red food coloring.

By the time the marauding menace was subdued by a hail of carbon dioxide in the basement of the Downingtown Diner, everyone recognized the villain for what it was, a blob, which became the final title for the film.

While Shorty Yeaworth was certain that *The Blob*, with dozens of Philadelphia-area teens filling extra roles in the film, was certain to be the talk of the teen set that summer, he hadn't counted on Dick Clark and his big announcement that *Bandstand* was going national.

It was the big break Clark had been building toward for a decade and he wasn't about to let it slip away. Clark started building on his business holdings in May 1957 when he bought a 25 percent share in the one-year-old Jamie records for a mere $125. At the time, Jamie had only released a handful of singles, none of them hits outside the Philadelphia area.

Besides pulling all the pieces together for a national television program, Clark was very busy that summer, emceeing as many teen dances as he could while hyping the *Bandstand* brand. He was also busy with a little rock & roll film that has been largely forgotten in the years since.

The movie was *Jamboree*, one of those early rock films that straddled the line between insipid ballads and the emerging raw sound that was replacing it. Rock & roll was still seen as a fad by many in 1957, a fad that was understood by young hepcats and misunderstood by older squares.

Alan Freed had pioneered the genre a year earlier with three films built around slim storylines of generational or cultural conflicts, and punctuated by the real stars—popular musical artists singing their hits. Clark, who saw himself as the heir apparent to Freed as the nation's No. 1 influencer of rock music, was eager to get his clean-cut, boy-next-door image into theaters as an alternative to Freed, whose image was considerably coarser, but whose musical acumen was light years ahead of his youthful Philadelphia counterpart.

Jamboree had some advantages over Freed's productions.

For one thing, it was being produced by a major studio, Warner Brothers. Its producer, Max Rosenberg, was familiar with the genre, too, having produced Freed's most recent epic, *Rock, Rock, Rock*, in 1956.

And, while Freed's productions piously presented him as the lone arbiter of good musical taste, *Jamboree* featured cameos from 19 disc jockeys, including two from England and two from Germany. This, presumably, would give ample promotional opportunities for distributors in major markets where these jocks held sway over young, impressionable listeners. Indeed, the film was originally titled *Disc Jockey Jamboree*.

Clark was also an investor in the film. He and Bernie Binnick, a veteran songwriter of the Philadelphia music scene, formed the Binlark Corporation in the summer of 1957 to invest in the film. Binnick, who would later be a partner with Clark and Tony Mammarella in Swan Records, was rewarded with a slot in the credits as "Assistant to the Producer."

Clark formed his fourth company that July, Sea-Lark (C-Lark) Enterprises, a music publishing firm that was wholly owned by the Clark family.

Clark spent the weeks leading up to the premiere of *American Bandstand* commuting between New York for the filming of *Jamboree* and hosting dozens of teen hops around Philadelphia.

Included in his 18-hour days were his duties on the Board of Governors of a new non-profit, the National Council of Disc Jockeys, which was formed to soften the image of rock & roll while "instituting national activities to enlist the participation of America's youth in public service endeavors."[10]

One major adjustment for the new *American Bandstand* concerned the music to be played on the program. The show would continue to air from 2:30 to 5 P.M. in Philadelphia, but the network was to pick up just the 90 minutes from 3 to 4:30. Only records that were available nationally would air during the network portion; leaving the remaining hour for records only available in the Philadelphia area.

There were other changes, too. Network officials revamped the set. Gone was the record shop backdrop; in was a wall of framed records. The *Bandstand* lectern was replaced by one that now read *American Bandstand*. The new lectern was smaller, making the 5-9 Clark appear larger on the screen. The opening theme song of the show would continue to be "Bandstand Boogie"—written by Charles Albertine, who shared writing credit with the deposed Bob Horn, and arranged by Les Elgart—but the camera would open with a shot of the dancers before pulling back to reveal a glittery, cutout map of the United States with *American Bandstand* superimposed on the screen. The fact that the cutout was made of cardboard with glitter glued to the edges is a testament to how low-budget the show was.

Some things remained the same, though—the phone on the lectern that connected Clark to the control room, the cool temperatures in the studio to offset the heat of the lights, the loudness of the music to aid the dancers and lip-syncing performers, the tape on the floor outlining the permissible dance areas and the miles of thick cable that tethered the cameras to America and kept dancers on their toes, sometimes literally, as they tried to avoid them.

Clark wisely retained the local production team. Veteran Ed Yates would oversee operations in the control room, working alongside trusty engineer Frank Kern. Tony Mammarella would continue as producer of the show and ABC consented to have the local WFIL camera crew provide the network feed.

Bandstand was not Yates' only responsibility. His day began at 6 A.M. when he oversaw the production of the station's popular

---

10. *1957 Radio and Television Yearbook.*

University of the Air. Between that and *Bandstand*, he was responsible for several other shows.

"As the years went by, my day was longer and longer," Yates said. "I never had a lunch at all. I brought candy bars with me to the control room."

Under Yates' guidance, *Bandstand* developed into one of the station's smoothest-running shows.

Records were delivered to the control room well in advance of air time. While the engineer played the records and controlled the show's audio, Yates controlled the cameras, directing their movement and picking the shots. Yates also was responsible for inserting the show's many live commercials.

Yates also made two major improvements in the way the show was produced.

"Those shows went fast," Yates said. "The music was usually fast and I wanted to get the shots fast, too."

But moving the bulky cameras through a throng of dancing teenagers proved difficult. Shuffling the massive Fearless Crane camera was practically impossible. Yates had the crane camera dollied to the rear of the studio, cranked as high as it would go and locked it in place. All long shots were taken with this camera, which allowed close-ups of Horn and, later, Clark.

After noticing that singers preferred to hold their own microphones when interviewed, Yates also got rid of the boom mike, which required an operator to push the mike around, a tricky and imprecise skill at best.

It was important to Clark that things go well with *American Bandstand*. A strong impression with the network could open many doors. But the competition would be keen. ABC was plunging full force into the music scene with a variety of programs.

Lawrence Welk, who had been with the network since 1955, had two shows—on Monday and Saturday nights. There was also the highbrow *Voice of Firestone* on Monday night and the folksier *Country Music Jubilee* on Saturday night.

Add primetime shows hosted by Frank Sinatra, Pat Boone, Patrice Munsel, and Guy Mitchell and the ABC-TV lineup for the fall of 1957 was saturated with music programming.

One genre conspicuously missing was rock & roll, even though *The Adventures of Ozzie & Harriet* featured young Ricky Nelson, who made his singing television debut earlier that spring.

ABC executives had hoped to include an Alan Freed program on the fall prime time schedule, but their plans hit an ill-timed speed bump just before *American Bandstand*'s premiere.

Ratings were strong for a pair of Freed specials in May—the first prime time network specials devoted to rock music—and Freed was rewarded with a 13-week run of a Friday night show, *The Big Beat*.

Freed took a cautious approach to the show's July 12 debut program, passing on the more popular hard rockers in favor of the Everly Brothers, Ferlin Husky, and Johnnie and Joe.

For his second show, however, Freed cut loose, bringing on Chuck Berry and Frankie Lymon. The show's close was intended to reflect the wholesomeness of the much-maligned music as the audience swarmed the stage to dance with the artists.

But, after the camera caught a beaming (and black) Lymon dancing with a white girl, the protests started rolling in, especially from the southern United States. The show's sponsors took notice but told Freed he could continue the show, as long as he only featured white acts.

Freed refused and after 21-year-old Jerry Lee Lewis gave a rousing rendition of "Whole Lot of Shakin' Goin' On" on the August 2 telecast, the show was dropped from the ABC lineup, nine weeks shy of a full run.

The lesson was not lost on Dick Clark as he wrapped up final preparations for his show's premiere.

August 5, 1957, was a typically hot and humid day in Philadelphia. Of more concern to Clark and WFIL-TV management was the strike that threatened to derail that afternoon's first broadcast of *American Bandstand* to ABC's 48 affiliate stations.

The National Association of Broadcast Employees and Technicians (NABET) threatened a walkout if the show went on air with a crew from WFIL-TV, which was represented by another union.

NABET members followed through with their threat with wildcat walkouts in New York, Chicago, Los Angeles, and San Francisco. The matter was temporarily resolved so most viewers in those cities saw most of *American Bandstand* that afternoon, but the incensed NABET workers later struck part of John Daly's news show and *The Lawrence Welk Show* before settling the matter for good just before midnight.

The premiere show had the glitches expected from a first-timer. Many print media outlets found the premiere of *American Bandstand* newsworthy.

IT'S MY SHOW NOW

J.P. Shanley of the *New York Times* News Service wrote:

> New York, N.Y.—Viewers who are of voting age are not likely to derive much pleasure from *American Bandstand,* the disk jockey show that began Monday on ABC.
>
> Those who have been voting for quite a few years, may, in fact, find this 90-minute session of music and dancing to be something of an ordeal. . . .
>
> Monday's program began with Elvis Presley's interpretation of "Teddy Bear." Some of the subsequent records were less atrocious but most of the lyrics were not memorable. . . .
>
> During the program, the studio from which it was televised was crowded with teenagers who danced as the records were played.
>
> They were an attractive group of youngsters. The girls wore pretty gowns and the boys were dressed conservatively. There were no motorcycle jackets and hardly a sideburn in the crowd.
>
> The quality of the dancing, however, was poor. There was also a shortage of boys. Quite a few of the girls had to dance with other girls and some of them looked grim about it.

Bob Bernstein of *Billboard* wrote:

> As a sociological study of teenage behavior, the premiere was a mild success. As relaxation and entertainment, it wasn't. Except for a hilarious series of scrambled commercials, which paired sound of picnics with hospital film and sound of Boy Scouts with nail polish film, the record show was rough going. . . .
>
> The bulk of the 90 minutes was devoted to colorless juveniles trudging through early American dances like the Lindy and the box step, to recorded tunes of the day. If that's the answer to the 'horrors' of rock 'n' roll, bring on those rotating pelvises.
>
> Technically, the opener was a shambles, reportedly due to an engineering strike at the show's point of origin, Philadelphia. A local smash, the series isn't going to help that city's reputation nationally as a quiet town. ABC-radio has just banned records. Why doesn't ABC-TV?

CHAPTER 7

BRANCHING OUT

As the reviews of the premiere of *American Bandstand* point out, the show had its problems. In the 1950s era of live television, mistakes were not only common, many viewers found them as entertaining as when things went right.

Nevertheless, Clark made every effort to connect with his national audience in as professional and low key a manner as possible. Acutely aware of the widespread generational polarization wrought by rock & roll and with the ill-fated result of Alan Freed's recent network experiment fresh on his mind, Clark consciously chose "safe" guests for the premiere—veteran song stylist Billy Williams and a pop quartet from Sheboygan, Wis., the Chordettes.

Williams was much in demand at the time as his rendition of a 1930s Fats Waller ditty called "I'm Gonna Sit Right Down and Write Myself a Letter" was racing up the charts. In honor of his first guest performer on *American Bandstand*, Clark recruited cameraman Marvin Brooks to climb a ladder with a sack of letters. The plan was for Brooks to drop the letters in such a way as to resemble a snowstorm. The special effect went awry when Brooks accidentally dropped a fistful of the mail, which appeared to strike Williams on the head.

There were other mistakes, too. On the third show, Paul Anka was caught in lip-sync hell when the record playing his "Diana" in the control room stuck in the middle of the chorus.

BRANCHING OUT

Eight of the 48 ABC-TV network stations that carried the premiere raised "strong objections" following the premiere but their complaints must have been resolved quickly. By the second week, the show was carried by 60 stations and A.C. Nielsen reported that 20 million viewers tuned into the show in its first week.

If Clark was troubled by the reviews or problems associated with hosting a new network show, he didn't show it. Quite the opposite, in fact.

"It took all of 20 minutes after we went off the air that first day for us to know we had a monster on our hands," Clark said. "The phones started ringing off the walls, and suddenly we had this extraordinary concentration of power."[1]

Clark's cool on-air demeanor undoubtedly soothed the nerves of parents everywhere.

Arnold Shaw, the author of *The Rockin' '50s*, called Clark "the great tranquilizer of the era, reassuring parents by his suave manner that rock 'n' roll was not bad and transforming the youngsters on his show into sunshine biscuits."[2]

Clark and Mammarella wisely had a contest from the start, designed to woo national sponsors to the program.

Viewers were invited to write, in 25 words or less, "Why I'd Like to Meet Sal Mineo." The contest drew nearly 30,000 entries in the first five days and sponsors soon followed. The first was Cheerios; the second was a little-known skin product named Clearasil.

For decades, science had been trying to come up with an effective treatment for acne, the scourge of teenagers everywhere. Entrepreneur Ivan DeBloise Combe teamed with chemist Kedzie Teller in 1950 to create a flesh-colored cream called Clearasil that dried up pimples.

Fortunately for Combe, his neighbor, Ollie Treyz, wanted *American Bandstand* to succeed as badly as did Dick Clark. Combe and Clark joined forces for a business relationship that proved immensely successful for both for many years.

It didn't take Clark long to learn that the $1,500 that ABC had budgeted for the program each week didn't go very far, especially when he was booking two acts per day just for the network portion of the show. But the resourceful Clark came up with a solution.

Though he variously referred to his system of payment as "kickbacks" or "check swaps," the bottom line was that no act was paid more than scale and many acts performed for free.

---

1. *Off the Record*, p. 103.
2. *The Rockin' '50s*, p. 176.

"We paid the people as long as we had a budget. When we ran out of the budget, either the record company would pay them or they'd swap the check back."[3]

Meanwhile, *American Bandstand* was fast gaining a reputation among artists as the place to be. In the show's first month guests included Gene Vincent, Jerry Lee Lewis, and Buddy Holly and the Crickets. Its influence extended to the kids watching the show, too.

Chartered buses from far outside Philadelphia often delivered throngs of teens to the WFIL doorstep, where they could live out their dancing fantasies. *Bandstand* parties popped up across the country every afternoon. Record sellers added TV sets to their stores and encouraged people to watch the show there.

In Cleveland, Ohio, WERE disc jockey Tom Edwards reported that the *Bandstand* influence "is reflected at my record hops, where the kids are now doing the new steps they've learned from the Philly kids."[4]

ABC officials locked in *American Bandstand* as a permanent fixture in its afternoon lineup after the four-week trial. Clark leveraged his new status with a bold move—taking over production responsibility for the show through his Click Corporation.

The tiny office at WFIL where Clark, Mammarella and Clark's secretary, Marlene Teti, each had a desk, overflowed with records and mail, including all sorts of unsolicited gifts from appreciative viewers. Eventually, a menagerie of stuffed animals was suspended from the ceiling.

Despite the burden of producing a 90-minute network television show five days a week, Clark knew that the time was right to take on new challenges to realize his professional ambitions.

ABC suggested that the best way to expand the *Bandstand* brand was to take it to prime time. Accordingly, the network offered him a 13-week run of a half-hour *Bandstand* variety show on Monday nights, beginning on October 7. Perhaps wary of losing their rising star, WFIL also offered him a prime time 7 P.M. Saturday night slot with a new local show called *Talent Trend*.

Clark accepted both offers, which put him in the unprecedented position of being on the air for 13½ hours each week, 8½ of those hours on national television.

---

3. *Up Close With Patsy Smullin*, California Oregon Broadcasting, Inc,, *May 13, 2001*.
4. *Billboard*, Sept. 9, 1957.

BRANCHING OUT

TV Guide ran features on *American Bandstand* in September and October. *Billboard* reported that *American Bandstand* ruled the Trendex ratings across its 90-minute time slot for September, 62 percent ahead of CBS and 35 percent higher than NBC. But even on its best night, prime time *Bandstand* badly trailed NBC's *The Price is Right* and CBS' *Robin Hood* in the Monday night ratings. It was gone by December.

There was little evidence that the rare professional setback rattled Clark. In fact, a group of Philadelphia teens from Bartram High School called the Juvenaires provided just the salve to soothe the wounds of defeat.

The Juvenaires had been formed in 1955 by 15-year-old David White. A young songwriter named John Madara heard the group singing on a street corner and began writing songs with White. In 1957, the duo wrote a song called "Do the Bop" and the Juvenaires sang it for Madara's vocal coach, Artie Singer. Singer took the group into the studio and recorded the song for his tiny Singular label, assigning it the number, S711: "S for Singular. The 7-11 because it was a crapshoot."[5]

Singer took the record to Dick Clark, who he knew from his days on the *Paul Whiteman TV Teen Club*. Clark liked the song but didn't care for the title. How about something a little more contemporary, like "At the Hop," he suggested.

Singer, assuming the revised recording would get airplay on Clark's *American Bandstand*, returned to the studio to record "At the Hop." He replaced lead singer Madara with Danny Rapp and renamed the Juvenaires Danny & the Juniors.

Clark liked the new version well enough to play it on the Philadelphia-only portion of the show, but wouldn't play it on the network until it had national distribution. Clark suggested that maybe they could assign the song to ABC's recording arm, ABC-Paramount. Oh, and one more thing . . .

"[Distributor Harry Rosen] comes to me and says, 'Artie, you're not going to believe this. Dick won't play the record unless you give him 50 percent of the publishing'," Singer said.[6]

Once the deal was made, Danny & the Juniors made a December 2 appearance on *Bandstand*, the song charted a week later and would eventually hold down the top spot nationally for seven weeks.

---

5. *Philadelphia Inquirer*, July 8, 1994.
6. *The Wage$ of Spin*, Character Driven Films, 2008.

While the drama over "At the Hop" was playing out, Clark was rolling out his first feature film, *Jamboree*.

The film's script was predictably lame, and the mix of musical acts was peculiar. Songwriter Aaron Schroeder, who wrote five No. 1 hits for Elvis Presley and later would sign Gene Pitney to his Musicor label, cranked out some real clunkers for *Jamboree*. Jazz greats Count Basie and Joe Williams lent some class to the proceedings but seemed woefully out of place.

Not as out of place as country warbler Slim Whitman, though, or "Ron Coby" (really Brazilian singer Cauby Peixoto), whose "Toreador," frankly, wouldn't be welcome anywhere. While strong performances by Jerry Lee Lewis (his screen debut) and Fats Domino nearly saved the day, the film was pretty much a yawner, though it did show how much influence Clark had during production, even before *American Bandstand* became a national sensation.

Take, for example, the matter of face time. All the disc jockeys (except for Clark and Chicago's Howard Miller), were limited to a few seconds while introducing a record or making a comment. Clark, however, managed to wrangle five separate spots for himself.

Clark also managed to keep performances by several Philadelphia acts from the cutting room floor—Charlie Gracie, Jodie Sands, and 17-year-old Frankie Avalon, who looked every bit his age as he cranked out "Teacher's Pet" with his band, Rocco & the Saints. And, to the producer's credit, rather than have main character Honey Wynn (played by actress Freda Holloway), sing Schroeder's insipid lyrics, another eventual Clark favorite, Connie Francis, overdubbed the vocals.

When the film premiered at Philadelphia's Stanton Theater in November 1957, a veritable who's who of the Philadelphia music scene attended, including some royalty from the kids who danced on *American Bandstand*.

Each of the 10 couples who were named finalists in the show's first jitterbug contest were invited to attend. That included Jack Fisher and his dancing partner, Dottie Horner. Fisher, who later produced a documentary, *Bandstand Days*, remembers the night well.

"They picked us up in a limo after *[Bandstand]*, took us to the dinner downtown (at the Chancellor Room, owned by Chancellor Records founder Bob Marcucci). Then we went to the premiere of the movie downtown. We all sat together at the movie theater," Fisher said.

BRANCHING OUT

While Fisher was excited by the night's activities—the limo ride, eating dinner with Frankie Avalon, attending the premiere of a motion picture as an honored guest—the evening had an abrupt ending.

"After all that . . . they dropped us off at the el. There you are, back to reality."

While *Jamboree's* appearance on the big screen undoubtedly buoyed Clark's confidence, November 1957 was a real roller coaster ride for him.

Although Ollie Treyz was being promoted to network president, Treyz did Clark no favors as he catered to another up-and-coming network star, Johnny Carson.

ABC was looking to Carson to rescue the afternoon quiz show *Do You Trust Your Wife?* The show had begun on CBS with ventriloquist Edgar Bergen as its host. Although CBS dropped the show, ABC picked it up.

The show was moved from Los Angeles to New York City and Carson was named as its new host, but the surprising success of *American Bandstand* tied up the most desirable slots for the program. In a curious compromise, ABC decided that the quiz show would be placed in the middle of the *Bandstand* slot although *Bandstand* would still be allotted 90 minutes each weekday.

Thus, *Bandstand* was moved from its 3–4:30 slot to a split schedule—3–3:30 and 4–5 P.M.—with *Do You Trust Your Wife?* taking the 3:30–4 P.M. spot.

The change outraged Clark, who refused to refer to Carson's show by name and openly campaigned against the intrusion, hoping that a flood of letters would bring ABC officials back in line. It didn't work and *Bandstand* was a split show for nearly a year.

Meanwhile, ABC's experiment with prime-time music shows wasn't going so well. Shows starring Frank Sinatra and Guy Mitchell were outright disappointments. *TV Guide* called the debut of *The Pat Boone Chevy Showroom* "about as exciting as a milkshake with two straws" and Clark's own Monday night show was axed at the end of its 13-week run.

Still, ABC thought Clark could bring *Bandstand*-like excitement to prime time. Network brass planned to move Clark's Monday night show to Saturday night, expand it to a full hour and pit it directly against Perry "Mr. Saturday Night" Como and his Emmy-winning NBC blockbuster at 8 P.M.

But they ultimately decided that Clark's as-yet-unsponsored show might be better suited to a more hospitable slot so they carved 30 minutes from *Country Music Jubilee* and gave the 7:30–8 P.M. spot to Clark, starting in early 1958.

Clark continued to expand his business empire in late 1957, incorporating his fifth and sixth businesses—Chips Distributing and Swan Records.

Clark paid $10,000 for his one-third share of Chips, joining Bernie Lowe and Harry Chipetz as co-owners. Lowe, who as Bernie Lowenthal played piano on Paul Whiteman's *TV Teen Club*, previously co-owned a record label with Bob Horn and Nat Segall and earlier in 1957 started the Cameo record label with Kal Mann and Dave Appell.

Clark's investment in Swan was a more modest $500, but he owned half of the label, while Tony Mammarella and Bernie Binnick owned 25 percent apiece. Binnick had joined forces with Clark earlier in 1957 to form Binlark Corporation to produce *Jamboree*.

Buoyed by his experience in shaping "At the Hop" for Danny & the Juniors, Clark tested his influence with another group before the end of 1957.

Earlier in the year, Clark had noticed that the dancers on *Bandstand* did an unusual, slow-moving line dance to "C.C. Rider" by Chuck Willis. Clark described the dance to Nat Goodman, manager of the Diamonds, as kind of a strolling motion and asked if he thought someone could come up with a song that captures that dance.

Clark's suggestion led to the Diamonds recording "The Stroll," the "rock & roll version of the minuet." Clark had the group lip sync the song on *Bandstand* on December 5 and the stroll became the first new dance to be popularized on the show.

The Diamonds' label, Mercury Records, bought a two-page ad in *Billboard,* offering "free stroll diagram cards' to deejays who requested them from the label's Chicago headquarters. Mercury followed that ad with another a month later, paying homage to Clark and the *Bandstand* influence by including a photo of Clark and some of the dancers on the show.

Dancing wasn't the only thing weighing on America teenagers in late 1957. There was trouble in Little Rock, where the Arkansas governor seemed hell-bent on keeping the city's biggest high school from integrating. There was also the draft notice that was going to take Elvis out of circulation—and, presumably, off the charts—for a while.

There was also the embarrassment of Russia beating us into space, not once but twice, with Sputnik 1 and Sputnik 2. There was further embarrassment when a Navy Atlas rocket carrying the first U.S. baby moon blew up just a couple of feet after taking off. The mainstream press called it "Flopnik" and "Stayputnik" but Clark thought *Bandstand* viewers could do better. His contest to name the first U.S. satellite drew more than 40,000 entries in the first week.

By the time the contest ended on December 18, more than 200 baseball players' names had been submitted, as well as some clever entries such as Minnie the Mooncher, Rocket 'n' Roll, Sir Launchalot and Looney Moon. The less-inspiring Ariel and Orbus were the winners.

Although record dealers were reporting that disc sales for the holiday season of 1957 were lagging 1956, *American Bandstand* was on a roll after being on the air for less than five months. Advertisers were eagerly buying up time, ranging from Wisk laundry detergent to Almond Joy to Popsicle. December Trendex figures had *Bandstand* beating its competition by 64 percent. Riding its coattails was *Do You Trust Your Wife?*, which saw its ratings bounce higher by 56 percent after it was coupled with Clark's show.

Ratings, advertisers and record sales were just a few of the ways to measure the success of *American Bandstand*. For Dick Clark, there was a simpler way to gauge the show's success—the mail received at Post Office Box 6, Philadelphia 5, Pennsylvania.

From *Bandstand's* earliest days, the show's regular dancers received mail from adoring fans. The mail was sorted off-camera but frequently was distributed on camera, perpetuating the practice. Clark took the letter writing to new heights when the show went national, first to impress the ABC brass who would decide the show's fate during its trial run, later for its utter wow factor.

Shortly after the show went national, Clark held the first *American Bandstand* fast dance contest. Early fan favorites Bob Clayton and Justine Carrelli were voted by viewers as the top jitterbuggers in the group, each taking home an AMF jukebox stocked with 200 records. Nice as those prizes were, Dick Clark was the ultimate winner as an astounding 700,000 votes were mailed in, cementing the show's popularity at a critical time.

Even without the draw of a dance contest, the mail flowed into the WFIL offices at a heavy rate. Clark hired several women to open and answer the mail, a task that seemed endless. On at least one occasion, Clark gave viewers a glimpse of the volume by bringing it into the studio and dumping it in the middle of the dance floor, apparently not realizing that the crew would have to remove it before the teens could return.

While it was clear entering 1958 that *American Bandstand* and Dick Clark were powerful attractions, the direction of the popular music business was not nearly as clear.

Billboard reported that despite the rise of rock & roll "there were indications, especially during the last four months of the year, that rock & roll popularity may be waning."[7]

A poll done by the Gilbert Youth Research Organization found that 55-year-old Perry Como was teenage America's favorite male singer. Elvis Presley, the acknowledged king of rock & roll who was the teens' favorite in a 1956 poll, came in fourth behind Como, Frank Sinatra, and Pat Boone.

Boone, who like Clark was seen by many as a clean-cut antidote to the emerging rock scene, was a 23-year-old Columbia University student and distant relative of American folk hero Daniel Boone. He had married at 18 and was the father of three young daughters by January 1958, when he was the host of a promising Thursday night musical program on ABC.

Since Boone had lip-synced to "April Love" on *American Bandstand* in November, it was time for Clark to return the favor.

Although Clark lacked the skills of a professional performer, his appearance on Boone's *Chevy Showroom* on January 2, 1958, nevertheless proved memorable. Clark brought along Danny & the Juniors, whose "At the Hop" was the No. 1 song in the country.

Clark was also popular with other media. *Modern Teen* magazine placed him on the cover, albeit in a small photo tucked in a corner, of its January 1958 issue, further enhancing Clark's growing reputation as a star maker. There was more to come.

Concetta Franconero was a Newark, N.J., musical prodigy, playing accordion at age 3 and winning on *Arthur Godfrey's Talent Scouts* at age 12. Although her dad pushed her to a career in show business, young Concetta wasn't so sure.

Torn between a scholarship to study medicine at New York University and music, she delayed her education to attempt a singing career as Connie Francis on MGM Records. Although her first 10 releases were flops, Francis did land a gig dubbing her vocals in place of Freda Holloway's in Clark's *Jamboree* movie.

---

7. *Billboard*, January 13, 1958.

BRANCHING OUT

Francis entered the studio for what she thought would certainly be her last session for MGM in 1957. With 16 minutes left in the session, she recorded one of her father's favorite songs, a 1923 tune called "Who's Sorry Now." Distributor Ed Barsky had left a copy of the song with Dick Clark in September 1957, but the record sat unplayed in Clark's office until the final days of the year.

Although MGM did, indeed, drop Francis after that session, she re-signed with them shortly after Clark finally played the song on *Bandstand* in early January 1958. A stunned Francis witnessed the national debut of her song on TV in her living room. Before the month was over, she was on *Bandstand* herself and the song was starting what would be a 22-week ride on the charts.

While Francis was ecstatic about the dramatic turn in her career, another resuscitation was in progress as a down-in-the-luck Philadelphia group was benefiting from *Bandstand's* magic touch. This time, though, it was Clark's associate Tony Mammarella who provided the spark.

The Gospel Tornados had formed in Philadelphia in 1955 but changed their name to the Thunderbirds when they switched to secular rhythm and blues. Group member Rick Lewis had written a sassy novelty tune while in the service about a henpecked husband and the Thunderbirds unsuccessfully pitched the tune, "Get a Job," to labels in Philadelphia and New York.

But Philadelphia disc jockey Kae Williams was impressed enough that he added the group to one of the shows he promoted at the Uptown Theater. Wanting to record the group on his Junior label, Williams suggested another name change and the Thunderbirds became the Silhouettes.

In October 1957, Williams took the group to the studios of WIP radio, recorded "Get a Job," released the record on Junior and started playing it on the radio.

Sales were strong, but Williams couldn't afford to expand distribution. Al Silver, the owner of Ember Records, bought rights to the record and switched publishing to Wildcat Music, which was owned by Milt Kellem and Mammarella.

With national distribution assured, Clark played "Get a Job" on *Bandstand*. Silver claims to have received orders for 300,000 records the next day. Pressing plants were so busy with "Get a Job," that they ran out of the trademark red Ember labels and pressed some copies with blue labels. The song quickly rose to the top of the charts and spent two weeks at No. 1.

Although the January report of the American Research Bureau cited *American Bandstand* as the top-rated daytime television program in the country, drawing an average 8.4 million viewers on its 105 ABC-TV outlets every day, network executives were apprehensive as the debut of Clark's Saturday night program approached.

Clark had reason to be concerned, too. The show was without a sponsor and he knew the network wouldn't be forking over its $15,000 a week budget for long. Since the show was to originate in New York, he would also be working with a new production crew.

ABC had tabbed Chuck Reeves as executive producer. Reeves, a jazz trumpeter with the Tex Beneke and Stan Kenton bands, had producer experience with *The Morning Show* and *The Gene Autry Show*. The show's producer, Louis "Deke" Heyward, was a staff writer on *The Garry Moore Show* and had won a Sylvania Award as head comedy writer for *The Ernie Kovacs Show*. He also created the popular *Winky Dink and You* children's show. Garth Dietrick of *Tonight* would direct.

Clark was allowed to bring along Mammarella as the show's associate producer. Since Clark was given free rein to book all talent from his home base in Philadelphia, Mammarella was crucial to the success of the show.

The show's format was also a cause for concern. Much of *American Bandstand*'s success was attributed to dancing teenagers. There would be no dancing on the *Saturday Night Show*, which would be staged in the Little Theater at 240 W. 44th Street.

The venue was in the heart of the Broadway theater district and, with a seating capacity of just under 600 [although for the *Saturday Night Show*, seating was said to be half that, or 300], was easily the smallest theater in the neighborhood. Built in 1912 at the height of the "Little Theater Movement," it was also the site of Johnny Carson's *Do You Trust Your Wife?*, the interloper that carved up *Bandstand* every weekday afternoon.

It was snowing when Clark boarded the train in Philadelphia on Saturday morning, February 15, headed to New York for the premiere. By the time he arrived, Manhattan was enduring near-blizzard conditions. To his surprise, New York police had barricaded the area around the theater and there was a blocks-long line of about 1,500 shivering teens.

Once inside, Clark and Heyward talked about what to do about the kids outside. Since less than half of them could squeeze

BRANCHING OUT

into the theater, Heyward suggested that they fill the studio for the 1:30 P.M. rehearsal, then do it again for the actual broadcast.

Fearful that the kids might eventually leave in the face of the bitter cold and continuing snow, Clark sent an aide out to buy hot cocoa for the throng outside the theater doors.

Clark had lined up an impressive array of talent for his first *Saturday Night Show*—Pat Boone, Chuck Willis, Connie Francis, the Royal Teens, and Jerry Lee Lewis. Although the show had more elaborate sets than *American Bandstand*, singers would lip sync to their songs, eliminating the expensive need for musicians to accompany the widely divergent styles of music that were to be presented.

This arrangement was fine with everyone, except Jerry Lee Lewis.

Lewis, who recently had closed a record-setting Alan Freed show at New York's Paramount Theater, brought his raucous band of musicians with him to the Little Theater, where he expected to bring the house down with his energetic and frenetic style. Sales for his most recent release, "Breathless," weren't going well and a strong live performance on network television just might turn the tide.

Reluctantly, Clark agreed to let Lewis perform live, also agreeing to have the president of Lewis' fan club handle the introduction.

Just before showtime, a bus of 40 Philadelphia teenagers arrived, courtesy of Clark, who thought that having a few rows of familiar faces from *Bandstand* might give the show the clout necessary to attract a sponsor.

But, when the New York teens got wind that some of their *Bandstand* favorites from Philadelphia were on the bus, many of them pressed forward to see for themselves. A group of noisy teens soon surrounded the buses, peering in the windows and slapping the sides, causing the bus to rock from side to side. Police intervened and escorted the *Bandstand* group into the theater.

The show went pretty much as planned. Jerry Lee Lewis was as explosive as his fans expected and Boone was characteristically cool. The show pulled a respectable 16.0 Trendex rating (up from the 5.8 of his predecessor), but still lagged NBC's *People Are Funny* (19.4) and CBS' *Perry Mason* (22.3).

Clark built on the success of the first show the next week. He opened the show with guitarist Bill Justis, whose *Raunchy* was rock & roll's first instrumental hit just a few months earlier.

He followed with Philly favorites Danny & the Juniors who first introduced their latest, *Rock and Roll Is Here to Stay*, then were presented their gold record for *At the Hop*. Billy and Lillie were on hand with their latest stroll song, *La Dee Dah* (on Clark and Mammarella's Swan Records) and the Chordettes gave America its first taste of *Lollipop*. Chuck Berry performed *Sweet Little 16* (which mentions *Bandstand*) and even Johnny Carson dropped by to show off his drum skills and promote his ABC-TV show.

Clark had brought his "A game" to Saturday night and Ed Noble noticed. Noble, the Lifesaver magnate who owned ABC before selling it to Leonard Goldenson in 1953, really didn't care for Clark's show but saw its potential as an advertising vehicle for his product, Beech-Nut gum.

Lifesavers had acquired Beech-Nut a year earlier. The longtime manufacturer of baby food had been pushing its gum products through major league baseball players like Stan Musial and Robin Roberts, but Noble wanted to broaden its appeal. What better way than to get behind the hottest disc jockey in the country and his millions of young followers?

Beech-Nut signed on with Dick Clark's *Saturday Night Show* beginning with his third show on March 1, 1958. Clark, who didn't allow teens to chew gum on *American Bandstand*, now found himself enthusiastically hawking the product every Saturday night: "Wrapped in green and made for a teen, Beech-Nut FlavorIFIC gum."

The IFIC part of the tagline soon became iconic. Ushers handed out complimentary packs of Beech-Nut spearmint gum and large green IFIC buttons to the audience as it filed in, ensuring that the sponsor's message would be driven home with every future audience camera shot.

One of Clark's guests on the first show sponsored by Beech-Nut presented a unique challenge.

John Zacherle was a Philadelphia native, an English literature graduate of the University of Pennsylvania and a member of a Philadelphia repertory theater company when he got the break of a lifetime—a recurring role on WCAU-TV's *Action in the Afternoon* television program.

Action was a bold experiment, a five-day-a-week live western, the only one on TV when it debuted on February 2, 1953. Interior shots were done in a studio; exterior shots were done in an employees' parking lot in Bala Cynwyd on the western edge of Philadelphia where a handful of mock buildings were hastily constructed to create the fictional town of Hubberle, Montana. Although background music was used to mask road noise from nearby City Line Avenue, it was not unusual to see motorcycles or airplanes pop into frames of the live western action drama.

Zacherle started as an extra on the show, filling many roles, before being added to the regular cast as Grimy James, the undertaker who was always seen in a moth-eaten black frock. The show lasted just one year, but Zacherle came to mind in 1957 when WCAU bought a package of Universal horror films and needed a host for its weekend *Shock Theater*. Zacherle, wearing the same frock coat he'd worn in *Action in the Afternoon*, became a new undertaker, Roland. The show was an immediate hit when it debuted that September.

Cameo record boss Bernie Lowe was tipped to Roland's exotic charms by his daughter, who suggested that a recording of the shockmeister might be a good thing for the label. Soon Lowe and Kal Mann were dashing off lyrics, Dave Appel was summoning his Applejacks band and Zacherle was headed to the studio.

Once the record was complete—"Dinner With Drac" on one side; "Igor" on the flip—it was taken to Clark to lobby for airplay. Clark thought the song had potential but objected to the gory lyrics on "Igor." He sent Lowe and Mann back to try again.

Apparently, Clark was not alone in his concern. Radio stations across the country were refusing to play the record. Columnist Dorothy Kilgallen, who spent much of the 1950s bashing rock & roll (excepting her alleged lover Johnnie Ray), pointed out that stations were put off by "Igor's" "blue lyrics."

Cameo came back with a new record—"Dinner With Drac, Parts 1 and 2"—which was acceptable to Clark, but there were other issues.

Although Clark started playing "Part 2" on *Bandstand*, he was having a difficult time getting Zacherle before the *American Bandstand* cameras at WFIL. WCAU was perfectly willing to allow Zacherley (as he was now known after adding the "y" to his name) appear on the show as himself, but they nixed any appearance in makeup or costumes that would make him resemble Roland. Plus, WFIL wasn't about to let him appear in any fashion since it would amount to a free plug for a rival station.

The apparent compromise was to book Zacherley on the *Saturday Night Show*, which was done on March 1, 1958. After

Zacherley later moved his TV show out of Philadelphia to New York, he was allowed to appear on *Bandstand*, which he often did for future Halloween-themed shows.

One of the less obvious effects of the success of Clark's *Saturday Night Show* was the straining of relationships between Clark and "the New York television music establishment," especially Alan Freed and Ed Sullivan.

Although Clark was born and raised in New York, because of his power base in Philadelphia he was perceived by many in the entertainment business to be an outsider. His move into New York City—Sullivan and Freed's turf—was seen as an affront.

In many ways, Clark and Sullivan were similar. Both were at their best when they had the most control. Both men became notorious for asking singers to tone down lyrics before being allowed to perform on their shows and both men were known to ban acts that didn't bow to their demands.

But, while Clark's affable on-air style masked the chain-smoking, sometimes hard-drinking, short-tempered and ruthless businessman that lay beneath, Sullivan's dour personality was readily apparent.

His stiff on-air demeanor would provide ample inspiration for countless impersonators in the decades ahead. Comedian Joe E. Lewis once quipped of Sullivan: "He was a man who could brighten a room simply by leaving it."[8]

Clark and Sullivan each had a stake in the popular music scene, too. For Clark, popular music was the very essence of his show. For Sullivan, a true television pioneer of the variety show, it was an increasingly popular segment of his program each Sunday night. In November 1955, Sullivan had devoted an entire show to rhythm and blues music, featuring then mostly unknowns (at least to prime-time television viewers) LaVern Baker, Bo Diddley and the Five Keys with radio disc jockey Tommy "Dr. Jive" Smalls on hand to co-host.

Since 1956, Sullivan had been locked in a heated Sunday night ratings battle with Steve Allen, whom NBC scheduled directly opposite Sullivan's CBS show with the express purpose of dethroning Sullivan from his perch as "King of Sunday night." This put Allen and Sullivan in direct competition for the hottest musical acts any given week. With Clark, the most influential disc jockey in the country, now in the mix, things got a bit testy.

---

8. *Vanity Fair*, July 1997, *The Ed Sullivan Show, Reconsidered*, by Nick Tosches.

BRANCHING OUT

That Sullivan would publicly feud with Allen and Clark should not have been a surprise. His feuds with Walter Winchell, Hedda Hopper, and Jack Paar were legendary.

"Harriet Van Horne of The New York World-Telegram & Sun wrote, 'Sullivan got to where he is by having no personality; he is the commonest common denominator.' In response, Sullivan wrote her an uncharacteristically short note 'Dear Miss Van Horne. You Bitch. Sincerely, Ed Sullivan.'"[9]

What really galled Sullivan about Clark, though, were his "check swaps," that resulted in some performers not receiving payment from Clark for appearing on *American Bandstand*. When Sullivan found out that singer Tony Bennett's payment for his Sept. 5, 1957, appearance on *Bandstand* was the then-union scale of $155 compared to the $5,000 to $7,000 that Sullivan had to shell out for a similar performance on his Sunday night show three months later, Sullivan took his complaint to the American Federation of Television and Radio Artists.

In Sullivan's complaint, he accused Clark of using "sleazy tactics" in a scheme designed to outwit AFTRA and defraud tax people.[10]

Furthermore, while reminiscing about the famous *Ed Sullivan Show* of January 6, 1957, when guest Elvis Presley was televised from just the waist up, Sullivan pointed out that the decision was made for the good of his audience: "The kids who came here were not the Dick Clark rabble. They were kids from good homes."[11]

As in any good feud, Clark had a different point of view.

"He [Sullivan] was a miserable bastard in those days. He tried to do us in, to kill the show. . . . Sullivan didn't understand the music, he was too busy booking trained seals, ventriloquists, and Russian dancing bears."[12]

Clark's differences with Freed were even more personal.

Freed is often credited for naming rock & roll while a disc jockey in Cleveland in the early 1950s. Indeed, after signing Morris Levy as his manager in 1954 and moving to WINS radio in New York City, Freed and Levy copyrighted the term "rock & roll," but found that collecting fees for using the phrase was an impossible task.

---
9. From edsullivan.com, 2014.
10. *New York News*, Ed Sullivan column, February 15, 1960.
11. *Philadelphia Inquirer.* July 11, 1958.
12. *Rock, Roll & Remember*, p. 131.

Freed found other ways to supplement his WINS paycheck, many of them questionable. One way was to cut himself in on the writing credits for songs that he had no hand in actually writing. Thus, when he was asked by *Billboard* columnist Ren Grevatt about what roles a disc jockey should be allowed to play in the music business, Freed said a deejay shouldn't be associated with record companies, distributors "or any phase of the record business," except for music publishing, which "was a different story."[13]

The comments appeared to be a direct slap at Clark, whose entry into the popular music spotlight had dethroned Freed as the country's rock spokesman. This doubtless rankled Freed, who preferred live performances by original music creators fresh off the street corners of America to the lip-syncing, neatly coiffed song stylists favored by Clark.

As Philadelphia record veteran Harold Lipsius put it, Alan Freed was the street hustler and Dick Clark was the altar boy.[14]

One thing Clark and Freed had in common, though, was to recognize and take advantage of an opportunity. In early 1958, that opportunity had arrived in the form of Jerry Lee Lewis.

Lewis, an early label mate of Elvis Presley, had the back story and talent that allowed him to quickly shoot to the forefront of the still-evolving rock music scene.

The son of dirt-poor farmers who mortgaged the family farm near Ferriday, La., to buy a piano so their prodigious son could learn with cousins Mickey Gilley and Jimmy Swaggart, Lewis and his cousins lurked around a black juke joint where they were enthralled by the boogie-woogie they heard.

Legend has the Lewis family selling 33 dozen eggs to bankroll a trip to Memphis where young Jerry Lee encamped outside Sam Phillips' Sun studio until he got a shot inside, where Elvis cut his earliest discs.

Sun eventually opened its doors and tried to capture on record the energetic—some might say manic—style that would make the blond, curly-topped Lewis a national sensation.

Lewis had made his national network debut, performing "Whole Lotta Shakin' Goin' On "on the *Steve Allen Show* just eight days before *American Bandstand* went national and was a guest on Freed's final *Big Beat* show on ABC on August 2, 1957. He appeared on *Bandstand* on August 19 and was the clear star of

---
13. *Billboard*, February 24, 1958, *On the Beat*, by Ren Gravatt.
14. *Record Makers and Breakers: Voices of the Independent Rock 'n' Roll Pioneers*.

BRANCHING OUT

Freed's record-breaking 1957 holiday concerts at the Brooklyn Paramount.

Clark had booked him on the first broadcast of the *Saturday Night Show* where Lewis brought the house down with his live rendition of "Great Balls of Fire" and performed his newest release, "Breathless," sparking sales of about 100,000 copies but the song was getting little exposure elsewhere. Its unusual rhythm made the song difficult to dance to and sales tapered off quickly.

Sam Phillips' brother, Judd, who handled Sun promotions and was Lewis' manager, was talking with Clark about booking Lewis back on the show to pump life into the song when they came up with an idea: why not come up with a tie-in with Beech-Nut?

The deal they cooked up was to have viewers mail five Beech-Nut spearmint wrappers and 50 cents to Sun and receive in return a copy of "Breathless." When Phillips suggested that Lewis do some sort of on-air jingle plugging the gum, ABC officials became leery. But when Phillips guaranteed that neither ABC nor Beech-Nut would lose a single penny through the promotion, the arrangement was agreed to.

Lewis performed "Breathless" again on the *Saturday Night Show* on March 8 and the people at Sun waited for the orders to roll in. What started as a trickle turned into a torrent.

"There were bets all over ABC-TV that we'd fail," said Phillips. "The first week we got fifty, maybe seventy-five orders. Next week, maybe five or six hundred, The third week, my God, fifty thousand! . . . We hadda cut it off in the end—the post office couldn't take it."[15]

Everyone at Sun was pressed into action, including session musicians, stuffing thousands of copies of "Breathless" into envelopes for mailing.

Beech-Nut reaped the benefit, too. It sold more spearmint gum in the first week after the offer was televised than it had in any week in its history, forcing its production plant into overtime.

The promotion was officially credited with sales of 48,000 records, a respectable number, but it was dwarfed by the 262,000 extended-play records Clark sold later in the year in a tie-in with Bosco, a chocolate flavored drink that was one of his *American Bandstand* sponsors. The first two volumes of *Dick Clark All-Time Hit*s were released via Bosco and were followed by *Volume 3* (Beech-Nut) and *Volume 4* (Dr Pepper).

---

15. *Hellfire*, p. 145.

Although these releases each featured six hit versions of songs by artists who appeared on *Bandstand*, that wasn't the case with Clark's first tie-in disc, *American Bandstand Favorite*s, that was released through Cheerios. That eight-cut EP included just two originals (both from Cameo Records)—"Butterfly" by Charlie Gracie and "Back to School Again" by Timmie Rogers. Although not generally known at the time, Clark held some of the publishing rights on both songs.

Clark's success in landing Beech-Nut as a sponsor and quickly capitalizing on the connection by extending his program's reach led *Advertising Age* to predict that Clark "may replace Arthur Godfrey as the number-one personal salesman."[16]

While *American Bandstand* had shaken up the world of daytime television in its first six months, Dick Clark's success in prime time with his *Saturday Night Show* amplified his role as a true shaper of the modern music scene. But to much of adult America, he was still something of a mystery. That would soon change.

---

16. *Rockin' in Time: A Social History of Rock and Roll*, p. 54.

CHAPTER 8

THE PHILLY SCENE

As *Life* magazine sent a reporter and photographer to Philadelphia to shadow Clark for a future article, *Billboard*'s Bob Rolontz kicked off a two-part series outlining "The Philadelphia Story" on March 10, 1958, with a story headlined "Drive, Talent, Hits, Clark Make Philly the Hottest."

Rolontz pointed out that since *Bandstand* went national, "record manufacturers, music publishers, promotion men, and artists flock into this city daily and the 30th Street Station of the Pennsylvania Railroad is like an annex to the Brill Building."

To Philadelphia insiders, though, the hub of activity was in Center City, near Rittenhouse Square. The Philadelphia building most analogous to New York's Brill Building was the Shubert Building. To passersby, it was the Shubert Theater, a magnificent facility that dominated the ground floor at 250 South Broad Street.

The floors above the theater, however, were where deals were made, careers were launched (or dashed) and where dreamers and schemers could pitch their hopes and ideas to one another. The Shubert was home to dozens of songwriters, managers, booking agents, vocal coaches and an eclectic collection of upstarts connected to the exploding music business in every conceivable way.

Right around the corner was another key building in the Philadelphia music industry. Although it lacked the grand style and history that gave the Shubert the stature of a local icon, the nameless office building was just as important.

Located across the street from the Philadelphia Academy of Music, 1405 Locust was mostly inhabited by lawyers and other 9-to-5 businesses, but it also housed the offices of Swan and Cameo records.

Philadelphia's fast-growing reputation had generated an explosion of independent record labels, most concentrating on local talent, and an extraordinary cadre of independent distributors.

Rolontz said the presence of *American Bandstand* made the Philadelphia distributors doubly important.:

> Since every manufacturer is competing to get a record started in Philadelphia and eventually on the national *Bandstand* show, the freebies are freer in this city than elsewhere and the arrangements that distributors have to appear to be more liberal, too.[1]

One of the people credited for Philadelphia's surge in influence was Bernie Lowe, one of Clark's partners in Chips Distributing. Lowe and fellow Philadelphian Artie Singer opened the 20th Century Institute of Music in 1947 where Lowe taught piano and Singer gave vocal training. Lowe eventually became musical director for Paul Whiteman's *TV Teen Club* at WFIL-TV where he met Clark.

Lowe, Nat Segall, and Bob Horn created the Teen and Sound labels. Teen was not noteworthy except that it launched the career of Freddie Bell & the Bellboys. The Bellboys' first pressing of Jerry Lieber and Mike Stoller's "Hound Dog" in 1955 eventually found its way to Elvis Presley, via Big Mama Thornton. Sound managed a pair of national hits in 1955 with Gloria Mann's "Earth Angel" and "Teen Age Prayer," but both labels were dropped after Horn was fired from *Bandstand*.

In late 1956, Lowe borrowed $2,000 to form a new label, Cameo, with Kalman Cohen (known professionally as Kal Mann). Mann had started in show business in the 1940s as a comedy writer and performed his own musical parodies in Poconos resorts. He operated an office above Lowe and Singer's downtown

---

1. *Billboard*, March 10, 1958.

music school and eventually began writing lyrics for Lowe and Singer's melodies.

Mann and Lowe broke through as songwriters when Nat "King" Cole recorded their "Take Me Back to Toyland" in 1955. That led to a one-year songwriting contract with brothers Jean and Julian Aberbach, owners of Hill & Range Music in New York.

Cameo was operating out of the basement of Lowe's home when he and Mann co-wrote a song called "Butterfly." They recruited a South Philadelphian, Charlie Gracie, to record the number as a demo for the Aberbachs. The Aberbachs passed on the song, allowing "Butterfly" to become Cameo's first hit record. It was a No. 1 national hit for Gracie, buoyed by airplay from Clark on *Bandstand*, which was still a local show.

Gracie's follow-up, "Fabulous," cracked the top 20 in the summer of 1957 but was eclipsed by another Mann-Lowe composition that the pair had written earlier for Hill & Range, "(Let Me Be Your) Teddy Bear," a chart-topper for Elvis Presley that summer.

Cameo had two other hits in 1957—"Back to School Again" by Timmie Rodgers and "Silhouettes" by the Rays—but it was John Zacherley's "Dinner With Drac" that firmly entrenched the label on the national scene.

Besides introducing America to "the Cool Ghoul," "Dinner With Drac" offered a glimpse of what lay ahead for Cameo. Mann's clever lyrics and Dave Appell's sharp arrangement and plucky guitar work were perfect matches for Zacherley's deadpan shockmeister persona.

Appell, who also worked on Gracie's "Butterfly" and "Fabulous" sessions, was another native Philadelphian who had returned home in time to participate in the 1950s rock & roll whirlwind. The Dave Appell Quartet was the house band for Ernie Kovacs' first TV show in Philadelphia in the early 1950s and jumped on the rock express as the Applejacks in the mid-1950s. Before joining Cameo as a $50 a week song arranger, Appell and his band appeared in Alan Freed's *Don't Knock the Rock* movie.

Appell had his hands on virtually every aspect of Cameo's business, from engineering and mixing songs to the actual production of the vinyl. Cameo's tiny studio soon became the first choice for the area's singers and musicians.

The studio, which had been built years earlier to record announcements for Philadelphia's trolley cars, took up less than 300 square feet and recording had to be done after 6 P.M. or on weekends to not interfere with other businesses in the building. A mike was strung into the men's room to create an echo chamber.

To many people, Cameo and Swan were the same company. Indeed, the labels shared office space in the Locust Street building in the late 1950s and Swan's first LP release—*Treasure Chest of Hits*—included just five songs that were Swan singles while including six Cameo releases and "Teenage Prayer" by Gloria Mann, an oldie originally released on Lowe's Sound label.

Although Dick Clark had no official business connection to Cameo, he and Lowe were business partners in Chips Distributing and Mallard Pressing Corporation, a South Philadelphia record manufacturing facility.

Clark's connection to Swan was more direct. He owned half of the label, with Tony Mammarella and Bernie Binnick owning the rest. Since the label debuted in late 1957, it had already had national hits with "La Dee Dah" by Billy & Lillie and "Click Clack" by Dicky Doo & the Don'ts.

Having successful national labels like Cameo and Swan in the same city proved crucial to the success of *Bandstand*, which depended on three guest stars each day, Monday through Friday. Whenever Clark needed someone on short notice, there were plenty of artists available. A third Philadelphia label also helped— Chancellor Records.

Clark had no official business ties to Chancellor either, but he enjoyed a close relationship to one of the label's co-founders, Bob Marcucci. Marcucci's plan to attend medical school at Penn State had been dashed when his parents divorced when he was 17. Instead, he worked at a variety of jobs in South Philadelphia to help support his mother. Ten years later, he borrowed $10,000 from his father to start a record label with a longtime friend and fellow songwriter, Peter DeAngelis.

They set up shop just a couple blocks east of Cameo and Swan, a few stories above the Forge Room restaurant in the Chancellor Hall Hotel. The landmark building provided the name and logo for their new enterprise.

It was a rocky start for Chancellor Records. The label's first record—"I Love My Girl" by locally popular vaudevillian Cozy Morley—was a bust. They nearly went bankrupt with their second offering—"Calypso Parakeet" by 9-year-old Patty Brandon—when they sent out hundreds of live parakeets to disc jockeys while promoting the disc, which also flopped.

THE PHILLY SCENE

Marcucci and DeAngelis finally turned the corner with a pop song by another Philadelphia singer, Jodie Sands. Sands' "With All My Heart" was a top 20 national hit in the summer of 1957, landing her a spot on the national portion of *American Bandstand* in the show's second week. More importantly, Sands' success led to a national distribution deal for Chancellor with ABC-Paramount and locked in a spot for Sands in Clark's *Jamboree* movie.

Sands not only joined fellow Philadelphian Charlie Gracie on the *Jamboree* roster but brought along another bonus, the band Rocco & the Saints, which featured two of Sands' Chancellor label mates—Andy Martin and Frankie Avalon.

Martin was the band's lead singer but it was 17-year-old Avalon who was the band's top attraction. As a youngster in music-rich South Philadelphia, Avalon became known as a child prodigy for his trumpet playing, winning numerous talent shows and landing on Paul Whiteman's show in 1951.

Marcucci had been tipped to Martin's potential as an up-and-coming rocker but was more impressed with the good-looking Avalon when he scouted Rocco & the Saints. He signed both singers and placed them in *Jamboree*. Martin was the opening act in the movie, dubbing "Record Hop Tonight" over an elaborately choreographed scene.

But it was the sparsely produced "Teacher's Pet" by the clean-cut, boyish-looking Avalon that stood out for most critics. Avalon found himself in Beltone Studio in New York City in late 1957 to record a new song written by Marcucci and DeAngelis, "De De Dinah."

The simple song proved to be more difficult to record than anyone expected. After more than 20 takes, they had managed to get through the song just a handful of times. Weary of the session, Avalon suggested that maybe he should just sing the song while holding his nose. That nasally infused final take was the one that finally made it onto vinyl and became the label's first million-selling record.

Other, smaller labels also flourished in Philadelphia in the wake of *American Bandstand*'s early success.

Bill Haley took a stab at label ownership with his Clymax Records in nearby Chester, pumping out a few rockabilly tunes and even giving Clark's fellow WFIL host, popular kid's show host Sally Starr, a shot at stardom with a single ("Rockin' In the Nursery") and LP (*My Gal Sal*). But even with the instrumental backing of

Bill Haley's Comets, neither release made a dent on the national charts.

Venton "Buddy" Caldwell was an upholsterer by trade who created two Philadelphia labels in 1958—first with V-Tone, followed by a subsidiary label, Len. Leonard Rosen, the songwriting son of song plugger Harry Rosen, plunged into the label business with Rhythm Records. Herb Slotkin, who began selling records on his Grand Records label out of his Treegoob's appliance store in the early 1950s, largely missed the early *Bandstand* boom but would recover to land a few hits a couple of years later.

Some of Philadelphia's top disc jockeys also owned labels in early 1958. Kae Williams, who also owned a record store and was the promoter of several local musicians, owned two of them—Junior and Kaiser. Jocko Henderson was a co-owner of Time and Main Line Records and Georgie Woods was a co-owner of Red Top Records.

While *American Bandstand* had accomplished a lot in its first six months as a national program, it was not at all clear that the program (or Clark) could maintain its phenomenal success.

For one thing, the show's concept was so simple, it was easily duplicated. *Billboard* estimated that more than 100 copycat shows had sprung up across the land. Some shows were content to piggyback on *Bandstand's* success, hitting the air just before or just after Clark's show. Others, however, took *Bandstand* head-on, airing at least part of their show at the same time as *Bandstand*. That included at least a few ABC outlets.

The most notable of these was *The Buddy Deane Show* out of Baltimore, just 100 miles southwest of Philadelphia. There are many parallels between Deane's show and *American Bandstand*. Both shows originated in 1957, with Deane's show premiering on Sept. 9, just about a month after Bandstand went national on ABC. Indeed, *The Buddy Deane Show* was created so Baltimoreans wouldn't have to go to the network for its teen dancing fix.

Deane's show was a success from the start, filling two hours every afternoon, six days a week. For the next six years, Deane pre-empted *American Bandstand* in the Baltimore market. Within six months, Deane was pulling down *Bandstand*-like numbers, some 55 percent of the late afternoon audience. Like *Bandstand* in its early years, Deane had his own committee of teens, called "The Buddy Deaners."

THE PHILLY SCENE

It was *The Buddy Deane Show* that provided the inspiration for *Hairspray*, the play (and eventual movie) about a fictionalized TV teen dance show that was written by Baltimorean John Waters.

Another 40 miles down the road, independent WTTG-TV was pulling big numbers in Washington, D.C., with *The Milt Grant Show*. Grant was another radio veteran who slid over to TV. His program started as a Saturday afternoon offering called *Record Hop* but was elevated to daily weekday status as it grew in popularity.

In Boston, *American Bandstand* was pre-empted on the local ABC outlet by a local program. WHDH-TV didn't officially hit the Boston airwaves until four months after *Bandstand* made its national debut and it took a while before Clark's show was supplanted by *Boston Ballroom*, but Bob Clayton's program would be a fixture for years to come.

Clark was quite familiar with two of his competitors. Jim Gallant was a newsman at WFIL-TV before Triangle Publications shipped him off to another Triangle station—WNHC in New Haven, Conn.—to launch a *Bandstand* clone, *Connecticut Bandstand*, in October 1956. Jocko Henderson, who gained fame at WHAT and WDAS in Philadelphia, had radio shows in Philadelphia and New York City for a couple of years and was a daily commuter between the two cities before hosting a TV dance show on New York's Channel 13, *Jocko's Rocket Ship*.

Some TV disc jockeys chose to challenge *American Bandstand* by playing different types of music, like cuts from LPs rather than 45s. Among these were Barry Kaye in Pittsburgh, Martin Block in New York City, and Bill Randle in Cleveland. Clark's success had provoked music broadcasters like Bob Martin, program director of WJBK in Detroit.

"We refuse to surrender to Dick Clark," Martin wrote to June Bundy, author of *Billboard's Vox Jox* column as published on February 24, 1958. "His success has been a great stimulant to every disc jockey in the country, but there is no reason in the world to drop from the competitive race because of one man's success."

The decentralization of the music industry that accompanied the rise of rock & roll was noted in an early 1958 report from the Music Performance Trust Fund, a nonprofit independent public service organization. which reported that records were being pressed in every state in the United States except for South Carolina and Wyoming.

Around the same time, Blair Television, a sales and marketing company for television stations, was touting the huge teen market by emphasizing to its more than 5,000 clients that teens bought 70 percent of all phonograph records sold in the U.S. Blair's message was clear: there's a lot of money to be made by catering to teens. Don't blow it.

Nobody was positioned better to take advantage of that market than Dick Clark. He had two immensely popular network TV shows that were focused on teenagers and their passion for music and he was building a business empire to take advantage of every area of the music business. But TV was relatively new and the public taste is notoriously fickle. He needn't look any further than his predecessor, Bob Horn, to see how one misstep could bring his meteoric rise to a flaming end. And there were reasons to be concerned.

It was true that *American Bandstand* had a Trendex rating nearly equal to the sum of the other two major networks and that half the audience on the 105 ABC affiliates that carried the program were adults. Clark received up to 45,000 letters a week and was earning an estimated $500,000 a year.

But the strong ratings were spotty. In New York, for instance, *Bandstand* pulled just half the rating it pulled in Philadelphia. In Chicago, the show ran a distant fourth in the ratings, trailing *Brighter Day*, *Queen For a Day* and *Mr. And Mrs. North*. Across the Midwest, in fact, ratings were erratic.

And, even though Clark was recognized as the nation's premier hitmaker, there was trouble brewing that even he couldn't control—the backlash against rock & roll itself.

Besides having a polarizing effect between parents from the big-band era and their offspring, the music had much the same effect among radio stations.

In Milwaukee, WISN tested rock's popularity by pre-empting its regular programming without warning, playing rock & roll instead. After 5 hours and 600 complaints, the station returned to its regular programming. Disc jockey Charlie Hanson then earned a spot in local papers with a photo of him burning 200 rock records in the station's courtyard. An ad campaign followed: "We gave them what we were told they wanted but they hated it!"

In San Francisco, KSFR-FM distributed window stickers that read "I Kicked the Junk Music Habit by Listening to KSFR." In

THE PHILLY SCENE

Nashville, WMAK disc jockey Leslie Scott was fined $25 for disorderly conduct after burning 600 Elvis Presley records outside the city's Parthenon Monument.

And in St. Louis, KWK declared a seven-day stretch as "Record Breaking Week" during which disc jockeys gave rock records one last on-air spin before smashing them. Buying rock & roll records was equal to buying girlie magazines in the minds of many.

While many stations doubtless were sincere in their opposition to the music, there was something else at play, too. For most of the 1950s, radio disc jockeys were the major factors in determining whether a record was a hit or not. Without airplay, a tune was doomed.

But that role now mostly belonged to Dick Clark. No matter how many times a song was played on a 50,000-watt clear channel radio station, it could not match the reach of *American Bandstand* or Clark's *Saturday Night Show*. A local disc jockey's power was further diminished by the emergence of a new format called Top 40 radio. Under Top 40 rules, deejays were restricted in what songs they could play, largely losing the ability to break out a hit on their own. The success of Top 40 pioneers like the Storz, Plough and McClendon stations fueled the trend from coast to coast.

Influential disc jockeys, who once were doted on by song pluggers and record labels, saw their influence—and income—decline. Their power was shifting to record dealers who began publishing Top 40-type sheets themselves and distributing them through retail outlets. Known as "ulcer sheets" to those in the music business, the sheets served as shopping lists for many teens who often bought records they hadn't even heard because they appeared to be popular on the sheets. Free records were now going to the dealers instead of the disc jockeys.

Stan Dale, a disc jockey at WAIT in Chicago, was vocal in his disdain for the Top 40 format. "It's the biggest cancer that ever hit the broadcasting industry," Dale said. "Radio has been reduced to nothing more than a glorified jukebox."[2]

Martin Block of WABC in New York offered an alternative to Top 40. Block teamed with Teenage Survey, Inc., to poll 60,000 people weekly to help him select discs to play on his show. In addition, Block established a "Platter Pickers Club" of teens who

---
2. *Billboard*, April 7, 1958.

could play a part in the selection process. WABC officials liked the concept so much they expanded it to all the station's programs and dubbed it "Operation 60,000."

Ironically, Top 40 pioneer Todd Storz was the organizer of the first three-day Pop Disc Jockey Convention in Kansas City in March 1958. Presumably, the convention was intended to bring some sort of order to the chaos that was pop radio in the late 1950s. That didn't happen. Indeed, the highlight of the affair was a blistering attack on rock & roll programmers by Mitch Miller of Columbia Records, the most esteemed artists and repertoire man in the entire USA.

Miller's speech to 900 disc jockeys and program managers, which drew the convention's only standing ovation, blasted stations for "lazy programming" and bowing "to the 8 to 14-year-olds, to the pre-shave crowd that makes up 12 percent of the country's population and zero percent of its buying power."[3]

Furthermore, Miller said, America's adults are tuning out and retreating to their living rooms where they can enjoy real music in the peace and comfort of their own homes.

Miller's speech drew national coverage and got mixed reviews from the radio community, reflecting the lack of consensus that permeated an industry that was trying to cope with a social shift never seen in America.

Dave Garroway, the genial host of the increasingly popular *Today* morning show on NBC-TV, tackled the changing scene in an unprecedented week-long survey of U.S. teenagers in April 1958. One of the segments included a live remote from the Ford Theater in Detroit where an Alan Freed tour was appearing. Freed brought along Jerry Lee Lewis as Garroway probed the popularity of rock & roll music among teens.

Meanwhile, a very different probe of the music was being conducted in Washington, D.C.

Sen. George Smathers, a Florida Democrat, had introduced a bill that would ban broadcast stations from owning interests in music publishing or recording. The Smathers bill was a thinly veiled slap at rock & roll music and an extension of the decades-long feud between ASCAP and BMI. Put simply, ASCAP represented "good music;" BMI represented the rest.

ASCAP (The Association of Composers, Authors, and Publishers) is the older of the two organizations, formed in 1914.

---

3. *Billboard*, March 17, 1958.

THE PHILLY SCENE

Broadcasters, fearful of a strike and increased ASCAP royalty rates, formed their own group, Broadcast Music, Inc. (BMI) in 1941. ASCAP remained the province of most pop music until the 1950s when BMI, which was pretty much limited to country, Latin American and race (blues) music in the 1940s, took off as rock & roll emerged.

ASCAP loyalists claimed that rock's rise was the result of a massive conspiracy among independent labels and radio stations. Without this forced feeding of such trashy music to America's youth, the modern music scene would return to the norm enjoyed by their parents, they reasoned.

Thus, Smathers was pressured to introduce his bill and hearings into the ownership issue were convened. Witnesses were heard but the bill went nowhere, largely because ASCAP songs got airplay over BMI songs by at least a 5-to-1 margin nationally and ASCAP's revenue from broadcasters had risen four-fold, from less than $5 million in 1941 to more than $20 million in the mid-1950s.

The Smathers bill was mostly a distraction, although lawyer Seymour Lazar did plant the seeds for further investigation, alleging that some disc jockeys commanded up to $500 a week in payola—payment from record companies to play their releases. Disc jockeys objected, of course, but the issue was far from dead.

Another issue that largely went unscrutinized before 1958 was the treatment of artists, particularly young artists. Buddy Knox was one of them.

Knox was a young musician from Happy, Texas, about 50 miles north of Lubbock in the same West Texas area that produced Roy Orbison and Buddy Holly. Like Orbison and Holly, Knox was drawn to Norman Petty's studio in nearby Clovis, New Mexico, where he struck gold with an early rock & roll favorite, "Party Doll."

But, like so many young musicians from that era, Knox was taken advantage of by more business-savvy music executives who took over his career. His experience was shared by countless young musicians across the country in the 1950s.

In a 1989 interview, Knox said that Norman Petty did his best to protect Knox's business interests, but that he didn't always follow Petty's advice.

"We didn't know nothing," Knox said. "They said 'Sign here kid and I'll make you rich. Here's $1,500. Sign this.' If you've only had

$35 in your pocket, $1,500 is the end of the world and you'd sign almost anything for it. And that's exactly what all of us done."

"Petty was very careful about who he did business with in New York because the New York guys are takeover type people. You come in there and they want everything, they want you to get out of the way while they make money off it. They just sit back on their fat butts in New York and collected the money and screwed everybody. And that's exactly what they all done in New York to all of us guys when we first came in. Most of us older guys don't care for New York."

For Charlie Gracie, the takeover people weren't from New York. They were from his hometown of Philadelphia.

Raised in South Philadelphia in an area full of haberdashers and pawn shops that he and his friends called "The Fence" because kids would steal things and pawn them there, young Gracie wanted to be a trumpet player like his idol, Harry James. But Gracie's dad, Sam, a hat maker at John B. Stetson, steered him to the guitar instead.

The guitar came easy to Gracie and he was soon hauling his guitar and amplifier around town to play clubs and at weddings. He appeared on the *Horn & Hardart Children's Hour* and got a shot on *The Paul Whiteman Show* in 1951 where he was a five-time winner, earning his family its first refrigerator. He caught the attention of Graham Prince of Cadillac Records in New York, cut a few sides with limited success and moved on to 20th Century, a Philadelphia label owned by Gotham Records' Ivin Ballen.

Record promotion at that time involved visiting popular disc jockeys like Georgie Woods, Jocko Henderson, and Bob Horn.

"You could go from station to station, walk in, hand your record and the guy would play it," said Gracie, whose travels also took him out of town, to places like York, Lebanon, Lancaster, and Reading.

Although Gracie found stardom to be elusive, he was getting regular work—including a few appearances on *Bandstand* and doing a Sealtest commercial on a circus program, *The Big Top*—and was making twice what his father was earning at Stetson. The Whiteman connection proved to be valuable, as the show's former musical director, Bernie Lowe, called him in late 1956 to ask about recording for his new label, Cameo. Lowe even visited the Gracie home, where he talked Gracie's dad into allowing Charlie to record a song he and Kal Mann had written called "Butterfly."

"Butterfly," which bore a strong resemblance to Guy Mitchell's No. 1 hit of "Singing the Blues," was recorded on the slim budget of $600 and became Cameo's first No. 1 record in the spring of 1957. With Gracie's success, Lowe felt that Cameo had the answer to Elvis Presley, who had broken through a year earlier. Rosemary "Little Ro" Fergione, a 16-year-old *Bandstand* regular, was the president of the Charlie Gracie Fan Club.

Gracie, who stood just 5'5" was practically dwarfed by his Guild guitar when he appeared on *The Ed Sullivan Show* on March 10, 1957, with another Philadelphia legend, basketball player Wilt Chamberlain. Gracie grabbed a singing spot in Clark's *Jamboree* movie and made two successful tours of England, where he inspired many young British teenagers, including Paul McCartney, Van Morrison and Graham Nash (who salvaged a Camel cigarette discarded by Gracie at a Manchester, England, concert, a memento he kept for decades).

Although two follow-ups to "Butterfly" made the U.S. charts in 1957, Gracie was more successful in England, where he had five straight No. 1 songs. Although he never duplicated the success of his first Cameo release, Gracie feels strongly that Cameo would have folded without "Butterfly."

"'Butterfly' *was* the company," he said. "If we didn't get a hit with this record, he [Lowe] would have gone broke at that point. You never would have heard of the other artists on the label that came after me."

By 1958, however, Gracie believed he wasn't receiving all the royalties he was entitled to. He sued Cameo and eventually settled out of court for $40,000. The lawsuit put the brakes on his promising career.

"I should have kept my mouth shut," he said nearly 50 years later. "But we're principled people. If I come to work for you for 8 hours, I want to be paid for 8 hours. I don't think there's anything wrong with that. But I didn't have enough experience in the business to keep my mouth shut."

"Once I left the company, I never got on [*Bandstand*] again."

While Gracie was left scrambling to keep his music career alive, Dick Clark found that his own connections were continuing to pay off. There were a few rumblings about *Bandstand's* contributions to the network's bottom line and the *Saturday Night Show* might need some tweaking, but Clark was not behaving like a man worried about his future.

NBC-TV was dropping hints that it might launch a network show to go head to head with *American Bandstand* before summer 1958 arrived and Clark's own network, ABC-TV, was talking about bumping the *Saturday Night Show* to a later time slot to accommodate a 17-week Billy Graham Crusade that started in May, but neither event happened.

There was concern about the overall U.S. economy in early 1958. A major recession was declared in the spring and unemployment headed to a decade-high 7.5 percent. The downturn was affecting the relatively new rock & roll package touring business. Three competing tours—Alan Freed's Big Beat tour, Irving Feld's Biggest Show of Stars and the Rhythm and Blues Cavalcade of '58—were reaping lower grosses than earlier tours.

Despite the bleak prospects, Clark pushed ahead with plans for an eight-week tour of his own. The tour, organized by Milt Shaw of Shaw Artists, was to begin at Ebbetts Field in Brooklyn, N.Y., on May 30.

The personable Clark was pursued by entertainment and news magazines eager to offer readers the story behind this fresh new face of the confounding new music. In an interview with Stephen Kahn of the United Features Syndicate, Clark said he had a 5-year contract with ABC for *American Bandstand* and a 7-year contract for his "exclusive services," although he is allowed up to 12 guest appearances per year on other networks.

Clark still conducted record hops, but not as many as in 1957, when he did 80 of them in the 60 days leading up to *American Bandstand*'s network premiere, meeting an estimated 100,000 teenagers in the process. Clark told Kahn that a dozen Hollywood studios were after him to make a movie and that he was considering cutting a record one of these days.

Clark admitted his meteoric rise to fame was "a little frightening" and claimed that ABC had mailed out 300,000 of his photographs since last summer. Teens from as far away as Texas had hitch-hiked to be on the show. "One Buffalo family did not notice a son was missing until he rock 'n' rolled onto the screen."[4]

Clark's income was approaching $500,000 and a new family getaway—a beach house on the Maryland shore—was nearly completed, but Clark said he'd been too busy to enjoy any of his new-found fame.

---

4. *Time*, April 14, 1958.

THE PHILLY SCENE

He clarified the beach house issue in a cover story in *TV Guide* (headlined "Pied Piper of Teenage Set") by declaring "it's an inexpensive, pre-fabricated house,"[5] adding that his three-bedroom apartment in suburban Drexel Hill cost him just $115 a month in rent. The apartment was also the site of a particularly significant broadcast of CBS-TV's *Person to Person*.

Person to Person was a popular interview program that was hosted by Emmy-winning journalist Edward R. Murrow. The 30-minute program was split into two 15-minute interview segments, each originating from a subject's home. Murrow had gained worldwide recognition for his live radio broadcasts from London during the bombing blitzes of World War II and a series of television reports that brought down Sen. Joseph McCarthy after a series of explosive anti-Communism hearings in the early 1950s.

Many people thought that *Person to Person*'s light and breezy style was a waste of Murrow's reporting skills (although he won an Emmy for the show in 1953). Murrow's interview with Dr. James Bryant Conant, ex-Harvard president, and top research director on the U.S. atomic bomb project, on April 25, 1958, may have appealed more to his critics than his other guest that night, a 28-year-old television personality who was unknown to most of the country just nine months earlier.

For Dick Clark, it was a chance to show off that $115 a month apartment to a national television audience. For days in advance of the telecast, CBS crews overwhelmed the Drexelbrook complex, stretching wires and taping down thick cables while creating what was essentially a television studio in Clark's apartment.

For Clark's part, he dutifully prepared wife Barbara, 1½-year-old son Dickie and family dachshund, Looie, for their biggest public appearance to date. In earlier interviews, Clark spoke of his interest in popular music, particularly jazz. He often hinted that he had a vast collection of recordings that he enjoyed at home. At least one story placed Clark's collection at 15,000 discs, more than most radio stations of the era. Truth was, Clark didn't have a collection at all and he spent the days before Murrow came calling rounding up LP jackets so he could at least create the illusion of a comprehensive record collection.

The show itself went well enough, but it was the after party that proved more significant. At the party, Clark's next-door neighbor, Ed McMahon, was persuaded to act as emcee.

---

5. *TV Guide*, May 24, 1958.

McMahon, born the son of a carnival pitchman, had followed in his father's footsteps as he worked his way through Catholic University in Washington, D.C., selling pots and pans door-to-door and "the famous Morris metric slicer" on the Atlantic City boardwalk.

After college, he held a variety of announcing jobs at WCAU-TV (including a stint as a clown on *Big Top Circus*) before his career was interrupted by duty as a Marine pilot in the Korean War. Returning to WCAU, McMahon landed his first network job as Sam Levenson's announcer on CBS' *Two For the Money* but was fired after two weeks when producer Mark Goodson objected to a McMahon joke.

For months, McMahon commuted between New York City and Philadelphia, looking for a new announcing gig. He eventually found it, thanks to a connection he made with Clark's Saturday night producer, Chuck Reeves, at the Drexelbrook party.

Reeves recommended McMahon as a replacement for Bill Nimmo, the departing announcer on Johnny Carson's *Do You Trust Your Wife?* (renamed *Who Do You Trust?* in July 1958). McMahon got the job, beginning a decades-long association with Carson.

Clark, meanwhile, continued to build on the momentum created by having two blockbuster television shows. He had expanded his business empire to nine corporations in March by incorporating three new businesses—Globe Record Corporation, Kincord Music Corporation and Rosho Corporation.

Under Globe, Clark launched the Hunt record label, which was distributed by Am-Par, a subsidiary of ABC-Paramount, the parent company of ABC-TV. Kincord was Globe's music publishing arm and Rosho was described as the "basic corporate vehicle for such literary rights of mine as might prove valuable." Clark also entered the apparel business with a line of Dick Clark musical shoes, bags and accessories through the Mary Jane Shoe Stores chain.

Clark's plans for a summer road tour were shelved after a disastrous stop in Boston by Alan Freed's Big Beat tour on May 3. According to press coverage in the days following the program at Boston Arena, there were robberies, stabbings, rapes and drug dealing during and after the show. Police charged Freed with inciting a riot, alleging that Freed came on stage after the house lights were turned on, interrupted the concert, and told the rowdy audience that "it looks like the police in Boston don't want you kids to have any fun."

THE PHILLY SCENE

It was never proven that Freed even made that announcement (a more likely suspect was Jerry Lee Lewis) and within days, police were forced to admit there were no robberies, no stabbings, no rapes and no charges of drug dealing in the area around Boston Arena the night of the concert, either. Eventually, all charges against Freed were dropped, but the damage was done.

Boston Mayor John B. Hynes proclaimed that rock & roll concerts were no longer welcome in his city and the Boston City Council followed up with a push to area clergy to help enforce the "Banned in Boston" movement. The national publicity brought the Big Beat tour to a screeching halt and threw future tours (like Clark's) in doubt. Even worse for Freed, the Boston fracas drew the attention of the FBI, which would dog him the rest of his career.

Freed, disappointed by the lack of support from his employer of four years, WINS radio in New York City, abruptly resigned from the station but soon found work at WABC radio in New York, the flagship station for the ABC radio network. There was even talk of a possible Freed television program on ABC-TV.

While the Freed drama was playing out, Clark dodged a bullet that could have sabotaged his career as well.

Although Clark and flamboyant rocker Jerry Lee Lewis enjoyed a mutually profitable business relationship, it was another Lewis relationship of a much more personal nature that led to the singer's four-year exile from Clark's TV empire.

Lewis, who had already been married twice before his 18th birthday, wed for a third time in December 1957, this time to a 13-year-old cousin, Myra Gale Brown, and while he was still married to his second wife. Lewis, who was about to embark on a tour of England, wanted to break the news during an appearance on Clark's *Saturday Night Show*.

Although Lewis was certain his growing legion of fans would offer a chorus of well wishes to the young couple, his manager, Judd Phillips, wasn't so sure. Phillips tipped off sponsor Beech-Nut and Clark about Lewis' plans.

Clark canceled Lewis' appearance, a wise decision given that when Lewis finally had a chance to break the news (on the tarmac of London's Heathrow Airport), he was met by nearly universal condemnation and cancellation of the entire British tour. It would be years before Lewis' career recovered despite an open letter apology that was printed in paid advertising in several entertainment publications.

Clark, meanwhile, continued to host the occasional record hop. That included regular Friday night hops at Willow Grove Park during the summer of 1958. For three other nights each week, Joe Niagara of WIBG conducted his hop business at Willow Grove, too.

Ratings for *American Bandstand* continued to be strong going into the summer of 1958, but ABC-TV executives were not happy with the revenue provided by its sponsors. In short order, Clark picked up five new national accounts and United Artists announced that it would start promoting its films on disc jockey shows, including *American Bandstand*, but it was too little, too late.

Even with the new sponsors, 20 percent of the available network advertising slots were left unfilled, prompting ABC-TV executives to cut the show from 90 to 60 minutes each day. *Pay Me*, a game show modeled after bingo, was assigned *Bandstand's* previous 3–3:30 P.M. slot.

On the other hand, Clark's *Saturday Night Show* was renewed and his plans to take a touring show on the road were resurrected with a planned 10-day opening run at the Brooklyn Paramount Theater over the Labor Day weekend. Increasingly, musicians from outside the Philadelphia-New York corridor were seeking professional assistance through one Clark business connection or another. One of these was Billy Lee Riley, a label mate of Jerry Lee Lewis at Sun Records in Memphis.

Lewis played piano on Riley's two biggest records—"Flying Saucer Rock & Roll" and "Red Hot." "Flying Saucer" did well regionally and "Red Hot" appeared destined to be a national success until label owner Sam Phillips threw all his promotional support behind Lewis' "Great Balls of Fire," allowing Riley to wither on the vine.

An angry Riley started to dismantle Phillips' studio in a drunken stupor before being coaxed back into the Sun fold. But Riley soon abandoned Phillips and Sun, driving to Philadelphia to meet with Clark. Clark was impressed enough to set up a recording session that afternoon with Swan Records.

"On the way over to the studio, we said, 'Aw, let's go back to Sam, he's the only one that understands us,' and we just drove back to Memphis, didn't tell nobody," Riley later recalled. "We were just suspicious of anyone from the North."[6]

---

6. *Good Rockin' Tonight*, Colin Escott, p. 177.

THE PHILLY SCENE

Riley didn't work out in Philadelphia, but a young guitar picker from Arizona did. The signing of 20-year-old Duane Eddy proved to be just the right medicine for Clark's latest business venture, a stake in the ailing Jamie record label.

Jamie, a spinoff label from the more successful Guyden, was in the red before Clark plunked down $125 for 25 percent of the label in May 1958, the same stake as co-owners Harry Finfer, Harold Lipsius and Samuel Hodge. Jamie had limped along with releases by the likes of Philadelphia lounge singer Marian Caruso and Al Jolson soundalike Norman Brooks before producer Lee Hazlewood and his business partner, Lester Sill, brought Eddy to Clark's attention.

Hazlewood first broke through on the national scene in 1956 when Sanford Clark recorded a Hazlewood composition, "The Fool," that went on to become a Top Ten hit. Al Casey, a guitar protege of Hazlewood's, was featured on many of Hazlewood's early productions but left to pursue his own guitar style.

Hazlewood, who was in search of a deeper, growling sound, found what he was looking for in Eddy whose sound was described as "plucking a string strung across the Grand Canyon."

Eddy used that sound to full advantage in what Hazlewood and Sill hoped would be their first national hit, a song titled "Moovin' & Groovin'." When several labels passed on the song, Sill went to Harry Finfer of Universal Distributors in Philadelphia, a co-owner of Jamie Records, who thought the song had potential, especially since it was an instrumental.

Good rock instrumentals were well-suited for *American Bandstand* and its many commercial breaks, where snippets of a song could be used as lead-ins and fade-outs. Clark was elated with Eddy's sound and a long and fruitful professional relationship between the two, including Clark's SRO Artists assuming Eddy's management, was begun.

"Moovin' & Groovin'" cracked *Billboard's* charts, but it was Eddy's follow-up that cemented the young guitarist's future. "Stalkin'" was plugged as the A-side of Eddy's next release but it was the flip side that proved to be the hit. For Clark, the switch occurred at one of the Friday night hops he emceed when he didn't bring enough records and was forced to play B-sides near the end of the evening.

When he played the B-side of "Stalkin'," a song called "Rebel Rouser," he was besieged by requests to replay the song. On

Monday, he flipped to "Rebel Rouser" on *Bandstand* and the song began a climb that placed it in *Billboard's* Top Ten. Hazlewood added a little mystique to the recording by adding to the label the tagline "From the production *Rebel Rouser* starring John Buck." There was no production called *Rebel Rouser*, nor was there a John Buck.[7]

In the summer of 1958, Clark took his *Saturday Night Show* on the road twice—to Atlantic City on June 21 and to Miami, Florida, on July 19. Eddy played a major role in the Miami show. He opened the show with "Moovin' & Groovin'," played "Rebel Rouser" while hoisted high on a forklift and closed the show with a new song, "Ramrod."

By Monday morning, Jamie had received 150,000 orders for "Ramrod," a song Eddy hadn't even recorded yet. Hazlewood, though, had recorded the song earlier by Casey. Hazlewood took Casey's version of the song, overdubbed a saxophone and added some backing yelps and hollers and had the record in stores within a week.

Whose guitar work is actually on Jamie's "Ramrod" has been debated ever since, but there's no question that Eddy was the lead guitarist for The Keymen, a group assembled by Clark and arranger Don Costa for a pair of LPs on ABC-Paramount, *Dance With Dick Clark -Volumes 1 and 2.*

Before the summer was out, Clark would add four more businesses to his empire, giving him 15 in all. Three of the new businesses were named after months of the year—January Music Corp. (music publishing), February Corp. (to handle a planned newspaper column) and March Productions Corp. (to handle Clark's personal appearances.) The fourth new business was Drexel Television Productions, Inc., which produced Clark's *Saturday Night Show.*

It was clear that Clark and *American Bandstand* were powerful forces in shaping America's cultural teenage landscape. Kids who a few months earlier were typical high school students were now national celebrities, just because an after-school dance was televised from coast to coast. The same could be said of many of the young stars who performed on *American Bandstand*, especially a pair of South Philadelphia teens who were groomed precisely for the unique opportunities presented by Dick Clark.

---

7. jerryosborne.com, Ray Cerri and Joel Whitburn, October 18, 1999

THE PHILLY SCENE

The first of these was Frankie Avalon. Born Frankie Avallone, Avalon was raised on South 13th Street, the same neighborhood that earlier produced Jack Klugman, Buddy Greco, Joey Bishop, Mario Lanza, Al Martino, and Eddie Fisher. He also lived just half a mile from Bob Marcucci, the co-owner of Chancellor Records who was guiding Avalon's career in 1958.

Marcucci and Chancellor co-owner Pete DeAngelis had distinctly different roles—DeAngelis concentrated on the music while Marcucci focused on professional development.

Marcucci went to work on Avalon from the start. The slight (5'7", 120 pounds) Avalon had the requisite good looks, was an adequate singer and had good footwork from his years as a boxer in the Police Athletic League. What he didn't have was the sophistication, experience, and confidence to deal with the adults in the music business or the press that Marcucci hoped would be interested in learning more about the teen who was more comfortable hanging around his neighborhood, drinking grape rickeys at Humphreys or eating pizza from Tessie's.

Fortunately, Dick Clark had engaged the services of a press agent around the time *American Bandstand* went national. That agent, Connie DeNave, had since branched out to take on young singers like Avalon and Connie Francis through her Image Makers company in New York. Marcucci soon linked Avalon with DeNave.

DeNave did more than issue press releases.

"The young people who were recording in those days had to be well-groomed and well-dressed, because the press thought that rock 'n' roll was the lowest form of life and that the people who sang it had just crawled out from under a rock," DeNave said.[8]

"They had to be trained never to smoke in public and never to have a glass in front of them, even a glass of water, when they were photographed because it might look like they were drinking and they would be finished overnight."

"They would do interviews over lunch and all they would order was hamburgers. In my office were over a hundred menus, and I would teach them to order snails, lobster."[9]

While Avalon was attending DeNave's "charm school," Marcucci and DeNave launched a promotional campaign in trade publications. Syndicated columnist Dorothy Kilgallen took notice.

---

8. *Like Young: Jazz, Pop, Youth and Middle Age*, Francis Davis, p. 323.
9. *When Rock Was Young*, Bruce Pollock, p. 61

"Mr. Sinatra will be so pleased to hear this. Frankie Avalon, a 17-year-old singer, takes trade paper advertisements announcing, 'Frankie now means Avalon'," Kilgallen wrote.[10]

Kilgallen's sniping didn't hurt Avalon one bit. In fact, *Billboard's* Joan Bundy, in reviewing *The Biggest Show of Stars for '58* in New Haven, Conn., called Avalon the "standout attraction," adding "the handsome young warbler may very well be the successor to Elvis Presley."[11]

But Marcucci was already in search of the successor to Avalon and by mid-1958 thought he had found him. Fabiano Anthony Forte was just 15 years old when he met Marcucci. Ironically, it was Avalon who made the introduction. That is unless you believe the story that was propagated after the South Philadelphia teen became known as simply Fabian.

According to urban lore, Marcucci discovered the photogenic young Forte on the stoop of the family row house as an ambulance arrived to assist his father, who'd suffered a heart attack. Marcucci, the story goes, promised to make Forte a star but Forte told him to go to hell. Marcucci was persistent, however, and since the family needed the money, young Forte eventually relented, became Fabian and a star was born.

Whether the finding-Fabian-on-the-stoop story is totally true or not, the important elements happened pretty much as described.

Before hooking up with Marcucci, Fabian was a typical 15-year-old. He liked playing football and was chosen by the principal of George C. Thomas Junior High to make the "farewell speech" to fellow eighth-graders in January 1958. He had a part-time job running errands at Bellevue Pharmacy. Music wasn't an important part of his life.

But when heart problems left his dad unable to work, Fabian reluctantly turned to music to keep his family afloat. True to his word, Marcucci began the process of creating the pop star that would eventually be known as Fabian. Fabian remained enrolled at Southern High School and kept his pharmacy job but he also rode the trolley that ran in front of the family home to take voice lessons under DeAngelis at the Chancellor studio. Working with DeNave, he began acting lessons, let others pick out his wardrobe and was placed on a $30 a week allowance.

---

10. *The Panama American*, November 29, 1958.
11. *Billboard*, April 21, 1958.

THE PHILLY SCENE

None of this came easily to young Forte. Fabian means "bean grower" in Italian and young Forte measured up. At 6-foot-tall and 165 pounds, he was a much more striking figure than Avalon. But the stress of preparing for his show business career caused him to lose weight, some 15 pounds in a short time.

"I was a fish out of water. I was awkward and didn't know what the hell I was doing," he later said.[12]

Before Fabian could appear before a TV camera, he needed a record. Before Clark would put him on *American Bandstand*, he needed a successful record. Working with arranger Roy Straigis, Marcucci and DeAngelis rushed Fabian into the studio for his first Chancellor session.

His first single, "Shivers," gained a little traction in Chicago and Georgie Woods gave it a few spins in Philadelphia, which apparently was good enough for Clark, who booked him onto *American Bandstand* for June 19, 1958.

DeNave plugged the appearance with a teaser display ad in the trades, reading: "The chicks are clucking over the fabulous FABIAN. Wait till You hear his new CHANCELLOR record.*" It was followed by: "*You'll hear it next week."

Instead of having Fabian lip-sync to "Shivers," though, Clark opted for the flip side, "I'm In Love." The record turned out to be a bomb. A follow-up: "Lilly Lou" (which Fabian lip-synced on Clark's *Saturday Night Show* in September) didn't do any better.

Arranger Straigis quit working for Chancellor and jumped to Cameo-Parkway where he went on to have an outstanding career. Reflecting on his Chancellor experience, he said, "I listen to those songs now and I want to shoot myself. I think, 'How could I do that?' But at that time the music was so schlocky you could get away with it."[13]

For Fabian, the image building continued and true stardom would come before the year was out.

Dick Clark's vision of integrating popular music into a profitable business plan was working well. He'd managed to work his way into practically every nook and cranny of the rock & roll business without making obvious enemies and while earning the adulation of millions of teenagers and older persons alike. He had the platform to push the music he liked and to shut down those who would drag him down.

---

12. *Goldmine*, Jeff Markus, February 15, 2012.
13. *Philadelphia Inquirer*, Ralph Vigoda, December 19, 1993.

He had help. The early rock pioneers who represented the brasher side of the music were largely out of the picture by mid-1958. Jerry Lee Lewis virtually self-destructed by marrying his cousin. Little Richard was going through a very public religious transformation. Chuck Berry was more focused on his St. Louis nightclub and buying up real estate than he was on his music and Elvis Presley—now U.S. Army Private Elvis Presley—was missing from the top of the *Billboard* charts for the first time since bursting on the national scene two years earlier.

Coupled with the success of more pop-oriented stars like Bobby Darin, Paul Anka, Ricky Nelson, and the Everly Brothers, Clark was perfectly positioned with his own stable of rising stars like Eddy, Avalon, Danny & the Juniors and (eventually) Fabian. Jimmy Clanton, a 19-year-old from Baton Rouge, Louisiana, also became a Clark favorite after Clanton's debut on *American Bandstand* to lip-sync "Just a Dream" netted sales of 100,000 records the next day.

Clark also had other interests to fill his time. He was a guest panelist on *What's My Line?* and Beech-Nut planned to sponsor him in a new Sunday night panel show called *Take a Good Look*. He indulged his literary aspirations by writing the preface to a trade book, *Popular Record Director,* and was reportedly working on a book about teenage slang.

As the first anniversary of *American Bandstand*'s network premiere approached, Bob Williams wrote an update on Clark and the show for readers of Philadelphia's *Evening Bulletin*.

Clark said that the "Date With Sal Mineo" contest that launched the show had been a huge success. While Clark took time to listen to 20 to 30 new records each day, he needed five clerks to handle the mail. Clark admitted that he was partial to the music of big band-era bandleader Glenn Miller and hinted that he collected Miller records.

He admitted 150 kids into the studio each day, holding back 30 to 50 spots each day for out-of-towners. Philadelphia-area regulars had *Bandstand Club* cards and the Committee of teenage proctors kept the dancers in line. Clark also told Williams he still was doing two or three record hops each week.

All in all, it had been a very good year for Dick Clark.

CHAPTER 9

A TIME OF RECKONING

While Dick Clark was enjoying a prosperous first year as host of the first national teenage dancing show, his predecessor, Bob Horn, wasn't faring nearly as well.

Immediately after his dismissal from *Bandstand*, Horn had hunkered down in the office of old friend, Nat Segall, above Big Bill Rodstein's bar.

At first, Horn had the option of continuing a radio program on WFIL, waiting for things to cool down over the drunk driving charge before being reinstated to his *Bandstand* position. Horn's reputation as a chain-smoking, hard-drinking, occasionally arrogant loudmouth didn't matter as much as the three-year contract he'd recently signed.

But that all changed when Philadelphia District Attorney Victor Blanc called WFIL to tip off station executives that he was investigating "teenage sex rings" and that reinstating Horn might prove embarrassing to the station.

Citing a morals clause in Horn's contract, he was cut loose but there was no public statement about why Philadelphia's most popular TV disc jockey was no longer working in the WFIL radio-television complex. And, despite his reputation for being self-centered and cold, Horn had a few supporters.

"I think some people loved Bob Horn," said *Bandstand* director Ed Yates, adding that the WFIL staff "didn't like the idea of Bob Horn leaving because he brought [*Bandstand*] to being No. 1."

Another supportive staffer was ad salesman Max Solomon.

"He was a very nice guy," Solomon said of Horn. "I think he was pretty good."

Many of the teens who danced on the show thought he was pretty good, too.

Jerry Blavat, the Committee member who led the teen protest against Horn's firing, wasn't Horn's only supporter.

Barbara Marcen remembers Horn paying for her singing lessons so she could record a song with her dance partner, Tom DeNoble.

"It was just like a family," Marcen said, noting that after Horn was fired, "a lot of us didn't go to the show again for a few weeks because we all wanted Bob Horn back."

Of course, the teens were unaware of Horn's allegedly bringing prostitutes into the WFIL studios after hours or the apartment he allegedly kept nearby for liaisons with a 13-year-old girl.

"When all that came out, that was quite a shock to all of us," said regular Mary Ann Colella.

Horn was indicted by a grand jury on the drunk driving charge on July 17, 1956, but remained free on bond. While splitting his time between his home in Levittown and his boat in Stone Harbor, Horn continued to host dances at his old friend Ray Jackson's Carman Roller Skating Rink and at the Starlight Ballroom in Wildwood, N.J. He also spent considerable time in New York, visiting another old friend, Lee Vines, the announcer for the Hallmark Hall of Fame television show.

Horn's record hops were immensely successful, drawing as many as 3,000 teenagers to his weekly dance in Wildwood and causing the local musicians' union to complain that the hops were cutting into attendance at live band dances.

In a desperate attempt to cling to his *Bandstand* connection, Horn registered the *Bandstand* title under Pennsylvania's fictitious name act, a tactic that ultimately proved futile.

On October 23, 1956, Horn's career slide accelerated when he was among a dozen people served with warrants issued by the Philadelphia District Attorney's office alleging morals offenses after a five-month, tri-state vice racket investigation. Also arrested that day was another well-known Philadelphia broadcaster, Steve Allison of WPEN radio.

Allison was the initial target of the probe, but Horn's association with 16-year-old Lois Gardner led to charges against him of statutory rape and corrupting the morals of a minor.

While Horn was clearly the city's most influential record spinner to the teenage crowd, Allison had a similar grip on liberal-minded adult Philadelphians. His late-night radio program was broadcast from the same ground floor studio used for Grady and Hurst's *950 Club* in the afternoon. At night it became the Ranch Room, a sort of quasi-nightclub where Allison, sometimes decked out in a tuxedo, could interview guests, play music or take phone calls from listeners. He was known as "the man who owns midnight."

Politically, Allison was the polar opposite of Walter Annenberg, owner of the *Philadelphia Inquirer* and WFIL-TV and radio. Annenberg was no friend of Allison, who frequently sniped at the *Inquirer*.

The format of Allison's show lent itself to late-night hanky panky. Food and drinks were served and there was little screening of the studio audience. The Ranch Room was a good place to mingle with people who wanted a taste of night club glamour and maybe make a solid professional connection or two.

There developed a cadre of regulars, similar to the young dancers on *Bandstand*. One of these was a young man named Bernard Jacobs, the owner of the Trend Model Agency. Jacobs, who would be cited as the "mastermind of the ring" investigated by Blanc, also brought models from his agency. Another Allison guest was James Worden, a dog breeder who often invited people he met at Allison's show to parties (some described them as orgies) at his family estate—called Hound Dog Hill—in Montgomery County. It was only natural that Jacobs' and Worden's worlds would intersect.

Things went smoothly until a teenage girl at one of Worden's soirees hooked up with a lout who went too far and the 17-year-old reported the rape to police.

District Attorney Blanc launched his investigation, complete with wiretaps, from a clandestine storefront on Chestnut Street in Center City. Through the investigation, it was learned that Gardner had done some "modeling" for Jacobs as a 15-year-old, at the same time she had an ongoing relationship with Horn.

The lengthy probe was quite productive, yielding more than two dozen suspects while shedding light on what proved to be a cottage industry catering to the broadcast and entertainment industries.

The first arrests came on October 4 when 44-year-old society photographer Michael Denning was charged with possession of obscene photographs and morals charges and Jacobs, 30, was charged with promising young girls modeling jobs, then luring them into vice activities.

Authorities piled up evidence from young girls and their parents before making their next arrests, of Worden, 42, and his wife, Cornelia, 53, on a variety of morals charges stemming from the parties on their estate. Obscene photos were also confiscated.

Horn and Allison weren't the only persons charged on October 23. Jack Barry, 30, a WPEN newsman, faced a variety of charges and Louis Cargill, 43, was charged with taking a 16-year-old girl from Philadelphia to the Barbizon Plaza Hotel in New York City and paying her $100 for sex. Others facing unspecified morals charges were Leonard Parkinson, 38, assistant chief of forms control and records in the Philadelphia Department of Records and Henry Bogdanoff, 34, the operator of a downtown camera shop.

All of the accused were scheduled for 2 P.M. hearings on October 24. Horn failed to show up, however, and his attorney, Louis Lipschitz, attempted to set up a private hearing instead. Chief Magistrate Joseph Hersch denied the request (and another) that would have barred the public.

About 300 people later crowded into the courtroom to hear Horn charged with statutory rape and corrupting the morals of a minor on numerous occasions. He was sent to Moyamensing Prison in a police car but was released two hours later on $5,000 bail. Allison was also free on $5,000 bail.

Blanc rescinded a two-year suspended sentence from a previous conviction for Jacobs and sent him back to prison while his attorney argued that Jacobs wasn't the ringleader he was painted to be and that the real masterminds were the people at WPEN who facilitated the illicit connections through Allison's show. Blanc also hinted that more arrests were coming in connection with an abortion related to a teenage victim of the ring.

Those arrests were reported on November 9 when a grand jury returned another 23 bills of indictment against five suspects. Eight of those charges were against Horn—four counts each of statutory rape and corrupting the morals of a minor. Photographer Joseph Kaytes faced one morals charge and the remaining charges, all related to a single abortion, were levied against three people—singer Joe Valino, 27; his manager, Nicholas Busillo, 35; and Mrs. Rachel White, 43.

Another charge was filed in Montgomery County, where Dr. A. Samuel Manstein, 43, was charged with two morals offenses committed on the Wordens' Hound Dog Hill estate. Manstein had been a witness at the January abortion trial of Milton and Rosalie Schwartz, following the abortion death of Mrs. Doris Jean Oestreicher, a 22-year-old food chain heiress who had died at the Schwartz apartment. Manstein was called to the apartment after her death.

Trials came quickly for most of those charged. Horn's was originally scheduled to begin on December 11, but was pushed back to January, first to January 2; then to January 28.

The Valino case came at a most inopportune time for the singer from South Philadelphia. His record, "Garden of Eden," first cracked the national charts the week that the first vice arrests were announced. The song received lots of airplay and good reviews and finally peaked at No. 12, but his future, which looked so bright a few weeks earlier, was threatened by the case that went to trial in December 1956.

Valino was charged with impregnating 20-year-old model Marian Melet and then arranging for an abortion performed by White. Though Valino proclaimed his innocence, he was found guilty and received a 17-year suspended sentence.

Though he went on to have a lengthy career in show business, Valino's only hit record was "Garden of Eden."

Entering 1957, Blanc's team had rolled up an impressive record. All 15 of the cases resolved to date had resulted in convictions, with just the three broadcast personalities left to try. Allison was facing a second trial since his first trial on December 26 resulted in a hung jury.

The first of the three was WPEN's Barry, who was charged with sodomy after Mrs. Donato Tursi, a 44-year-old widow, testified that she had sex with him in a second-floor room of the radio studio in mid-September.

Barry argued that he was on vacation in Vermont Sept. 2–10 and entered a hospital for surgery on his left arm on his return. His mother and wife testified that Barry had his arm in a cast for 10 days after the operation and hospital records backed up his story. Judge James E. Crumlish found reasonable doubt and found him not guilty, the first loss for Blanc.

Horn was next up, but before his January 28 trial, he found himself once again before a magistrate, facing another drunk driving charge.

Around 1:20 A.M. on January 22 Horn was driving west on Clearfield Avenue—a one-way eastbound street—when his green 1955 Cadillac sedan slammed into the rear side of a car driven by John McKnight, throwing McKnight's three children from the car and onto the pavement.

McKnight told investigating officers that Horn staggered and appeared dazed as he emerged from his car on the wet and foggy night. The officers said that Horn had a strong smell of alcohol and appeared to be intoxicated, with a flushed face, bloodshot eyes and thick speech.

Although Horn was immediately taken into custody, it wasn't until 2:35 A.M. that he was examined by police surgeon Dr. Gennario Squillace, who determined that Horn was not under the influence of alcohol at that time. Despite the surgeon's report, Magistrate Harry J. Ellick charged Horn with drunk driving.

McKnight, his wife, son John, 6, and daughter Donna, 2, were treated for cuts and bruises, but daughter Gail, 5, was unconscious with serious head injuries at the scene and was taken to Episcopal Hospital. John's head injuries were also later determined to be serious and he was admitted to the hospital, too.

When Horn's vice trial began on January 28, the two McKnight children were still hospitalized. Gail was in critical condition and in a coma with brain and internal injuries; John was slightly improved with a brain injury but was facing additional surgery for a skull fracture.

So Horn, who was still awaiting trial on his first drunk driving charge, had plenty on his legal plate as jury selection began for his vice trial. Horn entered a not guilty plea to all eight charges, but the Commonwealth chose to prosecute just the four counts of statutory rape.

The first witness for the prosecution was Gardner, 17 years old at the time. Gardner testified that she had met Horn in the summer of 1953 at the WFIL-TV studios. She was a member of the *Paul Whiteman TV Club* and sometimes did commercials for the station. She had watched Horn do a radio program one evening and he drove her to his Verona Apartment near 47th and Walnut streets, just a few blocks from the studio.

She testified that she saw Horn once or twice a week after that, through the end of 1955, and that they had "improper relations" on nearly every occasion after their first sexual encounter in his apartment just before her 14th birthday on November 18, 1953.

But the charges named in the indictment occurred in another apartment allegedly held by Horn, at 345 S. Hicks Street, on four separate dates. She also testified that Horn gave her cash gifts, including $100 on one of her birthdays. On her 15th birthday, he gave her a hi-fi phonograph worth $200, she said.

Gardner also testified that she spent 2½ days with Horn in Stone Harbor, N.J., in August 1955, alternating between his boat and the Shelter Haven Hotel. Under cross-examination, she admitted that at least two young women stayed in her home after they had abortions, including singer Joe Valino's paramour, Marian Melet.

Her cross-examination extended into the trial's second day when she told of meeting other personalities, including Sammy Davis Jr., whose apartment she admitted to visiting at midnight on one occasion with a date of her own. She said her current boyfriend, Johnny Christian, was married with three children but was separated from his wife.

Under relentless cross-examination by Lipschitz, Gardner admitted to having had sex with Louis Cargill, the industrialist caught up in the sting for taking another teen to New York for sex and who was convicted for that act.

She was finally dismissed from the stand before noon. The defense presented 13 witnesses (including Jerry Blavat) who testified about Horn's good character before Horn took the stand in his own defense that afternoon. He denied it all, calling Gardner "a psychopathic liar."

He admitted he sometimes gave Gardner birthday gifts—like the $100 and the record player. He said he'd been to her house a couple of times, but only as a friend. He denied that he had any apartments in the city.

He did admit that he frequently saw Gardner at a West Philadelphia restaurant where he ate dinner, but added that he saw lots of people there, like song pluggers and music publishers. It didn't make sense, Horn said, to make the lengthy commute from the WFIL studios to his home in Levittown between the end of his *Bandstand* show and the 11 P.M. start of his late night radio program. So he'd just hang around town, have a drink or two and eat dinner.

Horn also had alibis for each of the four dates he allegedly had sex with Gardner.

On the November 25, 1954, date (which was Thanksgiving), he said he attended a high school football game and then had dinner at home with his wife and four children. [Near the end of the trial, Gardner testified that Horn visited her between the end of the football game and before dinner with his family on that day. A parking attendant near the S. Hicks Street apartment testified that Horn had indeed parked his car in a lot near the apartment that afternoon and proceeded to enter the building.]

On January 15, 1955, he had arrived home early in the morning following an 11-day recuperative stay in Miami after losing his voice. He spent most of the day on a hunting trip with friends in Clinton, N.J., returned home in the early evening and played with his kids before going to bed early.

On February 17, 1955, he had dinner at Chubby's in West Collingswood, N.J., and watched singer Jaye P. Morgan perform before returning home around 1:30 A.M. On March 10, 1959, it was the Celebrity Room watching Sandy Stewart until 1 A.M. Horn claimed to have a "professional interest" in both singers.

Referring to the Stone Harbor trip in August, Horn said he saw Gardner about three hours on one of those days when he took several people on a boat ride. Horn's story was backed up by son Peter and wife Ann, who also noted that she saw Gardner at a nightclub party in 1954 and she appeared to be heavily made up and drunk.

The manager of the Verona Apartments said Horn hadn't had an apartment there and she never saw him there in the years in question. Furthermore, a 16-year-old acquaintance of Gardner said he'd known her for two years and that she had a bad reputation.

On the other hand, Horn's claim that Gardner had approached him in a Germantown Ave. restaurant, told him she was in some kind of trouble, and asked for $1,000 was contradicted by a bartender at the restaurant who said the girl was there first and that Horn and two other men later joined her.

As the case wrapped up, Horn testified that he was "a very gregarious person who likes people and after this is over I would like to see her again. I have no hard feelings, I have nothing against her."[1]

After three days, the case went to the jury, where they debated Horn's fate. He faced 15 years in jail and a $7,000 fine if found guilty on all four counts.

After seven hours of deliberations, the jury told Judge Edwin O. Lewis on February 1 that it couldn't reach a verdict. Although the vote was 10–2 for acquittal at one point, it was deadlocked at 6–6 by the time it approached the judge, who dismissed the jurors.

District Attorney Blanc promised a retrial within two months and turned his attention to the retrial of Allison, whose first trial had also ended in a hung jury. The vote in that trial was also 10–2 in favor of acquittal at one point.

Allison was acquitted in his second trial. That was good news for Horn supporters, but Horn's retrial was postponed when his lawyer was hospitalized in April.

Eager to find work in the broadcast industry, Horn was resigned to the fact that he'd have to leave Philadelphia. The *New York Daily News* reported on April 17, 1957, that Horn had been given a radio show in Allentown, Pennsylvania, but he actually ended up much further from Philadelphia than that.

Gordon McLendon, a Texas radio entrepreneur who loved tinkering with station formats, had bought KLBS in Houston in February 1957. He began revamping the station's announcing lineup to coincide with a call letter change to KILT that would take place in May.

A full-page ad in the *Houston Post* introduced the new announcers, including Eliot Field from Boston, Art Nelson from Dallas, Tom Fallon from Kansas City and Bob Horn from Philadelphia. But Horn wouldn't be using his own name; he'd be filling the 9 P.M. to midnight slot as Bob Adams, the same name he'd used in the early 1940s at WIP. But Texas would have to wait. Horn's retrial was finally set to begin on Monday, June 24.

In advance of the trial, Horn's lawyer, Louis Lipschitz, subpoenaed Doris Gardner, Lois Gardner's mother. He opted to have 16-year-old Jerry Blavat serve the papers since he knew both women. When Blavat arrived, he was greeted by a friend of Gardner's, John Falgiatore.

---

1. *Philadelphia Inquirer,* January 31, 1957.

Falgiatore allegedly told Blavat "this could all be cleared up for $3,000." After some discussion, Falgiatore said that Lois Gardner would leave town and not testify if she received $2,500. Blavat called Horn who called Lipschitz who called assistant district attorney F. Emmett Fitzpatrick, who was leading the prosecution.

The lawyers agreed to a sting, with Blavat turning over the cash to Falgiatore. When Falgiatore didn't show at the meeting place, Blavat called him. Falgiatore told him to bring the money to the Gardner house. As Blavat handed over the money, detectives swarmed in. Although no arrests were made, Blavat and Falgiatore agreed to take lie detector tests about the matter on Monday morning, prior to the start of the trial.

When Monday arrived, however, no lie detector tests were given. Horn surprised Judge Cyrus M. Palmer by waiving a jury trial while prosecuting attorney James N. Lafferty accused Horn of engineering the whole payoff stunt as a smokescreen. The trial was concluded in just two days and Palmer promised a decision on Wednesday, June 26.

Hundreds of fans, supporters and the merely curious spilled out from the courtroom and into the corridors of City Hall for the reading of the verdict. Horn arrived in a charcoal gray suit with yellow and black necktie and two-toned shoes. He took off his glasses and broke into a smile when Palmer read "Not Guilty." Palmer elaborated: the prosecution failed to prove its case and the bills of indictment failed to mention that Gardner was a minor.

With his first drunk driving trial still three months away, it was time for Horn to begin rebuilding his career. Ever since the state suspended his driver's license after the January accident, Horn had relied on others to drive him around. More often than not, that was Blavat. As he prepared to leave his family in Levittown while he established himself in Houston, Horn invited Blavat to accompany him to Texas. With most of the summer left before his senior year of high school, Blavat said yes.

For Blavat, it was a bittersweet summer. He developed a taste for pecan pie and landed a job with the distribution company of Harold "Pappy" Daily, the colorful country music publisher and founder of the Starday label. But he also had to watch as his old friend tried to resurrect a career from the ashes of self-destruction while another man was taking his creation to unknown heights.

"He read in the newspaper that Dick Clark was thriving in his absence and that *Bandstand* was going national, and his drinking increased," said Blavat. "As he became more despondent, I did what I could to rally him, alternating between 'Bob, you can't do this,' and 'You're going to be okay,' but there wasn't a platitude in the world that was going to help. He had it all and lost it all, and no one knew it better than him."[2]

Blavat returned to Philadelphia for the start of school in September. Horn returned a month later, to face his first drunk driving trial.

A jury of eight women and four men heard testimony beginning on October 1, 1957, about Horn's first drunk driving arrest in June 1956. Dr. Maxwell Cherner said Horn was drunk and not fit to drive and that of the three levels of intoxication, Horn was on the third level, just above unconsciousness. He said Horn's balance was impaired, his face pale and dull, his expression fixed and his pulse rapid. He staggered and had the odor of alcohol on his breath.

Arresting officer Russell Firesinger said Horn was swaying as he got out of his car and, when told he was being taken to the station, replied, "Go ahead. I know [Police Commissioner Thomas J.] Gibbons." On arrival and wearing dark glasses, Horn greeted the desk sergeant by saying, "I'm Bob Horn, *Bandstand*."

It took the jury just 15 minutes to deliver a guilty verdict and Judge Peter F. Hagen fined Horn $300 and placed him on probation for one year.

Horn opted for a non-jury trial as he stood before Judge Vincent A. Carroll five days later to face charges stemming from his January 22 accident. If Horn was counting on the testimony from examining Dr. Gennario Squillace that Horn was fit to drive 1 hour 35 minutes after the accident, it didn't work.

Judge Carroll called Horn's explanation that he got lost in the fog "a cock and bull story" and pronounced him guilty, though sentencing was delayed until October 25.

When Horn was sentenced to six months in jail, Horn's lawyer said he'd appeal, prompting Judge Carroll to raise Horn's bail from $500 to $3,000. When Lipschitz made a motion for a new trial, Carroll turned it down and criticized Horn for his "defiant attitude."

Lipschitz pleaded for leniency, noting that Horn barely earned enough to support his family. "He is as low mentally as a man can be and still desire to live," Lipschitz said.

---

2. *You Only Rock Once*, Jerry Blavat, p. 72.

"He may be on the brink, he may be prostrate, but he is still defiant," Carroll said.[3]

Horn returned to Texas as his appeal moved through the courts. With the criminal case adjudicated, John J. McKnight began legal action in civil court.

On November 14, 1957, McKnight sued for $17,500 in damages for himself, his wife, and daughter, Donna, in Common Pleas Court. On November 15, the parents filed suit in U.S. District Court for $375,000—$250,000 for daughter, Gail; $75,000 for son, John D.; and $50,000 for the father, John J. McKnight to cover medical expenses. The suit claimed that both children may be permanently impaired as a result of the accident.

Horn continued on-air for a few months but found himself ill-suited to the job. As host of *Bandstand*, he had the backing of the entire WFIL-TV staff. As the late-night disc jockey at a small Texas radio station, it was just him, a couple of turntables and a console to operate himself. He shifted to advertising sales, where he was the station's top producer. Then came another round of legal problems.

In April 1958, Horn was indicted by a federal grand jury on a charge of evading federal income taxes for the years of 1953–55. Although Horn paid taxes of $14,192.68 on an income of $57,368.45 reported for those years, U.S. Attorney Harold K. Wood said Horn should have paid $23,629.40 on an income of $80,238.45.

The difference was payola, said Wood. The court record shows most of the payments were made by record distributing companies—John Harold Co., David Rosen Inc., Stuart F. Louscheim Co., Gotham Record Corp., Universal Record Distributing Corp., Edward S. Barsky Inc., and Marnel Distributing Co. Wood said the investigation had been ongoing for several years and didn't deny that evidence of other payments to jocks might have been turned up.

Horn pleaded not guilty at a May 1958 arraignment and trial was set for July.

On June 19, the Pennsylvania State Superior Court unanimously upheld Horn's drunk driving conviction, leaving his six-month jail sentence in place. He ultimately served three months.

His tax evasion trial was delayed until September, but he lost his job at KILT two months earlier. Reunited with his family in Houston, Horn was in the process of starting his own ad agency,

---

3. *Philadelphia Evening Bulletin*, October 25, 1957.

called Bob Adams Advertising, when he changed his plea from not guilty to no defense.

After an examination by probation officers, Horn was given a two-year probationary sentence and fined $500 by U.S. District Judge John W. Lord in the tax case. Horn was given nine months to pay the fine and was also instructed to make a partial payment of his tax bill, which had grown to $15,000 with interest and penalties.

Lawyer Lipschitz described Horn as "despondent and destitute," adding that he would have to pawn one of his wife's rings to get money for his return to Texas.

Judge Lord said he understood that payola was a recognized source of revenue in Horn's business.

"No doubt he is guilty, and no doubt many others in the same situation are shaking in their boots," he said.[4]

---

4. *Philadelphia Evening Bulletin*, November 7, 1958.

CHAPTER 10

WHATEVER IT IS... HE'S GOT IT

Payola wasn't a word you heard very much in 1958 unless you were connected to the music business in some way. It was simply a fact of life that in order to get your song heard—and that mostly meant on the radio—you would probably have to do something extraordinary to distinguish it from the crowd.

A special gift here, some cash there. Maybe dinner, a few drinks, something for the wife. A few extra records, perhaps, or maybe even a piece of the publishing. Whatever it took. It all was perfectly legal, but given the rapid rise of rock & roll, it had the oily sheen of something rancid.

Comedian Sid Caesar's funniest bit on the season premiere of *The Chevy Show* in the fall of 1958 was a sendup of a televised teenage dance show. Caesar and Shirley MacLaine ruled the dance floor as a teen couple always mugging their way in front of the camera. In the windup, deejay Art Carney plopped a record on the turntable while declaring, "I'm especially fond of this record because I get an awful lot of money for plugging it."[1]

---

1. *Billboard*, November 10, 1958.

WHATEVER IT IS... HE'S GOT IT

Although few persons outside the business had concerns about payola, some stations tried to head off criticism before things got nasty. Their efforts didn't do away with the dubious practice of pay-for-play, but they did bring it out of the closet.

In Hollywood, Calif., KDAY instituted a "test record" plan where $400 guaranteed eight plays a day for 10 days for a song that had been approved by the station's programming department. If a regional breakout was the goal, the station had a tie-in with five other West Coast stations for $1,200.

In Pittsburgh, KDKA set up "clinics" where song pluggers had up to 20 minutes to introduce their newest records to the announcing staff and managers. Jockeys were not limited to the clinic picks, though, and record pluggers were still free to visit the station whenever they wanted.

One tactic used by labels to circumvent charges of payola was to make their artists available to disc jockeys at no charge for record hops or stage shows, allowing the DJ to profit legitimately through perfectly acceptable tie-ins based on actual record sales.

Stage shows, long the province of Alan Freed, were an area Clark had yet to add to his business résumé. His plans for a touring stage show in the fall of 1958 never came together, but Clark hadn't abandoned the notion.

After marking a highly successful first year of *American Bandstand*, Clark took much of August 1958 off. It could hardly be called a vacation, though.

Each day in his absence, Tony Mammarella read "letters from Dick." Mammarella shared emcee duties with disc jockeys from around the country. This included popular hosts of similar dance shows, like Jim Lounsbury from Chicago and Jim Gallant from New Haven, Conn., and some from much smaller markets, like Ron Scott of the ABC affiliate in Ames, Iowa.

Each of the substitute deejays was allowed just one day on the show. The "one-show rule" kept the guest hosts from learning too much about the day-to-day operations of the show and prevented them from developing a following that could jeopardize the regular host.

Clark presented a show that August at the Hollywood Bowl that proved immensely successful. Billed as "A Salute to Dick Clark," the first rock & roll show at the Bowl drew an overflow crowd of 11,800 teens who turned out to hear a lineup of 15 acts, including Duane Eddy and Jimmy Clanton. According to *Variety*, the show grossed a respectable $29,000.

Eddy was the only Hollywood Bowl act to follow Clark to the Minnesota State Fair three days later, where he was joined by Eddie Cochran, Dale Hawkins, Jack Scott, the Olympics, and others. The Minnesota program proved to be a huge disappointment, however, when just a few hundred teens showed up.

Undeterred, Clark and producer Deke Heyward proceeded with plans to take the *Saturday Night Show* to another fair, this time in Atlanta, Georgia.

Fairs had long been seen as rural attractions, where country music ruled and teens stayed away. Singers didn't like them because the sound was uniformly bad on fair stages.

But packagers of rock stage shows saw opportunity in fairs. They upgraded sound systems and provided the entertainers that teens loved. Using emcees from local radio stations who freely advertised the shows, attendance was on the increase (the Minnesota State Fair notwithstanding.)

The Southeastern Fair at Lakewood Park in Atlanta was a chance for Clark to test an integrated stage show in a southern locale for the first time. The racial divide was still strong in the south in 1958 and Clark received numerous threatening phone calls and letters, many directed at the program's lone black singer, Sam Cooke. The threats drove Heyward to buy a gun. But, despite the threats, the show went off without a hitch, setting several records in the process.

The *Saturday Night Show* remained a strong fixture in the ABC-TV lineup (Beech-Nut said gum sales had doubled since the company began sponsoring the show) as *American Bandstand* slipped into its new hour-long slot on Sept. 29, 1958, a position it would hold for the next three years.

The network was still looking for new opportunities for Clark, but plans to launch the panel show *Take A Good Look* in the fall of 1958 were scrapped when Beech-Nut pulled out of its sponsorship and no replacement could be found. The show finally did take to the air a year later, but with Ernie Kovacs as host instead of Clark.

One of *American Bandstand*'s most enduring features was the Top Ten board, which listed the top songs of any particular day. With its prominent location near Clark's lectern, the board was seen dozens of times on every show. The songs on the board didn't directly represent sales, airplay or general popularity. Instead, they were songs selected by Dick Clark and Tony Mammarella.

WHATEVER IT IS . . . HE'S GOT IT

Some in the music business reasoned that songs about *Bandstand* had a better chance of being played on the show, turning them into hits that might find their way onto the Top Ten board. Thus, there was a surge in *Bandstand*-related records in the show's early years.

Country singer Charlie Rich took this approach, recording a song called "Philadelphia Baby" in August 1958. Bobby and His Orbits followed with "Bandstand Dancing" and Vic Wayne delivered a catchy tune with "The Girl I Saw on Bandstand."

Not only did the tactic fail, but it also created something of a backlash, at least in Wichita Falls, Texas, where disc jockey Abe Lincoln refused to play any record that referred to *Bandstand*.

Despite the Wichita Falls boycott, just one year into his run as a national television personality, Dick Clark was building on the fame spawned by *Bandstand*. In the fall of 1958, ABC-Paramount released what would be the first of two *Dance with Dick Clark* LPs (the second would come a year later). Nine of the 24 instrumentals on the two LPs were songs in which Clark owned the publishing.

Just as successful for Clark were his publishing companies in New York, managed by Vera Hodes. Hodes, a veteran of the music publishing business, had previously worked for George Goldner and his Gone Records empire.

Clark also had that endorsement deal with Mary Jane shoes and a brand of Bobby Sox with his picture on the package resulted in 120,000 orders in the first three weeks. Next up: teenage dresses and blouses.

No wonder, then, that *Billboard's* June Bundy wrote that Clark was considered "one of the hottest merchandising and promotional properties in TV."[2]

Clark quietly disbanded his committee of *American Bandstand* regulars in October 1958, replacing it with the Dick Clark Fan Club, as he mounted a public campaign to reinforce his image as the very best surrogate father or brother a teenager could have.

Apparently, overseeing a popular dancing show for teenagers made Clark an expert in all areas of the teenage experience.

After making an appearance on New York *Herald Tribune* columnist Hy Gardner's television show, *Hy Gardner Calling*, Clark fielded questions on teenage issues from a studio audience of 200 high school editors. He also started a weekly teen advice column

---

2. *Billboard*, November 10, 1958.

in the Sunday newspaper supplement magazine, *This Week*, called *Dick Clark Speaking*.

The week before his column began, Leslie Lieber made the case for Clark's expanding role as a teen expert in a feature article in *This Week*, headlined "Why Everybody Loves Dick Clark." In the article, Lieber told of how even the normally brusque New York police had praise for Clark's tranquilizing effect on teens. Noting that 60 private police were normally needed in support of the 100 city police assigned to rock shows down the street at the Paramount Theater, Clark's *Saturday Night Show* required just two. "The worst thing these kids do is feed sugar to the horses," an unidentified police spokesman is quoted in Lieber's article.[3]

A *TV Guide* article—entitled "Whatever it is . . . He's Got It"—also let it slip that Clark was known to attend the rehearsal for the *Saturday Night Show* in his slippers and that his feet swelled up just before a *Bandstand* show once because of an allergic reaction to some blueberries he had just eaten.[4]

The media frenzy to learn more about Dick Clark extended to his wife as well.

Darol Gelber of the Philadelphia *Evening Bulletin* offered up a Sunday profile of Barbara Clark that pointed out that the blonde, blue-eyed, soft-spoken wife of America's favorite teen dance show host liked rock & roll, loved to dance and was sometimes mistaken for Grace Kelly.

Although she had taught at Gradyville Elementary School near Media, Pennsylvania, in the early years of their marriage, she was now a full-time wife and mother to young Dickie, born less than two years earlier. She and hubby listened to records or watched TV on quiet evenings at home and occasionally slipped away for dinner or a movie.

She went with Clark to New York every Saturday for his network show but noted that a downside to fame was that kids frequently drove by their house and they had to have an unlisted phone number.

Was it any wonder, then, that the Philadelphia County Council of the American Legion honored Clark for his work with teenagers at an October 1958 dinner in the Warwick Hotel?

While Clark was riding high, there was still a lot of competition for the Philadelphia teenage audience. That competition mostly

---

3. *This Week*, November 16, 1958.
4. *TV Guide*, October 10, 1958.

came from radio station WIBG. The station, popularly referred to as "Wibbage," had begun as an outlet for weekly church services in 1925. Indeed, the station's call letters stood for "I Believe in God."

But the station's format changed to dance band music in the 1940s and, following its sale to Storer Broadcasting in 1957, moved into rock & roll. By 1958, WIBG had moved from sixth in Pulse and Hooper ratings in Philadelphia before Storer took over, to No. 1. Its lineup of Bill Wright Sr., Hy Lit, and Joe Niagara made it *the* radio station for teenagers.

But WIBG had adopted the controversial Top 40 format in 1958. Besides using a limited playlist (a format that had increased ratings at other Storer stations), WIBG jocks were required to submit a list 24 hours in advance of the records they wanted to play the next day.

Clark, of course, had no such restriction. And, while his expanding business connections opened many doors, he also took many cues from radio, especially Philadelphia radio. James Brown, an aspiring R&B singer, tried to use that path to get his recording of "Try Me" on *Bandstand* in late 1958.

When playing at the Uptown Theater in North Philadelphia, Brown met a Philadelphia disc jockey who told him he could get "Try Me" played on *American Bandstand* for $1,000. Since Georgie Woods, Jimmy Bishop, Kae Williams, and Jocko Henderson all hosted shows at the Uptown around that time, it's not clear which DJ made the promise, but Brown plunked down the $1,000.

Later, as he and his band watched from a Macon, Ga., night club, "Try Me" came up on Rate-a-Record and did poorly.

"We were going crazy, saying, 'Naw, naw, this can't be true.' I was thinking, 'I paid that jock a thousand dollars for *this*?',"[5] Brown later said.

"Try Me" wasn't the only miss for Clark, who claimed he listened to upwards of 200 new records each week and could tell within a minute whether a tune had any hit potential. One notable song that slipped through Clark's fingers was "Philadelphia USA" by the Nu Tornados, a group of high schoolers from Philadelphia, recorded with the assistance of the locally popular Ferko String Band.

The song, a jaunty tune in the style of the Philadelphia string bands that dominated the city's Mummers' Day parades, was

---

5. *James Brown: The Godfather of Soul*, pp. 103–105, 1986.

co-written by Al Scalise and Bill Borelli. Borelli thought the song had more potential than he could satisfy with his own small label so he shopped it around, starting in Philadelphia. Clark was among those taking a pass on the song.

Also passing on the tune was Bernie Lowe. Lowe, still reeling from the Charlie Gracie lawsuit and settlement earlier in the year, was finalizing the sale of his Cameo Records to elevator music king Muzak for $250,000 when he was offered "Philadelphia USA." Although the Muzak deal fell through at the last minute (reportedly "because Lowe suffered an attack of sentiment"[6]), Lowe rejected the song and Borelli had to go outside Philadelphia to find a home for the tune.

He found it in New York, with Carlton Records, a new label that was riding high thanks to the success of a Detroit area rockabilly singer, Jack Scott. Borelli also found a willing promoter in the Philadelphia Chamber of Commerce and the song went on to become a top 30 hit. The Nu Tornados eventually appeared on Dick Clark's *Saturday Night Show* and were rewarded with a half-time performance before 100,000 at the Army-Navy game at Philadelphia's Municipal Stadium.

Noting "Philadelphia USA's" success, Clark wasted no time in making up for his mistake. Using a sound-alike group, the Quaker City Boys, Clark's Swan Records rushed out "Teasin'," a song that debuted just a month after Borelli's song, and pushed it to a top 40 spot with a chart run that virtually matched that of "Philadelphia USA."

The episode showed that Clark's business sense and powerful influence made it possible to turn a profit, even when making a mistake. Others in the business might mount a challenge, but there was no doubt who was in control.

In early fall 1958, a trio of Los Angeles teenagers called the Teddy Bears recorded a song inspired by the words on the tombstone of the father of the song's writer, Phil Spector, who was studying to become a court reporter. "To Know Him Is to Love Him" became a surprise regional hit, first in Fargo, N.D.; later in the Minneapolis-St. Paul, Minn., area.

Dore records owner Lou Bedell gave his friend Dick Clark a call. "Could Clark give the disc a few spins on *American Bandstand*," he asked.

---

6. *Billboard*, December 1, 1958.

WHATEVER IT IS . . . HE'S GOT IT

"Depends," said Clark. "Who's got the distributing?"

When Clark found out that his Jamie Records partner Harry Finfer had the distributing through Universal, he agreed to give the disc a shot.

Within three weeks, the record was being played on Top 40 stations across the country. Within six weeks, it was in the Top 10. Clark invited the Teddy Bears to Philadelphia for an appearance on *Bandstand*. It was Spector's first airplane ride and one week after Finfer drove the group from the airport to the WFIL studios for their *Bandstand* appearance, "To Know Him Is to Love Him" was the top song in the country.

Clark had planned to celebrate his 29th birthday in grand style—with a star-studded *Saturday Night Show* on November 29, 1958. The stars showed up for "Dick Clark's Birthday Show," but an airline strike grounded most of the 50 winners of a "Name Nameless" contest that were to be flown in for the program. The grand prize winner, a 13-year-old girl, did show up and was serenaded by Frankie Avalon.

Several of Clark's good friends, like Bobby Darin, Pat Boone, Sal Mineo, Connie Francis, and Danny & the Juniors made appearances on the *Saturday Night Show*. Clark returned the favor to Darin by writing an article for *Motion Picture* magazine entitled, *Bobby Darin: The Richest Kid In the Slums*. Clark further exercised his literary chops by writing another article—*My Views on Teen Love*—for a new magazine called *Stardom* in December.

As Christmas 1958 approached, a hot new song on ABC-Paramount got Clark's attention. Lloyd Price was rising up the charts with an old R&B song, "Stagger Lee," which was intended to be the B side of his newest release. The song, which told the story of a murder in St. Louis in 1895 after a drunken argument, had been softened by the addition of the pop singing group, The Ray Charles Singers, as the label tried to cross over onto the popular music market.

But the song was still too violent for Clark, who had booked Price for an early December appearance on *Bandstand*. If you want to appear on my show, Clark said, you'll have to change the lyrics.

That's exactly what Price did. In the new "*Bandstand* version," there was no gambling, barroom, .44 pistol, begging or shooting. Instead, there was some arguing, apparently over a girl and a loan gone bad. Price made his appearance, the song reached No.

1, and Clark turned his attention to other matters, like the family Christmas card.

Clark wanted to do something different for the holidays, something that represented his status in the TV music business. He decided to produce a special record that would serve as an audio Christmas card, perhaps a song like "Jingle Bells" as it might be sung by popular singers of the day.

When he floated the idea by Bernie Lowe, Lowe just happened to have what he saw as a perfect solution. A young kid from Southern High had been begging him to do some recording at Cameo. Turns out the kid also did impressions. Clark said to give him a call.

It was just the break young Ernest Evans had been looking for. Born in South Carolina, Evans spent his early years on a cotton and tobacco farm. Around the age of 10, the family moved to an apartment in South Philadelphia, where he was introduced to indoor plumbing and electricity. A self-taught piano player, Evans also showed promise as a singer, prompting a sixth-grade teacher to enroll him at the nearby Settlement Music School.

By the time he reached high school, Evans was entertaining classmates with his musical impersonations, often with classmate Tommy Enos. He joined a singing group called the Quantrells, picking up the nickname Fat Ernie while entertaining fellow students outside the Southern cafeteria and at the school's annual talent show, Stunt Night.

He spent summers doing farm work back in South Carolina and took a part-time job at a sandwich shop in the Italian Market but when he found he could make more money cutting up chickens, he took that job. It was there that he picked up the new nickname of Chubby from a fellow worker. He also got the attention of his boss, Henry Caltabiano, for his singing. At first, he sang to himself. Then, the customers started to notice.

"People would come in to hear me sing and buy chickens," Chubby recalled.[7]

Evans hoped that his musical skills would lead to rock stardom, as it had for fellow South Philadelphians Charlie Gracie, Frankie Avalon, and Fabian, who was a year behind him at Southern High School. Even good friend Enos was already cutting records for small Philadelphia labels as Tommy Lane.

---

7. *San Mateo Times*, November 20, 1961.

WHATEVER IT IS... HE'S GOT IT

Although Evans made the rounds of the Philadelphia labels, he found no takers. His boss, Caltabiano, was supportive. Even better, he was friends with Kal Mann at Cameo, who tipped off Lowe about young Chubby Evans.

"Henry was listening to me one day when I was cutting loose for the customers," Evans said. "When he came over to talk to me I thought he was going to tell me to go about my [chicken] business and leave the singing alone. . . . Instead, he asked me if I wanted to cut a record."[8]

When he found out the record would be cut by Cameo, he was doubly pleased.

"I had gone to that record company like a hundred times. . . . They kept throwing me out! But, I kept going back."[9]

When Evans showed up at the Cameo studio to rehearse the song, he met Dick and Barbara Clark as he was practicing his Fats Domino imitation. Barbara Clark asked him what his name was.

"Chubby," he said.

"Oh," said Barbara Clark, amused by the juxtaposition of Chubby copying Fats. "Chubby, um, Checker, like Fats Domino?"

They laughed at the time, but the name stuck. The Christmas card was so popular, that Mann suggested that they rework the song for the commercial market. As Mann began crafting a similar song to the tune of "Mary Had a Little Lamb," Henry Caltabiano changed his name to Henry Colt and took over management of his discovery, Chubby Checker.

As Christmas 1958 approached, disc jockeys dusted off old standards by Bing Crosby, Perry Como, and Frank Sinatra. There were new offerings, too, by the likes of Pat Boone and the Mickey Mouse Orchestra from Disneyland, but the hottest record around was a novelty tune from the same man who had wrought "Witch Doctor" a year earlier.

Ross Bagdasarian, doing business as David Seville, pretty much owned the 1958 Christmas market with "The Chipmunk Song," a jaunty tune that told the tale of three mischievous chipmunks in voices that sounded suspiciously like speeded-up versions of Bagdasarian himself. In the weeks leading up to Christmas, "The Chipmunk Song" was selling as many as 200,000 copies in a single day.

---

8. *Winnipeg Free Press,* December 17, 1960.
9. *Goldmine,* December 28, 1990, Wayne Jancik.

The song found a happy home on *American Bandstand*, as did "16 Candles," an up and coming hit by a previously obscure group, the Crests. Clark was doubly happy to watch "16 Candles" ride up the charts since his January Corp. owned the song's publishing. Song publishing, an important part of Clark's business empire, was expanding in December 1958 with the acquisition or Arch Music, his first holding affiliated with ASCAP. SRO Management was doing well for Clark, too, with the addition of rockabilly singer Dale Hawkins to the roster that already included Duane Eddy and LaVern Baker.

Clark made an appearance on Patti Page's ABC-TV prime time variety show on December 15, a week before he was featured in a *Life* magazine article, headlined "Rock 'n' Roll Rolls On 'N' On." The *Life* article was less than flattering, however, claiming that rock music "has little musical eloquence—is a singer's highly personal way of shouting or moaning lyrics" and appeals primarily to girls ages 8 through 16.[10]

Furthermore, the article referred to Clark as "The Dictator" and described *American Bandstand* as a show "on which teenagers dance to records [and] is an institution based on his defense of teenage behavior and taste in music."[11]

Christmas was still a festive occasion for fans of *American Bandstand*. The set was brightened with a Christmas tree decorated by the WFIL staff and Clark danced with his wife on Christmas Day.

But the final week of 1958 was marred when a 20-year-old man was stabbed in a fight after leaving a Clark record hop at the Sunnybrook Ballroom in Pottstown, Pennsylvania. The fight, which occurred in a parking lot after Clark had left the building, was witnessed by about half of the estimated 2,000 kids who had attended the hop.

"We've had some 600 dances like this in various places and this is the first time there has been any trouble," Clark told the *Associated Press* the next day. "I'm very sorry it happened."[12]

The new year of 1959, however, got off to a good start. Clark, who was never able to persuade Elvis Presley's manager Col. Tom Parker to allow Presley to appear on *American Bandstand*, did

---
10. *Life*, December 22, 1958.
11. Ibid.
12. *Associated Press*, December 27. 1958.

manage to land a phone interview with the Army private on his 24th birthday, January 8, 1959.

Clark, who dedicated the entire program that day to Presley, finally made connections for a 4½-minute on-air interview. Presley said that he was studying map reading and learning how to grease a Jeep. In his off-duty hours, he said, he strummed his guitar. "I don't want to get out of practice if I can help it," he explained.

After Clark informed Presley that he was voted favorite male vocalist and had the favorite record of the year in the 1958 *American Bandstand* popularity poll, Elvis responded: "You'll never know how happy I'll be, boy, when I can return to the entertainment world, because once you get a taste of show business, there's nothing like it."

When it came to the entertainment world, Clark and Presley were kindred spirits. Just as Presley had Colonel Parker to look out for his affairs, Clark had assembled a team to help him navigate his way.

Through ABC-TV, it was press agents Mari Yanofsky and Connie DeNave who spread the Clark gospel. Anyone who asked could learn that Clark was 5'9", had a 32-inch waist, wore size 8 shoes and liked steak and onions as well as hot dogs and chili.

Lawyer Marvin Josephson guided Clark in his myriad business dealings while Vera Hodes kept an eye on his publishing interests from her New York City office. Tony Mammarella, who had been with *Bandstand* from the very beginning, and Marlene Teti Pauls, his personal secretary, kept things running smoothly around their small WFIL-TV office.

Plus, there were his business partners: Bernie Binnick (Swan Records, Binlark); Harold B. Lipsius, Samuel Hodge and Harry Finfer (Jamie Records); Bernie Lowe (Chips Distributing, Mallard Pressing . . . and co-owner Cameo Records) and Harry Chipetz (Chips).

His team had put Clark in an enviable position. As 1959 began, *American Bandstand* was seen on more than 100 stations across the country. Ratings service Arbitron reported that *American Bandstand* easily outdistanced runner-up *The Price Is Right* as the highest-rated daytime show in the U.S. Trendex reported that *Bandstand's* rating nearly equaled that of the NBC and CBS competition combined.

The record business was continuing to evolve as rock & roll matured and showed signs of sticking around for a while. Record sales in 1958 produced about the same volume as in 1957 but had turned around in the last six months after a sluggish start.

Stereo records were gaining a foothold in the LP market, but the old model of record stores driving sales was rapidly crumbling. Record racks were popping up in department stores, drug stores, and supermarkets, where these "traffic builders" accounted for about one-quarter of all U.S. sales in 1958.

Mail order record clubs were siphoning off millions of dollars in pop LP sales. RCA, Capitol, and Columbia were well established by the end of 1958 and more clubs were on the way. Dot Records was working on a club that would pool independent labels; Liberty was considering joining forces with the Diner's Club and MGM was talking about teaming up with Mercury.

One of the big benefits for the clubs was the special fourth class postage rates that applied to their records. Boston Congressman Torbert MacDonald, however, said he'd work to eliminate that benefit that subsidizes "rock & roll, jazz, and hillbilly musicians . . . musical illiterates. We should make it more difficult for the phonographs of our teenagers to blare from coast to coast daily and nightly with this trash," MacDonald said.[13]

Warner Brothers saw a way to work around higher postage rates by creating a club through retailers instead. One Chicago entrepreneur proposed selling records at living room "parties," similar to those practiced by Tupperware.

Just about every Hollywood movie studio got into the record business, too, in 1958, including Warner Brothers and 20th Century Fox.

American Bandstand's success continued to heavily influence program directors around the country in early 1959. There were dozens of similar shows in local markets around the U.S., many of them subscribers to the syndicated "Top 10 Dance Party."

NBC-TV finally unveiled its answer to Clark's *Saturday Night Show* on January 11, 1959, with Buddy Bregman's *The Music Shop*. Reviewers panned the show, described by *Billboard's* Joan Bundy as "a patent imitation" of Clark's show, adding that Bregman "lacks polish, poise and an authoritative manner—all of which enable Clark to establish an easy rapport with his kid audience."[14]

---

13. *Billboard*, March 9, 1959.
14. *Billboard*, January 19, 1959.

WHATEVER IT IS . . . HE'S GOT IT

Longtime Clark rivals Buddy Deane and Alan Freed persisted in their attempts to outdo the Philadelphia show with twists of their own.

In Baltimore, Deane launched a new show on ABC-TV aimed at young adults. *Buddy Deane's Dance Party* invited 60–80 young adults to lunch at the Gold Room of Marty's Mark Plaza where they could also dance, watch musical stars perform and be interviewed by Deane. Deane's target audience was clear as the show also offered a babysitting service.

Alan Freed had bounced back from his 1957 cancellation at ABC-TV to host a daily weekday 5–6 P.M. record hop show on WNEW-TV in New York City and a weekly telecast on ABC-TV in the hour following Clark's *Saturday Night Show*. Freed promised a greater emphasis on talent and more elaborate productions than Clark's show plus, like Deane, he invited parents and older couples to dance on the program.

Despite Freed's Saturday night program, Clark remained the only television deejay with national reach six days a week. Clark's national standing gave him a unique position in the ABC-TV pantheon. The network's vice president of standards and practices, Grace Johnson, had the duty of ensuring that ABC programming was acceptable to the communities the network served. Within her division was music rights supervisor Harold Parkyn whose duty was to rule on whether songs were appropriate to be played on ABC programs.

Parkyn admitted that there was a double standard employed for *American Bandstand*. Rock & roll, after all, was more dependent on its beat than its words, so some songs got a pass for Clark's show where they might be rejected for a show like Patti Page's. Parkyn was tested in early 1959 when Link Wray's "Rumble" became a breakout national hit. The problem was that rumble was a term that was usually associated with gang violence and, even though the song was an instrumental, its raw rhythms caused it to be banned at many radio stations, including in New York City, which was in the midst of a teenage crime wave.

Parkyn initially banned the song on ABC, too, but Clark, who had scheduled Wray for a *Bandstand* appearance, objected. A compromise was reached and when Wray appeared on Clark's show, he performed the song, but its title was never mentioned.

While Clark was adept at wielding his considerable power, things didn't always work out the way he intended. Such was the case with singer Tommy Leonetti.

Leonetti, a 26-year-old pop singer from North Bergen, N.J., appeared to be a perfect fit when he was booked for Clark's *Saturday Night Show*. A clean-cut song stylist with a modest track record, Leonetti looked more suited for *Your Hit Parade* (which he occasionally appeared on) than a rock & roll program.

But testimony before the U.S. Senate's Racket Committee on February 20, implied that a former Leonetti manager from years earlier had used threats of violence to get Leonetti's records played on Chicago jukeboxes. Hearing this, Clark's *Saturday Night Show* producer Chuck Reeves called Leonetti's manager and canceled the appearance, less than 24 hours before it was to take place.

News of the cancellation created a strong backlash. Media critics blasted Clark for his rush to judgment. Clark's professional rivals seized the opportunity. Jim Gallant of New Haven, Conn., snagged the next booking of Leonetti, for *Jim Gallant's Bandstand* on WNHC on February 28. Steve Allen booked him for his national show the next night.

Even Alan Freed got into the act, securing Leonetti for his March 27 Easter show at the Brooklyn Fox Theater. Clark, meanwhile, relented and booked Leonetti for a later appearance.

Clark, who first dabbled in movies with his *Jamboree* in 1957, was being lured back to the big screen in early 1959 as Freed was already wrapping up production on his fifth rock & roll film with *Go Johnny Go*, which starred Jimmy Clanton, a favorite teen singer among *American Bandstand* fans.

The casting of young male singers in movie roles was a trend among Hollywood studios who saw big dollars in transferring that on-stage charisma to the big screen.

Elvis Presley started the trend years earlier, but the pace quickened following the emergence of *American Bandstand*. And it wasn't just for exploitative rock & roll movies. Ricky Nelson was getting good reviews for his dramatic work with John Wayne in *Rio Bravo*, Paul Anka had a major role in *Girls Town* and Pat Boone and Tommy Sands were both in *Mardi Gras*.

But the trend struck closer to home when Frankie Avalon was signed to star with Alan Ladd in Warner Brothers' *Guns of the Timberland* and Fabian landed a four-picture deal with 20th Century Fox.

Clark, who had created Drexel Television Productions the previous summer to produce his *Saturday Night Show*, expanded his Drexel company to include movies. By March 1959, he had three new companies under the Drexel banner—to produce motion pictures with United Artists and Columbia and to produce television shows in addition to the *Saturday Night Show*.

The new businesses promised to keep Clark busy—producing five movies in the next 18 months (two starring him), four to six musical specials on ABC-TV in the next year, hosting a new version of *This Is Show Business* starting October 8 on ABC-TV and, possibly, dramatic TV shows for prime time and daytime audiences. Clark also promised to continue doing weekly record hops in the Philadelphia area, which he used "as a testing ground for new records and chats with the youngsters to find out what they like and dislike about everything from books and movies to his sponsor's product."[15]

His first movie assignment was to do promotional work for Columbia's *Gidget*. Columbia also sent him to the Kellman Laboratories in Philadelphia to take a series of film tests.

Kellman Laboratories grew out of News Reel Laboratories, the brainchild of Louis W. Kellman, a film pioneer who dreamed of making Philadelphia a major film center. Kellman had been producing commercials, documentaries and industrial films in the Philadelphia area since 1930.

Kellman branched out into theatrical releases in the mid-1950s when he shot what would become a film noir classic, *The Burglar*, starring Dan Duryea. The film, which was shot in Philadelphia and Atlantic City, also was the first starring role for Jayne Mansfield. Future NFL Films narrator John Facenda had a small part, as did disgraced WPEN announcer Steve Allison, who was brought down in the same vice sting that ended Bob Horn's Philadelphia career.

Kellman sold *The Burglar* to Columbia Pictures for a tidy $200,000 profit which allowed him to beef up his Philadelphia staff to about 50 employees by the time Clark showed up for his screen tests. Things must have gone well at the tests for Clark soon was doing the narration for one of Kellman's trade films, *The Wonders of Philadelphia*.

Clark started planning his first major film production in March 1959 when Drexel Pictures Corporation purchased the movie rights to *Harrison High*, a best-selling novel written by 22-year-old John Farris. Bobby Darin and Fabian were said to

---
15. *Billboard*, March 9, 1959.

be competing for two of the top roles in the film, which would be co-produced with Columbia Pictures.

But there was no doubt who would be playing *the* lead role, a mild-mannered yet firm and sensible teacher who could diffuse the most incendiary teenage situation. Directing Clark in that role would be Paul Wendkos, the director of *The Wonders of Philadelphia* and, more importantly, *The Burglar*.

Movie production wasn't the only new business Clark added in early 1959. Although he now managed singers, recorded their songs, pressed their records, distributed them and played them on national television, there were still unexploited areas of the teenage market.

How about someplace to store those 45s? Clark teamed up with Tony Mammarella and song plugger Ed Barsky to form Raye Products, a manufacturer of record-carrying cases, which were given away during *Bandstand*'s Rate-a-Record segment. Mammarella, A.N. Albertini (better known as Four Aces lead singer Al Alberts), and J.R. McCausland joined Clark in creating Startime Industries, a manufacturer of stuffed animals (Platter Puss, Cuddle Pups) plus Autograph Hounds, stuffed dogs that were seen frequently at the *Bandstand* autograph table.

Clark and Mammarella entered the cosmetics business, too, with Post-Grad Products but a Clark-endorsed creme hair conditioner proved to be a rare miss in the Clark business empire.

Clark made a stab at his own personal rock stardom with a Cameo release called "Jenkins Band." Clark, who performed under the fake name of Stan Newman, described the release as perhaps the first rap record, though he later conceded the record was a failure.

"It was the worst thing you ever heard," he said. "Talk about a white man trying to sing with absolutely no soul!"[16]

What Clark lacked in soul, he more than made up for with his business acumen. The roster of businesses he held a stake in grew to 23 in early 1959 when he formed Claban Publishing Corporation with his wife. Claban was to coordinate publication of a magazine with Banner Magazines, Inc.

The Real Dick Clark hit newsstands late that spring. For 35 cents, readers got 66 pages of pictures and articles about Elvis, Frankie Avalon, Connie Francis, Pat Boone, and Bobby Darin,

---

16. *Knight-Ridder News Service,* Doug Adrianson, November 11, 1989.

plus a cover article by Clark, "What Makes Me Blazing Mad: Dating and Love."

While his behind-the-scenes partners at Chips Distributing were scouting Manhattan for a site to expand their business into New York City, Clark was meeting with British music talent agents Lew and Leslie Grade and Jack Good as the Brits were lining up talent for a show to premiere in London in the fall called *Oh Boy*.

Clark's popularity continued to grow.

Ivan Combe, pleased with the increased sales of Clearasil since he bought time on *American Bandstand*, expanded Clark's role to a company spokesman in print advertising, where he was also seen promoting the *Gidget* movie and Gayla bobby pins. Clark was named the chairman of the National Teens Against Polio for the 1959 March of Dimes and he joined Steve Allen, Dick Clark, Dave Garroway, Earl Wilson and Patti Page as judges for the queen of the Music Industry Trade Show sponsored by the National Association of Music Merchants.

On April 9, Clark was honored by the Golden Slipper Square Club and the next day received the man of the year award from the Philadelphia Guild of Advertising Men at their annual dinner dance, where he admonished the advertisers to not talk down to teens, who, he said, are more sophisticated than most advertisers realize.

Although the cover headline on the July issue of *TV, Movie, and Record Stars Illustrated* teased "Dick Clark Asks: Are Teenagers Really My Friends?," there was no question about the answer.

As WFIL owner Walter Annenberg dined with the Richard Nixons, their teenage daughter, Tricia, learned that Annenberg was associated with the same station that broadcast *American Bandstand*. "Oh, you must know Dick Clark!," she cried. "Can you get me a couple of his autographed pictures?"[17]

While Clark's enormous influence let him take advantage of just about every trend, his status was far from unchallenged.

In Philadelphia, Joe Grady and Ed Hurst—who nearly were the first hosts of *Bandstand* in 1952—were awarded their own dance party show in April 1959 when they began the *Grady & Hurst Bandwagon* on WRCV-TV for two hours every Saturday afternoon. Philly radio station WIBG increased its power from 10,000 to 50,000 watts and celebrated by giving listeners prizes ranging from candy bars and cigarettes to a new car.

---

17. *Philadelphia Daily News*, April 24, 1959.

Nationally, though, disc jockeys felt besieged as management at station after station fell under the spell of Top 40 radio. While limited playlists restricted a DJ's ability to break out new hits, the format proved popular with listeners who were more likely to hear the familiar songs they preferred.

Promotion men, too, were threatened by the format and its inherent shift of power from the disc jockey to the program director. RCA Victor promotion man Dave Hollis was particularly critical of the changes in Detroit, where he alleged that four of the five rock stations had gone to the Top 40 dark side.

"Detroit radio has turned into a jukebox," Hollis said. "A promotion man in Detroit is turning out to be a thing of the past."[18]

The specter of a Top 40 America was deemed so heinous as to spark talk of a national organization to represent disc jockeys. Although many disc jockeys saw themselves as strong independent cowboys operating in a wild west fraught with danger, the fear of losing their independence to the playlist was danger enough to merit serious consideration of a DJ's union as soon as the upcoming second national disc jockey conference in Miami.

Indeed, the first panel discussion scheduled for the Memorial Day conclave was titled *The Pros and Cons of Formula Radio*. Another session, *What Next Mr. Music Man?*, included Alan Freed on the panel.

Clark, though, mainly stayed above the fray. His success at the Southeastern Fair in Atlanta in 1958 landed him a sweet offer from the Michigan State Fair for Labor Day 1959—two shows a day for four straight days at the State Fair Coliseum.

Philadelphia teenager Fabian finally had a modest hit with "I'm a Man," igniting a heavy Clark-led promotion for the 15-year-old's follow-up, "Turn Me Loose," in which it was promised the lad's last name would be revealed on the *Saturday Night Show* (it was.)

Fabian's high school classmate, Ernie Evans, was also finding recording success as Chubby Checker. Bernie Lowe and Kal Mann took the format of Dick Clark's Christmas card recording a step further, creating a novelty tune called "The Class." The song capitalized on Checker's ability to impersonate popular rock singers. When it came to re-creating David Seville's Chipmunks, Checker and another south Philadelphia teen, Bobby Rydell, provided the

---

18. *Billboard*, March 23, 1959.

WHATEVER IT IS... HE'S GOT IT

speeded-up vocals. The song became the fourth release on Lowe and Mann's new Parkway label and netted Checker his first appearance on *American Bandstand*.

The always busy Clark was preparing for a new challenge in the spring of 1959, his first prime-time music special for ABC-TV. Originally planned as a 90-minute spectacular in May, the show finally took shape as an hour-long special entitled *The Record Years* and was scheduled for June 28.

The date conflicted with NBC's *This Is Your Life*, which wanted to feature Clark on its season finale on June 24, when Clark would be deep in preparations for his prime-time special. A compromise was reached when NBC decided to tape the program three weeks earlier. Besides eliminating the conflict, that option also gave NBC precious time to alert a potentially huge teen audience by leaking word of Clark's appearance.

Although host Ralph Edwards introduced each episode of *This Is Your Life* by surprising the subject of that night's show, Clark undoubtedly was tipped off before he appeared on camera for a bogus panel show about teenage music. Clark's wife and parents were there. So were Roger Clipp, Lew Klein and Tony Mammarella from WFIL. Singers Frankie Avalon, Fabian, Connie Francis, Andy Williams, and David Seville also took part in the 30-minute tribute to the 29-year-old Clark, one of the youngest subjects ever to be featured on the show. In his review of the program for United Press International, William Ewald said "The *This Is Your Life* show was a pretty pale one. But that was no one's fault. Nothing much seems to have happened to Clark."[19]

Nevertheless, Edwards described Clark in his introduction as "a spokesman for the great wholesome majority of American teenagers," a theme carried throughout the program and forward to Clark's own special four days later.

Clark saw the special as a great opportunity for his Drexel production company to prove itself in prime time and vowed to sink any profits into the show's production "to make it a glittering example of what he and his TV team can do."[20]

So, instead of spending the evening of his seventh wedding anniversary with his wife, Clark spent the night with musicians while presenting *The Record Years*, which was described as a "tribute to the recording industry." Lip-syncing was the order of

---

19. *Philadelphia Evening Bulletin*, June 25, 1959.
20. *Philadelphia Inquirer*, June 26, 1959.

the day for guests Johnny Mathis, Les Paul & Mary Ford, Fabian, Stan Freberg, Fats Domino, Stan Kenton and his orchestra and the McGuire Sisters.

As he promised in the lead-up to the program, Clark showed off some of his own dancing skills with the McGuire Sisters, but it was his defense of teenagers and their music that proved to be the highlight of the show. Using his star-studded cast, Clark pointed out the silliness of past eras with their songs like "Ta Ra Ra Boom De Aye" and "Three Itty Fishies" and antics like goldfish swallowing or wearing sloppy joe sweaters and zoot suits.

Then, with a decided Clarkian flourish, he brought out a troupe of well-dressed, perfectly behaved thoroughly modern teenage dancers.

Clark's effort was hugely rewarded. According to Trendex ratings, *The Record Years* drew more than half of America's viewing audience and beat such stalwart opposition as *Alfred Hitchcock, The Chevy Show, The Loretta Young Show,* and *Richard Diamond.*

A fringe benefit was the cash Clark pocketed as a spokesman for one of the show's big sponsors, AMF Pinspotters. AMF, a major player in the surge in popularity of bowling in the late 1950s, hired Clark—a notorious non-athlete—as the cover boy for a booklet called *Bowling Fun* that was distributed through North American bowling centers.

More in line with Clark's public image was his tie-in with DuPont for a line of teenaged girls clothing called "Dance Band Fashions." Under this arrangement, Clark's photo was to be used in promotional materials by some 35 manufacturers whose items were made of DuPont nylon, dacron or orlon.

As the second anniversary of *American Bandstand* approached, Clark added a few more businesses to his empire. He and his wife formed two corporations—Salutem and Wallingford Realty—to handle land purchases in Maryland and Delaware and he set up three more corporations to deal with Swan Records entities—Anita Pressing (with Mammarella and Bernie Binnick, for pressing of Swan records), BAE Music (for ASCAP publishing) and Request Music (for BMI publishing).

Through his SRO Productions, Clark teamed up with successful tour packager Irvin Feld to create Clark-Feld Productions and revealed plans for an ambitious 52-day fall tour called *The Dick Clark Caravan of Stars* to start on Sept. 18.

WHATEVER IT IS ... HE'S GOT IT

Clark also announced that his planned fall TV series, *Dick Clark's World of Talent*, would air on Sunday nights (opposite the popular *What's My Line?*) instead of Wednesdays and would be sponsored by cigarette manufacturer P. Lorillard Company. In addition, Clark revealed that he'd be taking the entire month of August off so he could spend the month in Hollywood filming his first feature film *Because They're Young*.

Since his California plans would take him out of Philadelphia for his anniversary show on August 5, Clark taped two weeks of shows in advance, including the anniversary show. Besides receiving congratulatory on-air phone calls from Fabian, Frankie Avalon, and Duane Eddy, Clark also conducted a brief phone chat with Elvis Presley, who was still with the U.S. Army in Germany. Clark filled the remaining two weeks of his absence with guest deejays and moved the *Saturday Night Show* to Hollywood for three weeks beginning August 22.

With everything in place for his August "recess," Clark headed for Hollywood. But, on the first day that the taped programs were to begin, word leaked that something was amiss. Pat Molittieri, a 16-year-old Bartram High School student who was one of the most popular young dancers on *American Bandstand*, told a reporter that Clark had banned her from the show after her picture appeared on the June cover of *'Teen* magazine.

Not true, said Clark. She quit to write for the magazine, he said.

But, by the time the taped second anniversary *American Bandstand* show hit the air two days later, dedicated fans of the show weren't gushing over the Elvis phone interview.

They were asking, "What happened to Pat?"

CHAPTER 11

THE REGULARS

Pamela Beasley was upset.

While watching *American Bandstand* from her home in the small town of Madisonville, Texas, shortly after the show went national she couldn't believe what she was hearing: some kids on the show debating which city was the capital of Florida.

"I was just outraged that these teenagers didn't know," Beasley recalled.

So, she did what any self-respecting 11-year-old of the 1950s would do—she got out pen and paper, made up a list of every state capital in the U.S. and mailed it to the show. One day, after rushing home from school, she flipped on the TV and saw Dick Clark reading her letter on the air.

"He started to quiz the kids in the audience about the various states," she said. "It was really kind of funny."

Although Beasley's fleeting fame was atypical of the *American Bandstand* experience for the millions of American young people who tuned in every day, her interest in the kids who danced on the show was very mainstream.

From the show's beginning, it was apparent that the kids were every bit as important to *Bandstand's* success as were the host and the music played. Bob Horn knew that; so did Dick Clark.

Philadelphia wasn't the only city to try a teen dancing program in the early 1950s. Indeed, most popular radio disc jockeys of the

THE REGULARS

era gave TV a shot. The common denominator was the dancing teens. Beyond that, programming was diverse, and sometimes just plain weird.

For some reason, several stations thought viewers would like to see their hosts pantomime to popular records. *Paul Dixon's Song Shop* in Cincinnati was so successful with the format that the Dumont network brought Dixon to New York City for a national version of the show that lasted less than a year.

Chicago was a hotbed of teen dancing shows in the early 1950s where Howard Miller's show included records and interviews of guests but was killed by filler camera shots of hanging mobiles, dogs in playpens and dolls. Ray Rayner at WBBM-TV thought teens playing charades was a good idea to supplement his role as a pantomime singer.

Jim Lounsbury of WGN-TV, whose *Bandstand Matinee* would go on to enjoy a lengthy run in the Windy City, had the right mix of guest interviews and teen dancers but was a victim of his own success when more than 2,000 kids tried to jam into his 400-capacity studio for an appearance of the McGuire Sisters. After the police riot squad was summoned, station officials pulled the show off the air for a week so management could come up with a better method of crowd control.

Horn never had to call out the riot squad for *Bandstand*, but he did have to let kids into the studio in two shifts.

Philadelphia's reputation as a "breakout city," where potential hits could rack up big sales and get the attention of the major national labels, was cemented by the show's first bona fide dance craze, the bunny hop.

Ray Anthony's recording of "The Bunny Hop" took off after Horn started playing it on *Bandstand*. The dance took off, too, and soon all of America was hopping to the song's staccato rhythms. While "The Bunny Hop" became a ticket to fame for *Bandstand* regulars Harvey Sheldon and Irma "Dimples" Eininger, the song became something of an albatross for bandleader Anthony who, although he graciously played the song for adoring fans for the next four decades, never felt its simple structure adequately displayed his orchestra's considerable talents.

Harvey and Dimples were so popular with the WFIL-TV audience, fan clubs were created for them and other popular *Bandstand* couples, like Blanche McCleary and Mickey Cullen and Jim Hudson and Carmella Raffa.

Horn soon learned that when he took the teens to dances outside the Philadelphia area they were recognized as celebrities.

"If you would go to another dance, people would know who you were," said Earle Drake, one of Committee member Barbara Marcen's regular dance partners on *Bandstand*. But, said Drake, his future wife didn't see the *Bandstand* dancers as anything special when she saw them at a St. Lawrence dance. "She didn't think much of any of us. A bunch of stuck-up kids."

Horn and Tony Mammarella walked a fine line, making the dancers entertaining and natural enough to hold viewers' attention, but not so entertaining that they took over the whole show. Rules about dress and behavior were instituted and enforced, usually by Mammarella.

"Sometimes girls would wear sweaters that were too tight. [Mammarella would] make them go home," Marcen said. "He wouldn't let them on the show. Sometimes, if somebody did something wrong, say you got in a fight or something or an argument with somebody, you'd get banned from the show for a week."

The most common offense was jostling for face time before the cameras. Even though television was fairly new in *Bandstand's* early years, teens quickly learned that a lit-up red tally light on a camera meant that camera was live. It was *Bandstand* director Ed Yates who came up with the technique of moving a dissolve lever ever so slightly, lighting up two camera's tally lights at the same time.

"I could fool those kids," Yates said. "Nobody would know which camera I was really using."

For the most part, there was little on-camera drama among the *Bandstand* regulars during the Horn years. A few of them aspired to a show business career, but most just wanted to hang out with friends and dance.

Although *Bandstand* was preempted for a few months in the spring of 1954 for live broadcasts of the McCarthy congressional hearings, many of the regulars showed up at the studio anyway. At first, they tried dancing without music but Yates graciously started piping music into the studio. Occasionally, the hearings would recess early and an abbreviated version of the show would be broadcast.

A few of the regulars during the Horn era achieved some local show business fame through their *Bandstand* connection. Lucille Napoli was a professional singer and a dancer at the Varsity Club

THE REGULARS

and Ginny O'Callahan took her contest-winning jitterbug moves from West Catholic into tryouts for movie roles. But the biggest *Bandstand* star of the Horn years was Tommy DeNoble.

DeNoble was a decent dancer, but not the show's best. He was, however, among the show's best dressers, with a signature suit featuring lavender and pink stripes running down the legs and flat-toed shoes. And DeNoble danced with just about any girl who showed up. Viewers, especially female viewers, noticed the charismatic young teenager.

When the 15-year-old sophomore from St. Thomas More scheduled a visit to the Friday Night Halloween Dungaree Dance at Sacred Heart Hall in Mahoney City, Pennsylvania, in 1954, the parish took out a newspaper ad to announce the planned appearance of "That popular, versatile dancer, singer, pianist, and member of the committee on Bob Horn's *Bandstand*."[1] The dance drew more than 1,000 teenagers.

Before becoming one of the first regular dancers on *Bandstand*, DeNoble had sung on *The Horn and Hardart Children's Hour* on WCAU. During his high school years, he started his own singing group, the Stardusters. After high school (and after leaving *Bandstand*), DeNoble recorded a song called "I Want to Go With You," which was written by Philadelphia ad man Les Waas. Although the record went nowhere, DeNoble did have a minor hit with "Count Every Star," a record that earned him a guest spot on *American Bandstand* in 1960.

DeNoble's musical career didn't last long, but he was a Philadelphia TV fixture for decades, first as Sgt. Sacto on Channel 48, later as an engineer at Channel 29.

Horn built the show's popularity throughout his nearly four-year run as host. He created a special committee, with "Preferred" written on the back of membership cards in lipstick by his secretary, Shirley Rubin.

Horn also encouraged the regulars to attend his Wednesday, Friday and Saturday night hops at the Carman Roller Skating Rink, Willow Grove Park and in Avalon, N.J. Special broadcasts from the annual picnic at Woodside Park and in the Arena next door allowed him to pack in crowds not possible in Studio B.

Promotion men valued the opinion of the *Bandstand* regulars. They'd often round up a bunch of them for a record party where

---

1. WHYY-TV, Philadelphia, documentary, *More Things That Aren't There Anymore*, 1994

they could solicit their thoughts on recent releases, a practice frowned upon by Horn and Mammarella.

Mary Ann Colella, whose years at John W. Hallahan Catholic Girls High School coincided with Horn's years helming *Bandstand*, was one of his biggest supporters.

"I spent half my *Bandstand* years in the school's discipline office for wearing my uniform on *Bandstand*," she said. "They never called me by name over the loudspeaker. They would say, 'Would the girl who was on TV dancing yesterday with her uniform please come to the discipline office?'"

When Horn was replaced by Dick Clark in the summer of 1956, Colella was among the large group of regulars who protested the move.

"None of us were crazy about Dick Clark because we felt he inherited this job, where we felt [*Bandstand*] should have went to Tony Mammarella," she said.

Like most of the *Bandstand* regulars, Colella didn't listen to Clark's radio show. Their only contact with him was when he did commercials on the show.

"He reminded me of a young punk," Colella said. "He just wasn't personable. We were spoiled."

Although Horn's very public drunk driving arrest was well known, the charges that he was fooling around with a young girl were just rumors at the time.

"We didn't believe what he did . . . none of us thought of Bob Horn that way," Colella said. "So here's someone new coming in and Tony Mammarella doesn't get the job. . . . It was a bad time for us. We figured, 'Oh God, what's going to happen to the show now?'"

* * *

Although the protest led by Committee head Jerry Blavat was brief, Dick Clark still faced tough scrutiny by the show's young dancers and their parents as he took over hosting duties of Philadelphia's most popular afternoon television program.

Fran Saddic, who regularly rode the trolley from South Philadelphia to *Bandstand* from 1954 through 1956 and acquired the nickname "Franny with the Bangs" for her hairstyle, was barred from attending the show by her parents after the Horn sex scandal broke.

THE REGULARS

Another popular regular, Joanne Montecarlo, was also barred from the show after Horn's dismissal.

"Tony Mammarella called my house and told my father that they were getting this new host who was a clean-cut family man," Montecarlo said. "Between Tony and my mother, my father was finally convinced. [My sister] Carmen and I went back to the show."[2]

Mammarella was key to the show's continued success. Mammarella was as South Philadelphian as they came, although he was delivered by his physician father on Sept. 24, 1924, on a Labor Day outing to Atlantic City, N.J. Growing up in the heart of the Italian Market area, Mammarella had hoped for a career as an actor after his U.S. Navy service in World War II but had settled comfortably into a broadcasting career at WFIL where he met his wife, Agnes. As producer of *Bandstand* from the beginning, Mammarella was a favorite of the teens who visited the show.

"Tony was a doll baby," said Colella. "I don't think there was one person that worked for WFIL at the time that we didn't like. I think mainly it was that they appreciated the kids. They needed the kids. Without the kids, there's no show."

Ron Caponigro was another regular whose *Bandstand* dancing career spanned the Horn and Clark years. Caponigro, who would later be known as Ron Joseph (or R.J.) in his own broadcast career, was drawn to the business at an early age. As a 9-year-old in 1950, he appeared on the children's show, *Ghost Riders*, on WCAU-TV. In 1954, he was a panel member on Phil Sheridan's *Radio Rangers* on WCAU radio. He attended the same church as legendary Philadelphia newsman John Facenda.

Before debuting on *Bandstand* in 1956, Joseph published and edited *The Upper Darby Tower* newspaper. He barely had time to learn the ropes of being a *Bandstand* regular before Horn was ousted. Although Dick Clark was not well-known among the *Bandstand* kids, Joseph took comfort in the fact that he was practically a neighbor; Clark was living in Drexelbrook, not far from Joseph's home in Drexel Hills.

"I stayed on because of Tony Mammarella," Joseph said. "I wanted to learn the business. Tony was like a father to me. He taught me everything."

When Clark, too, learned that young Joseph was aiming for a broadcasting career, he became a mentor as well. Since he was

---

2. *The History of American Bandstand*, p.9, 1976.

familiar with the area, Joseph often drove Clark to hops at Frolics' Ballroom in Allentown or the Starlight Ballroom in Wildwood, N.J. During the drives, Clark would offer insights into the business.

Clark also arranged for Joseph to receive a birthday cake on air, an act that became a tradition in the years to come. Clark also made appearances at Joseph's 16th birthday party in his home and at an assembly at Upper Darby High School, where Joseph was a student.

"Our class decided to pay him a talent fee of $500 for the appearance, however, on stage during the program he returned the check to me and the class treasurer and said it was a personal favor to Ronnie," Joseph recalled.

Joseph also occasionally made the trip to New York City for the *Saturday Night Show* where he helped in commercials for Beech-Nut gum and Pepsodent toothpaste.

Joseph vowed that when he launched his TV broadcast career that Clark would be his first guest. Clark probably never thought that day would come when he agreed to the arrangement, but he fulfilled that pledge in 1962 when young Joseph debuted his *Spotlight on America* program on WPCA-TV.

Another early favorite was Rosemary Beltrante of South Philadelphia, winner of an early Horn slow dance contest with partner Jackie Starr. Her reward was an evening gown ensemble, courtesy of *Seventeen* magazine. The ensemble of an evening gown and accompanying stole, shoes, gloves, and jewelry were perfect for the aspiring model.

Beltrante was known as "Big Ro," a designation necessary to differentiate her from another regular of the same time, Rosemary "Little Ro" Fergione. Beltrante was also the first of three Beltrante sisters to become *Bandstand* regulars—sisters Mary and Susan succeeded her.

Frank Spagnuola was another teen from South Philadelphia who made the *Bandstand* transition from Bob Horn to Dick Clark. After cutting classes at Bishop Neumann High School to attend the show with buddy Jerry Blavat, Spagnuola was one of the dancers upset with Horn's firing and who refused to dance to the first song played by Clark after he assumed permanent hosting duties.

But Spagnuola eventually relented and in the last dance competition before the show went national, won a calypso contest with another popular early regular, Dottie Horner. Horner, who usually appeared on the show without makeup, often received fan mail asking if she was a Quaker, prompting a response from her mother that she was "a good Catholic girl."

One of the most popular of the early regulars was another Neumann student, Bill Cook. Cook, who ran track in high school and worked part-time in his dad's trash hauling business, wanted to be a professional dancer and entered at least four *Bandstand* dance contests, winning a fast dance contest with Barbara Levick in 1960.

Cook was known as a fun-loving prankster, something that evidently came through on air. Cook's popularity carried over when the show went national. He and fellow dancer Frank Brancaccio once flew from Philadelphia to Cleveland for a weekend at a fan's request. He later was a road manager for Freddie Cannon, made a brief attempt at a singing career and was pictured on two Cadence record album covers with another popular regular, Justine Carrelli.

Carrelli and her early dancing partner, Bob Clayton, were the first national "*Bandstand* couple."

Carrrelli arrived at *Bandstand* first, as a 12-year-old junior high student from Tilden Junior High. When her first attempt to get into the studio failed, she returned with her older sister's birth certificate.

Clayton, who lived in Wilmington, Del., was a dancer on Grady and Hurst's dance show in Wilmington when he noticed Carrelli on *Bandstand*. Since he had a 2:30 P.M. study hall, Clayton figured he could drive the 32 miles up Route 13 from P.S. DuPont High to the WFIL studio in time to dance on *Bandstand*. It was a trip he would make practically every school day for the next three years, dodging trucks and collecting a fair number of traffic tickets in the process.

Clayton wasted little time in squiring Carrelli to the dance floor and when the show went national, fan clubs sprung up around the country as they were dubbed "America's sweethearts." Clayton's fan clubs boasted some 150,000 members at the couple's peak and when Carrelli once mentioned on air that she liked tiaras, within a week she had one, encrusted with small diamonds.

Like many of the teens who danced on *Bandstand*, Clayton and Carrelli frequently attended record hops in the area.

"You'd go out to a dance and people would back away to give you room," Clayton said in the documentary, *Bandstand Days*.

"And, if there was prize money involved, [we'd win] hands down. There were many times I said, 'I'm not the best dancer here'. . . but, because of the popularity, whatever the prize was, they gave it to you."

Clayton and Carrelli put their fast-dance skills on display in Dick Clark's first *American Bandstand* contest, jitterbugging to Chuck Berry's "Rock & Roll Music." Clayton naively assumed DuPont school officials were unaware of his daily skipping of study hall to attend the show, until the day of the fast-dance finals.

"The principal of the school got on the intercom about one o'clock. He said, 'I guess you all know that Bob Clayton, one of our students, is in this dance contest in Philadelphia and we all want to wish him well and I only have one thing to say: If you don't win it don't come back.'"[3]

By the time all the votes were tallied, Clayton and Carrelli were declared the winners. Already popular before the dance contest, the couple's popularity skyrocketed after their victory. Adoring fans sent Carrelli dolls and clothes and peppered her with questions about her striking blonde hair. More significantly, the couple caught the eye of Orlando Scaltrito, a local guitar player whose pedigree included a stint with Bill Haley's Comets.

Scaltrito (who was also known as Bob Scale or Bob Savar) was venturing into the record business. Working with songwriter Joseph Matarazzo (known professionally as Joe Matt), Scaltrito soon had Bob and Justine in the studio to record "Dream Girl" and "Drive-In Movie" for his Fransil label.

Scaltrito probably saw the record as his ticket to the big-time music business. What it turned out to be, however, was Bob and Justine's ticket off the show.

Since Clayton was closing in on his 18th birthday, his exit was rapidly approaching anyhow but for 16-year-old Carrelli, it was a devastating blow.

"The show's producer called me into the office and gave me the bad news," she later said. "I thought my life was over."[4]

Her experience would be repeated many times over the remainder of *American Bandstand*'s run in Philadelphia. Dancers would reach the mandatory "retirement age" of 18 or simply lose interest in the show and stop showing up. A few boys were dismissed because the school they attended was not an accredited

---

3. *Bandstand Days, documentary,* Teleduction, 1997.
4. Response to book project questionnaire, 1998.

high school. Still, others would be thrown off for fighting or for committing the capital sin of trying to cash in on their *Bandstand* fame.

Cameraman Marvin Brooks understood the teenagers' predicament.

"They became celebrities," Brooks said. "All of a sudden you're turned into the national limelight and you're getting fan mail and calls. It really got to some of them. They think they're stars. They started doing interviews. That's when some of them were thrown off the show."

While many fans and the regulars themselves thought dismissal was too harsh a penalty for their misdeeds, Brooks came to the defense of Clark.

"He was just trying to protect them. It wasn't done to hurt the kids. They didn't want anything to hurt the show."

Although fans continued to show interest in Clayton and Carrelli for two years after they left the show, it didn't take viewers nearly that long to find a new couple to idolize. By mid-1958, Kenny Rossi and Arlene Sullivan were the new *Bandstand* sweethearts.

Although many young dancers were drawn to *Bandstand* by watching their peers dancing on screen, Sullivan and Rossi went to the show because of their mothers.

Sullivan's mother was a big fan of the show in the Bob Horn years, knowing the names of more of the regulars than her daughter. Rossi's mother watched the show, too, and often mused about what her son might look like on screen.

Sullivan appeared on the show first. Her first attempt was on the day Horn was fired and, although she had a front-row seat to the brief picketing led by Jerry Blavat, she didn't get in. A few more failed attempts followed before a chance meeting with Carrelli at a party led to the reigning queen of *Bandstand* ushering the future queen into the studio for the first time. Soon she was sneaking out of her last-period music class every school day to begin the trolley and bus ride to the studio.

Rossi's *Bandstand* debut came more than a year later when he walked the two blocks from his school, West Catholic High School for Boys, to appear on the show, which was still local. Within days, though, the show went national, and Rossi, who was still a month shy of his 14th birthday, was on the dance floor with Sullivan. At first, they claimed to be brother and sister but their real relationship became clear after a spotlight dance.

Rossi may have been the most popular boy on the show during its Philadelphia run. Girls, especially, were attracted to his dark brown eyes and hair to match. He'd often appear in his school uniform—but with a V-neck sweater worn backward to cover his tie—plus a sport coat and fashionable white buck shoes.

At the peak of his popularity, Rossi estimates he had as many as 300 fan clubs. The father of one of his fan club presidents once drove his daughter from Fall River, Mass., just so she could meet Rossi in person. He was bombarded with thousands of fan letters a week and received more than 100 sets of cufflinks for his 15th birthday in September 1958.

Sullivan was nearly a year older than Rossi and just as popular. On her 16th birthday in November 1958, she arrived home from *Bandstand* to find her family porch overflowing with gifts from fans.

Sullivan appeared shy on camera yet spent many hours off-camera with fans. On more than one occasion, runaway teens found their way to her family's doorstep in Southwest Philadelphia, seeking refuge. She developed real friendships with some of the singers who appeared on the show, including Paul Anka and Annette Funicello. On Annette's first appearance, the popular Mouseketeer looked up at Sullivan from her seat behind the autograph table and declared, "I should be getting your autograph, Arlene."[5]

Rossi and Sullivan were a regular couple for most of the 16 months they were together on *American Bandstand*. During that time, they won one of *American Bandstand*'s dance contests, the calypso contest in 1958.

While the dancers competed to Billy & Lillie's "La Dee Dah," fans across the country were mailing in their votes.

"I sent in 300 postcards voting for Ken and Arlene," said Marian Driscoll, an ardent viewer of the show from Ohio. "I actually thought they would check the cards, so I disguised my writing and made up names."

When all the votes were tallied, Rossi and Sullivan were the winners, each taking home a three-wheel 1957 BMW Isetta automobile for their efforts.

Although Rossi and Sullivan will be linked forever in the minds of many *Bandstand* viewers, their personal relationship was brief.

---

5. *The Sandpaper*, October 4, 2002.

THE REGULARS

Rossi also dated perhaps the show's most popular dancer, Pat Molittieri, and Sullivan once dated singer Danny Rapp of Danny & the Juniors.

Rossi's *Bandstand* tenure was cut short when he opted to try for a singing career, though Clark claimed to have cut him from the show for accepting money for appearing at a Passaic, N.J., dance hall, an allegation Rossi has long denied. But the attempted recording career began at roughly the same time when he cut a record entitled, ironically, "Problem Child," for the local Adelphia label.

Sullivan soon followed him out the *Bandstand* door, ending what she described as a "McCarthy-like experience" when Clark summoned her and a group of fellow 17-year-olds into a room and told them they were banned from the show for unspecified reasons.[6]

Myrna Horowitz, another popular dancer on *American Bandstand* in the late 1950s, was most noticeable not for her dancing skills, but for the fact that she was on her feet at all. Horowitz wore a full-length brace on her left leg as a result of her battle with infantile paralysis as a 6-year-old.

One of Horowitz's best high school friends was Harvey Robbins, another popular Bandstander from that era. For months, Robbins tried to persuade Horowitz to attend the show. Finally, when Horowitz learned that her favorite actor, Tab Hunter, was scheduled to appear on *Bandstand* in February 1957 to lip-sync to his latest record, "April Love," Horowitz gave the show a try.

She met Hunter, had a good time and returned several times. With Robbins keeping a protective eye on his friend, Horowitz soon made friends and found herself dancing on the show. When the show went national, she started receiving hundreds of fan letters a week, many praising her for her courage. On her 16th birthday in February 1958 she became a member of the *Bandstand* Committee.

At first, her family was against Horowitz appearing on national TV, fearing it would only lead to teasing and taunting. Indeed, she did face some hostility from other teenage girls who were treated at the same rehabilitation hospital, but only because they couldn't get on the show as Myrna did.

Almost every weekend, Horowitz went with her *Bandstand* friends to parties or record hops around Philadelphia. Horowitz

---

6. Response to book project questionnaire, 1998.

once served as president of the Freddie Cannon Fan Club and hosted a party for him at her parents' house, a party that was documented in an article in *'Teen* magazine.

In 1959, Horowitz required surgery on her bad leg, an operation that kept her bedridden for 16 weeks. Throughout the ordeal, Clark kept *American Bandstand* viewers updated on her progress. The flood of get-well cards and letters hastened her recovery, Horowitz said.

Two of the more popular girls on *American Bandstand* in the late 1950s were two of the most telegenic as well—Frani Giordano and Carole Scaldeferri.

Giordano was a cut-up with a quick sense of humor which was often on display at Pop Singer's drug store, a favorite hangout of the regulars and their fans. The affable Singer, who often provided birthday cakes on-air to his favorite regulars, once arranged for Giordano to take the train to New York City for Clark's *Saturday Night Show*, even providing a letter to get her in. The letter was rejected, however, by two guards at the door. Giordano managed to get inside only when a classmate of hers, Fabian, popped outside a stage door and vouched for her.

Giordano came from a well-to-do family that operated a large produce and fruit market in South Philadelphia. The family beach house at Sea Isle, N.J., a converted yacht club, provided a venue for countless summer gatherings of regulars over the years.

A pert blonde, Giordano was a particular favorite of male viewers and she frequently received invitations from fraternities and colleges to be their prom queen.

Scaldeferri was the dark-haired equivalent of Giordano. She was meticulous about her appearance and created a stir once when she appeared on the show without lipstick. On another occasion, she changed dresses in the middle of a show, prompting hundreds of letters. She was known for wearing colorful headbands, many of them gifts from adoring fans, and ballerina shoes.

Singer Ral Donner was a fan of Scaldeferri, describing her as a "knockout." Once, during an appearance on *American Bandstand*, Clark concluded his interview with Donner by saying: "See that gorgeous creature over there? She's gonna lead you to the autograph table." Donner said he "looked up and there was Carole, that was a thrill!"[7]

---

7. *Goldmine*, November 1979.

THE REGULARS

To non-regulars who attended the show, the camaraderie among the regulars was abundantly clear.

"Some of the regulars back then just seemed like they were, what's the kind word to say, snobbish?" says Bob Tharp, a West Philadelphia High School student who occasionally attended the show from 1955 through 1957. "They were in their own little pack."

Rick Fisher, who was a semi-regular for much of Dick Clark's Philadelphia reign, says the behavior of the regulars was understandable.

"The regulars were kids. They were cliquish," Fisher said. "They had their little groups. It was probably very hard to break into that in the beginning, but once you got in there, I think it was very family-like."

Stan Marks, a student at Lincoln High School in Northeast Philadelphia, "took a bus and two trains to get down there [to *Bandstand*]." Describing himself as shy, young Marks had a crush on Arlene DiPietro, a popular regular. Classmate Allen Durbin, also a regular on the show, told Marks he would dance a slow dance with DiPietro and have her cross her fingers for him.

"I ran home and watched TV. Sure enough, they were coming around. He turns his back toward the camera and she's got her fingers crossed for me. Needless to say, I was pretty excited."

Soon after that, Marks accompanied Durbin to the show with the intention of meeting DiPietro.

"Wouldn't you know it, she was home sick that day," Marks recalls.

Still, Marks had at least one memorable *Bandstand* experience. His first dance on the show came during a "multiplication" dance, where Clark would yell "change" and each dancer would find a new partner. During a change, Frani Giordano selected Marks.

"I thought I would go through her, I was so close. She would grab on tight."

Jack Fisher, who in the late 1990s produced a documentary called *Bandstand Days*, took a circuitous route to fame as a dancer on *American Bandstand*. Fisher was a regular on Joe Grady and Ed Hurst's dance show in Wilmington. Fisher developed quite a following with Grady and Hurst.

"I was a much bigger personality on Grady and Hurst," Fisher said. "I was their guy. I was like the Bob Clayton of the show."

Deciding to check out Clark's show right after it went national, Fisher's entrance to the show was ensured when he was recognized by regulars Dottie Horner and Rosemary "Big Ro" Beltrante outside the studio. Soon he and Horner were jitterbugging their way into the finals of Clark's first fast dance contest. He also experienced some resentment from at least one of the regulars.

"Sid Payne didn't like me because his girlfriend was Joanne Montecarlo and she liked me. On ladies choices, she would ask me to dance. . . . One day, we were slow dancing on the show. We went by each other and started jawing at each other. Tony [Mammarella] saw that and pulled us both over and said 'If that happens again, you're both out of here'."

Once *Bandstand* went national, the dancing teens enjoyed fame beyond their wildest expectations. Fan clubs sprang up and the mail flowed. Some regulars didn't bother to answer their fan mail while for others it became a family affair with parents and siblings taking part in the postal ritual.

Bolder fans pressed for face-to-face meetings and many of the regulars obliged. Whether at the hops and dances they attended with Dick Clark or on their own, it was relatively easy for out-of-state teens to connect with their *Bandstand* faves. Sometimes the regulars even visited their fans on their own turf.

Marian Driscoll of Cleveland, Ohio, was a fan of Arlene Sullivan's dancing partner, Kenny Rossi, and copied Sullivan's dress and hairstyle while corresponding with as many *Bandstand* regulars as she could.

Although Driscoll received up to 10 letters a day, it was correspondence about Sullivan's connection to Cleveland that piqued her interest. The pair eventually met in Cleveland and a friendship ensued. They went horseback riding together and shared sleepovers where Sullivan would belt out show tunes, like "Let Me Entertain You" from *Gypsy*. Sullivan even showed up at Driscoll's high school the night Driscoll was crowned homecoming queen.

Driscoll made several trips to Philadelphia to visit her *Bandstand* friends, including one memorable visit in the summer of 1959 when she and a friend rode a Greyhound bus to meet up with regular Carole Higbee. Like many Philadelphia visitors, Driscoll did some shopping at Wanamaker's Department Store and sipped Cokes at Pop Singer's drug store, a favorite *Bandstand* hangout.

Unlike most visitors, she got to hang out with Higbee, Kenny Rossi, and Eddie Kelly. The group spent one afternoon at Willow Grove amusement park.

THE REGULARS

"As we walked down the carnival game aisle, one of the game operators yelled 'Hey *Bandstand*. Come try your luck.' That is how well-known the regulars were."

Ray Otto was a Brooklyn, N.Y., native whose *Bandstand* connection began at Dick Clark's *Saturday Night Show* in New York City. Every Saturday morning Otto and some friends took the bus to the Little Theater where they'd spend the rest of the day.

From Dick Clark's arrival around 11 A.M. through the afternoon dress rehearsal and the actual *Saturday Night Show*, the streets around the theater were an exciting place to be.

"Every hour or so, a cab would come up in front of the theater," Otto said. "You knew it was somebody that was going to be on the show that night. It was an area where you'd see a lot of stars anyway, because of all the theaters around there."

Otto was there when a busload of regulars from Philadelphia pulled up.

"People went wild outside. You don't realize how popular they were. I don't think they realized themselves how popular they were. They went crazy in that line outside the theater. I remember the whole line broke when that bus came and they heard the regulars were on it. They were trying to look in, get in and see them."

Otto made a couple of trips to Philadelphia to see *Bandstand*, thanks to a written invitation from Justine Carrelli who wrote: "If you're ever in Philadelphia, come and see me."

The first time he tried, Carrelli wasn't home, but her mother invited him and a friend into her home, even though her daughter had already been dismissed from the show.

"It's hard to believe that these people had to put up with all of these fans showing up at their doors unannounced. And they were so gracious about it. She invited us in and gave us something to eat. I wonder how often that happened."

Otto, who also was invited into regular Barbara Levick's Philadelphia home, once tried to return the favor at his own home in Brooklyn. The occasion was a birthday party for regular Allyn Markert.

Otto and a friend prepared for an expected 35 guests for the Sunday party. When he awoke for Mass around 7:30 A.M. on Sunday, he found a half dozen strangers gathered on his stoop.

"They were fans. They heard the regulars were coming to my house."

By the time of the party that afternoon, Otto estimates that about 20 regulars, plus friends, filled the house. Things got out of hand. Some people were making long distance calls from the family phone and some of the regulars started bickering among themselves.

"I had to walk around the block a few times, thinking, 'Geez, when is this going to end'?" Otto said.

To make matters worse, some of the regulars brought their own 45s to dance to.

"One of the records was missing at the end of the day," Otto said. "They were accusing my friends. . . . I finally found it among my records."

In 1958, Linda Zimmerman was a 13-year-old from Winchester, Ind., who jumped at the chance to visit Philadelphia with a good friend, Karla Ertle, and Ertle's parents. Ertle, who was a year older than Zimmerman, came bearing gifts for her *Bandstand* favorites, Rossi and Sullivan.

"I think she gave Arlene a stuffed animal," Zimmerman recalled.

A dinner invitation from the Ertles to the young *Bandstand* stars paved the way for a whirlwind three-day visit that included trips to *Bandstand*, a local amusement park and a record hop emceed by Dick Clark.

When Zimmerman returned a year later, she brought with her an aluminum key to the city of Winchester, Ind., made by her machinist father. After presenting the key to Clark on air, the Zimmermans went to dinner with Rossi and Sullivan only to be thrown out of the restaurant.

"We were asked by the restaurant's proprietor to leave as soon as we were seated," Zimmerman said. "We were told that the appearance of the regulars made the tables quit turning over, people wouldn't leave the restaurant after they'd eaten."

If the ejection was the downside to *Bandstand* fame, Zimmerman got to experience a bit of the upside later that night at an amusement park.

"It was really fun when people would recognize Arlene and Kenny and then look at us, scratching their brain cells to see if they could figure out if we (me, my sister, Sheri, and friend) were regulars, too. People kept coming up to us asking for our autographs!"

If *American Bandstand* was the No. 1 Philadelphia destination for American teens in the late 1950s, Pop Singer's drug store had

THE REGULARS

to be No. 2. Many teens who visited the show also visited Pop's, hoping to meet a regular in person, maybe even have a picture taken with them out front.

There was nothing special about Pop's other than its location down the street from the WFIL studios. Simon "Pop" Singer was a pharmacist by trade but had converted his drug store into a luncheonette in the 1950s. It was typical for the era, a narrow space with a row of booths on one side, a soda fountain on the other.

There was a jukebox, phone booth, and racks of candy, gum, snacks, magazines, newspapers, and comics, plus various sundry items. The walls next to the booths and tabletops were decorated with carved or written names. Pop was known to plop into a booth to visit with his regular customers and he expected everyone who occupied a precious seat to buy something.

It was a small, noisy place (the Philadelphia el ran practically overhead), but very popular with the *Bandstand* crowd. Pop was well known for delivering birthday cakes to some of his favorites live on *Bandstand* and he voluntarily drove teens to area dances. His personalized stationery featured two jitterbugging dancers.

Dick Clark loved Pop and when he said "We always had our lunch delivered from Pop Singer's. Worst food in the world! Grease!"[8], it was with reverence. Clark hand-delivered personalized copies of each of his books and once gave Pop an engraved wristwatch. Connie Francis once gave Singer a musical cigarette lighter that played *Who's Sorry Now*.

For the regulars who planned ahead and managed to get out of school early enough, Pop Singer's was a pre-*Bandstand* staging area. They'd muster their forces, then move out.

"It was almost like a processional," said Rick Fisher. "Around 3:10, 3:15, they all lit up cigarettes and they'd walk up the street one block to the studio. They walked by everybody but wouldn't ever speak to anybody outside. It was almost comical. They did have a definite star attitude when they walked up the street."

After the regulars claimed their spots inside the WFIL doors, the competition for the remaining openings began. Those lucky enough to make it into the studio were almost all struck by how small it was. And colorful. After all, most had only seen it on a small black and white TV screen.

"There were all these winding halls to get to the studio," Rick Fisher recalled. "It was so different than what it looked like on TV.

---

8. *Philadelphia Inquirer*, November 7, 1985.

This was a mish-mosh of colors and it was half the size of what you would have pictured it to be. There was a line with tape that you were never allowed to dance in front of because the cameras would move in that area. Dick Clark had a microphone that he would call your name if you were camera-hogging. He'd call your name. That meant to come to the back."

Charlie Heffernan, a senior at St. Peters High School in Staten Island, N.Y., and his buddies wrote letter after letter trying to get on *Bandstand* but were rejected each time. A friend, however, cracked the code. Instead of writing to the posted address for tickets, Jimmy Sullivan instead wrote to director Ed Yates, whose name appeared on the closing credits. It worked and Heffernan finally got a pass to his beloved show.

But his trip to Philadelphia on the Feast of the Immaculate Conception school holiday was not nearly what he expected.

"I remember lining up on Market Street," Heffernan said. "I remember how organized it was, how strict they were with kids. They checked your appearance and told you once you're in the building 'No talking' and they told you where to put your coat.

"I also remember how unfriendly Dick Clark was to everybody. Not hostile or not yelling, but the charm disappeared once the red light went off. At the end of the show we were all sitting in the bleachers and once the light went off he turned to us and said, 'You have to stay where you are. We'll tell you when you can leave.' They dismissed us by section."

The musical guest that day was Danny & the Juniors.

"We went into the bathroom to use it and Danny & the Juniors were in there and they were all lined up along the mirror, combing their hair. And my 6'4" friend, who was a bit of a wise guy, says 'Which one of you guys is Danny?' One guy says 'I am' and he says "How about getting your group out of here so somebody else can comb their hair'."

"Some of those kids from Philadelphia were aggressive about being in front of the camera. In fact, my friend was jostled and he tussled. One of the kids made a comment like 'We'll get you after the show.' So, when we walked out, I didn't know what we were going to face out on the street. Actually, we faced nothing, it was just talk."

For Ray Otto, visiting *Bandstand* was "almost an overwhelming experience . . . the lights, very bright, and I remember the music being very loud."

THE REGULARS

Bruce Aydelotte, who visited *Bandstand* from his home in Vineland, N.J., said you had to use your imagination when watching the show from the bleachers in Studio B.

"You were sitting there in those bleachers and [the singers] were close enough, almost, to touch them and it was weird because they lip-synced . . . you could hear the song and you knew they weren't really singing but you still believed it because you wanted to believe it."

If you were transported to a teenage Nirvana during the course of the show, you were quickly brought back to earth once Clark signed off and the crew went to work on the curtains behind Clark that served as a backdrop.

"At the end of the show they would whip those curtains open and there would be just a cement wall with a big garage door. An overhead garage door. It wasn't very classy," Aydelotte said. "The stagehand would just whip that door up and the sunlight would come streaming in. . . . You'd walk outside and, man, the sun would hit you and blind you."

That burst of sunlight every weekday meant that Bandstandland was shutting down for a while. Come back tomorrow, after you've hung out with your guy or gal, finished your homework and shared some time with your siblings, parents and Uncle Miltie.

For some of the regulars, however, the 22 hours between shows could be agonizing.

"These were plain people that really thought that they were stars. They really did believe it," says Rick Fisher. "These were basically working-class kids who went to the show. They were absolutely idolized but they didn't seem to have any specific talent, other than being good dancers. And not even trained dancers."

But across the land, the *American Bandstand* regulars were seen as trendsetters as teens everywhere copied their hairstyles, clothing, dance moves, and language. Though they were popular in Chicago, Los Angeles, and Miami, that popularity wasn't as intense in Philadelphia.

"For some reason, in certain parts of the city, they were disliked," Fisher said. "I guess because they were famous."

Ray Otto saw this firsthand as he walked from the *Bandstand* studio with Barbara Levick to her house after the show.

"We met this group of people. They started harassing her from across the street. She knew who they were. She said she went through this all the time. They'd call her names and stuff like that."

"She said just ignore them. They go through this every night. She said Bill Cook even had a worse time with them. It was sort of a revelation to me at the time."

Even a popular dancer like Kenny Rossi experienced the downside to celebrity. Envious classmates taunted him daily between classes, sometimes spitting on him as they declared "dancing is for sissies."

"I was in a fight every day," says Rossi. "The brothers at West Catholic would have to walk me out the door, down the street, and they would walk me far enough to see me walk into the show."[9]

Nicholas Fiorentino, who as Nicky Blue was a popular dance partner of Arlene DiPietro, wasn't nearly as popular in his own neighborhood.

"I had to take a lot of hits back in the neighborhood because a lot of the guys would say, 'You're one of the guys. You shouldn't be on that show, you shouldn't be doing that. A real guy doesn't go on those shows.'"[10]

Justine Carrelli was shoved in the halls of her school and had her lunch stolen after she became popular on *Bandstand*. Rosemary "Little Roe" Fergione often ate lunch alone "because of *Bandstand*."[11] Ray Smith says "the kids at school called me Mr. *Bandstand*. I took it as a compliment; they meant it as an insult."[12]

Bunny Gibson transferred from St. Hubert's High School after someone threatened her life, saying they were "going to kill all the lousy Bandstanders." And it wasn't just the kids.

At St. Hubert's, where students were required to walk single file down the halls without uttering a word, nuns undid Gibson's beehive hairdo and made her sit in the back of the classroom "because she had breasts and refused to allow her to be the "May Queen" because she liked boys."

The Jimenez sisters—Carmen and Ivette—were among the first Hispanic dancers on *Bandstand* and were among the most popular. But they were abused by students and staff in their parochial school, often the targets of racial epithets.

"The nuns declared that we were dancing to the 'devil's music,'" said Carmen Jimenez, who was escorted to school by police

---

9. *Main Line Today*, January 2004.
10. *Philadelphia Inquirer*, April 18, 2012.
11. *Bandstand Days*, 1997.
12. Response to book project questionnaire, 1998.

THE REGULARS

after her life was threatened. "They'd often keep me after school so I wouldn't go [to *Bandstand*]. Eventually, my understanding dad transferred me to a public school—but didn't tell my mom for two months—so I could go to the show."[13]

Even something as seemingly innocent as a dance can create controversy. Some of the sexier dances were seen as "dirty dancing" by some, but that wasn't what you'd expect from a dance known as the strand, which is kind of a slow-motion jitterbug.

Two *American Bandstand* regulars, Jimmy Peatross and Joan Buck, introduced the strand to *Bandstand* viewers through a series of spotlight dances on the show in 1959. The dance caught on and Clark casually asked the couple where they'd learned the dance. We made it up, they said. But they had really learned the dance from some high school classmates who were black.

Peatross later said, "We had to say we made it up on the air. We weren't allowed to say that the black people taught us."[14]

Buck offered a clarification. "It wasn't that [Clark] said, you can't say black people. He didn't say that. . . . We really didn't want to say that "Oh, black people taught it to us."[15]

"After we said we made it up the next day we had about 50, 100 people after us to beat us up outside the show," Peatross said. "All black. They came after us. Dick Clark got us protection."[16]

The teens who had it the worst were the gay kids. Some regulars estimate that as many as half of the male regulars who danced on the network show during the Philadelphia years were gay.

"In Philadelphia, where you lived, you were a *Bandstand* faggot," said regular Frank Brancaccio. "Back then, girls and sex were different than they were in the 60s and 70s. . . . Girls weren't putting out then so the boys used to play with the boys."

Eddie Kelly, who says he knew he was gay when he was 11 or 12 years old, says "back then it wasn't too cool to be gay. We were dealing with it, but not so sure. Those are difficult years."

American Bandstand "was like a safe haven for gay people," Kelly says. Life was much different outside the studio.

"My high school years were horrible," Kelly said. "The show had such a terrible reputation for homosexuality. I was so glad

---

13. *Philadelphia Inquirer*, May 2, 2002.
14. *The Twist*, a film by Ron Mann, 1992.
15. Ibid.
16. Ibid.

to go to a private school because the minute I walked out of my house and I used to have to take a trolley car and the elevated line to school . . . I was bullied beyond words because I went on *Bandstand*. I lived in a very rough area but I do feel that all the regulars in their own neighborhood were accepted but the minute you left that neighborhood, you really had to be careful that you wouldn't get beaten up and stuff like that. It was rough."

Things got so bad that Kelly transferred to a business school which led to his being barred from the show because the school was not an accredited high school.

Clark was aware of the many gays on the show and cautioned them to avoid the city's gay hangouts, like the area around Rittenhouse Square. Some regulars went there anyway, keeping an eye out for the detectives Clark had reportedly hired to follow them. Clark denied hiring detectives but claimed to have seen regular Larry Giuliani in the area himself and confronted the young teen.

Since Clark considered Giuliani a ringleader who encouraged other kids to go to the square, Clark immediately barred him from the show. Giuliani wasn't the only one booted from *American Bandstand* because they hung around Rittenhouse Square.

"At night [Rittenhouse] was crowded with homosexuals," Brancaccio acknowledged. "It was just someplace where we all used to congregate and walk around and talk to each other. But it was a gay hangout. Three people—Joe Fusco, Harvey Robbins, and Frankie Lobis—were thrown off the show for going to Rittenhouse Square. . . . For some reason, I was never thrown off the show and Clark never bothered me about it and yet I was one of the offenders, too."

Clark's efforts at keeping Bandstandland squeaky clean knew no bounds. Not even the most popular kids were exempt from Clark's amateurs-only rule. So when he saw Pat Molittieri's picture on the cover of the June 1959 issue of *'Teen* magazine with the headline, "Meet 'Bandstand's' Dance Queen," it was just a matter of time before she'd join the growing legion of banned regulars.

That day came on June 24, 1959.

Bobby Rydell was a musical guest that day and Linda Zimmerman was in the studio, one of several days she attended that week while visiting from Winchester, Indiana.

During the show, Zimmerman witnessed an altercation between Molittieri and another regular, Peggy Leonard. The dustup came when Molittieri re-entered the studio after escorting a young man who had become ill back to his parents. Re-entry was not allowed under Clark's rules, a point Leonard apparently made strongly upon Molittieri's attempt to return to the dance floor.

Skirmishes among friends were not unusual on *Bandstand* and Zimmerman thought little about it until later. After the show, she had spent time with Arlene Sullivan at Pop Singer's before they left in Zimmerman's parents' car headed to Sullivan's home.

On the way, they passed the *Bandstand* studio where they saw Molittieri walking down the sidewalk in tears. The next day, when Molittieri didn't show up at the show, Zimmerman asked Sullivan what was up. When told that Molittieri had been banned from the show, Zimmerman assumed it was because of the fight the day before.

Truth was that Clark had asked Molittieri to explain her appearance on the *'Teen* cover. Molittieri explained that it was more than a one-shot deal, that she would be writing a column for the magazine.

That's it, said Clark. You're done here.

CHAPTER 12

NEW DIRECTIONS

It should not have surprised Dick Clark that one of *American Bandstand*'s most popular dancers would pop up in a magazine aimed at teenagers. Teen magazines were hot in 1959 and no teens were hotter than the *Bandstand* kids.

It was only natural that fan magazines would latch on to the emerging teen market, given its huge numbers, relative affluence and seemingly insatiable appetite for all things rock & roll.

The radio and movie fan magazines of the 1930s and 1940s had barely begun edging into television when the rock tsunami hit. By 1959, it had swept into magazine stands and drugstores with full force.

The teen magazine culture has its roots in Philadelphia as Walter Annenberg's Triangle Publications—owner of WFIL-TV, the birthplace of *American Bandstand*—launched *Seventeen* magazine in 1944. *Seventeen* was aimed at young girls ages 11–17 and was a major force in recognition of the then-new term "teenager" and the demographics the term represented.

But *Seventeen* was too conservative to fully embrace the rock movement of the 1950s. That ground was claimed by the new kids on the block—like *'Teen, Dig, 16,* the myriad song hit magazines published by Charlton or the dozens of other magazines that sprung like the first crocuses of spring and disappeared just as quickly.

Pat Molittieri had aligned herself with one of the more successful of the upstarts.

Charles Laufer, the 30-something founder and editor of *'Teen* saw in the teenage publishing market the same golden promise that motivated Dick Clark in the popular music field. A high school basketball star from New Jersey, Laufer was lured to California by a high school classmate. There he graduated from the University of Southern California before becoming a high school journalism and English teacher in Norwalk, Calif.

Dismayed that his students weren't reading enough, Laufer launched a teen-oriented magazine called *Coaster* in 1955. He changed the name to *'Teen* in 1957 and by the time he got around to hiring Pat Molittieri two years later to be a star columnist, he was locking horns with Clark.

When the flap over Molittieri's hiring spilled over into the mainstream press, Laufer had had enough. Many *'Teen* critics felt the magazine went overboard in its coverage of the *Bandstand* teens and alleged that the magazine must be working closely with Clark.

Indeed, Linda Zimmerman wondered the same thing.

Three months after witnessing Molittieri's last day on *Bandstand*, she sent a letter to *'Teen* magazine "with some critical things concerning *American Bandstand*."

"Only two days after I mailed my letter from Indiana to Hollywood, I received a letter from Dick Clark mailed from Philly!" she said. "He defended some of his actions in his letter to me. I was quite shocked at receiving the letter from Philly only two days after I'd mailed a letter to Hollywood. I figured out that Dick Clark had to have some connection with *'Teen* magazine."

Nothing could be further from the truth, Laufer wrote in a *'Teen* magazine editorial headlined, "Why Dick Clark Dropped Pat, Ken, and Justine," in the February 1960 issue of *'Teen*.

Laufer wrote of "strained relations" between the magazine and Clark that had lasted more than a year and said the magazine's editors were "very upset" when Clark's people continually stonewalled the magazine's efforts to run stories and photos of the show's regulars adding that "letters poured in by the thousands" requesting such articles.

Laufer tried to clear the air in the article about the recent disappearance of some of the show's more popular dancers.

Molittieri was hired to work with writer Steve Kahn to write stories about the regulars. Clark resisted and Laufer said he received two calls from a New York public relations firm asking the magazine to refrain from writing about the *Bandstand* regulars.

Laufer went on to report that Justine Carrelli was booted from the show on February 13, 1958, when she told Clark she intended to cut a record. Kenny Rossi was cut loose after he was accused of accepting money for appearing at a series of record hops in Passaic, N.J.

Laufer concluded his editorial by stating that all recent stories on the *Bandstand* teens were done "without any cooperation from the Clark camp" and promising that the magazine would continue to serve its readers "regardless of any outside influences."

Gloria Stavers over at *16* magazine, on the other hand, had a much more friendly relationship with Clark.

The magazine itself was a ripoff of *Seventeen*, touting itself as "The Magazine for Smart Girls." More precisely, *16* was for *young* girls.

"*16* is for the girl who is too old for daddy's knee, but too young for the boy next door," Stavers often said.[1]

The magazine was founded by literary agent Jacques Chambrun in May 1957. Its first issue featured Elvis Presley on the cover and sold for a mere 15 cents. The magazine was largely a two-man production—editor Desmond Hall and writer George Waller—though from the start "Georgia Winters" was listed as editor on the magazine masthead. The fictional chief was actually a combination of Waller's first name and Hall's middle name.

The Presley issue sold out quickly, setting the course for *16*'s future—feature stories on young male singers who appealed to teen and pre-teen girls. The magazine published as a quarterly that first year with Waller cranking out copy from his home. Fortunately for Chambrun, the magazine was a success. It was a publishing "Hail Mary" for the flamboyant Chambrun who had gained a reputation in the publishing world as a con man.

He was alleged to have fraudulently appropriated rights payments from some of his famous clients (among them Grace Metalious, Aldous Huxley, W. Somerset Maugham, and H.G. Wells),

---

1. *Who's Your Fave Rave?*, Randi Reisfeld and Danny Fields, 1997, p. vii.

and lesser-known writers as well. His grandiose, French persona was apparently a winning one, though he likely was a native New Yorker. His taste for the good life doubtless accounted for *16*'s swanky digs at 745 Fifth Avenue in New York City, an art-deco masterpiece once known as the Squibb Building at the southwest corner of Central Park. The building was well-known for its ceiling murals in the lobby and for over half a century the legendary toy emporium FAO Schwarz occupied the ground floor.

It was at one of Chambrun's frequent lavish parties that Stavers first met the *16* impresario.

Born Gloria Frances Gurganus in Wilmington, N.C., she married Frank Staveridis shortly after high school and, finding herself stranded in Ithaca, N.Y., ditched Staveridis to seek her own fame in New York City as Gloria Stavers. She found it quickly, parlaying her glamorous looks (*Saturday Evening Post* writer William Kloman described her as "a stylish blend of Katherine Hepburn and Julie Andrews"[2]) into successful gigs as a runway and advertising model for the Hartford, Powers and Conover agencies.

She found her way into the gossip columns of Walter Winchell and Earl Wilson while being escorted through the city's hot nightspots by some of the city's best-known celebrities. She's rumored to have dated Mickey Mantle in his prime and was a longtime lover of comedian Lenny Bruce.

But health issues stemming from a childhood bout with rheumatic fever and a chronic bad back were threatening the 30-year-old Stavers' livelihood in early 1958. She was considering switching to the other side of the camera as a fashion photographer before her fortuitous meeting with Chambrun.

Chambrun was immediately taken with Stavers. Upon learning she'd had a smattering of journalism experience on the sports desk of the Goldsboro (N.C.) Argus newspaper and writing safety manuals for an auto club, Chambrun hired her as a sort of girl Friday at $50 a week.

One of her initial responsibilities at *16* was to open fan mail and handle subscription requests. Every night she'd take home bags of mail from teens and pre-teens pouring out their prepubescent souls.

"I believe them and I know what they're going through," she said for the *Saturday Evening Post* article. "It hurts. We try to help."

---

2. *Saturday Evening Post*, November 4, 1967, "Meet Gloria Stavers," William Kloman.

It was easy for Stavers to rise through the *16* ranks. The barebones operation barely had any staff at all and the magazine itself was printed on the cheapest newsprint available. By the end of 1958, she had inherited the name "Georgia Winters" and the duties of editor-in-chief. Her time in front of the camera as a model allowed her to observe the skills of high fashion photographers and, using a Rolleiflex camera, she assumed the role of chief photographer for *16*, even persuading Chambrun to spring for a few pages of slick stock paper each issue to showcase her photographic work.

She was also writing most of the articles that appeared in the magazine. Not wanting to be under the thumb of advertisers, Chambrun accepted no advertising for *16*. Not wanting to antagonize the subjects of the magazine's articles, Stavers based her stories on press releases and rarely printed a contrary word about the stars who were responsible for the magazine's very existence.

Stavers had the uncanny ability to put herself in the shoes of the young girls the magazine was trying to reach, assimilate what they were looking for and then give it to them. Despite the magazine's title, *16*'s target audience was girls ages 11 to 14.

"Sixteen-year-old girls rarely read fan magazines, but most 13-year-olds want to be 16," Stavers said. "I have this button in my head. I push it and I become thirteen again, and I remember all the things I longed for . . . other magazines can't reach these children the way I can."[3]

Just as Dick Clark was creating Bandstandland in his own vision, Stavers was creating *16*-land, where young girls could fantasize about their favorite celebrities without fear of adult scorn or contradiction.

Clark's introduction to Stavers would come through his connections to two other women holding power positions in the New York City pop music world—Connie DeNave and Rosalind Ross.

DeNave was the well-connected, tough-talking press agent who once worked for ABC-TV before becoming Clark's personal press agent. Not only did she crank out press releases practically around the clock for the clients of her Image Makers PR firm, but she also ran a "charm school" for young rockers out of her office at Laurie Records.

Philadelphians Frankie Avalon and Fabian were among the young rockers who were taught the niceties of public expression

---

3. *Saturday Evening Post*, November 4, 1967, "Meet Gloria Stavers," William Kloman.

NEW DIRECTIONS

while also being warned of the pitfalls that loomed for young, testosterone-driven celebrities. DeNave also ran dozens of fan clubs for her clients and hired "screamers" to incite crowds wherever her young charges appeared.

Fan club memberships were sold for a buck apiece, and a separate division of Image Makers was created just to open the hundreds of envelopes stuffed with dollar bills that were delivered each morning before returning to the sender an autographed picture and a membership card.

Many of DeNave's press releases were perfect fodder for Stavers' magazine, of course, with the bigger name stars often steered to Stavers directly, so they could be properly "interviewed" and photographed. Many of these interviews took place in Stavers' apartment where she reportedly kept bottles of champagne in her refrigerator for "the boys."

Ross had risen to power as a booking agent at General Artists Corporation. Starting in GAC's Variety Department, Ross started a campaign to create a rock & roll division within the company, an idea resisted by many of her peers who viewed the music as simply a fad that wasn't worth their time. Ross persevered, however, and by 1959 she was helping Clark put together the acts that would make up the first *Dick Clark Caravan of Stars* that fall.

Clark's relationship with Stavers began in 1958 after DeNave pitched a story that found its way into *16*. Headlined "Dick Clark: Top Tune Spotter," the article launched a mutually beneficial relationship that would last throughout *American Bandstand*'s Philadelphia run.

"She had her finger on the pulse of what kids were thinking, which impressed me," Clark said. "Gloria helped *American Bandstand*, and the show helped *16*. it was a two-way street. We kept track of the kids and who was popular. She would publish stories about them; we would have them on as guests."[4]

To the most devout *American Bandstand* watchers, *16* must have looked like the show's official magazine. Stavers definitely had her finger directly on the pulse of young America. Her *Swinging the Breeze* column (written under yet another alter ego, Gee Gee), which was subtitled "What's happening here, there, everywhere," may have been the first successful teen-oriented gossip column. She also printed letters from the magazine's readers

---

4. *In Their Own Write: Adventures in the Music Press*, Paul Gorman, 2001, p. 100.

BANDSTANDLAND

(*You're Telling Me*) and jammed as many as a dozen young stars on the cover with cartoonish drawings that followed a single theme each issue, giving the magazine a unique newsstand presence.

The magazine included a jokes page, an advice column by Barbara Hearn ("Elvis' best home-town girlfriend") that debuted in issue No. 1, a Kwestion Column by deejay Clay Cole, articles written by fan club presidents and a Stavers innovation, stars answering "40 Intimate Questions."

Readers could join the *16 Club*. For $2 members received a special code key that allowed them to decipher secret messages in each month's magazine. Of course, there was also the membership pin plus a deluxe edition of the *16 Club Secret Star Directory*.

When Frankie Avalon bought a new house, *16* readers were invited to submit potential names, à la Elvis' Graceland.

When it came to *American Bandstand*, there were virtually no limits to how the magazine capitalized on the popularity of the show's regulars. There was *Bandstand Portrait, Bandstand Beat, Bandstand Newsletter* and *Bandstand Mailbox*. You could send in questions to be answered by *Bandstand* regular Arlene Sullivan. You could vote for your favorite *Bandstand* couple, even create your own by matching male dancers with girls.

You could "Win a day with your favorite regular," *IF* your one-page letter explaining why you wanted such a day was selected from the mailbags full of similar letters. If a day with a regular wasn't quite your cup of tea, maybe you'd prefer to win a date with regular Mike Balara. Or maybe with South Philadelphia singing star Bobby Rydell.

Contests were popular in *16*. In many issues, readers were invited to select their Top 10 favorite celebrities from a couple dozen or so that were pictured. It was not unusual to see photos of *Bandstand* regulars among the choices, alongside Elvis Presley, Fabian, and Annette Funicello. At least one issue even listed Robert Forte, a nonperforming brother of Fabian. A poll to determine "your favorite regulars," listed 49 regulars and, in case that wasn't enough, included space for write-ins.

One of the more elaborate contests offered a "regular wardrobe" delivered to the winner by regular Mike Balara. Among the offerings were a "dressy dress" from Frani Giordano, a pocketbook from Norman Kerr, a pair of pajamas from Arlene DiPietro and perfume from Frankie Vacca.

NEW DIRECTIONS

The regulars were so popular with *16* readers that articles like "It's Square to Be a Beatnik!" could be bylined "By Arlene," no last name required.

Readers were encouraged to submit their own drawings of *Bandstand* regulars, some of which were printed in *16*. A professional artist named Josh King did a series of cartoons called "Betty Goes to Bandstand," which carried a storyline about the regulars through more than a year's worth of issues. King also did another *Bandstand*-oriented cartoon for the magazine called "Kelly." King's skills were further utilized with a series of "pin-up portrait drawings" of recording stars and a few regulars, including Arlene Sullivan and Kenny Rossi, for 50 cents apiece.

Photos of the regulars were included in one of the magazine's $1 specials. There were also several series of $1 magazines entirely about the *Bandstand* regulars—*All About Us* and *Your Secret Bandstand Album* were published for at least three years and when sales dipped, *Regulars' Fun Time* was launched.

So important was the *Bandstand* franchise to *16* that Stavers enlisted the aid of Steve Brandt, described as "a slight, pockmarked, intensely nervous young man"[5] who lived in an expensive suite at the Beverly Hotel on Lexington Avenue in New York. Brandt's duties were to work himself into *Bandstand's* inner circle and provide photos for the magazine.

Brandt became friends with several of the regulars, including Arlene Sullivan, Joe Wissert and Larry Giuliani. When doing his *Bandstand* duties, Brandt sometimes stayed with the family of another regular, Frani Giordano. Brandt's *Bandstand* photos did, indeed, pop up in *16* where he was sometimes described as "*16*'s private eye photographer," but his contributions weren't limited to the visual. He often wrote articles, like "The Story of My Life" by Mike Balara "as told to Steve Brandt."

Published circulation numbers for *16* varied wildly, but were probably in the 150,000–250,000 range with overall readership much higher, probably in the millions. No other magazine could claim the same *Bandstand* clout, but they tried.

'Teen, of course, had Molittieri, who relocated to Hollywood to pursue her dream of becoming a star. *Pat's Party Line* was a magazine staple, but Molittieri had loftier ambitions. She enrolled in the Hollywood Professional School, where Mouseketeer Cubby

---
5. The description comes from Clay Cole in his book.

O'Brien was a classmate. Tuesday Weld and Annette had also attended the school, which accommodated working entertainers.

'Teen publisher Bob Peterson invited many of those young entertainers to his home for a welcome party in Molittieri's honor. Among those attending were *Bad Seed* star Patty McCormack, singers Jan and Dean, *Leave It to Beaver* star Tony Dow and several Mouseketeers, including Sharon, Darlene, and Doreen. When *'Teen* did a story about how the Mouseketeers were coping professionally after the show's cancellation, the group photo accompanying the story included Molittieri.

'Teen founder Laufer started the Teen Magazine record label and Molittieri's "The USA" (written by Paul Anka) backed with "Say That You Love Me" was the label's first release. Molittieri toured to plug the record yet found some time to continue dancing—doing the Cha Cha Cha with Tommy Cole at Disneyland and gracing the dance floor of the Coconut Grove with Bobby Burgess at her 17th birthday party.

Despite her career aspirations, she never forgot her Philly roots. She frequently included a "Flashes from Philly" section in her *'Teen* column and was always open to visitors from back home, like regulars Billy Cook and Carole Scaldeferri who made the trek west.

Molittieri soon adapted to the mornings-only class schedule at Hollywood Professional and spent many afternoons hanging out at the community pool with the UCLA students that were her neighbors. She dated singers Tony Cosmo and Mike Clifford, had a small role as an extra in Connie Francis' *Where the Boys Are* and was seeking work in TV commercials when she decided to give it all up and return to Philadelphia.

Pat's Party Line was still going strong, however, when *Teen Screen* magazine hired another popular regular, Myrna Horowitz, to write a *Bandstand* column for that fledgling publication. Horowitz had just "aged out" (turned 18) of *Bandstand* and was finding the transition tough. She worked three mornings a week at Swan Records and spent many afternoons in the back of WFIL's Studio B, just watching her friends dance.

The offer from *Teen Screen* editor Sheldon Heiman was a godsend. Molittieri had written about Horowitz in *'Teen* and Horowitz herself had written about her close relationship with Dick Clark in *Modern Screen*.

Heiman gave Horowitz the opportunity to write up to 750 words every month about her favorite people, the kids who danced on

American Bandstand. She was encouraged to mention as many regulars as she could "in a chatty vein" and Heiman reminded her that she would be competing with her old friend Molittieri.

There were some technical details to be worked out—two carbons, double-spacing of copy, deadlines two months in advance of publication—but Horowitz jumped at the chance to pocket $25 every month for work she loved, plus $5 for every photo she sent in.

The relationship was profitable for both sides, as *Teen Screen* tripled its readership during Horowitz's tenure before folding in 1963.

One other magazine to make a serious bid for a share of the *Bandstand* audience was *Dig*. *Dig* covered the same music, fashion and other trendy topics that the other teen magazines did, but from a different perspective.

The magazine's founder, Lou Kimzey, was more interested in souped-up cars and motorcycles than he was in jitterbugging teens, but his love of hot rodding was not so out of step with teens of the era.

Kimzey was a native Californian whose first job after earning an art and design degree from Woodbury College in Burbank was as art director for *Road & Track* magazine. His wife was circulation director at the magazine and sometime in the early 1950s, he got rid of his cherished customized 1941 Buick convertible and purchased his and hers MGs in green and red.

Through the mid-1950s, Kimzey served as art director for a variety of car publications and in 1957, struck out on his own with Teenage Publications, publisher of a variety of teen-oriented magazines, including *Modern Teen* and *Dig*.

Dig called itself "America's Coolest Teenage Magazine" and, in at least one respect, lived up to its billing. Unlike its competitors, *Dig* had a monthly dance column, penned by Dick D'Agostin. D'Agostin was a California dance champion as a teenager and a rocking piano pounder, to boot. D'Agostin played in Eddie Cochran's band and had a role in a 1958 Kimzey B-movie production, *Hot Rod Gang*, which also featured Gene Vincent.

In case the dance column wasn't enough to corral the *American Bandstand* crowd, Kimzey also hired one of the show's regulars, 15-year-old Gary Levin, to cover the Philadelphia show from the inside. Levin proved to be perceptive beyond his years, even providing a detailed article on "Why Dick Clark Banned So Many Regulars," exactly the kind of story shied away from by most of the teenage press.

There was a literal glut of teen-oriented magazines on newsstands in the late 1950s, most of them biting the dust after an issue or two, and many of them had cover stories on Dick Clark or *American Bandstand* before their demise.

The photogenic Clark found himself on the cover of *TV Life*, *'Teen*, *Photoplay*, *TV World*, *Hit Parader*, *Movieland & TV Time* and *Hep Cats*, to name a few. He even made the cover of *Uncensored*, which promised "What Dick Clark Really Hides" within its pages.

Alan Freed, America's best-known disc jockey before Dick Clark, never enjoyed the same adulation from the press, though he did have a profitable working arrangement with Gary Filosa, the publisher of *Rock and Roll Roundup*.

Filosa was on the staff of Esquire magazine in 1956 when he started Filosa Publications International and launched *Rock and Roll Roundup*, which he believed was the first "specific and unique" rock & roll magazine. In 1957 he published his first *Rock & Roll Annual*, which was sold at the door of Freed's rock & roll concerts. It became Filosa's biggest seller with over 10 million sold at Freed concerts.

* * *

Dick Clark had carefully planned his late summer absence from *American Bandstand*—four weeks to star in his first feature film in California and one week for personal appearances before returning to his daily duties in Philadelphia.

As was typical with Clark projects, he had enormous control over the film. Although it was billed as a joint production between Columbia Pictures and Clark's Drexel Pictures, it was apparent who was calling the shots.

It was Clark who snapped up the movie rights for the film. The project was initially titled *Harrison High*, the name of the John Farris novel that the movie was based on. Somewhere along the way, though, James Gunn's adapted screenplay was retitled *Because They're Young*.

You would think Clark would have been a shoo-in for the leading role, but Milt Young, a Philadelphia-based Columbia spokesman for the film said Clark had to take a screen test for the part.

"Dick took the one test. When the director saw it, he told him: 'You have nothing to worry about'," Young said.[6]

Clark surrounded himself with familiar faces from Philadelphia.

---
6. *Philadelphia Daily News*, April 14, 1960.

NEW DIRECTIONS

Two of the young lead parts went to a pair of 23-year-old Philadelphia natives who were already getting rave notices. James Darren wasn't quite sure which direction his career was heading after starring in and singing the title song from the movie hit, *Gidget*. Michael Callen brought equally impressive credentials after wowing them on Broadway as Riff in *West Side Story*.

Another Philadelphia actor in the cast, Rudy Bond, was a graduate of Elia Kazan's famed Actors Studio and Columbia music director Morris Stoloff, who helped with the film's music, snared three Academy Awards after leaving his native Philadelphia. The film's producer, Jerry Bresler (a two-time Oscar winner) went to Swarthmore and director Paul Wendkos worked with Clark on the trade film, *Wonders of Philadelphia*, and broke into the feature film business with *The Burglar*. Even Clark's *American Bandstand* producer, Tony Mammarella, was cut in on the action. Although he had little to do with the actual production of the movie, Mammarella was credited for acting as "script consultant."

Because They're Young was a drama, but its musical contributions were considerable.

The title song was co-written by three successful songwriters—Aaron Schroeder, Don Costa, and Wally Gold. Schroeder, who had a hand in writing 17 songs for Elvis Presley—including five that reached No. 1—had worked with Clark before, in writing music for *Jamboree* two years earlier. Costa was the a.&r. director for ABC-Paramount records and Gold would later write Lesley Gore's teen anthem, "It's My Party."

Darren sang "Because They're Young" for the film, but his version of the song never cracked the U.S. popularity charts. Duane Eddy's instrumental version fared much better, reaching No. 4 on the *Billboard* charts, the biggest hit of Eddy's career. The movie also included Bobby Rydell, whose "Swingin' School" was the young Philadelphian's third straight top 10 record.

Musical score duties fell to a young contract player with the Columbia Studios Orchestra, Juilliard-trained jazz pianist Johnny Williams. It was Williams' first assignment to write a complete score, but he would go on to write many more, winning five Oscars and 22 Grammies as John Williams.

The female leads in the cast were also accomplished.

Tuesday Weld, who was just shy of her 16th birthday when filming began, was something of a "teen queen" despite her youth, having made her big screen debut three years earlier in Alan Freed's *Rock Rock Rock*. Clark's on-screen love interest was

Australian-born Victoria Shaw, the wife of actor Roger Smith. Although Shaw stood three inches shorter than her co-star, Clark wrote in his autobiography that he had to stand on two telephone books to kiss her.

For the first two weeks that Clark was busy filming *Because They're Young* in Hollywood, *American Bandstand* viewers were fed taped programs that were recorded earlier in the summer. Then guest hosts took over. As he had done the year before, Clark allowed the guest hosts just one day each on the national stage. For most of these one-time *Bandstand* hosts, it was the highlight of their professional careers, an achievement often noted in their obituaries decades later. Such was the case even for Owen Forrester, the youthful host of *Dance Party* in Atlanta, Ga., who went on to become a federal judge.

With *Bandstand* in capable hands during his absence, Clark was able to concentrate on other matters. Besides the daily rigors of filming, Clark moved his *Saturday Night Show* to Hollywood for three weeks beginning on August 22. He also was gearing up for his first Caravan of Stars tour, which was scheduled to begin in Baltimore on Sept. 18 and run for six weeks before finishing in Milwaukee on Halloween.

As something of a Caravan preview, Clark reprised his successful *Salute to Dick Clark* concert of 1958 at the Hollywood Bowl. Many of the artists who performed at the Bowl followed Clark for a series of Labor Day concerts at Fairgrounds Coliseum at the Michigan State Fair in Detroit.

Although Clark relinquished several hours of national network time during his absence from *American Bandstand*, he was as popular as ever. Besides hosting the *Saturday Night Show*s from Hollywood, he continued to be a hot commodity for the print press.

Bob Thomas of the Associated Press secured enough time with Clark to allow the affable host to expound on the joy he reaped from being with teenagers for up to six hours each day. "It's like working in a bakery," Clark told Thomas. "If you're around it long enough, you'll learn how to bake."[7]

Rose Perlberg took a deeper dive into Clark's professional life with an article in the September 1959 edition of *Movieland and TV Time* headlined "Dick Clark Reveals: How I've Changed."

In the article, Clark confessed that he was "up to my eyeballs in the business" and "I wish I could be in three places at once, but

---

7. *Associated Press*, August 28, 1959.

NEW DIRECTIONS

I can't." Clark estimated that he worked up to 60 hours a week, but his associates put the figure at closer to 75 hours.

"I remember when Steve Allen showed me his huge scrapbook of articles filled with lies about him," he mused. "I remember Steve shaking his head and saying he could never understand why they were written. And now *I've* got a book like that."[8]

Before returning to Philadelphia, Clark had one more obligation—the four nights of concerts at the Michigan State Fair, where General Artists Corporation wanted to test the drawing power of rock & roll in a venue more typically filled with country acts. The rockers proved to be a huge success, smashing attendance and revenue records by drawing more than 63,000 fans and grossing more than $73,000.

American Bandstand's pull on the pop music market was once again in evidence when Fabian's latest release, "Come On and Get Me," drew advance orders of more than 200,000. The record was soon reissued, however, when listeners complained that Fabian's vocal intro to the B-side, "Got the Feeling," sounded like he was singing "when we were fucking cheek to cheek."

Sal Mineo's manager bought a full-page ad in *Billboard*'s August 31, 1959, issue to thank Philadelphia "for the sensational all-out support" of Mineo's 'Make Believe Baby,' a song that failed to make *Billboard*'s Hot 100.

Clark had plenty of reasons to be upbeat as he returned to Philadelphia.

His investment in Swan Records proved to be a wise one. Billy and Lillie, the Quaker City Boys and Dicky Doo & the Don'ts got the label off to a solid start with a string of successful records, and a recent discovery, Freddy Cannon, was poised to make the label even more profitable after breaking big with "Tallahassee Lassie."

One of WFIL's competing stations in Philadelphia, WPEN, had banished rock & roll from its playlists by the time Clark returned and the ABC network showed it shared Clark's belief that music was good business by loading its fall schedule with musical specials from Frank Sinatra, Bing Crosby, Pat Boone, and Eydie Gorme and Steve Lawrence. The network also announced that it would air Elvis' first post-Army special the next spring.

As Clark settled back into his *American Bandstand* hosting duties, he also was a judge in the "Miss Good Grooming Contest"

---

8. *Movieland and TV Time*, "Dick Clark Reveals: How I've Changed," September 1959.

at the *Inquirer's* Beautyrama show at the Hotel Sheraton. On his first *Saturday Night Show* from New York since his return, Clark plugged *Because They're Young* and brought in a co-star, 16-year-old Roberta Shore, to sing "Love At First Sight."

There were two new Clark ventures on the horizon as well—the Caravan of Stars and a new prime time show for ABC-TV, *The World of Talent*.

With the Caravan, Clark was emulating Alan Freed's Big Beat package tours, taking a large contingent of rock acts on the road for one-nighters in places that rarely had an opportunity to see young hitmakers in person. Clark had joined forces with promoter Irvin Feld, who assembled the Caravan's musical acts for GAC.

The Caravan would be headlined by Paul Anka and also included Lloyd Price, Annette Funicello, Duane Eddy, Jimmy Clanton, LaVern Baker, the Coasters, the Drifters, the Skyliners, Bobby Rydell, and Phil Phillips. Little-known comedian and impressionist Arnold Dover was hired as the MC for the shows where Clark did not appear.

The tour opened in Baltimore on Sept. 18 and immediately hit a snag. Although scheduled for Boston Garden the next night, the tour had to make an abrupt detour to Scranton, Pennsylvania, when GAC learned that the Garden would need to be converted to a concert venue in just hours after an afternoon hockey game, something tour officials were not comfortable with.

Meanwhile, Clark concentrated on his new network show, scheduled to premiere on Sunday, Sept. 27. Clark confided to *New York Herald Tribune* columnist Marie Torre that "I'm worried about this one. After all, It's a gamble, a complete departure from the sort of thing I've been identified with."[9]

The World of Talent had a format similar to an earlier CBS program, *This Is Show Business*. Three young performers were to appear each week, do their act and then be critiqued by a panel that included regular Jack E. Leonard and two celebrity guests.

With the addition of the Sunday night show, Clark became the only TV personality to have a scheduled network program every day of the week, but since *World of Talent* was taped, he had Sundays free for his family.

By the fall of 1959, Clark was dealing with the constantly changing music environment with relative ease, but there were

---

9. *New York Herald Tribune*, Sept. 17, 1959.

rumblings in Washington that environment could be threatened by events beyond his control.

Congress was involved in a highly publicized quiz show scandal that was knocking some popular prime time television programs off the air. The scandal began a year earlier with a New York grand jury looking into cheating allegations, compelling Congress to take a look itself.

The probe mostly involved the other two major national networks, CBS and NBC, but every network was caught up in the reform effort. One of ABC's concessions was to drop the quiz portion of Johnny Carson's *Who Do You Trust?*, the program that interrupted *American Bandstand* for 30 minutes each weekday afternoon.

The primary targets were two of the most successful packagers of game shows, Jack Barry and Dan Enright. When investigators for Sen. Oren Harris' Subcommittee on Legislative Oversight learned that Barry and Enright also owned Top 40 radio stations, it opened up a whole new area of potential inquiry that could help bring the rogue producers back in line.

Pennsylvania Sen. Joseph S. Clark also hinted that the radio business could be in line for further Congressional scrutiny.

Joe Clark was in his first term in Washington after serving several years as Philadelphia's mayor. As a recently elected mayor in 1952, Joe Clark had started a television show on WFIL called *Tell It To the Mayor* around the same time Bob Horn was launching *Bandstand*. One of the lessons Joe Clark apparently learned from Horn was that disc jockeys get a lot of perks.

In a speech to the Danville, Pennsylvania, Rotary Club in late September, Joe Clark said that he was sponsoring bills to tighten rules that allow businessmen to engage in tax-deductible gift exchanges. Pointing out that record companies and publishing firms take full advantage of these tax loopholes, Joe Clark said he had found Congressional support for a bill that would allow the IRS to hire more auditors.

An IRS spokesman, responding to Joe Clark's message, said: "that they are aware of the existence of payola, and in 1958 successfully prosecuted a case against a Philadelphia radio personality [presumably Horn] for failure to report some $9,000 in payments."[10]

---

10. *Billboard*, Sept. 28, 1959.

Dick Clark, who already was vested in at least 28 businesses at the time of Joe Clark's speech, was uncomfortable talking about his own income. This was abundantly clear in a landmark interview the *Bandstand* host gave to another Philadelphia icon, Pete Martin of the *Saturday Evening Post*.

Martin was as legendary in his field as Dick Clark was in his. A Virginia native, William Thornton "Pete" Martin had risen from a hardscrabble childhood to a long and distinguished career with the *Saturday Evening Post*. His work appeared alongside articles by Agatha Christie, William Faulkner and F. Scott Fitzgerald, poems by Robert Frost and wrapped in covers illustrated by Norman Rockwell.

When television threatened the magazine's advertising base in the 1950s, Martin stepped up with a column entitled "I Call On . . ." Martin's column subjects read like a Hollywood Who's Who—including Clark Gable, Lucille Ball, and Marilyn Monroe. Martin also was ghostwriter for several celebrity biographies and wrote credited biographies of Bing Crosby and Bob Hope.

Martin's ability to put his subjects at ease and to coax interesting, often obscure, details from their personal lives was a major factor in reversing the *Post's* declining circulation numbers and keeping the Philadelphia-based magazine afloat through the 1950s.

The "I Call on Dick Clark" interview session resulted in a contentious generational clash that found Martin pressing into areas Clark clearly found annoying while he tried to steer the conversation back onto more *Bandstand*-friendly turf.

As Martin pointed out several times in the course of the interview that ran in the *Post's* October 10, 1959, issue, he was no fan of rock & roll and had little understanding of or compassion for the behavior of modern teenagers. Martin, who was twice the age of Clark (58 years old vs. Clark's 29), spent his teenage years between the start of World War 1 and the beginning of prohibition, and was already well out of his teens when Clark was born.

Clark noted the age difference several times in the interview, teasing that Martin may have already forgotten the waltz of his youth and noting that "as we grow older our minds close in certain areas, music among them." For his part, Martin tagged Clark with several unflattering labels—The Czar of the Switchblade Set, The Kingpin of the Teenage Mafia and The Dictator of Popular Music—and when Clark noted that Elvis Presley was reflecting an art form popular with teens, Martin responded, "If rock 'n' roll is an art form, it's a degenerative art form."

Throughout the interview, Clark defended teenagers and their behavior and lashed out at his critics. "I'm always puzzled as to why anybody should dislike me apparently because I am associated with young people, and because I defend teenagers' musical likes and dislikes," Clark told Martin.

At times during the interview, Martin noted, Clark was clearly irritated by some lines of questioning and his replies took on a "cold edge."

One of those times was when Martin asked whether Clark had had "any trouble with young girls having crushes on him," an apparent reference to Bob Horn's morals charges.

"I've never had an incident," was Clark's terse reply.

"What do you mean 'incident'?" Martin pressed.

"I mean I've never been embarrassed in that way, by a male or female," Clark said.

At one point when the matter of Fabian and his lack of talent came up, Clark pointed out that he and Fabian shared at least one trait: they were the victims of "biased journalism."

Clark claimed that many journalists were "preoccupied" with how much money he made. As Clark often pointed out in interviews, he was successful, sure, but he was also just like everyone else.

The interview took place in Clark's Drexelbrook apartment.

"I think you will agree that it is not pretentious," Clark told Martin, referencing his home. "The rent is $110 a month and we've had the same furniture for years. I mentioned a piece of ground that my wife scrimped and saved to buy on the Maryland coast. Three or four years later we had saved enough to put a prefab beach house on it."[11]

By the end of the article, Clark had managed to shift the conversation to his childhood, his success with *American Bandstand* and a plug for his latest effort, a book he jokingly referred to as "How to Live With Yourself In Spite of Being a Teenager."

The book was actually entitled *Your Happiest Years* and was published by Clark's Rosho Corporation, a company he'd originally set up in 1958 to handle anticipated package tours of rock stars but the unusual name, a contraction of "road show," was never used for its original purpose.

---

11. *Saturday Evening Post*, "I Call on Dick Clark," By Pete Martin, October 10, 1959.

Your Happiest Years was a book of advice for teenagers, a topic Clark felt particularly well-qualified for. Besides dispensing generic advice, the book also contained anecdotes from Clark's personal experiences and included several family and business photos.

While Clark was seen as a staunch defender of teenagers and wholesome living in general, the tone of *Your Happiest Years* was a real downer for those teens who espoused the very independence that was represented by the music Clark played on *American Bandstand*. If there was a theme to Clark's book it was to obey your parents and get ready for a life just like theirs.

He told the story of a girl he knew who stayed at a friend's home one night without informing her parents. Her frantic father went out looking for her, wrecked the family car, and emerged as a cripple.

Clark warned of the consequences of too much makeup, not enough deodorant, long hair and going steady. How can you be ready for adulthood if you don't heed Mom, Dad, and Mother Nature?

For maturing girls he cautioned:

> A young woman should begin in her teens learning the things that keep a home running smoothly. She can watch how her mother cooks and bakes. There are also many opportunities for a daughter to observe how Mother handles Dad when he's had a tough day at work. Mom can always use some help around the house, with dishes, cleaning, cooking, and a million other things a girl should know to qualify for that band of gold.[12]

And for boys:

> A pinball machine may be a lot of fun when you're seventeen, but at twenty-two, it's no date for a dance, and it won't sew up those ripped shirts when you're thirty.[13]

Although Clark had clearly set his career course by the teenage compass, he was always looking for opportunities to expand his reach to an older, more mature audience. As he frequently pointed out (including in the Pete Martin interview), over half his audience consisted of adults.

---

12. *Your Happiest Years*, p. 136.
13. *Your Happiest Years*, pp. 126–127.

His prime time shows, featuring rock & rollers of the present and pop singers more familiar to the older set, were attempts to bridge the gap between young and old. Clark even occasionally put his own performing skills on the line, like lip-syncing to his own recording of the old standard, "Bye Bye Blackbird," on Perry Como's *Kraft Music Hall* on NBC on October 14, 1959.

As Clark rehearsed for the Como show, many of the older music fans he sought were mourning the death of Mario Lanza, the popular singer from South Philadelphia who had shot to fame portraying the famed opera star Enrico Caruso earlier in the decade. Lanza, who as Alfredo Cocozza had been a football star and powerful weightlifter at Southern High School, won great acclaim for his starring role in *The Great Caruso* in 1951.

Ironically, several other natives of South Philadelphia had transitioned from strong recording careers into movie roles by the time of Lanza's death.

James Darren was a breakout star in *Gidget*, was in the cast of Clark's *Because They're Young* and was signed to co-star with another *Bandstand* favorite, Sal Mineo, in *The Gene Krupa Story*. Two other singers who grew up within three blocks of Darren were also hoping to carry their recording popularity into movies.

Nineteen-year-old Frankie Avalon was at work on his first movie, appearing with John Wayne in *The Alamo* and Fabian's first movie, *Hound Dog Man*, was set to premiere in Philadelphia on November 11.

Clark took advantage of Fabian's star power, inviting *American Bandstand* viewers to write in with an essay on "Why I would like to have dinner with Fabian." Winners would be flown to Philadelphia for the *Hound Dog Man* premiere and would have dinner with Clark and Fabian.

Meanwhile, the *Dick Clark Caravan of Stars* had hit another snag in Kansas City, where police stopped the show after fights broke out among the audience. Some news outlets called the October 17 disturbance a riot, a description Clark described as overblown.

"I have received three different versions as to what happened," Clark told the *Associated Press*. "I understand the situation came to a head after the show was over and the dance was going on. All of my people had gone by then."

Police reports showed that 49 people were arrested and witnesses said there were at least 30 fights. A gun was reported to have been fired, but police claimed the noise was from firecrackers. Most of those charged with drunkenness and creating a public disturbance were adults, although some teenage boys were found hiding in a women's restroom. They were sent home to their parents.

The melee threatened to cancel the rest of the tour, which was an experiment for Clark and GAC Super Attractions. Promoters Irvin Feld and Tim Gale had lined up radio sponsors for each stop, no small feat considering many of the stations considered themselves competitors of *American Bandstand* in their markets.

In the wake of the Kansas City disturbance, Kansas City Police Chief Bernard Brannon called for a new city ordinance to control rock & roll concerts. In Minneapolis—an upcoming stop on the Caravan tour—police chief Milton Winslow urged that the October 28 show be canceled. Winslow got his wish when Minneapolis promoter T.B. Skarning pulled the plug on the show, which was co-sponsored by WDGY. Skarning claimed that ticket sales had ground to a halt and that 50 people had requested refunds after the Kansas City incident. Omaha radio station KOIL also withdrew its support for a concert in that city and it was canceled, too.

As it turned out, those were the only stops canceled and the tour rolled on, albeit with increased security. At Municipal Auditorium in San Antonio, Texas, on October 22, cast members threw an impromptu on-stage 17th birthday celebration for Annette Funicello as an additional 25 San Antonio police officers looked on.

As Dick and Bobbie Clark were finally abandoning apartment living and moving into a new $38,000 split-level home at 308 Dogwood Lane in Wallingford, Clark received an unusual request.

Could he meet with ABC-TV president Oliver Treyz in his New York office on Wednesday, November 11?

Sure, Clark replied.

I wonder what's up, he thought.

Bob Horn

Promotional ad for *Bandstand* in *TV Guide*, which was owned by Walter Annenberg, who also owned WFIL-TV.

Bob Horn addresses the studio audience in the early years of *Bandstand*. (Photo courtesy of Rob Graham, Bob Horn's grandson)

Tony Mammarella (right) looks on as Bob Horn holds the lion cub that was part of a successful *Bandstand* promotion in 1956. (Photo courtesy of Tony Mammarella family)

Dick Clark often cited the flood of mail into WFIL as proof of the show's popularity. On at least one occasion, he flooded the studio floor with bags of mail to prove his point.

For years, Tony Mammarella and Dick Clark shared a small office near the *American Bandstand* Studio B. (Photo courtesy of Tony Mammarella family)

One of Tony Mammarella's many duties on *American Bandstand* was keeping things orderly, even before teens were allowed in the studio. (Photo courtesy of Tony Mammarella family)

Many of the photos taken in the *Bandstand* studio during the Philadelphia years were taken by local photographer Edgar Brinker. Here Dick Clark gives last-minute instructions to Brinker before an ice skating party televised nationally on *American Bandstand*. (Photo courtesy of Edgar Brinker family)

Two of the most important players in the day-to-day success of *American Bandstand* were director Ed Yates (seated) and Tony Mammarella. (Photo courtesy of Ed Yates family)

Ed Yates had a unique vantage point of *American Bandstand* from his director's chair. (Photo courtesy of Ed Yates family)

In the wake of the payola hearings in 1960, *Modern Screen* magazine published an article in which Dick Clark praised his wife for her support during those trying months. They divorced the next year. (From *Modern Screen*)

A promotional photo for Dick Clark's role as a teacher in the film *Because They're Young*.

Dick Clark interviews former regular Myrna Horowitz in a 1970 *American Bandstand* reunion show.

Dick Clark promotional photo from 1961.

Hear about Clearasil from DICK CLARK on "American Bandstand" on ABC-TV Network.

Dick Clark's effective representation of pimple-starving Clearasil on television carried over to print media as well.

SCIENTIFIC CLEARASIL MEDICATION

'STARVES' PIMPLES

SKIN-COLORED, *Hides pimples while it works*

CLEARASIL is the new-type scientific medication *especially* for pimples. In tubes or new squeeze-bottle lotion, CLEARASIL gives you the effective medications prescribed by leading Skin Specialists, and clinical tests prove it *really* works.

WFIL-TV 46th & Market Streets Philadelphia 39, Pa.
AMERICAN BANDSTAND with Dick Clark
American Bandstand is holding a reservation for you to visit the program on WED JAN 2 1962

Dick Clark

NOT TRANSFERABLE - VOID IF SOLD - SEE REVERSE SIDE

No. 19221

Getting a ticket to *American Bandstand* was a big deal for a teenager in 1962.

Bunny Gibson and Eddie Kelly made one of the more popular couples on *American Bandstand* in the early 1960s. (Photo courtesy of Bunny Gibson)

Best friends Diane Iaquinto and Marlyn Brown were popular regulars in the early 1960s. (Photo courtesy of Diane Iaquinto Celotto)

American Bandstand regulars Diane Iaquinto and Charlie "Rubberlegs" Hibib were a couple at the Junior Prom at Nazareth Academy High School on February 23, 1963. (Photo courtesy of Diane Iaquinto Celotto)

American Bandstand regulars Mary Ann Cuff and Carmela Montecarlo share a laugh outside the studio. (Photo courtesy of Chuck Zamal)

One afternoon before he left for *American Bandstand*, Chuck Zamal found five girls from his New York fan club at his door. Naturally, they wanted a picture. (Photo courtesy of Chuck Zamal)

Although Dick Clark was already in great demand by many print publications, he formed Claban Publishing in 1959 to put out his own magazine, *The Real Dick Clark*.

16 magazine was saturated with *American Bandstand* coverage during the show's Philadelphia run and jumped into the special magazine competition with *All About Us*.

'Teen magazine capitalized on its relationship with former *American Bandstand* regular Pat Molittieri to publish the special magazines *Bandstand Blast* and *Bandstand*

The *Betty Goes to Bandstand* cartoon page was a popular feature of *16* magazine in the early 1960s.

Pat's Party Line column in *'Teen* magazine continued to tout *American Bandstand*'s Philadelphia roots even after Pat Molittieri danced her way to Hollywood in pursuit of an acting and recording career.

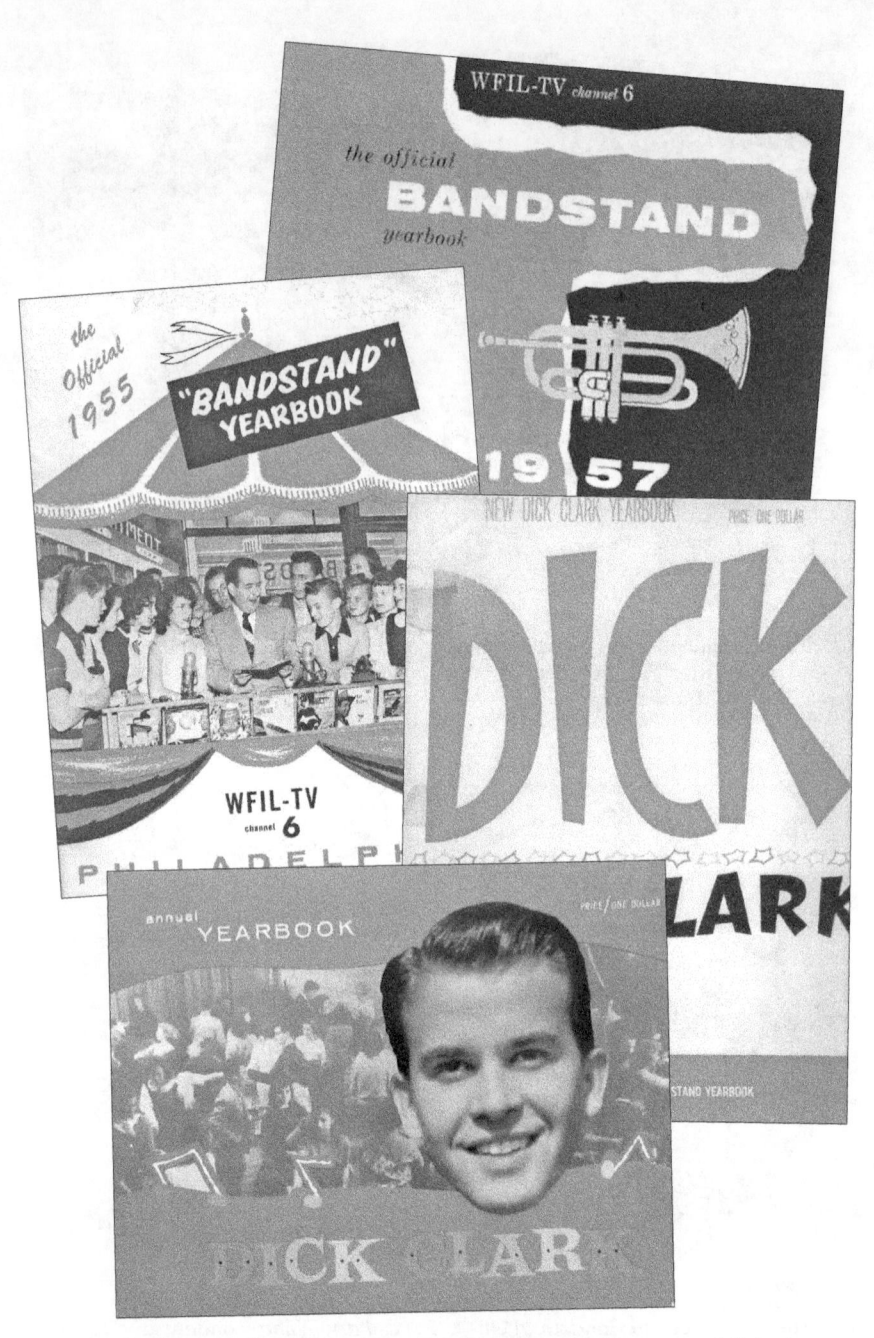

When it was still a local show, two *Bandstand* yearbooks were published—one featuring Bob Horn, one featuring Dick Clark. Two more yearbooks were published in the *American Bandstand* Philadelphia years, but as Dick Clark yearbooks.

The old WFIL studios are now the home of the Philadelphia Enterprise Center, which has a mural honoring the *Bandstand* legacy on one of its walls. Bunny Gibson and Joe Terry of Danny & the Juniors stand in front of the section of the mural that shows Gibson and her Bandstand dancing partner, Ed Kelly. (Photo courtesy of Bunny Gibson)

Sharing a post-*Bandstand* moment are former *American Bandstand* dancers Arlene Sullivan, Rick Fisher and Carmen Jimenez. (Photo courtesy of Rick Fisher)

Dick Clark frequently got together with the *American Bandstand* dancers over the years. Here he's with Bunny Gibson. (Photo courtesy of Bunny Gibson)

Gathering at the Bandstand mural in Philadelphia are ex-*American Bandstand* dancers Lou DeNoble, Frank Brancaccio, Terry Cellie and Rick Fisher. (Photo courtesy of Rick Fisher)

For decades, Davey Frees kept memories of *American Bandstand* alive with his fan club and *Bandstand Boogie* newsletter. Here he shares much of the *Bandstand* story with the author in his "Bandstand room."

CHAPTER 13

PAYING THE PIPER

NOVEMBER 11, 1959
Fabian Forte woke up to one of the biggest days of his life.

He'd come a long way in the months since he hung around Politano's candy store in his South Philadelphia neighborhood or delivered medicine to ailing neighbors in his part-time job for Bob Grobman at Bellevue Pharmacy. Longtime friends knew he was destined for greater things than serving on the student council at George C. Thomas Junior High.

As legend has it, Fabian was plucked from his rowhouse stoop by Chancellor Records owner Bob Marcucci to join neighbor kid Frankie Avalon in Chancellor's growing stable of young singers

That had worked out, too, and Fabian became a big recording star, earning an estimated $12,000 a week. He had to drop out of school to pursue his recording career but Marcucci arranged for schooling on the road. Fabian could now afford things that were out of his reach a few months earlier, like a typewriter so he could practice for his typing class, a guitar so he could learn to accompany himself and his own telephone extension so he could talk to his friends from the privacy of his own bedroom.

Things worked out for Marcucci, too. A week earlier, Chancellor Records had moved from the Chancellor Hall Hotel to larger quarters on Vine Street, from where it hoped to add a TV production unit in the future.

Dick Clark and *American Bandstand* had been instrumental in building public interest in Fabian, whose career took another fortunate turn when movie producer Irwin Allen spotted the teen heartthrob on *The Ed Sullivan Show*. Allen rushed in with a seven-year movie contract in the hopes that Fabian would follow Elvis Presley's path to screen stardom.

For his first film for 20th Century Fox, Fabian was slotted into a lead role in *Hound Dog Man*, a film based on the best-selling novel by Texan Fred Gipson. Gipson was a hot property at the time following the successful movie adaptation of another of his novels, *Old Yeller*.

Producer Jerry Wald had tried to get Tuesday Weld for the female lead, but Weld was unavailable because she was working on Clark's *Because They're Young*. Wald's second choice, Jayne Mansfield, also was unavailable so the role went to Dodie Stevens, a favorite of Wald's teenage sons. Like Fabian, Stevens was better known as a recording artist with a hit recording, "Pink Shoelaces."

The film was to premiere in Philadelphia on November 11, at the grand Fox theater at 16th and Market streets. Dick Clark would lead a motorcade to the premiere.

But first, Clark had that meeting in New York with Ollie Treyz.

* * *

When Clark arrived in New York, he was surprised to find ABC-Paramount president Leonard Goldenson and several other network executives in Treyz' office. Although Goldenson and Clark had never met before, the two men had a few things in common—they were both strong-willed, smart businessmen who recognized an opportunity when they saw one and each was accustomed to getting his way.

Goldenson was the grandson of Russian immigrants and his father had been a successful merchant in the western Pennsylvania coal country town of Scottdale. The Goldensons were one of just four Jewish families in Scottdale, a town of 6,000. Leonard Goldenson worked for a coal company and steel mill while in high school and developed a love for the movies thanks to his father's part ownership of the town's two movie theaters. Young

Goldenson was also fascinated by radio and built a crystal set so he could tune in to broadcasts of one of the nation's first radio stations, KDKA in Pittsburgh.

Goldenson attended college at Harvard and worked summers at a Pittsburgh brokerage firm where he learned to be skeptical of Wall Street types. Nevertheless, he dabbled in stocks while attending Harvard Law School, building up a sizable nest egg. Although he got out of the stock market just before the crash of 1929, his father wasn't so lucky. Young Leonard loaned his father money to keep the family business afloat in the early years of the Depression.

Work was hard to find after Goldenson finished law school, but he finally landed a $50 a week job as a law clerk. The contacts he made in the months he spent looking for work would later prove invaluable, as was the lesson he learned after passing on an opportunity to invest in a new play, *Tobacco Road*, after friends talked him out of it. The lesson: always trust his own instincts.

In 1933, Goldenson joined Paramount pictures in Boston. He later moved back to New York, where he soon found himself in charge of the vast string of Paramount-owned theaters. By the start of World War II, Goldenson had visited every one of Paramount's theaters and earned a promotion to vice-president.

His frequent trips to Hollywood resulted in close ties to movie moguls of the day, like Louis B. Mayer, Jack Warner, and Samuel Goldwyn. After a Supreme Court decision in 1948 separated Paramount Pictures from its theaters, Goldenson was named the president of the branch known as the "theater company."

While most in the movie business saw television as the enemy in the early 1950s, Goldenson saw an opportunity. After persuading his bosses that owning its own TV network would provide a new outlet for Paramount's Hollywood movies, Goldenson negotiated a $25 million merger with the American Broadcasting Company.

By the time the merger was finalized in 1953, ABC owned just five stations and needed programming if it was to compete successfully with the other three networks—NBC, CBS, and DuMont. Goldenson's first success was *Make Room For Daddy* starring Danny Thomas. In late 1953, Goldenson made a deal with Walt Disney, who was scrambling for money so he could fulfill his lifelong dream of creating an amusement park for children.

Disney had already been turned down by NBC and CBS, but Goldenson saw an opportunity to latch onto some quality programming and maybe make some money, too. The final agreement resulted in ABC-Paramount owning a 35 percent stake in Disney's venture, which would be called Disneyland, plus all concession profits for 10 years. Disney would also provide one hour of programming each week and give ABC access to the company's extensive film library.

Disneyland (renamed *Walt Disney Presents* in 1958) premiered in 1954 and was quickly followed by other Disney-produced successes like *The Mickey Mouse Club*.

By late 1956, Goldenson finally put together the programming "dream team" that eventually brought *Bandstand* to network television.

Bob Kintner had been grandfathered in as head of the ABC network for three years following the merger but Kintner's time was up in late 1956 and Goldenson wasted no time in replacing him with Ollie Treyz. Treyz had been something of a whiz kid as head of ABC's Research and Sales Department at the time of the merger but left a year later to become president of the Television Bureau of Advertising after a dispute with Kintner.

Goldenson made two other important hires around the same time: Jim Aubrey joined ABC as head of programming and talent and Dan Melnick was hired as manager of program development. They joined Ted Fetter, whose letter to Dick Clark had opened the lines of communication between the network and *Bandstand*.

It was Treyz and his pioneering use of demographics that ultimately landed *American Bandstand* on the network schedule, but in late 1959 payola threatened to undermine two years of unqualified success for the program as Treyz and Goldenson sat across from Dick Clark.

Goldenson got right to the point.

"Have you ever taken payola?" he asked Clark.

After Clark assured his boss that he had never accepted money for playing a record, had never refused to play a record because he wasn't offered money and had never accepted any form of payola from anyone, Goldenson asked Clark whether he had any interest in music publishing, records or anything else related to the music business.

Well, yes, Clark said. He did have part ownership in a few music-related businesses.

After Goldenson admonished Clark for not revealing his business ties earlier, Clark defended himself, saying he didn't think he was doing anything different from others in the industry.

Goldenson saw it differently. He had faced a similar situation years earlier when he was in charge of Paramount's theaters. Goldenson thought things were sliding in Detroit, where a lawyer turned businessman named George Trendle was supposed to be managing Paramount's theaters. But Trendle seemed to be focusing on another venture of his, radio station WXYZ, where he had created two popular radio series—*The Lone Ranger* and *The Green Hornet*.

That won't do, Goldenson told Trendle. You've got to decide: the theaters or radio? Trendle chose radio. Now, Goldenson gave Clark a similar ultimatum: you'll have to get rid of the outside business interests if you want to stay on the air at ABC-TV.

Clark said he'd need some time to think about it and returned to Philadelphia for that afternoon's *American Bandstand* broadcast. According to Clark, that's when he first told Tony Mammarella that he wanted to meet with him that night to talk about the New York meeting. According to Mammarella, he learned about the New York meeting a day later, during a dinner on November 12 at Bookbinder's restaurant with the winner of the "I want dinner with Fabian" contest.

It was at that dinner, Mammarella says, that Clark was called to the phone and returned with news of an after-dinner meeting that evening at Clark's house with Clark's manager, Marvin Josephson. You should come, too, Clark told Mammarella.

At Clark's home, they were met by Josephson and Clark's lawyer, Charles Seton, who outlined the conditions Goldenson had laid down for Clark and Mammarella if they were to continue on *American Bandstand*—divestment of music-related business interests and signing of affidavits stating they'd never taken payola.

Clark had already decided to divest, plus he wanted to make his own statement to ABC executives that he'd never taken payola. But it was all new to Mammarella, who in a way had much more to lose.

As the public face of *American Bandstand*, lucrative business opportunities were constantly flowing Clark's way, but Mammarella operated behind the scenes, doing much of the hard work but reaping few rewards. He did own a quarter of Swan Records, but that was just half of what Clark owned. He also held a stake in music publishing (Wildcat Music) with Milt Kellem of New York and was invested with Clark in companies that made stuffed animals and record carrying cases.

While these investments enabled Mammarella to buy a nice home for his family in New Jersey, they paled in comparison to Clark's business deals that made him an estimated $500,000 a year. Nevertheless, Mammarella wasn't sure he wanted to give up his music interests.

As far as making a statement to the network went, Mammarella never felt that he was an employee of ABC-TV. WFIL paid him for his work on *American Bandstand* and Dick Clark, through Drexel Productions, paid him for his work on the *Saturday Night Show*. Clark, on the other hand, might want to think twice before issuing any statement, he thought. He pulled Clark aside to discuss the matter.

What about those gifts you got from that Los Angeles record guy? The diamond ring he gave you and the diamond necklace and mink coat he gave Barbara?

Nonsense, Clark replied. They were just gifts, plus I reimbursed him later.

Sure, said Mammarella. Pennies on the dollar. It will look bad.

Truth is, both men had received many gifts from their music business associates over the years, mostly token gifts during the holidays—like bottles of liquor and inexpensive jewelry. Each had scrupulously noted these gifts and reported them as income on their tax returns to avoid problems with the IRS.

But, while Clark carefully managed his business affairs through proper legal channels, Mammarella confessed to Clark that not all of his business dealings had been so dutifully documented.

There was some "private consulting work" he had done for a couple of record companies a couple of years earlier, work he was paid for. And, yes, records by both of these companies were played on *Bandstand*, before and after the "consulting work."

Clark told his longtime associate that his "consulting" would probably sound a lot like payola to investigators and that maybe he should quit the show.

After a long, agonizing night, Mammarella made his decision—he would stay in the record business. On Friday, November 13, 1959, he arrived early at the *Bandstand* office, wrote a short note of resignation and went home.

* * *

PAYING THE PIPER

Dick Clark could be forgiven if he was feeling apprehensive.

After all, in a span of a few short days when he and Bobbie should be enjoying their new life in a brand-spanking new home, he'd been kicked out of the music business and just lost his closest associate, the man who helped create the very program that had vaulted him to unbelievable fame and riches in the past two years.

And it wasn't over yet.

The threat of a congressional investigation had really shaken things up at the network where executives were asking anyone in a position to be offered payola whether they had done so. If payola meant taking something of value in exchange for playing a record on the air, Clark figured he was in the clear. Besides, he told anyone who would listen, payola wasn't illegal. Indeed, it was a standard operating procedure in most businesses. In Washington, it even went by another name—lobbying.

Payola was as old as the music business itself.

In the 1880s, librettist W.S. Gilbert and composer Arthur Sullivan found that paying singers to perform their compositions was the easiest path to success in Victorian-era musical theater. Without payola, *The Pirates of Penzance* or *The Mikado* may have never survived past the 19th century.

Crooner Al Jolson was persuaded to record some songs only after he was cut in on song royalties in the vaudeville era, a time when the Music Publishers Protective Association fought against, but couldn't stop, payola.

Even Paul Whiteman, on whose WFIL-TV program Dick Clark once pushed Tootsie Rolls, was the beneficiary of payola in the radio era when the popular bandleader served as "musical advisor" to publisher Leo Feist.

Payola was largely an accepted—and ignored—facet of the radio business until the 1950s. In December 1950, *Variety* reported that payola to DJs was at an all-time peak.

Keystone Records of Philadelphia brazenly launched a promotion plan in 1952 that overtly touted payola as part of its business plan. For two daily plays of its releases, which cost $1 apiece, Keystone would reimburse stations eight cents, to be divided equally among the station manager, disc jockeys, station librarian and the station itself for each record sold.

No wonder Abel Green of *Variety* penned a series of editorials in 1954 headlined "Payola—Worse Than Ever."

Nothing brought payola into the national spotlight more than the rise of rock & roll, which owes its very existence to the long-simmering feud between the two major music licensing organizations—ASCAP and BMI. In the years since BMI was formed in 1941, the two organizations became increasingly bitter rivals.

The growing popularity of BMI's offerings, coupled with networks abandoning their radio programming as they transitioned to television, gave rise to an explosion of independents—independent radio stations playing records provided by independent record labels.

Another big change was occurring in America in those postwar years—the emergence of teenagers as an economic force. These teens were the most affluent youth in U.S. history, arriving during and after the dark days of a punishing World War, yet coming of age at a time when America's future never looked brighter.

While young people in many other parts of the world were struggling to rebuild shattered cities and societies, American teens were chuckling to *I Love Lucy* on television, cruising their hometown streets in jalopies en route to drive-ins to watch movies starring Marlon Brando and James Dean, and listening to music. Since many of these teens had part-time jobs, they had money to spend, and if they were going to spend it on records, they were going to spend it on music they liked.

They were no longer limited to popular tunes recorded by singers their parents' age and put out by the same record labels that had filled record store racks for decades. Nor were they limited to the network radio of the previous generation, with its big band remotes, assorted dramas and comedy programs featuring stars who came from the vaudeville era.

Simply by turning a radio dial, new types of music could be heard—music with strange beats, odd lyrics and that was curiously fascinating. Increasingly, a new genre emerged. That music became known as rock & roll.

Outside of friends and family, the adult with the most influence over a teenager in the 1950s probably wasn't their teacher or preacher. It was more likely to be a disc jockey from the local radio station. Deejays not only served up the music the kids liked, but the deejay was also an advocate for the growing ranks of teens who were increasingly bewildering to their elders.

At the root of the deejays' popularity, though, was the music. Deciding what music to play wasn't always an easy matter for disc jockeys who came from the big band era.

PAYING THE PIPER

The real problem at radio stations wasn't a scarcity of material catering to the evolving tastes of America's youth. It was just the opposite. Dozens of new labels sprung up each month and disc jockeys and program directors were inundated with many more records than they could possibly listen to, leaving them with difficult choices on what to put on the air.

The major labels had long employed promotion men to plug their records so it was only logical that the independents do the same. Everyone was looking for an edge. Whether it was cutting a deejay in on songwriting credits, plying him with booze and loose women or simply offering cold, hard cash in exchange for a few plays, there was plenty of temptation to go around.

Ironically, it wasn't one of the nationally known deejays who was responsible for bringing payola to the nation's attention in the late 1950s. While much of the initial attention was focused on Dick Clark at *American Bandstand* in Philadelphia or Alan Freed and his myriad operations from his home base in New York City, it was really a radio station executive in Omaha, Nebraska, who set the stage.

Todd Storz had started his radio career after World War II in Hutchinson, Kansas, then worked as a disc jockey in Omaha. In a co-venture with his father (of locally popular Storz beer fame), the 25-year-old Storz bought KOWH, a nondescript station that owes its call letters to a previous owner, the *Omaha World-Herald* newspaper, in 1949. Young Storz started tinkering with KOWH's programming, finally arriving at a formula that would be copied around the country for decades to come.

Storz came into radio at an opportune time. The national radio networks were more interested in television and had scaled back their radio efforts. Only in his mid-20s, Storz didn't bring the baggage of network experience and practices that burdened many of his rival station executives.

He mostly stayed true to the music and news format that had proved successful in the past, but with a few twists. Almost every newscast opened with a local story. Storz pioneered the news tip, where listeners could get paid for a solid news tip, a gimmick that resulted in 6–8 stories every day and set KOWH apart from its Omaha competitors. Storz was also fond of giveaways and contests, another successful tactic that built an audience. He had buried treasure and mystery Santa contests. Listeners could have dinner with their favorite jocks, even win a fully furnished house.

But Storz' greatest innovation was in the music he played. As a GI, he noticed that restaurant patrons played the same songs over and over again on the jukebox. At the end of her shift, the waitress would drop her tip nickels into the box and play the same songs she'd heard all night. Why not give people what they want, Storz thought? Top Forty was born.

KOWH deejays had great leeway in showing their on-air personalities, but when it came to picking the music, they had little choice. Top Forty playlists meant playing the same song at about the same time each day and maybe more than once during a deejay's shift. Consistency was the name of the game at a Storz station.

There was a slight opening, though. There were slots for past hits and for songs the deejays thought could become hits. Storz' mantra was "I won't play anything that isn't a hit, can't be a hit or wasn't a hit."[1]

As Storz built what would become the Mid-Continent Broadcasting Company by buying stations in Kansas City, New Orleans, Minneapolis, and Miami, he had an opportunity to test his format in other areas of the country. In each case, his station climbed to the top of the Hooper Ratings.

Naturally, others noticed. Plough Stations and Gordon McClendon were among the nation's independent chains that copied Storz' Top Forty format. Disc jockeys—especially disc jockeys who were accustomed to selecting their own records for their shows—hated the format, which limited their freedom of selection.

George "Hound Dog" Lorenz, one of the nation's most popular deejays, blamed the format when he quit WKBW in Buffalo, N.Y., in July 1958, calling it boring and saying it shut the door on new artists. Around the same time, KLAC in Hollywood reported that five key deejays quit because of the format and Ed McKenzie left WXYZ in Detroit. Chicago disc jockey Stan Dale called Top Forty "the biggest cancer that's ever hit the broadcasting industry."[2]

Still, the format proved popular with station managers across the country, even in Philadelphia where WIBG rose to the top of the ratings in late 1958 after adopting the format. Storer Communications had taken over the station earlier in the year, and "Wibbage" (as it was known) soon found itself riding the coattails of one of the city's hottest deejays, Joe Niagara.

---

1. *Television Magazine*, "The Storz Bombshell," May 1957.
2. *Billboard*, April 7, 1958.

PAYING THE PIPER

Mindful of the implications of payola, WIBG management required its jocks to submit a list of songs they intended to play 24 hours in advance and limited night-time jocks to playing songs from a playlist of 100 songs. Daytime disc jockeys were even more restricted, to a playlist of just 50 songs.

Stations across the country tried various methods to battle payola in the hopes of staving off governmental intervention.

Since payola had been linked only to rock music, some stations abandoned the genre altogether. In Rocky Ford, Colo., KAVI station manager Ken O'Donnell pledged his station would play strictly "good family music" and proceeded to have his station's disc jockeys break one rock & roll record every 10 minutes until the station's 500-disc library was destroyed. "Any announcer on my staff who plays a rock & roll record in the future will be fired on the spot," O'Donnell said.[3]

Other stations sought to bring payola into the open by offering overt "pay for play" schemes. In Detroit, WJBK had a "sound special," where $300 bought one play per hour for a week. Another Detroit station, WKMH, offered a similar scheme for LPs.

WNEW in New York City, one of the top rock stations in the country, started referring to its announcers as "personalities" instead of disc jockeys. The more erudite personalities were forbidden to use jargon on the air and any songs they wished to play had to be pre-approved.

"For example, [station manager Jack] Sullivan said they will play Frankie Avalon, but won't play Fabian because his vocal quality is considered too poor."[4]

WNEW news director Martin Weldon convened a panel of four station personalities to discuss payola in a one-hour special. Naturally, none admitted to accepting payment for playing a record but Pete Myers conceded that his decision wasn't entirely a principled one.

"I have always turned it down because—well, maybe I am afraid of being caught. Probably that's it," Myers said.[5]

Dick Clark wasn't afraid of being caught. He'd done nothing wrong, he thought. Nevertheless, there were still some unresolved issues to be worked out. Hopefully, things could be settled when he was in New York for the *Saturday Night Show*.

---

3. *Billboard*, July 13, 1959.
4. *Billboard*, July 27, 1959.
5. Billboard, November 16, 1959.

SATURDAY, NOVEMBER 14, 1959

It wasn't the Saturday that Tony Mammarella had hoped for.

He had been looking forward to this day for some time. His boss and longtime friend Jack Steck was getting married. Steck, a 62-year-old widower and WFIL-TV program director, was marrying Florence Bendon, a popular singer that Steck had once fired from the WFIL staff decades earlier in a cost-cutting move.

Steck, who had hired Dick Clark and fired Bob Horn, was one of Mammarella's closest friends at the station that Mammarella had resigned from just the day before. It was with a measure of sadness that Mammarella and his wife, Agnes, attended the wedding of his old friend who was also the godfather to their 1-year-old daughter, Palmina.

Although the weekly trip to New York he'd made for nearly two years as producer of the *Saturday Night Show* was no longer necessary, Mammarella was headed to the city for a different reason—to meet with Clark about that affidavit and how best to go public.

The Saturday afternoon meeting with Clark, Clark's attorney Charles Seton and Clark's manager Marvin Josephson was brief. Clark's camp wanted to know the extent of Mammarella's previously undisclosed involvement with record companies, anything that might help Clark in upcoming investigations. When Seton suggested that Mammarella hire a good criminal lawyer, it was clear to Mammarella that he was to be made the scapegoat of any *Bandstand*-related payola probes.

I'll get a criminal lawyer when I commit a crime, Mammarella huffed, and returned to Philadelphia. Clark and Mammarella had been good friends, working within an arm's length from each other in their tiny, shared WFIL office for more than three years.

"In many ways, Tony was like a brother to me," Clark wrote in *Rock, Roll & Remember*. "But in the end, I found I really didn't know him. I certainly didn't know he had received money from several record companies in exchange for consultation."

It would be months before Clark and Mammarella had a civil conversation with each other.

Clark went ahead with his *Saturday Night Show* with Fabian, Jimmy Clanton, and Johnny & the Hurricanes, but his concentration was elsewhere. He was to meet with Leonard Goldenson on Sunday morning.

PAYING THE PIPER

SUNDAY, NOVEMBER 15, 1959
Clark arrived at Goldenson's home in Mamaroneck, N.Y., with manager Josephson and lawyer Seton, hoping to reassure his bosses that he had never accepted payola. To Clark's camp, that simply meant that he had never accepted specific payment in return for playing a specific record. That narrow definition of payola was much different than the working definition being used by the House committee that was investigating the practice.

In a confidential memo later sent to committee members by committee chief counsel Robert Lishman, investigators had uncovered 21 areas of music payola to investigate. These included favored treatment for record companies in which the deejay held a financial interest, record hops to promote a deejay's outside interests and deejays having a financial interest in artists performing on their programs—all areas which appeared to pertain to Clark.

Goldenson was worried. He had just recently learned of the depth of Clark's investments in the music industry and was concerned that Clark may have used *American Bandstand* to promote his own records, which was in violation of the network's conflict-of-interest policy.

"It looked like Dick and *Bandstand* might go down the drain," Goldenson said.[6]

In order to get to the bottom of this mess, Goldenson brought help to the meeting—his vice-president, Sy Siegel, and ABC general counsel Ev Erlick. The group set up shop for what promised to be a long day in the projection room of Goldenson's home theater. Even tucked away in the relative seclusion of Goldenson's own home, Clark mustered teenage support.

"My daughter Loreen was a teenager then and a big fan of Dick Clark," Goldenson said. "She kept trying to find ways to come in and watch. Somehow she got an idea of what we were doing, and became very worried that some harm might come to Dick."[7]

The meeting went well into the evening as the ABC executives grilled Clark on his music holdings and what role they played in selecting music for *American Bandstand*. Clark apparently defended himself well. His business ties played no role in what he played on the show, he said. The public decides what's a hit and

---
6. *Beating the Odds*, p. 163.
7. Ibid, pp. 163–164.

a million plays can't turn a dog into a best-seller. As to why he invested in record companies, pressing plants and music publishing, Clark responded that anyone who doesn't invest in the business he knows best is a damned fool. And, about that payola stuff, Clark steadfastly denied that he had ever taken any sort of payment to play a specific song. Goldenson bought it.

"When the day was over, I satisfied myself that Dick was clean," Goldenson said.[8]

The gathered assemblage proceeded to hammer out an affidavit that would satisfy both parties. When they were finished, they had a nine-page document that detailed the 33 businesses Clark owned or partially owned, including the music-related businesses he would be divesting from as part of the agreement to stay on with the network; his insistence that his business interests played no role in his selection of music for *American Bandstand* and that he had never received any payments in exchange for playing specific records.

There was one sticking point, however. The 18th paragraph referred to Tony Mammarella as a *Bandstand* staffer who, unbeknownst to Clark, had engaged in activities that would likely be construed as payola.

Goldenson, hoping that Clark would be spared if another villain were offered, had insisted on the reference, but Clark objected. Tony was like a brother to him, he argued. He deserves better. Goldenson relented and the paragraph was re-written, changing "Tony Mammarella" to "one of my programming associates."

Clark signed the affidavit.

MONDAY, NOVEMBER 16, 1959
Tony Mammarella and his wife, Agnes, were summoned to a 10 A.M. meeting at WFIL with Roger Clipp and George Koehler. The meeting was cordial, but there was no cause for celebration as they discussed Mammarella's formal separation from the station he had called home for most of his professional career.

When the Mammarellas returned home, they found Tony's mother was agitated after receiving what she said was a threatening phone call from a man claiming to be an investigator. Seeing his mother distraught was enough for Mammarella.

Now, he needed a lawyer.

---
8. Ibid, p. 164.

Mammarella wasn't the only person who thought the threat of a House investigation was more than a possibility. But most people thought the probe would begin in New York, just as the probe into quiz shows had. Indeed, two New York City newspapers—the *Journal American* and the *Post*—were reportedly working on extensive payola series.

Murray Kaufman, a popular disc jockey at WINS in New York, tried to head off any House probe by sending a letter to the subcommittee "wherein he said he spoke for '900 members' of a disk jockey group, and demanded an apology for the payola inferences."[9]

Kaufman's action prompted Bill Williams of rival station WNEW to quip: "This fellow representing himself as a spokesman for disk jockeys is like the bat boy speaking for the New York Yankees."[10]

The threat of a payola probe apparently was too much for a New York City public relations firm that had been retained by Clark. When word got out that Clark's business ties might sink the *American Bandstand* ship, Barkas & Shalit, Inc. bailed out. One of the partners, Gene Shalit, went on to become a popular member of NBC's *Today Show* crew, but Clark never forgave him, often referring to him as a "jellyfish" for abandoning Clark at a critical time.

TUESDAY, NOVEMBER 17, 1959
Marvin Josephson delivered a bombshell, issuing a statement that told the world what had been going on behind closed doors for the previous week: Dick Clark was getting out of the music business.

No, he wasn't quitting *American Bandstand*, just getting rid of some record manufacturing and music publishing companies. These investments were never a secret, Josephson said. Anyone who read Pete Martin's piece in the *Saturday Evening Post* a month earlier should know that.

Newsmen scrambled to learn more. They staked out the WFIL studios, where they tried to corner Clark after *American Bandstand* wrapped up for the day.

Sorry, fellas, can't talk right now he said as he piled into a car driven by his father and headed to New York City for his regular Tuesday night taping of *World of Talent*.

---
9. *Billboard*, November 16, 1959
10. Ibid

Tony Mammarella, however, was happy to make a statement.

He never took money for scheduling records on *Bandstand* or the *Saturday Night Show* he said. In fact, he said, he did thousands of favors for others without receiving any sort of payment. Yes, he was in a couple music-related businesses but that's not unusual in the entertainment business.

Mammarella even pointed to his own mortgage as proof he wasn't on the take—an $11,000 balance on a $19,000 home after nine years in the business.

But it was Clark that people really wanted to hear about.

As Clark was headed to New York, ABC issued a statement that must have put many teenagers at ease:

"Because of great public interest in certain areas of television programming, the American Broadcasting Co. is thoroughly investigating its own programs, with particular emphasis on those which feature disc jockeys and popular music. . . .

"We have concluded our investigation with renewed faith and confidence in Dick Clark's integrity."

But what those teenagers didn't know was that Clark had spent part of Tuesday afternoon with House investigators.

WEDNESDAY, NOVEMBER 18, 1959
Reporters at the *Philadelphia Evening Bulletin* had been working on a *Bandstand* scoop all week—a flap over a swimming pool, of all things.

Clark had run a contest earlier in the year where *Bandstand* viewers were invited to suggest names for a stuffed cat he displayed on the show. Sherry Lynn Stevens of Cleveland won the contest with the name "Platter Puss." First prize was a swimming pool.

The only catch was that the pool was to be built on a $5,000 lot in Punta Gorda Florida, which wouldn't even have an access road for another two years. But the Stevens' family wanted the $2,500 pool built in Cleveland so they sent registered letters to Clark and Tony Mammarella. When the letters were returned unopened and stamped "Unclaimed," they took their story to the *Cleveland Press*, which reported on the issue.

The controversy finally landed in the lap of WFIL program director Lew Klein, who passed the information on to Clark, who told Mammarella to see that the pool was built in Cleveland.

But, as the pool story was unfolding, reporters were shifting to the developing story about Clark getting out of the music business. You would think that Walter Annenberg's *Inquirer* would have had the inside track on any coverage of Clark, who was employed at another of Annenberg's properties, but it was the *Bulletin* that had the early lead in the Philadelphia payola sweepstakes.

It was *Bulletin* TV and radio columnist Bob Williams who gave House subcommittee chief counsel Robert Lishman a call earlier in the week that something big was going on with Clark, something probably worth investigating. It was Williams' call that prompted Lishman to send investigators Charles Howze and James Kelly to Philadelphia to interrogate Clark and Mammarella with instructions to report back by the end of the week.

Howze and Kelly managed to corner Clark briefly in his WFIL office on Tuesday afternoon before *Bandstand* and spent some time with Mammarella at his home in Delaware Township, N.J. They met with Mammarella again on Wednesday, for three hours in his lawyer's office in the Philadelphia National Bank Building.

Mammarella filled them in on his business activities. He was a partner in two publishing houses—Wildcat Music (BMI) and the Milton Kellem Co. (ASCAP), which was named for his partner, a well-known Philadelphia bandleader and restaurateur, who wrote more than 40 songs. The Wildcat connection proved especially profitable with the publishing of "Get a Job" by the Silhouettes, a song that received considerable airplay on *American Bandstand*.

Even more profitable was Mammarella's $7,000 cut of Charlie Gracie's "Butterfly." The song was written by Cameo's Bernie Lowe and Kal Mann, who (according to Mammarella) insisted he take writing credit for the song. Yes, Mammarella confessed, he was the Anthony September credited on the record as a songwriter. When it came time to share the songwriting cash, though, it was split three ways. Each man's take on the song, which sold an estimated 600,000 copies, was $7,000.

Nevertheless, Mammarella insisted, he had never accepted payola.

"As far as I am concerned, there was never a single kickback," he said. "That is ridiculous."[11]

The investigators had scheduled a second meeting with Clark following Wednesday's *American Bandstand* broadcast. Before

---

11. *Philadelphia Evening Bulletin,* November 19, 1959.

that meeting, though, Clark had a bit of tidying up to do. He took his case to the court of public opinion, addressing the huge teenage army of Bandstandland. At 4 P.M., the camera zoomed in on Clark at his most comfortable place in the world, standing at the lectern of *American Bandstand*.

"Hello," he said, staring straight into the camera that was radiating his familiar smile from coast to coast. "You and I have talked many times in the past. Maybe some of you are looking in today for the first time.

"If we've never met, my name is Dick Clark. You know it's always been the ambition of every television performer, every entertainer, every singer, every night club performer to get his name in the papers.

"My name has been in the papers, on television and radio quite a bit in the last 24 hours. You've probably wondered what on earth it's all about.

"All this morning and a good part of this afternoon, people have called me, said wonderful things and sent me telegrams.

"And patted me on the back and said, 'Don't worry, everything will be all right.' It's a very wonderful thing to know you have friends, amongst which I hope I count you.

"Now if by any chance you haven't heard as yet of the ABC statement in my behalf regarding the investigation of the music business, I would like to read it to you, because if you haven't read it I'd like to have the opportunity of my telling you about it."

Clark then read the ABC statement that exonerated him. After reading the statement, Clark leaned into the camera and said: "I want you to know as a friend that I appreciate, as I said before, your kind words and encouragement and the fact that the people I work for stand behind me.

"Here's *American Bandstand*."

Teenagers in the audience applauded and the theme music began.

THURSDAY, NOVEMBER 19, 1959
As word of Howze and Kelly's questioning of Clark and Mammarella in Philadelphia spread, a subcommittee spokesperson leaked news that other Philadelphia disc jockeys were also being investigated and that their tax records had been examined by IRS investigators in recent months. After Philadelphia, the probe was

titled *Rockin'*. On Clark's show, Laine mimed his latest Columbia single, obviously aimed at the teen market, "Rockin' Mother."

So, for three minutes that Saturday night, an aging singer who was struggling to stay relevant in a business that his producer thought was slipping into mediocrity sang a feeble song to an audience full of teenagers more attuned to Eddie Cochran and Fabian on a show hosted by a man who just days earlier pledged to get out of the music business.

Should anyone be surprised that "Rockin' Mother" never made the charts?

* * *

The very fate of Bandstandland was in jeopardy as Dick Clark prepared for what he hoped would be a routine *American Bandstand* on Monday, November 23, 1959. Things had sure changed in just a few days. Although he had been cleared by ABC, Clark knew that payola was far from settled in the public's mind.

But while Alan Freed was dealing with the disgrace of having been fired from a prestigious radio job, Clark at least had the solace of knowing that he had fended off public criticism, at least for a while.

It was just dumb luck that a color portrait of a clean-cut and smiling Clark was the cover photo of the November 24 edition of *Look* magazine. Inside were several more flattering Clark photos and excerpts from his book, *Your Happiest Years*.

Not so flattering was the article in that week's *Life* magazine entitled "Gimme, Gimme, Gimme on the Old PAYOLA." The four-page article attempted to explain payola to its readers. In addition to an essay from Ed McKenzie, the deejay who quit his job at a Detroit station eight months earlier in protest over "formula radio," the article included 13 pictures, including one of Clark and his recently deposed cohort, Tony Mammarella, in the WFIL office they shared. There was even a glossary of payola terms, like "dead presidents" ($20 and $50 bills).

Readers of the *Life* article may have been left with the impression that deejays faced all sorts of temptation from unscrupulous record promoters and salespeople but, fortunately, were governed by a solid moral compass that allowed them to resist the evils all those dead presidents represented.

The reality, however, was quite different.

Freed wasn't the only disc jockey to lose his job over the weekend. In fact, Detroit DJs lost three of them in a 36-hour span., all from WIBG's sister station, WJBK. Thomas Clay was the first to go. Clay was fired on Saturday night after he admitted to accepting $6,000 to plug records. Don McLeod resigned the next day for undisclosed reasons, and Dale Young, the host of WJBK-TV's *Detroit Bandstand,* also resigned.

The station's newscasters were not immune, either. They were forbidden to comment on either the quiz show scandal or the developing payola probe, but that didn't stop the station's most respected TV news anchor, Jac LeGoff, from editorializing on air about payola, putting the practice on a par with a businessman buying lunch to woo a prospective customer. LeGoff was axed, too.

Even though Freed had lost his radio job, he still had his daily afternoon dance show on WNEW-TV. Until Monday, that is, when he was told he could host the show just through the end of the week, when Bill Hayes, the singer who scored a big hit with *The Ballad of Davy Crockett* a few years earlier, would be taking over.

Freed was livid about losing two jobs in three days, especially after seeing ABC throw all its support behind Dick Clark. House investigators caught up with Freed in New York early in the week and spent two days questioning him about his business and poring over his finances.

The incensed Freed also squeezed in an interview with *New York Post* columnist Earl Wilson that appeared mid-week.

In the interview, Freed conceded that his firing from WABC was a result of his own hubris. "I've never been able to accept a station manager telling me, you've GOT to do something," Freed told Wilson. Freed also freely admitted that he'd accepted gifts, but that he'd never taken payola.

"I've never taken a bribe," he told Wilson. "I would throw anybody down the steps who suggested it. Somebody said to me once, 'If somebody sent you a Cadillac, would you send it back?' I said, 'It depends on the color'."

Freed said he resented being labeled a disc jockey when he was actually "an entertainer, motion picture star, and a few other things." He claimed to have information on unnamed others who had accepted money to play records and hinted that he may share his information with the District Attorney and investigators in Washington. But he didn't hesitate when asked about Dick Clark.

"I feel this guy [Clark] should be investigated. If I'm going to be a scapegoat, he's going to be one, too. He's on about 300 stations, I'm on one," Freed said.[15]

Although Wilson managed to track Freed down long enough to do a phone interview for his column, Freed was hard for others to find that week as he shuffled around New York City. New York City detectives spent much of Wednesday looking for Freed to serve a subpoena and had just about given up when they saw him on screen in his *Big Beat* program on WNEW-TV. After the show, they cornered Freed in the lobby and ordered him to appear before a grand jury on November 30.

Elsewhere in the Post that day it was reported that Clark would be summoned to Washington to testify before the Harris Subcommittee on December 9. But a subcommittee spokesperson quickly clarified that Clark's appearance was likely several weeks away, because of the many tips the committee was receiving. The subcommittee was to convene again on December 9 but to continue its probe of Boston industrialist Bernard Goldfine, whose gifts to former presidential aide Sherman Adams had come under scrutiny.

As House subcommittee investigators fanned out around the country, two other federal agencies were preparing to launch their own payola investigations.

The Federal Trade Commission was looking into the possibility that payola violated the agency's rules against unfair practices, like commercial bribery. Federal Communications Commission Chairman John C. Doerfer scheduled public hearings to begin on December 7 after receiving a complaint from the American Guild of Authors and Composers that payola ran much deeper than disc jockeys.

Guild president Burton Lane was especially critical of ABC's forcing Clark out of the music business because "ABC is permitted to own and operate far greater music interests of its own, which include the important recording company, known as Am-Par Record Corp."[16]

Am-Par had grown so rapidly since its 1955 creation that many in the business considered it one of the country's major labels. Label president Sam Clark once said he was reluctant to sign anyone over the age of 17 to a recording contract. Besides being owned

---
15. *New York Post*, Earl Wilson, November 25, 1959.
16. *Associated Press*, November 24, 1959.

by ABC-TV's parent company, the label had another connection to Philadelphia. Director of sales Larry Newton had started his record career in Philadelphia 20 years earlier and was responsible for Am-Par's deal to press, sell and distribute Chancellor records.

And Lane's claim was true. There were no signs that Leonard Goldenson was planning to shed Am-Par from ABC's corporate stable.

On Friday, Alan Freed prepared for his final *Big Beat* dance show. He arrived at the studio wearing the red plaid jacket he had worn to all openings and closings since his first wife, Jackie, gave it to him in 1952. Freed was in a jovial mood, talking and dancing with the teens who filled the studio. Then he interrupted the playing of Little Anthony & the Imperials' "Shimmy Shimmy Ko Ko Bop" to announce that this would be his last show. After the show, he held a press conference, once again denying that he'd ever taken payola but acknowledging he'd accepted checks from record companies and distributors for "consultation work."

Dick Clark made it through the week without directly addressing payola, politely refusing comment to all inquiries. Almost lost in the payola hubbub was the fact that ABC was canceling his Sunday night show, *World of Talent*.

The show had poor ratings from the start and critics panned it for being dull and failing to live up to its promise of delivering promising young amateurs to its stage. Beginning on December 20, *World of Talent*'s slot would be filled by re-runs of *21 Beacon Street*.

Despite the distractions, Clark had welcomed a reporter from New York who asked to follow him around for a couple of days, presumably to write a story sympathetic to Clark's plight. After the reporter returned to New York, Clark and his wife went out for a dinner date with friends, leaving their son, Dickie, in the care of a babysitter.

The babysitter was soon visited by a man claiming to be the reporter. When he was told the Clarks weren't home, he entered the house anyway, telling the babysitter "That's all right. I can get what I want just by glancing around."

Clark blew up when he returned home and learned what had happened.

"I wished he were still there, in the house, so I could belt him one in the nose," Clark said.[17]

---

17. *Modern Screen*, "Thank God For Barbara," August 1960.

PAYING THE PIPER

* * *

Alan Freed, who had spent the better part of two days talking to House investigators a week earlier and who proclaimed he had no involvement in all this payola business before a press contingent just a few days earlier, suddenly clammed up.

As instructed, Freed appeared before a New York City grand jury on November 30, 1959, but never actually testified. When representatives of the district attorney's office were informed that Freed would be asserting his Fifth Amendment rights and would not be answering any questions, his appearance was scratched. Instead, DA Frank Hogan issued a subpoena for Freed's television records.

Things may have been put temporarily on hold in New York, but there were curious goings-on in Boston. At one point it was reported that five disc jockeys were leaving station WILD because their contracts had expired. They were simply too expensive for the station, a spokesman said, adding that payola was not a factor.

However, two of the five had ties to an infamous disc jockey convention in Miami the previous Memorial Day weekend. WILD deejay Joe Smith had been on the convention planning committee and Stan Richards later admitted that a $117 clothing bill from the Miami gathering was paid for by a record company.

When it came time to explain his actions, Richards said that payola "seems to be the American way of life, which is a wonderful way of life. It is primarily built on romance: 'I'll do for you. What will you do for me?'"[18]

The quote reportedly outraged President Eisenhower but pretty well mirrored the attitude of payola's supporters at the time. The outrageous behavior of the music industry in Miami was the spark that finally ignited the House probe.

The convention was the brainchild of Todd Storz, the Omaha-based creator of Top 40 radio. Storz had held a moderately successful similar convention in March 1958 in Kansas City, Mo. Ironically, many of the 900 attendees were critics of Top 40. The biggest news coming out of Kansas City that weekend came from keynote speaker Mitch Miller who blasted radio stations for

---
18. *Life*, May 16, 1960, p. 122.

catering to "the pre-shave crowd" at the expense of the adults in their audience who "are yearning for a break from the noise on the radio."[19]

Things would be different in Miami, Storz vowed. There would be bus tours of South Florida for the wives while their husbands attended seminars and workshops. Pres. Eisenhower filmed a welcoming address to be followed by a presentation by Dr. Shane McElroy of Ike's Council on Youth Fitness who urged jocks to use their airtime to promote youth fitness.

Best of all, it wouldn't cost disc jockeys a thing, according to promotional material distributed before the convention:

"No cost to DJs and station management personnel for any of the functions. These are completely underwritten by America's leading record companies. Thus, expenses are limited to transportation and hotel accommodations, all of which are tax-deductible, according to competent legal counsel."

Some of the biggest names in the radio and television business would be appearing on panels, like Buddy Deane, Art Ford, Gordon McClendon, and Martin Block. And, of course, those record companies would be bringing along a few of their artists, so many, in fact, that there would be an all-star concert on Saturday night at convention headquarters, the swanky Americana Hotel.

ABC-Paramount was providing limousine rides from the airport to the Americana and Columbia was giving each deejay a record carrying case. Dot Records rented the Goodyear blimp, which was often seen floating above Bal Harbour, pulling a streamer promoting Pat Boone.

Capitol Records said they would stage a recording session with Peggy Lee and George Shearing at a Friday night cocktail party. RCA Victor was offering a special recording suite where deejays could record interviews with entertainers or have photographs taken to be mailed to their hometown newspapers. The convention would officially kick off with a Thursday night cocktail reception (hosted by Mercury Records), but many deejays arrived as early as Monday, taking advantage of special Americana early bird rates as low as $10 a night.

Miami mayor Robert King proclaimed May 24–31 as "Disc Jockey Week in Miami," citing their "admirable dedication to the improvement of the standard of their profession and of popular music in general."

---

19. *Billboard*, March 17, 1958.

PAYING THE PIPER

Following a convention-opening breakfast (hosted by United Artists Records) on Friday, Harold Fellows, president of the National Association of Broadcasters, delivered the keynote address in which he warned that deejays should not be so self-absorbed as to think they are more important than the station that employs them.

However, Fellows said, "It is wonderful to know that all of you are sufficiently serious about your professional pursuits that you can and will take the time in such a forum as this, to counsel with each other. Broadcasting will be the better for it, you will be the better for it, and America, which needs you in all her homes, will be the better, too."[20]

Then the 2,500 people (including just one female, Ann Wagner of WFBM in Indianapolis) in attendance took part in a weekend of "professional pursuits" that would later be detailed in a *Miami Herald* story provocatively headlined, "Booze, Broads, and Bribes." *Variety* described it as a drunken orgy and Marc Fisher called it "a bacchanalia" in his book, *Something In the Air*.

It was obvious from the start that the deejay confab had much more to offer than the Americana's Gaucho Steak House, Dominion Coffee House, and Carioca Lounge. In fact, only a fraction of the deejays in Miami that weekend, about 720 of them, were registered hotel guests, most staying elsewhere, courtesy of the record companies.

Upon arrival, each deejay was given $1 million in play money, courtesy of RCA Victor. They could win even more by gambling in games that were rigged in the deejays' favor or they could stop by the RCA suite for a free drink and pick up another $5,000 each time. At the end of the convention, they could use the play money at a real auction for real merchandise, including color television sets, trips to Europe and a Studebaker Lark.

You might think that Saturday night's all-star show that featured at least 17 acts, including Pat Boone, Peggy Lee, Vic Damone, Andy Williams, and Count Basie, would be the biggest attraction of the weekend. You'd be wrong.

The convention was a non-stop affair, where free-flowing alcohol and bikini-clad women were in ample supply around the clock. At the Panama Records suite, for example, self-service faucets were labeled "Martinis" and "Manhattans." Author William

---
20. *Billboard*, June 1, 1959.

Barlow said, "the convention featured one of the largest contingents of hookers ever assembled in a Miami Beach Hotel."[21]

"In the words of Paul Marshall, who attended the event, '[Atlantic Records'] Ahmet [Ertegun] hired a certain number of hookers. However, he got them gowns and introduced them as the cream of Miami debutante society. And he told them he would double their fee if they did not have sex with the guests."[22]

If gambling with play money wasn't a deejay's thing, he could partake of the real thing, with the right connections.

Even the least known of the deejays in Miami could find room on a yacht fully-loaded with booze and an all-female crew. Once the yacht was a few miles off the coast, inhibitions and clothing were discarded and the partying got serious. Some of the better-known, hit-making jocks piled onto a plane for a quick hop to Cuba, where new dictator Fidel Castro hadn't yet shut down the nightclubs, casinos, and brothels.

Marshall Chess, the 17-year-old son of Chess Records co-founder Leonard Chess, would later remember that he smoked marijuana for the first time at the Miami convention and witnessed a circle of people throwing down $100 bets on how long a specific sex act would last.[23]

"It was the greatest party I have ever been to in my life," recalled former Cleveland deejay Joe Finan. "I was there ostensibly to give a speech on public service. I gave it, but I was so juiced and so hungover I don't even know what I said. But I will never forget the hookers down there."[24]

As big as the Saturday night concert was, it was the after-party that was the hottest ticket of the weekend. Morris Levy, the owner of Roulette Records (and former manager of Alan Freed), was bankrolling an all-night, poolside recording session by Count Basie's Band that would also include a late-night barbecue dinner and an early morning breakfast for those who could stay up all night.

Besides paying the band and all expenses for the recording session itself, Levy paid a little over $15,000 for the barbecue/breakfast. It was the breakdown of those expenses that proved eye-popping. Breakfast cost Levy $2,360 and the barbecue was

---

21. *Voice Over: The Making of Black Radio*, William Barlow, p. 187.
22. *The Last Sultan*, p. 128.
23. Ibid
24. *The Pied Pipers of Rock 'n' Roll*. p. 34.

another $4,205, but the bar tab was a staggering $8,850. That included 2,000 bottles of bourbon.

When Edward E. Eicher of Americana Hotel later testified before the Harris Subcommittee looking into payola, he was asked why the discrepancy between the breakfast bill and that for alcohol.

"Bourbon costs a little bit more than eggs," Eicher replied.[25]

There probably was some legitimate business conducted in Miami that weekend, but it clearly wasn't what made the news. The Miami papers were not kind in their appraisal of the gathering. Besides the *Herald's* attention-grabbing headline, the *Miami News* called the deejays "little tin gods." At least one newspaper account said it was the prostitutes—not the disc jockeys—who held most of RCA's play money at the convention's conclusion and were the highest bidders for the top items at the auction.

The bad press continued for weeks as *Time* called it "The Big Payola," *Newsweek* called it "the flip side of paradise" and *Life* printed a photo of deejays tossing hundreds of dollar bills into the air in the Americana lobby.

Alan Freed, who was in Miami that weekend but managed to stay out of the public eye, lightheartedly said he spent the weekend protecting his wife, Inga, from Mitch Miller, who he alleged was making passes at her. At one point, a jovial Freed playfully tossed Inga into the pool.

Ultimately, Miami was too much for America's disc jockeys to overcome. Todd Storz had entered the weekend saying he wasn't willing to underwrite a third convention. It just took too much of his time.

But Bill Gavin, a former deejay whose *Gavin Report* was a must-read for Top 40 stations, was attempting to rally deejays into a national organization that could take the lead in organizing similar events in the future. After Miami, he claimed to have at least 50 interested jockeys and music directors.

But the damage was done. There would not be a third convention.

* * *

With Alan Freed squarely in the cross-hairs of payola probers in Washington and New York, Dick Clark had some time to

---

25. United Press International, February 2, 1960.

regroup and work on his own response should he be summoned to Washington, which seemed inevitable.

While Freed was asserting his Fifth Amendment rights at the courthouse, the *New York Post* was reporting on Clark's ties to Sun Records. It was the promotion of Jerry Lee Lewis' "Breathless" in early 1958 that had captured the attention of *Post* reporter William H.A. Carr.

At the time of the promotion, Clark was struggling to find sponsors for his then-new *Saturday Night Show*. While wooing Beech-Nut Gum, Clark and Sun owner Sam Phillips came up with a scheme that looked like a win-win-win. If viewers sent in five Beech-Nut Gum wrappers and 50 cents, they would be mailed a 45 of "Breathless."

Clark promoted the song on his shows, which boosted sales for Sun and proved the show's teenage appeal to Beech-Nut officials. Lewis gave up his royalties for records sold in the promotion, as did publishers of "Breathless" and the flip side, "Down the Line." Clark received a check for $2,746.82 for his role in the promotion.

The Sun deal certainly didn't fit Clark's narrow definition of payola, but investigators weren't so sure. It was just one of the areas they were looking into as regulators struggled to learn if there was a real problem in the music business and if they should be stepping in. By early December, it was clear that the matter wasn't going away anytime soon.

The Federal Communications Commission ordered each of the nation's 5,000-plus radio and television stations to report, under oath, whether any of their employees had accepted secret payments to plug persons or products.

The Federal Trade Commission said that it would soon take action against several record companies for payola deals that may have violated federal laws barring unfair methods of competition. The National Association of Broadcasters said it would help by increasing its monitoring of commercial advertising by 400 percent, from 20,000 hours in 1959 to 100,000 hours in 1960.

It became apparent to ABC network executives that the ripples from the expanding federal investigations still threatened *American Bandstand*. They decided someone would have to keep an eye on Dick Clark down there in Philadelphia. They settled on a recent hire, Chuck Barris.

Barris seemed uniquely suited to the task. He was a native Philadelphian and a graduate of Drexel Institute of Technology, where he had been an all-East lacrosse player and a columnist for the student paper.

Following college, he moved on to New York, where he landed a job as a page at NBC-TV. He soon moved into a management training program. After completing the program, Barris was assigned to daytime TV sales before the entire department was wiped out a few months later in an efficiency move. He knocked around Europe for a few months, tried selling Teleprompters for a bit and took a temporary gig promoting an Ingemar Johansson-Floyd Patterson heavyweight fight, but was unable to find steady work.

Even his marriage to Lyn Levy, the niece of CBS co-founder William S. Paley and whose father served on the CBS board, didn't help. Barris had even applied for work as a spy with the CIA around the same time he was hired by ABC. After the payola investigation broke, ABC's head of daytime television, Julian Bercovici, recruited Barris to keep an eye on Clark.

It would only be for a few weeks, Barris was told. You can commute down there every day and report back to us on what you see. So, outfitted in a new, corporate suit, Barris began his daily commute—1 hour and 45 minutes each way by train—a commute that would last several months.

Clark and his boss, George Koehler, knew why Barris was there, but the rest of the WFIL staff was in the dark about Barris' duties. Since Barris spent time with Ed Yates in the control room and with Walt Beaulieu in the remote truck, some thought he was in training to become a director. Since he spent time talking to salespeople and setting up commercials, some thought he was some sort of advertising coordinator.

But mostly he just hung around, playing chess with announcer Charlie O'Donnell or engaging guests in conversation.

"I shook Brenda Lee's hand and told her she had a great future in the business," he wrote in his book, *The Game Show King*. "She thanked me and walked away. I had no idea she already had nine gold records."

Announcer John Carlton, who often drove Barris to the train station in the evening, found Barris to be engaging with a "delightful sense of humor," but conceded that "he was a little bit off to the side." Ad man Les Waas found Barris' presence to be annoying since they were about the same size and wore similar clothing. "People were always confusing us," Waas said.

Barris, who enjoyed his daily train rides because it gave him a chance to catch up on his reading or squeeze in a quick nap, was grateful for the job but found his hours in the *American Bandstand* studio to be largely a waste of time.

"It was so ridiculous," Barris said in an Archive of American Television interview. "If I left at 6 o'clock, what's to say [Clark] couldn't be doing nothing nefarious after 6 o'clock? It was so silly. I spent my time writing these dumb little reports every day. . . . They piled up in cartons."

Plus, Barris said, "everybody in the studio hated me. They thought I was Benedict Arnold, a major spy that had come to spy on them, but Dick loved me because he knew I was his lifesaver."

CHAPTER 14

PAYOLA

However Chuck Barris spent his days at WFIL, he didn't spend much time hanging out with those ubiquitous record promotion men he was told to keep an eye out for. Ever since news of the payola probes broke, they were scarcely seen.

"All you do with a new record today is leave it at the station," one song plugger complained about the changing Philadelphia scene.[1] Philadelphia was not unique.

"No longer are the lobbies of the Brill Building [in New York City] or its annex thronged with diverse music businessmen, wildly ecstatic over a newly recorded song or a newly released disk. . . . Disk jockeys cannot be reached by phone, distributors are out of town, a.&r. men are suddenly vacationing and many record company officials are answering their phones in soft, whispery voices."[2]

The networks were running scared, too. NBC's mandatory notarized questionnaires from employees extended the query to music business interests of relatives as well. The network even threatened to pull a payola skit from its popular *Bob Hope Show* but relented after Hope complained. CBS threatened to fire any employee accepting questionable gifts and any deejay who failed

---
1. *Billboard*, December 14, 1959.
2. *Billboard*, December 7, 1959.

to turn in his next day's playlist on time. It also banned mentions of products not directly related to a show's sponsors, a once-lucrative income source.

Individual stations, feeling the threat of losing their licenses (even though the FCC hadn't pulled a license since 1932), took payola seriously, too. At WCPO in Cincinnati, general manager Mort C. Watters, invited two dozen local record distributors to the station so he could outline the station's code of ethics that barred deejays from accepting free lunches or gifts valued at more than $5.

In Cleveland, two popular KYW disc jockeys were fired after it was determined that they had accepted payments from the local RCA Victor distributor. Although Joe Finan and Wes Hopkins claimed the payouts were "listening fees" for acting as "consultants," their protests were undermined by the fact that the distributor made payment by check with each check listing the specific record that was to be plugged. Payments were made in a third-floor restroom, dubbed "the payola booth."

Nationally, however, Alan Freed continued to be payola's poster boy.

Life magazine's December 7, 1959, issue ran a short article with five photos under the headline, "Payola Axes King Freed." The article detailed Freed's income as a consultant to record companies, which he described as "the backbone of American business."

One of the photos showed Freed accepting a scroll of appreciation from song pluggers that was presented to him at his final radio show. "Payola, payola, that's all you've been hearing," Freed told *Life*. "These are the nicest guys in the business."

The *New York Post* reported that Roulette Records held a mortgage on Freed's Greycliff mansion in Wallachs Point, Conn. Freed was fond of telling visitors the story behind each of the 16 rooms in the stucco house that overlooked Long Island Sound.

"Over there," he'd say, pointing to the den, "you see that room? That was built by Frankie Lymon! And there, you see the bedroom? Chuck Berry did that for me. . . . Over there, that's Atlantic Records' pool."[3]

Freed's lengthy association with Morris Levy also piqued the interest of congressional investigators. Dubbed "the Octopus" by

---

3. *Rockonomics: The Money Behind the Music*, p. 81.

Variety magazine, Levy had his hands in virtually every facet of the music business. A onetime proprietor of New York jazz club Birdland, Levy also owned several record labels at one time or another, including Roulette. Among his vast music holdings was a songwriting credit for Lymon's biggest hit, "Why Do Fools Fall in Love."

Levy befriended Freed when the Moondog arrived in New York from Cleveland and once was Freed's manager. He was also the money behind the all-night barbecue and recording session that concluded the debauchery of the infamous deejay convention in Miami.

New York district attorney Frank Hogan was eager to look into Freed's relationship with Levy. While Hogan's investigative team questioned Bobby Darin, Les Paul and Mary Ford about Freed, the Federal Trade Commission was zeroing in some of Dick Clark's associates in Philadelphia.

Under federal law, the FTC viewed payola as an unfair method of competition and a deceptive practice. Less than a month into its investigation, the FTC warned that complaints would be filed before Christmas. On December 4 they issued their first complaints, alleging that three record companies and five independent distributors from Philadelphia had paid unnamed disc jockeys to play records. Among those charged were five of Clark's recent business associates: Bernie Lowe, Ed Barsky, Harry Chipetz, Harold B. Lipsius and Harry Finfer.

Although Clark had told ABC-Paramount president Leonard Goldenson that he would get entirely out of the music business, the *New York Post* reported on December 16 that Clark had not yet divested himself of his holdings and that ABC executives had little information about what Clark's business connections actually were.

When reporters Alfred T. Hendricks and William H.A. Carr asked ABC public relations vice-president Michael Foster what Clark's business ventures were, Foster replied: "I'm damned if I know. . . . I doubt if anyone at the network knows."[4]

When they asked Chuck Barris (identified as network supervisor for Clark's shows), he said: "The names of the companies will not be made public at this time . . . I'm not quite sure myself how many companies there are."[5]

---
4. New York Post, December 16, 1959.
5. Ibid.

The *Post* story identified at least 11 companies in which Clark still had a financial stake. The only company they found that Clark had gotten out of was Mallard, a record pressing company. Clark would not talk to the reporters and his manager, Marvin Josephson, would not comment.

Although payola had shaken the music business, few Americans seemed to share that concern.

A national poll by Elmo Roper found that 37 percent of respondents hadn't even heard of payola. From a list of national issues, 89 percent thought juvenile delinquency was a major issue, followed by the arms race and corrupt union leaders. At the bottom of the list, at 34 percent, was "disc jockeys taking money from record companies."

Kevin Sweeney, president of the Radio Advertising Bureau, called payola "the most over-played news story of 1959."

Some TV dance shows had been canceled since news of payola broke, but similar teen dance shows in Chicago, Washington, D.C., and Baltimore claimed to be flourishing, with waiting lists of sponsors who wanted to advertise on their shows.

One hot seller aimed at the pre-teen market that Christmas season was Abbey-Teen's $8.95 dress shirt that featured press-on photo decals of Frankie Avalon, Fabian, and Clark, among others. Avalon and Fabian were on hand at the WFIL studios on New Year's Eve as Clark hosted a 90-minute *New Year's Eve Party* on the ABC-TV network.

As the countdown to a new decade began, Clark had to be saying to himself: I hope 1960 starts a lot better than 1959 ended.

* * *

All the buzz about payola had gotten the attention of President Dwight D. Eisenhower. As the FCC and FTC ramped up their investigations, Pres. Eisenhower asked U.S. Attorney General William P. Rogers to look into the matter. Ike's concern was whether existing laws and staffing were adequate to deal with the problem.

On December 31, 1959, Rogers reported back to the President. Statutes were adequate, he said, but they needed to be used more effectively. He suggested that the FCC and FTC clean house before legislative action be taken.

That wasn't what Oren Harris wanted to hear. As chairman of the House Interstate and Foreign Commerce Legislative Oversight

Committee, he was itching to start hearings into the whole payola business. After weeks of delays, he decided to start hearings in Washington on February 8, 1960.

Satirist Stan Freberg placed deejays in the curious position of having to decide whether to play a song about their plight with his record, "The Old Payola Blues." The clichéd storyline of the song went like this: record producer plucks good-looking teenager who can't sing from the streets, records him and then pays a disc jockey to help turn the song into a hit.

In a direct swipe at Fabian, the teenager in the song (named Clyde Ankle) protests that he can't sing. The record producer says that's OK, his pretty face and pompadour are good enough. When Clyde asks, "Well, do I get to pose beside a tiger?" (which Fabian had done for the cover of his *Hold That Tiger* LP), he was told "Nah that's been done. Maybe we'll get you a moose."[6]

On January 8, 1960, Dick Clark had scored another coup—an on-air phone interview on *American Bandstand* from Germany with Elvis Presley on Presley's 25th birthday. Interest in Elvis was running especially high since he was soon to be discharged from the Army and he was rumored to be setting up a joint television program with a teen favorite from another era, Frank Sinatra.

But the *New York Post* was still focused on payola. The same day that Clark talked to Elvis, the *Post's* William H.A. Carr reported that Clark had secured most of the rights to "16 Candles" by the Crests at no cost to him and netted some $10,000 in royalties after turning the song into a hit that sold some 600,000 copies.

The song was relatively obscure before Clark became involved. On December 15, 1958, the title, copyright, all the mechanical rights, and half of the performing rights to "16 Candles" were shifted to Clark's January Music Corp. Clark was listed as president in corporation filings; his wife, Barbara, was secretary and his mother-in-law, Mrs. M.M. Mallery, was vice-president.

Before Clark's company acquired the publishing, Clark had played "16 Candles" just four times in 10 weeks. After January Music acquired the song, "16 Candles" was played 27 times in 13 weeks and shot up the charts.[7]

January Music was established by Clark to handle songs licensed through BMI, the most popular music rights organization of the rock & roll era. ASCAP devotees derisively referred to BMI

---

6. Freberg Music Corp. (ASCAP), 1959.
7. *Anti-Rock: The Opposition to Rock 'n' Roll*, p. 93.

as "Bad Music Incorporated," but with the rise of rock & roll, it started to be known as "Big Money Incorporated," a distinction that further fanned the flames of resentment in the ASCAP community.

A few ASCAP members had filed a $150 million antitrust suit against BMI in 1953, accusing it of conspiracy to dominate the market. In 1958, ASCAP lobbyists led a failed effort to push Congress to divorce broadcasters from ownership in BMI.

In testimony before the FCC on January 11, the two sides again squared off. ASCAP president Stanley Adams accused BMI of using payola to force its records on deejays and once again called upon the FCC to force broadcasters to divest themselves of any BMI holdings.

BMI board chairman Sydney M. Kaye responded by calling ASCAP's charges a diversionary tactic intended to cover up ASCAP's own misdeeds.

The BMI-ASCAP dispute was of little consequence to Clark, who had bought Arch Music for the express purpose of handling ASCAP-licensed songs. Just like January Music, Arch was among the music-related businesses that Clark was trying to sell as part of his agreement with Leonard Goldenson.

Another of Clark's businesses, Jamie Records, had also been recently charged by the FTC with using payola to influence disc jockeys. At WFIL, station executives for parent company Triangle Publications announced that screening committees at each of Triangle's broadcast stations would in the future decide which records to play. In addition, the station would buy those records, estimated at 50 per week at each station.

Meanwhile, Rep. Oren Harris had his staff busily preparing for the subcommittee hearings. In mid-January, he dispatched investigators Oliver Eastland, Charles Howze and James P. Kelly to Chicago to look into payola charges there. Harris had a $410,000 budget for the hearings, which were expected to last a week. He expanded his staff of 25 by adding six new investigators and two new clerks.

Clark tried to maintain business as usual. He launched a "Name the Mascot" contest on the *Saturday Night Show* to coincide with the premiere of his movie *Because They're Young*.

When his old neighbors from Mount Vernon, Arthur and Kathryn Murray, asked him for help in re-energizing their NBC network dance show with young talent, Clark was more than willing to help. The Murrays offered to devote a show entirely to Clark and his career and he reciprocated by offering a tribute to their contributions to dance on his *Saturday Night Show*.

Clark found moral support from the Trenton, N.J., Junior Chamber of Commerce, which presented him with the keys to the city for his "wholesome influence on the Nation's youth."

One of *American Bandstand*'s most popular regulars, Myrna Horowitz, defended Clark in the January 1960 issue of *Modern Screen* magazine., saying "I, for one, am behind Dick Clark, no matter what."[8]

But life was anything but usual for Clark.

"I remember having to go to the corner drugstore, to a phone booth, to call my lawyer, because I knew our phones were tapped," Clark told Joe Smith in a 1986 interview. "Government agents broke into my house. They were a tough bunch of cookies."[9]

Clark's lawyer had warned him early on that it was possible that New York City district attorney Frank Hogan might serve him with a subpoena to appear before a grand jury. Hogan would have to serve the subpoena in New York so Clark was told to be cautious when in the city.

"For the next six months, I sneaked in and out of New York City," Clark wrote in his autobiography, *Rock, Roll & Remember*. "Ed McAdam drove me up by car. When we got to the Lincoln Tunnel I would lie down in the backseat, pulling a blanket over myself. I'd stay there until we got to the stage entrance of the Little Theater. Once Ed gave me the all-clear sign, I dashed out of the car into the theater. Then we locked the theater doors while we did the broadcast. I felt like a damned fugitive."[10]

Clark's bosses at ABC apparently had some empathy for what their star afternoon attraction was going through, although it was more likely the knowledge that Clark shows were responsible for a hefty chunk of the company's bottom line that led to "a modification" (i.e., "a raise") of Clark's seven-year contract with the network.

The negotiations took place in January but weren't made public until two months later because, as ABC vice-president Tom Moore said in March "the less said about Clark at this time the better."[11]

---

8. *Modern Screen*, "Dick Clark I Love You," January 1960."
9. *Off the Record*, p. 105.
10. *Rock, Roll & Remember*, p. 191.
11. *New York Herald Tribune*, Marie Torre column, March 28, 1960.

Although the Harris Subcommittee public hearings didn't begin until February 8, the subcommittee held closed-door sessions in late January with several of Clark's business associates.

That included Harry Chipetz and Bernie Lowe, Clark's partners in Chips Distributing. Testimony showed that Clark's $10,000 investment in Chips netted him $23,000 at the time of divestment. Chipetz also testified that Chips paid DJs close to $20,000 in 1958 and 1959, but added that he had no idea whether Clark was aware of the transactions.

Lowe, who also was co-owner with Clark of Mallard Record Pressing, testified that Mallard didn't really own any record presses but had an arrangement with Stenton Music that guaranteed Stenton one million pressings a year. The arrangement grossed Mallard $800,000 from May 1958 to November 1959, according to Lowe. Clark's investment of $7,500 had grown to $30,534 at the time of divestiture.

Lowe, who also co-owned Cameo Records, acknowledged that he paid Clark $7,000 out of gratitude for Clark's help in pushing Cameo's first big hit, "Butterfly." Lowe testified that Clark refused the payment at first "but agreed to accept a check for $7,000 made out to his mother-in-law, Margaret Mallery. When she cashed the check, Mrs. Mallery wrote on the back of it, 'Reimburse loan'."[12]

George Paxton of Coed Records ("16 Candles") and George Goldner of Gone Records testified that "they had surrendered, without charge, complete copyright interests to music publishing firms owned by Clark with the understanding this would foster their music's promotion. Goldner said a representative of the Clark firm had asked for the copyrights and that Clark had subsequently played all but one of the records for which he received the copyrights from him."[13]

But the star of the closed-door sessions was Tony Mammarella, whose appearance before the committee stretched over two days.

Committee members were impressed that Mammarella had risen from switchboard operator and WFIL-TV cameraman to producer of the highest-rated daytime show on television where he described one of his duties as "riding herd" of an enthusiastic throng of teenagers each weekday afternoon.

But they really wanted to know how he landed on four weekly payrolls that paid him an aggregate $753 a week. Two of them

---

12. *All Shook Up: How Rock 'n' Roll Changed America*, p. 156.
13. *CQ Press*, a publication of the Congressional Quarterly.

were easy. He'd always been an employee of WFIL, he explained, and Clark paid him for his *American Bandstand* producing duties through Clark's Drexel Productions. Mammarella's *Bandstand* connections also paved the way for his two other jobs—as 25 percent owner of Swan Records (with Clark and Bernie Binnick) and half-owner (with Milt Kellem) of Wildcat Music Publishing.

But there was more. In all, committee investigators claimed that Mammarella had received checks from 11 other record companies and distributors for what Mammarella claimed was "listening" or "consulting." He also received income from other interests, like Milt Kellem Music, Inc. (a Wildcat affiliate); Raye Products, Inc. (part-owned by Clark, which produced Dick Clark record carriers) and Startime Industries Corp. (with Clark, which produced stuffed animals Platter Puss and Cuddle Pup).

Mammarella also acknowledged that he got one-third of the royalties from record sales of Charlie Gracie's hit, "Butterfly," by virtue of being cut in as a writer, under the nom de plume, Anthony September.

The music business continued to shift under the weight of payola. Many more radio stations, fearful of the stigma of playing rock & roll, switched to more melodic tunes like those from the *Hit Parade* era of just a few years earlier. Major labels, which had been slow to adapt to rock, openly welcomed the trend while independents, accustomed to recording guitar- and drum-based combos on a shoestring budget felt financially threatened by the more lush pop arrangements. Even Todd Storz, the Father of Top 40 Radio, fell in line. "If the public wants Chinese music, we'll give them Chinese music," he said.[14]

The trend towards pop was likely a factor in Clark losing a coveted spot to Pat Boone in negotiations for the 1960 Michigan State Fair. Clark's preview of the Caravan of Stars had posted attendance and sales records during its four-day run to open the 1959 Michigan fair. But that spot went to Pat Boone for 1960, although Clark was offered a three-day slot following the Boone run.

Many expected Clark to be the first witness when the House subcommittee opened its public hearings on February 8, but subcommittee chairman Oren Harris told the press that Clark's appearance would come later since there was so much material to be investigated.

---

14. *Billboard*, January 25, 1960.

Investigators for the House subcommittee, the FCC and the FTC were joined in the field by investigators for the Internal Revenue Service, whose Los Angeles office had been tipped off about alleged irregularities with at least one West Coast distributor. With so many investigators in the field, it was inevitable that there would be conflicts.

In Boston, the FTC arranged to pick up records from a TV station at 10 A.M. one day only to find that House investigators had picked them up an hour earlier. A similar clash occurred with the books of a record firm Clark had an interest in. Clark protested that he was being harassed and had his lawyers arrange a meeting between Oren Harris and FTC boss Earl W. Kintner to straighten things out.

Harris told the press that he hoped the payola hearings wouldn't take more than a week or two so congressmen could get down to the greater task of creating legislation that would bring the music business back in balance. In any case, Harris said, the hearings couldn't extend into July because it was an election year and political conventions would take center stage at that time.

Although the Senate was mostly leaving payola in the hands of their colleagues in the House, Washington Senator Warren Magnuson summoned several broadcast leaders, including ABC's Leonard Goldenson, to Washington for a mid-February roundtable to discuss how the FTC and FCC might more effectively deal with the payola scourge.

Not to be one-upped, Harris Subcommittee member John W. Bennett of Michigan proposed legislation on the eve of the hearings that would provide for fines of up to $5,000 or imprisonment of up to two years for persons who use the airwaves to "deceive and defraud the American people."[15]

In a preview of the hearings, syndicated columnist Drew Pearson wrote that several record companies accused of paying off disc jockeys had opened their books to government investigators. One of the companies, King Records of Cincinnati, claimed to have made its payments by check, a practice put in place ironically, after dealings with Clark's *Bandstand* predecessor, Bob Horn.

As the company was preparing to issue regular cash payments to Horn, government agents showed up.

"After a visit from T-men, the company insisted upon paying Horn by check," said King vice-president John Kelly. "He refused

---

15. *New York Times News Service*, William M. Blair, February 6, 1960.

to accept checks. Subsequently, he got into deeper trouble on morals and drunkenness charges."[16]

Pearson also wrote that a major Philadelphia distributor, Lesco, had also provided investigators with a complete list of payments made to disc jockeys in recent years. Company president Edward Cohn had earlier acknowledged that Philadelphia was one of the worst cities in the country for payola, estimating that 20 of the city's 200 deejays willingly accepted the payments.

However, Cohn said, "Dick Clark doesn't take a cent and never would."[17]

Prior to the start of the hearings, it was learned that the subcommittee was taking a hard look at the deejays' convention in Miami the previous May. As part of the probe, the subcommittee subpoenaed records of the Americana Hotel. The Disc Jockey Association, which was hastily formed to counter the bad publicity generated from the Miami meeting, had been scrambling to find its footing ever since. Just before the hearings, the group announced that it had finally settled on a place (Minneapolis, Minn) and a date (April 8) for its first business meeting. The DJA also reached out to the FCC for assistance in drafting a code of ethics for the fledgling organization.

Oren Harris finally gaveled in the first public hearing of the subcommittee on Monday morning, February 8. There were eight other members of the subcommittee—four Democrats and four Republicans.

Harris made it clear that disc jockeys were not the only people to be questioned. The subcommittee would also call song pluggers, record promoters, distributors and manufacturers and officials of radio and television stations, Harris said, pointing out that quality declines when side payments are the reason materials are chosen and such practices constitute unfair competition to honest businessmen.[18]

After Harris' opening remarks, the subcommittee immediately went behind closed doors to hear testimony from former Boston disc jockey Norman Prescott. In the 2½ hour session, Prescott claimed that he had been clean for his first 10 years in the business before succumbing to "the payola virus" in 1957. In two years he pocketed $10,000 in payola before quitting his job in disgust over the practice last year.

---

16. *Washington Merry-Go-Round*, Drew Pearson, February 6, 1960.
17. *Associated Press*, November 20, 1959.
18. *Associated Press*, February 8, 1960.

He was aware that management of WHDH and WBZ pushed specific records when he was employed at those stations but it was when he worked at WORL that he realized how pervasive payola was. It was in the early 1950s after a new LP by Johnnie Ray landed on Prescott's desk. He played the Columbia release on the air only to learn that WHDH's Bob Clayton had an exclusivity deal with Columbia that entitled him to first plays of Columbia releases. A delegation of Columbia representatives descended on the WORL studios to make their displeasure known.

Clayton was just one of several Boston disc jockeys of the early 1950s paid under the counter to service certain labels and distributors, Prescott said. In July 1958, WBZ station manager Paul G. O'Friel sent Prescott and fellow DJ Bob Given on a road trip to New York to solicit free albums to replenish the station's depleted record library. They returned with at least 1,000 albums, including up to 300 from Columbia's Mitch Miller.

In open session that afternoon, another Boston deejay, Dave Maynard, acknowledged receiving $6,800 from distributors in the previous three years. But Maynard, who was on suspension from WBZ at the time, claimed the payments were not payola but were for promoting records at teenage dances that were not broadcast. Similarly, another suspended WBZ personality, Alan Dary, claimed that the $400–500 he'd received were Christmas gifts, not payola.

The first day's session drew a sparse crowd, surprising organizers who had expected the overflow crowds that the quiz show hearings had drawn a few months earlier.

The Boston portion of the week's hearings wrapped up on Tuesday, when bandleader Lester Lanin, a Philadelphia native, testified that he had been shortchanged while participating in a promotion sponsored by WBZ.

Subcommittee counsel Robert Lishman then brought Joe Finan, who had been fired from KYW in Cleveland in November, before the panel. Finan unabashedly conceded that he'd supplemented his $40,000 a year salary with income from record companies, but insisted it was purely for services rendered, including "evaluating the commercial worth of [his clients'] records; [and] acting as consultant to 'verify' if a record was worth the cost of promotion."[19]

---

19. *Billboard*, February 15, 1960.

For his consulting, Finan pocketed $16,100 in 1958 and 1959 from 15 record companies, including $450 from Cameo to plug Bobby Rydell's first hit, "Kissin' Time."[20]

Finan's testimony, Chairman Harris said, "certainly helped to point up a sad situation in the broadcasting industry. Apparently, they forget about operating in the public interest."[21]

A former Finan associate, Wesley Hopkins, took the stand on Wednesday to defend the $12,000 he'd received in "listening fees" from record companies, including Cameo. It was not "pay for play," Hopkins insisted, he just wanted to make sure good records weren't "lost in the shuffle." Like Finan, Hopkins had been fired from KYW in November. Both were done in by check stubs and flaps with song titles written in that were turned over by record distributor Main Line.

Wednesday turned out to be the last day of hearings in what was a short opening week since Congress needed to take a long weekend to celebrate Abraham Lincoln's birthday. Before breaking, though, Lishman released damning details of the infamous Miami convention.

Nineteen record companies ran up a tab of $117,664 at the Americana Hotel during the May 29–31 convention, with $68,144 of that for receptions, cocktail parties, and similar events. That included the $15,415 Roulette Records spent for the all-night Count Basie recording session—for bar charges, a barbecue and breakfast.

"I've heard the three Bs description of the convention, but not as a bar, barbecue and breakfast," quipped Rep. John Moss of California, referring to the Miami newspaper headline, "Babes, Booze, and Bribes."[22]

As subcommittee members from the House of Representatives began their long holiday weekend, the FCC said it wanted Congress to provide fines of up to $5,000 or imprisonment up to one year for those who conduct deceptive broadcast practices, like payola. On the same day, National Association of Broadcasters president Harold E. Fellows told an audience in Boston that he preferred self-regulation.

It had been nearly three months since payola had divorced Dick Clark from at least half of his burgeoning business empire,

---

20. Ibid.
21. *New York Times News Service*, William M. Blair, February 10, 1960.
22. *New York Times News Service*, William M. Blair, February 11, 1960.

yet after one week of Congressional hearings, it still wasn't clear what it all meant.

When Oren Harris called the hearings to order, payola was not in violation of any federal law. Indeed, to some, it "combated conformism and racism in the music business."[23]

One unnamed record executive saw the whole process as an unwarranted witch hunt:

> It was bizarre, that's the only word I can think of, that one American business was singled out for industrial gift giving. At the same time record people were being thrown in jail, professionals in Washington were doing the very same thing. They're called lobbyists.[24]

If song pluggers had been pushing Gershwin tunes or Lerner & Lowe compositions, payola would never have been seen as such a threat. But that wasn't the case.

"Payola gave a special boost to rock and roll.," an unnamed record executive said. "Payola gave record buyers—the young, the diehard music fans, and the followers of rock and roll—greater influence over station programming."[25]

Entering this latest chapter of the ASCAP-BMI wars, ASCAP was doing quite well with its Broadway show tunes and network television exposure, while BMI tunes were winning with the market of the future, America's teenagers. ASCAP backers and rock haters saw common cause in payola. Maybe it was just the ticket for putting an end to this cacophonous threat.

A quick study of the members of the Harris Subcommittee would be cause for optimism among the ASCAP faithful.

At 56, Chairman Harris was the oldest member of the committee. He also had the most service time in the House of Representatives, having served continuously since he was first elected from Arkansas' fourth district in 1940.

In 1957, Harris was chairman of the House Commerce Committee, which held authority over the Federal Communications Commission, when he and House Speaker Sam Rayburn hired New York University law professor Bernard Schwartz to look into the operation of several independent government agencies.

---
23. *In Praise of Commercial Culture*. p. 166.
24. *Rockonomics*, pp. 78–79.
25. *In Praise of Commercial Culture*, pp. 167–168.

PAYOLA

One of the things Schwartz found was that Harris had bought 25 percent of an El Dorado, Ark., TV station for $5,000 ($4,500 of which was a promissory note) and later presided over a previously stalled license renewal and power expansion for the station. When Harris didn't see this as a conflict of interest, Schwartz leaked the information to the press, prompting Harris to quickly sell his interest in the station and fire Schwartz.

Harris was also an avowed segregationist who was among 101 Senate and House members who in 1956 signed the Southern Manifesto, a proclamation that vowed to resist federal efforts at racial integration. Two other subcommittee members also signed the Southern Manifesto—Walter Rogers, 51 (D-Texas) and John Flynt, 45 (D-Ga.).

Harris had also served on a steering committee that helped defeat a bill establishing a Fair Employment Practice Committee, a measure designed to check racial bias, and was a staunch defender of Arkansas Governor Orval Faubus when Faubus challenged the Supreme Court's decree that Little Rock's schools must be integrated.

Harris also apparently had a large ego. During the first week of the payola hearings, Harris wrapped up testimony early one afternoon so committee members could attend a 4 P.M. unveiling of a painted portrait of Harris. The portrait, commissioned at committee expense, was hung in the committee room.[26]

Seven of the nine subcommittee members were law school graduates and the youngest was 41 years old, a full 11 years older than Dick Clark. All had been teenagers or young adults in the big band era, a time when ASCAP tunes dominated the nation's airwaves.

John Bennett, 55, (R-Mich.) had already proposed legislation that would fine or jail payola offenders and at least two other subcommittee members were no-nonsense law and order types.

Samuel Devine, 44, (R-Ohio) was a former track teammate of 1936 Olympics star Jesse Owens and had served as an FBI agent during World War II. During his time in the Ohio state legislature, Devine pursued Communists as chairman of the Ohio Un-American Activities Committee.

Peter Mack, 43, (D-Ill.) was known as "the flying Congressman" ever since a 1951 trip where he flew his own single-engine

---

26. *New York News*, February 13, 1960.

plane, The Friendship Flame, to 59 countries. The plane ended up in the permanent display of the Air and Space Museum at the Smithsonian Institution.

In 1958, Mack, who was concerned about youth gang violence, sponsored legislation that would become known as the Switchblade Knife Act of 1958. As passed, the law made it illegal to purchase, sell or import automatic knives in interstate commerce.

Illinois was the only state with two members on the subcommittee. The second was William Springer, 50 (R.-Ill.). Besides being the youngest member, Steve Derounian, 41, (R-N.Y.) had gained national recognition for his stern questioning of Charles Van Doren in the quiz show scandal hearings. The ninth member, John Moss, 44 (D-Calif.) was a former appliance store owner and real estate salesman who had entered the House in 1953.

The hearings began their second week on February 15 as the subcommittee again zeroed in on Boston, but expanded its interrogation to record manufacturers and distributors.

Cecil Steen of Records, Inc., admitted that he paid $2,000 to Boston deejays. Gordon Dinerstein of Music Suppliers, Inc., also testified that his firm had paid Boston disc jockeys and record librarians, but only "to create and maintain goodwill." Some of that money involved the Am-Par Record Corp., a wholly owned subsidiary of ABC-Paramount, which was also the parent company of *American Bandstand*.

Am-Par president Sam Clark (no relation to Dick Clark) testified in a closed session that ABC-TV was so careful not to plug its "owned" records that he found it difficult to get Am-Par tunes played on *Bandstand*. But chairman Harris countered that claim with a 1959 analysis of *American Bandstand* that showed that Dick Clark played more Am-Par discs (nine records, 30 plays) than Columbia (8, 28), RCA (8, 22) or MGM (8, 21).[27]

The subcommittee finally got some linkage to Dick Clark on Friday, February 19, when disc jockey Joe Smith of WILD in Boston acknowledged that he had benefited from the success of "16 Candles" by the Crests. The tune became a national hit when Clark started playing it regularly after publishing was transferred to Clark's January Publishing. Smith jumped on the bandwagon and started plugging the tune after Coed Records started paying

---

27. *Billboard*, February 22, 1960.

Smith 2 cents for every copy of the record that was sold in the Boston area.

Harris wrapped things up soon after Smith's testimony, telling reporters that it would probably be at least a month before the hearings resumed. The subcommittee needed some time to be briefed on the results of the FCC and FTC probes, plus legislative hearings on ethics in government were to begin in mid-March.

Ironically, as FCC chairman John C. Doerfer was briefing the subcommittee on FCC payola findings, the New York *Herald Tribune* broke the story that Doerfer was guilty of some payola transgressions himself. The *Herald Tribune* reported that Doerfer had spent six days and nights aboard the yacht of multiple radio-TV station owner George B. Storer and also received free air transportation to and from Florida for the excursion.

Doerfer initially denied the allegations to newsmen but confessed before the Harris Subcommittee. Pres. Eisenhower soon replaced Doerfer with Frederick Ford.

As the Doerfer story broke, subcommittee member John Bennett tried to give Doerfer cover by demanding that the House panel immediately summon Dick Clark to Washington for interrogation. The ranking Republican claimed that the committee had already received evidence that Clark had accepted expensive gifts of furs and jewelry and had held an interest in 17 companies.

"His activities pinpoint, more than anything else, the evils of payola," Bennett said.[28]

Chairman Harris disagreed, noting that the FTC was still waiting to examine Clark's books, which were in the committee's possession. Committee counsel Robert Lishman also informed committee members that a team of investigators, attorneys, and accountants on loan from the General Accounting Office was still working to unravel Clark's complex business holdings.

Lishman further reported that some people were reluctant to provide information because they feared reprisals from Clark.

Hearings were unlikely to resume before mid-April but that didn't stop Clark's fans from writing early to congressional staffers in search of tickets or reserved seats for his testimony (they didn't exist). Clark had retained 55-year-old Washington lawyer Paul Porter, a former staffer in Pres. Franklin D. Roosevelt's administration and one-time head of the FCC, to be his attorney.

---

28. *Associated Press*, March 4, 1960.

Clark's movie, *Because They're Young*, was scheduled to premiere about the time the hearings were to resume and a *'Teen* magazine poll for its March issue found that Clark trailed just Pres. Eisenhower as the person that young people most admire and respect.

But there were signs that Clark's grip on popularity with his young fans might be slipping.

His column in the *This Week* Sunday newspaper magazine had been dropped. Elvis' stint in the Army was coming to an end in late March, and Col. Tom Parker was busily stoking the teen press with Elvis tidbits, like the $125,000 he would receive for singing four songs in his first post-service appearance on a Frank Sinatra special.

TV and radio stations continued the trend back to pop, including WNEW-TV in New York where Alan Freed had aired his last rhythm & blues dance show just a few months earlier. After trying rock & roll with new host Bill "Davy Crockett" Hayes for a while, station brass decided to abandon rock altogether.

Philadelphia station WRCV took dead aim at the Clark TV dance franchise when it said it would broadcast live a teenage prom from Convention Hall the evening of March 10. NBC planned to carry parts of the prom nationally in a test to see whether a network show was possible.

Just like *American Bandstand*, jackets and neckties were required for boys and slacks were verboten for girls in what WRCV described as a "Look Right, Dress Right, Feel Right" policy. Since the dance was slated to go until 11 P.M., the city issued special cards allowing the dancing teens to be out past the city's 10 P.M. curfew.[29]

If any of this was bothering Clark, he didn't show it. On Sunday, March 20, he was spotted sunning himself under an umbrella at the Ocean Manor Hotel in Fort Lauderdale, Fla. When approached by a reporter, Clark said: "Biggest reason I'm here is to get away from reporters."[30]

Before returning to Philadelphia, Clark went to Phoenix for the late-March premiere of *Because They're Young*. A Phoenix girl had won the premier honor for her city by winning the "name the mascot" contest promoted by Beech-Nut. While in Phoenix, Clark

---

29. *Billboard*, February 15, 1960.
30. *Billboard*, March 28, 1960.

was gracious with the press, as long as they didn't ask him about payola.

Around the same time, a House spokesman confirmed that Clark had been subpoenaed to appear before the Harris committee, tentatively on Thursday, April 21. The spokesman also said that as many as 30 other people from the Philadelphia area had been subpoenaed and some 80 of Clark's business associates had been interviewed.

On April 11, *Billboard* unveiled what it called "the most exhaustive study ever made on TV record and dance party shows." The magazine promised that the study of 74 programs in 61 cities in 32 states would eventually be published in a book. The study revealed that there were only two network record and dance programs—*American Bandstand* and Clark's *Saturday Night Show*.

Nielsen and ARB ratings for October 1959 indicated that Clark's *Saturday Night Show* pulled in nearly 19 million viewers, 10.5 million of which were adults.[31] The Disk Jockey Association meeting in Minneapolis, on the other hand, drew fewer than 50 people (compared to the estimated 2,500 that attended the Miami Convention a year earlier), but the DJA did adopt a code of ethics which called for disc jockeys to "avoid acceptance of favors from interested parties" and have no outside interests unless approved by station management.

But now even House members who were not on the Harris committee were getting into the act. Rep. Emanuel Celler of New York introduced an anti-payola bill invoking criminal penalties for givers and takers of the bribery. Rep. Thomas "Tip" O'Neill of Massachusetts was asking the FCC to check the licenses of stations involved in payola. Calling teens a "captive audience," O'Neill said they must be protected from "a type of sensuous music unfit for impressionable minds."[32]

As Clark prepped for his House appearance, he added a wrinkle to *Bandstand*—taking viewers inside the home of Frankie Avalon. *Because They're Young* had arrived at Philadelphia's Viking theater and Clark was drawing favorable reviews for his portrayal of a high school teacher.

Ernie Schier of the Philadelphia *Evening Bulletin* wrote that "while [Clark] isn't likely to capture an Academy Award nomination, he conducts himself with ease and dignity in the major

---

31. *Billboard*, April 11, 1960.
32. Ibid.

role. . . . He's a likable smoothie who projects with warmth. He might very well find another career on the screen, and a less troublesome one."[33]

"Less troublesome" doubtless had appeal to Clark as his House appearance drew closer. But the payola hearings also gave much of America its first detailed peek into the Dick Clark phenomenon.

Teenagers certainly knew who Clark was and people in Philadelphia knew who he was, but much of America was ignorant about this young man who had suddenly burst on the national scene. Who was he, anyhow?

Profiles of Clark that popped up in newspapers during the run-up to his Congressional appearance were overwhelmingly positive. They were mostly based on ABC-TV press releases or the features that proliferated in the teen press after *American Bandstand* went national. Payola was off limits.

American newspapers that were members of the *Associated Press* had access to a "personality in the news" feature about Clark written by Noah Halper and released on the eve of Clark's Washington appearance.

In the 700-word piece, Halper writes of Clark's fortuitous rise to the *Bandstand* podium, his ability "to reach the kids," how he overcame a skin disease and the death of his brother to become popular in high school, how he courted his high school sweetheart right to the altar, how his modest lifestyle includes "a 1959 passenger car and an older inexpensive station wagon," how he enjoys trips to the Maryland shore to visit his not-wealthy in-laws and how seriously he takes his role as a father.

Quoting an unidentified associate, Halper wrote: "Dick is a real devoted father. He has a special time set aside for his son every morning. By the time he gets through work every day the boy is asleep. Dick worked hard to get here and he still works hard."[34]

Halper didn't totally ignore the reason for doing the story, addressing Clark's payola status in a succinct 32 words in the story's 12th paragraph: "Since his name first was linked with payola he's had little to say publicly, other than his utterances on his shows and his words in a syndicated column of advice to teenagers."[35]

Halper's article reflected the mood of much of America at the time—that Dick Clark was a good guy and that payola wasn't a

---
33. *Philadelphia Evening Bulletin*, March 18, 1960.
34. *Associated Press*, April 29, 1960.
35. Ibid.

big deal. One unidentified 16-year-old girl summed up the view of many when she said: "Even if I found out that Dick Clark took payola, it wouldn't make any difference. He makes us teenagers happy."[36]

* * *

Oren Harris had a scheduling issue as his House subcommittee resumed its payola hearings on Monday, April 25, 1960. According to the subcommittee's published schedule, it was set to open hearings the following Monday on an issue deemed much more important by Congressional watchdogs—a potential scandal in the Federal Power Commission's regulation of the natural gas industry.

To meet that schedule, Harris would have to wrap up the payola hearing by the end of the week, an unlikely possibility especially since star witness Dick Clark had yet to appear. That wasn't Clark's fault. He repeatedly asked to appear before the subcommittee only to be told it wasn't time yet. Eager to get Clark's story on the record, his lawyers again asked if they couldn't open proceedings on April 25. Just as with previous requests, the answer was no. Instead, the hearings re-opened with closed-door testimony from Alan Freed.

Freed was still miffed over his treatment by ABC management. In his testimony, Freed claimed that the network had a dual policy—one for Clark and another for everyone else. While Clark was allowed to use his self-created narrow definition of payola in the affidavit he signed for the network, Freed said he wasn't given that option. Instead, he was also asked to answer questions about his interests in publishing and musical copyrights.

Freed said he would not have been able to answer no to some of the questions on the network affidavit but, had he been presented with the same option that Clark had, he would have come out "clean as the driven snow."[37]

Freed, who was fired from WABC radio for failing to sign the network affidavit, further claimed that he was pressured by ABC vice-president Mortimer Weinbach to "lay heavy on [ABC-Paramount-owned] Am-Par Records and play only Paramount Theaters" in his stage shows."[38]

---

36. *Newsweek*, May 2, 1960.
37. *Billboard*, May 9, 1060.
38. Ibid.

Freed claimed that Clark was given preferential treatment by ABC because of his hefty contribution to the network's bottom line. Freed said that Clark grossed about $12 million annually for ABC (a figure the network later rejected), while Freed brought in just $250,000.

The committee also heard from George Paxton and Marvin Cane of Coed Records in Monday's closed-door session. They told how "16 Candles" languished in the charts until Dick Clark obtained the publishing and started playing the song heavily.

Open sessions resumed Tuesday morning with testimony from Paul Ackerman, music editor of trade publication *Billboard*. Ackerman agreed that payola should be a crime and recommended that the music industry launch a self-policing program with some sort of music czar, similar to the commissioner of baseball.

Another *Billboard* staffer, research director Thomas Noonan, acknowledged under questioning that Dick Clark "probably was the most important single individual" in the exploitation of records.[39]

But much of Tuesday's hearing was given to a detailed statistical analysis of the songs actually played on *American Bandstand*.

From the start of *American Bandstand*, Clark had meticulously recorded on index cards the name and play date of every record played on the show. From the show's premiere on August 5, 1957, through November 11, 1959, that resulted in 15,000 index cards. In an effort to show the subcommittee that his influence was far less than had been thought, Clark hired a New York statistical and electronic data processing firm to analyze the cards and come up with a presentation for the subcommittee.

But clarity wasn't what Clark had in mind when he sent Bernard Goldstein, vice-president of Computech Inc., into the House hearing room.

"I spent $6,000 creating the biggest red herring I could find—something that would shift the subcommittee's attention away from my scalp," Clark later wrote.[40]

Clark hoped that Goldstein's analysis would overwhelm the subcommittee with facts and numbers that supported Clark's position of innocence in all payola matters. Computech, after all, had done similar work for the U.S. Government.

---

39. *CQ Press*, a publication of the Congressional Quarterly.
40. *Rock, Roll & Remember,* p. 204.

"Goldstein arrived with half a dozen suitcases, stuffed with 300 pounds of information," Clark wrote.[41]

Goldstein began his presentation by testifying that Clark played songs in which he had a financial interest 4,230 times in the two-year period, which equated to roughly 27 percent of the songs he played on *American Bandstand.* While Goldstein's claim was far less than what subcommittee investigators expected, his numbers didn't go unchallenged.

Under strong questioning, Goldstein admitted that the numbers he used included the (not Clark-affiliated) *Bandstand* theme song, which was played twice each show. The study also included several months right after the show began its network run and before Clark started building his extensive musical empire and therefore had no songs to push. The analysis also failed to flag any songs in which the ABC network or Clark's friends and business associates had an interest.

Rep. John Moss of California called the whole exercise "statistical gymnastics" designed to put Clark in the most favorable light. But the subcommittee had its own view of those 15,000 file cards and on Wednesday brought in three statisticians of its own who offered a quite different interpretation.

Joseph Tyron, a teacher of economics and statistics at Georgetown University, testified that his study of the Computech survey led him to the "inescapable conclusion" that Clark favored records in which he had a financial stake.[42]

Tryon claimed that Clark "clearly and systematically favored the records in which he had some interest. He favored them first by playing them more often, he favored them by playing them longer, he favored them by playing them earlier relative to when they became popular. And it also appears that he favored those in which he had the strongest interest—he favored those records most."[43]

The two other statisticians—Morton S. Raff of the U.S. Bureau of Labor Statistics and Joseph F. Daly of the U.S. Census Bureau—noted in a 95-page staff analysis that there were at least 270 errors in Computech data and several statistical flaws in the Computech study. The staff analysis also pointed out that Clark often played records in which his financial interest wasn't with the song being played but, rather, with the flip side.

---

41. Ibid.
42. *Associated Press,* April 27, 1960.
43. *All Shook Up: How Rock 'n' Roll Changed America,* p. 157

Two other witnesses on Wednesday shed light on how some of Clark's "financial interests" played out.

Harry Finfer was vice-president of two Philadelphia companies—Universal Record Distributing and Jamie Records. Finfer testified that Universal had paid Philadelphia disc jockeys some $35,000 over a two-year period in 1957–59 but that Dick Clark was not among them.

Georgie Woods of WDAS was the biggest beneficiary of Universal's largesse at $6,375, but Tony Mammarella was No. 2 on the list at $4,000. Finfer told the subcommittee that Mammarella was paid for listening to records and offering advice, except for $500 that was a gift in honor of his newborn child.

Realizing that Clark's advice could also be valuable, Finfer offered Clark a 25 percent stake in Jamie Records for an investment of $125. In July 1959, Jamie put Clark on the company payroll (retroactive to May 1958) at $200 a week "for giving Jamie the benefit of his advice and experience."[44]

When Clark was forced to divest, he sold his stake in Jamie for $15,000, a profit of 11,900 percent. In all, Clark had grossed more than $31,500 for his $125 investment.

Finfer's detailed records gave investigators an accountant's peek into how widespread payola was in the Philadelphia area. The $35,000 of Universal money was spread out to 30 disc jockeys, including some of the biggest names in Philadelphia radio—Lloyd "Fat Man" Smith, Joe Grady, Ed Hurst, Tom Donahue, Joe Niagara, Georgie Woods, Hy Lit, Mitch Thomas, Larry Brown, Mammarella, Kae Williams, Red Benson and Jocko Henderson. The list even included $15 paid to Billy Dupree at WDAS.

Finfer turned over a similar list of 22 people who shared $20,000 in payouts to promote Jamie records. One big difference was the scope of the Jamie payments, which covered a much larger geographic area (including Nashville, Cleveland, Detroit, and Miami) and payments to managers and promotion men in addition to deejays.

Songwriter Orville Lunsford of Chillicothe, Ohio, testified how Clark's influence, too, extended well beyond Philadelphia.

Lunsford assigned copyright of his song, "The All-American Boy," to Fraternity Records in Cincinnati, Ohio. He soon received a call from Harry Carlson, president of Fraternity, who told him

---

44. *All Shook Up: How Rock 'n' Roll Changed America*, pp. 154–155.

that Dick Clark was prepared to push the record, but only if Fraternity had 50,000 copies of the record pressed by Clark's Mallard Pressing Co. in Philadelphia.

Carlson later disputed Lunsford's story, which claimed Mallard pressed the records in January 1959.

"Almost immediately," Lunsford said, "I heard my song played every other day on Clark's show, *American Bandstand*, and on the other Dick Clark show also. The record became a big hit in the nation for a while."[45]

Harris had wanted to conduct the hearings in the subcommittee's meeting room but found it had been reserved by a 4-H Club so he took his group into executive session in a smaller room.

Reporters covering the hearings were caught off-guard with the lack of a public hearing that day, but a reporter for the *Associated Press* managed to corral three subcommittee members for an update on the proceedings.

Rep. John Moss (D, Calif.) said "it appears Clark took a profitable form of payola.

"His methods were different but he appears to have explored every possible avenue for cashing in. He has meticulously put together a vehicle for avoiding the appearance of payola without losing any of the benefits."

Rep. John Bennett (R, Mich.) said: "I think it is pretty convincing that Clark was involved in payola the same as all the other disc jockeys but on a much larger scale."

Rep. Peter Mack (D, Ill.) said: "The only question now is determining the degree."[46]

With the stage now set, it was time to put those questions to Clark himself.

FRIDAY, APRIL 29, 1960
Dick Clark looked splendid in his dark blue serge suit, neatly pressed white shirt, dark blue tie, and shiny black loafers as he entered the House caucus room carrying a leather dispatch case. He looked every bit the youthful TV host as he paused to chat with his wife, Bobbie, who was wearing a corsage as she took her seat in the House gallery, alongside Clark's parents, Dick Clark Sr. and Julia. All four had taken the train from Philadelphia for this historic day.

---

45. *Associated Press*, April 28, 1960.
46. Associated Press, April 28, 1960.

Clark took his spot at the witness table with his Washington lawyer, Paul Porter, right behind him. Although Capitol Police had prepared for a standing-room-only crowd, there were a few empty seats in the 240-seat gallery. Although there were hundreds of teenagers at the Capitol that day, very few dropped in for the hearing.

At 10 A.M. the nine members of the House Subcommittee on Legislative Oversight filed into the chamber, taking their seats in an arc in front of and towering above Clark.

Chairman Oren Harris gaveled the hearing to order and, after a brief exchange of pleasantries, asked Clark if he had anything he wanted to say before the proceedings began. Clark said he did and proceeded to read from a 34-page prepared statement. It took 40 minutes.

> Gentlemen, I feel that I have been convicted, condemned and denounced even before I have had an opportunity to tell my story. . . .[47]
>
> I want to make it clear immediately, that I have never taken payola. In brief, I have never agreed to play a record or have an artist perform on a radio or television program in return for a payment in cash or any other consideration. . . .[48]
>
> On this program [American Bandstand], I play records and interview recording stars. The recording stars perform and teenagers dance. I seek to provide wholesome recreational outlets for these youngsters whom I think I know and understand. . . .[49]
>
> As everyone who has any familiarity with television is aware, television performers cannot look forward with any assurance to long runs or continuing popularity.
>
> Television can be an extraordinary fickle medium and I realize that my position could be a precarious one to sustain . . .
>
> So, because of the frequently erratic nature of the television business, I sought the opportunity for diversified investments of my energies and resources. I sought out investments and opportunities which would continue after my performing popularity had waned or disappeared. It was then most natural

---

47. *Hearings Before a Subcommittee of the Committee on Interstate and Foreign Commerce,* Government Printing Office, 1960.
48. Ibid.
49. Ibid

> for me to look to the music industry, the field I knew best, for such investments. . . .[50]
>
> So I set about acquiring interests in, or forming, companies active in the fields of music publishing, record manufacturing, record pressing, and record distribution, in addition to companies active in television production, motion picture production, literary rights and arranging personal appearances. I also made investments in other fields as opportunities presented themselves, such as real estate.

"The various corporations just grew," Clark said. He insisted that none of these concerns had been set up to "exact tribute" from the music and record industry in return for his playing their tunes on the air. He conceded that some songs and records "were given to my firms at least in part because I was a network television performer."

> However, the conflict between my position as a performer and my record interest never clearly presented itself to me until this committee raised questions of payola and conflicts of interest.[51]
>
> In not one of these instances did it occur to me that I was engaging in any impropriety. I followed normal business practices under the ground rules that existed.[52]

In the course of his statement, Clark carefully outlined his professional career from Syracuse and Utica, New York, to the helm of television's top-rated daytime program. He also gave details on each of the 33 businesses in which he had held a financial interest prior to divestiture, a number much larger than most in the gallery expected. Clark explained what each business did, who his partners were and his financial stake in each one.

Clark told how he happened to help write "At the Hop" and admitted that he and his wife, Bobbie, "had inadvisedly taken" jewelry as a gift from Lou Bedell of Dore Records. He defended the Computech survey, noting that he volunteered the information before the subcommittee had requested it (at his own expense) and that he undertook the analysis in good faith.

---

50. Ibid.
51. Ibid.
52. Ibid.

Clark also defended the kickback scheme that allowed him to have talent perform on *American Bandstand* for free. Under the system, which Clark claimed was standard procedure in the business, his production company, Click, gave the artist a check for union scale, the artist then turned the check in to the record company, which issued a check for the same amount back to Click. Besides, Clark said, he doesn't do that anymore.

Clark reaffirmed his belief that a hit lay in the grooves of a record and that no amount of play or exposure could turn a dog into a hit. He also took issue with subcommittee counsel Robert Lishman's recent remarks about fear of reprisals by potential witnesses.

"I have never in my life threatened reprisals or used devious methods in negotiating with the hundreds of artists, managers, record companies, publishers and songwriters I have dealt with in my career . . . Should any man accuse me of exacting tribute or using coercion, this man would not be telling the truth," Clark said.[53]

While Clark's position of influence on the record-buying practices of America's teenagers was unique, his ownership of businesses related to his profession wasn't. Indeed, many of the biggest stars of the day had the foresight to diversify their investment portfolios.

Many (including Clark's boyhood idol Garry Moore) created production companies to produce their own television programs. Lucille Ball and Desi Arnaz owned Desilu, Frank Sinatra had Hobart Productions, Jack Benny had J & M Productions and Jack Webb had Mark VII Productions.

Two of the more successful show business stars-turned-entrepreneur of the era also had shows on ABC-TV. Lawrence Welk's Teleklew, Inc., was so successful that it had outgrown its modest one-story building in Santa Monica, Calif., and was planning a move into a new six-story Lawrence Welk Building.

The entertainer whose business interests most closely aligned with Clark's was, ironically, Pat Boone, whose physical features and soft-spoken personality were so close to Clark's that they were often confused for each other.

Boone's Cooga Mooga, Inc., was one of the most successful music-related firms of the early rock era. Through Cooga Mooga,

---

53. Ibid.

Boone owned a music business and merchandising branch for radios, record players, wrist watches, bathing trunks, scarves, gloves, shirts, sweaters, charm bracelets, petticoats and buck shoes (both white and "pre-dirtied tan").

Boone was also a successful author, whose *'Twixt Twelve and Twenty* sold more than 300,000 copies. In 1959, Boone and the Townsend Investment Company bought two radio stations—KNOK in Dallas (gospel music programming) and WDKA in Nashville (pop music).

Though Clark had shed his music-based investments by the time of his appearance before the House subcommittee, two stories that sounded a lot like payola hadn't been resolved—the $7,000 he received from Bernie Lowe for his help in promoting "Butterfly" and the expensive gifts he had received from Lou Bedell of Dore Records. Clark addressed both issues before the subcommittee.

Clark said he had, indeed, received $7,000 in royalties from "Butterfly" from Lowe and admitted that he played the song until it became a hit. Lowe gave him the money out of gratitude, Clark said. It wasn't payola because he had made no commitment to play the record at all.

"The public and the members of the investigating committee simply do not understand the meaning of the term 'payola'," Clark said, adding that there is payola only if a disc jockey agrees to push a record in return for money or other things of value. Clark admitted that he pushed records and had received money, but denied that there was an agreement.[54]

The gifts from Bedell were simply gifts, Clark testified, though he acknowledged that he was embarrassed to receive them.

The first gift was a fur stole given to Clark's wife. Clark insisted on paying Bedell for the stole and wrote out a check for $300. Clark later learned that the stole actually cost $1,000 and that Bedell had charged the cost as a business expense for his record company.

The next gifts were even more valuable—a necklace to Bobbie and a ring to Clark. The items, again charged off as a business expense by Bedell, were valued at $3,400.

Again, Clark claimed that the gifts didn't meet his definition of payola.

Bedell, on the other hand, explained: "If the man next door makes $150,000 for me, by golly, I'm going to buy him a Cadillac."[55]

---

54. Ibid.
55. *Newsweek*, May 2, 1960.

And Bedell was very appreciative of the help Clark provided in elevating "To Know Him Is to Love Him" to the top of the charts.

The record by the Teddy Bears (which included a teenage Phil Spector) had languished until breaking out in Fargo, N.D. A Minneapolis radio station started playing the song and orders for the record picked up in the Twin Cities, but Bedell wanted a national hit so he called Clark in Philadelphia to ask if he would play the song on *American Bandstand*.

"The first thing Clark wanted to know was if Universal Distributors . . . was handling the Dore record in Philadelphia. It was, and that bit of good fortune may have led Dick Clark to listen to it."[56]

Although Clark had no direct business connection to Universal, two of its three owners—Harry Finfer and Harold B. Lipsius—owned half of another business Clark had a 25 percent interest in, Jamie Records.

"Having assured himself of his own financial interest in the success of the record, Clark activated his hit-making machinery. In the third week of September, he played the record on his show, and the climb began. It hit number 40 on the Top Forty list on October 11, 1958, then number 16 a week later. By late October it had reached number 4. Two weeks later, Clark called Bedell and asked him if the Teddy Bears would agree to appear on *American Bandstand*."[57]

Shortly after that, around the time of Clark's 29th birthday, Bedell presented the jewelry gifts.

Rep. John Moss (D, Cal.) responded to Clark's explanation of the gifts with sarcasm, saying that the broadcast music field manifests "more brotherly love than any other on earth—people cannot restrain themselves from giving away their wealth."[58]

Subcommittee counsel Robert Lishman opened the hearing's questioning of Clark by taking a detailed look at Clark's finances. Lishman pointed out that since 1957 Clark had received $167,750 in salary and $409,020 in increased stock values on investments of $53,773.

When Lishman asked Clark to confirm that he had made more than $800,000 in less than three years, Clark claimed ignorance of the matter.

---

56. *He's a Rebel*, p. 36.
57. *Reckless: Millionaire Record Producer Phil Spector and the Violent Death of Lana Clarkson*, pp. 67–68.
58. *Hearings Before a Subcommittee of the Committee on Interstate and Foreign Commerce*, Government Printing Office, 1960.

"One thing I've never fallen in love with was accounting," Clark said, noting that his wife wrote the family checks. "The only thing I ever failed in my life was mathematics."[59]

"Apparently you know how to count," Rep. Steven Derounian of New York declared derisively, "and I think more students in the country are going to want to fail math if they can be as successful as you are."[60]

Derounian went on to describe the affidavit Clark had prepared for ABC as "a Christian Dior affidavit," tailored to his need. "You say you did not get any payola, but you got an awful lot of royola."[61]

"My only crime is that I made a lot of money out of businesses in which there was very little investment," Clark said.[62]

Derounian criticized Clark for playing Duane Eddy songs on *American Bandstand* more often than Elvis Presley tunes, alleging that Clark favored artists in which he had a financial stake. Clark countered by pointing out that he had no financial interest in many *Bandstand* favorites, like Bobby Darin, Connie Francis, Fabian, and Frankie Avalon.

Clark conceded that it may look as if he intentionally played records he had a financial stake in but said he "did not consciously favor such records. Maybe I did so without realizing it. I would note that until this committee's activities, no one had really pointed out the inconsistency of performing records and owning an interest in record and music companies."[63]

After Clark restated that payola was a strict agreement to play a specific record for a specific reward, Lishman responded: "You know, we have had twenty or thirty disk jockeys here, and not one ever stated that he 'agreed' to take payola. It is always some kind of a telepathic understanding that if everything is going good, in appreciation for what they are doing somehow miraculously they get their money."[64]

Rep. John E. Moss (D, Calif.) joined in on the theme, saying a "unique facet" of the television industry was the ability to communicate without agreement, by "intellectual osmosis."[65]

---

59. Ibid.
60. Ibid.
61. Ibid.
62. Ibid.
63. Ibid.
64. Ibid.
65. Ibid.

Although the subcommittee persistently tried to establish Clark as a shrewd businessman whose primary motivation in selecting music for *American Bandstand* was to fatten his own bank account, Clark saw things much differently. His job was to find the music that his youthful audience wanted to listen to and dance to. He described himself as a "professional crystal ball gazer."

When Lishman pointed out that 30 records from one of Clark's firms were played 650 times to promote them, eventually realizing high spots in the *Billboard* ratings, Clark used Lishman's numbers as proof of his ability to predict hits.

Although the morning questioning had been testy, Clark was granted a favor not afforded other hearing witnesses—the luxury of leaving the chamber through a back door for the lunch recess, allowing Clark to avoid the horde of reporters clustered outside the hearing room doors.

After lunch, however, Clark moved purposefully through the crowd, flanked by two policemen, signing autographs and taking time to address the cameras, reaffirming his claim that he had never taken nor condoned the issuing of payola.

In the afternoon session, Lishman continued the attack. Frank Sinatra, Perry Como, Frankie Laine, and Bing Crosby were popular and sold a lot of records, Lishman said. Why don't you play them on your show?

Clark tried to explain that not all singers were popular with the *Bandstand* crowd, that it took someone like him to make certain the show remained relevant and popular with his audience.

Lishman returned to Clark's business connections later that afternoon. Three large charts were wheeled into the hearing room, full of diagrams and names of people and corporations, connected by a tangle of lines. Chairman Harris looked at the charts and concluded that this would be a good place to stop for the day.

Harris told Clark to return on Monday. Clark asked if things would wrap up in time so he could host *Bandstand* that afternoon. Harris said no.

Reporter Clark Mollenhoff of the *Des Moines Register* reported that Clark became angry when told he'd have to return for a second session. In fact, Mollenhoff wrote, Clark's testimony ran the gamut of emotions that day, describing him as "polite, overly polite, sad, sarcastic and sometimes a little angry."

ABC reinforced Clark's importance to the network's bottom line when it released information that Clark's television shows accounted for 4 percent of the network's TV billings in 1959. Trade publications put the network's total billings at $130 million for the year, meaning Clark's shows were responsible for $5.2 million of that total.

Before Clark resumed his testimony on Monday, May 2, the subcommittee released transcripts of earlier closed-door sessions with New York record manufacturers and music publishers George Goldner and George Paxton.

The subcommittee had learned that Clark owned copyrights to 162 songs and that 90 percent of them were handed over to Clark firms free of charge. When asked what was the difference between giving a man copyright and a $1,000 payment, Goldner said he didn't "know the difference."[66]

Live testimony opened with House investigator James Kelly telling the subcommittee that ABC's initial statement supporting Clark that claimed a company investigation had cleared Clark of any wrongdoing was inaccurate. Upon questioning by investigators, ABC officials admitted that there had been no investigation and that the statement of support was based solely on Clark's denial that he had done anything wrong.

When Clark took the witness chair, he was asked at length about what he knew about Tony Mammarella's payola involvement. Clark insisted that he was unaware of the "consulting fees" reaped by the man who sat an arm's length from him in their tiny WFIL-TV office until Mammarella hinted that he was involved in some things "that would be difficult to explain." Clark told him he didn't want to know any more about it but found out more a few days later.

Clark also confirmed that he had induced ABC officials to soften the wording of a reference to Mammarella, without naming him, in the affidavit Clark executed for ABC denying that he had received or solicited payola.

Lishman then spent the rest of the morning going over the charts that detailed virtually every business transaction Clark had conducted since taking over *Bandstand* and introducing documents into the record.

Clark and his lawyer retreated to a private room during the lunch hour to map out their afternoon strategy when there was a knock on the door. It was Lishman, and his 14-year-old son,

---

66. Ibid.

Robert Jr. Would you mind giving Robert an autograph, the senior Lishman asked Clark?

"It was at that point that the light suddenly came on in my head," Clark later wrote in his autobiography, *Rock, Roll & Remember*. "I realized the whole thing was a shuck. This man had been saying terrible things to me in public, really gunning for me, and then he turned up with his kid for an autograph!"[67]

In the afternoon session, Rep. Moss accused Clark of collecting $7,000 in fees from American Airlines for plugs that were in violation of Section 317 of the Communications Statute.

The plugs, which came at the end of the *Saturday Night Show*, hinted that guests on the show had used the airline for travel to the show. Under questioning, Clark said he didn't know if guests actually used the airline and that he wasn't knowledgeable about the details of the arrangement since it had been negotiated by the network. He did admit, however, that he pocketed all of the $7,000.

The rest of the afternoon session degenerated into discussions of Fabian's talent and squealing teenage girls.

Reps. Derounian and Springer claimed that by any measure, Fabian was lacking in the basic skills you would expect in a popular singer, Clark countered by saying he was only giving the public what they wanted, and they really liked Fabian. Derounian said the entire Fabian phenomenon was created by Clark, not an eager public.

Chairman Harris took the discourse even lower when he asked Clark, "What do you do . . . that causes all these fine young people in attendance in these shows to squeal so loud at a particular time? Do you have some kind of a cue that you give them to do it?"[68]

Even Harris must have realized it was time to wrap things up. But, before ending the proceedings, he said to Clark:

> You are obviously a fine young man. You started in this business young and you are attractive to young people. Therefore, your responsibilities with your influence can be great. . . . I do not think you are the inventor of the system; I do not think you are even the architect of it, apparently. I think you took advantage of

---

67. *Rock, Roll & Remember*, p. 216.
68. *Hearings Before a Subcommittee of the Committee on Interstate and Foreign Commerce*, Government Printing Office, 1960.

a unique opportunity to control too many elements in the popular music field, through exposure of records to a vast teenage audience.[69]

As Clark was headed back to Philadelphia and the relative comfort of Bandstandland, ABC-Paramount president Leonard Goldenson was headed to Washington to testify in what promised to be the final day of the hearings.

Before Goldenson's testimony, however, the subcommittee released its detailed report on its analysis of the 15,000 index cards representing songs played on *American Bandstand*. Staffers Rex Sparger and Bill Martin compiled the data which showed that Clark gave preferential treatment to songs in which he had a financial interest.

Ben Hoberman, station manager of WABC in New York and the man who fired Alan Freed for not signing a network affidavit about payola, testified about the station's contract with Freed that would have paid him $40,000 a year, but would have charged him $10,000 for on-air promotion of each of the three holiday concerts Freed was planning for the upcoming year.

If Dick Clark were held to a similar standard for promoting records in which he had a financial interest, the *New York Times* reported, the tab would come to $25 million.

Goldenson found himself taking pointed questions from several subcommittee members.

Yes, he admitted, there had been no network investigation of Clark prior to its public statement of support. And yes, it was true, he'd never met Clark before the kerfuffle that ultimately led to Clark's divestment of his music holdings. Goldenson also admitted that the network had never investigated Tony Mammarella, even though Mammarella and Clark had an extremely close working relationship.

When it came to Freed's claim that Clark's signing of a "Christian Dior" affidavit represented special treatment by the network, Goldenson said there was no significant difference in the documents Freed and Clark were asked to sign.

When Rep. Moss brought up Freed's claim that he was told to "lay heavy on Am-Par [an ABC-Paramount subsidiary] records," Goldenson called Freed a liar.

---

69. Ibid.

An angry Moss responded by asking Goldenson, "If it is necessary for a deejay to divest of music interests—why not a network? What's the difference?"[70]

Goldenson responded that Am-Par "as a corporate, but separately—and virtuously—administered subsidiary of a network, would not be so susceptible [as an individual deejay]."[71]

Rep. Bennett pointed out that as much as 4 percent of Am-Par's gross was used for payola; Goldenson called it "promotion." Rep. Mack took Goldenson to task for apparently thinking that with Freed fired, Clark out of the music business and with Mammarella gone that the whole sordid matter of payola at ABC was over and done with.

Indeed, the entire subcommittee announced it would go into executive session within days to hammer out anti-payola legislation before the rapidly ending 86th Congress concluded business.

"The announcement summed up the Committee's outspoken dissatisfaction with the 'unrealistic' testimony of the ABC network president, and the stand-pat claims of innocence by Clark, as holding out any promise of voluntary reform by the broadcasters."[72]

At the end of 19 days of testimony, the subcommittee released figures, based on a mail survey, that showed 130 record distributors had handed out $263,244 in payola in the past two years to 207 disc jockeys and other radio-TV personnel and to 12 stations themselves.[73]

Trade publication *Variety* noted that each of the subcommittee's 57 witnesses were asked to define payola. Over the course of the hearings, payola came to be known by other terms, too:

Chairman Harris used the term "plugola" to describe the practice of broadcasting a plug for anything commercial without identifying it as advertising for which there was compensation. Rep. Derounian used "royola" in a reference to Clark's outside royalty interests in disks he favored on his television shows.

By the end of the hearings, Clark's multiple revenue streams were so unique that Lawrence Laurent, TV columnist for the *Washington Post*, created a term only applicable to the *American Bandstand* host: Clarkola.[74]

---

70. Ibid.
71. Ibid.
72. Ibid.
73. Ibid.
74. *Variety*, May 4, 1960.

With the payola hearings now behind him, Clark redirected his energies. On May 4, he treated *American Bandstand* watchers to a filmed tour of Bobby Rydell's Philadelphia home. On his *Saturday Night Show* on May 7, Junior & His Friends lip-synced to "Who's Our Pet, Annette," a forgettable little ditty but for the fact that the song was written by Paul Anka for his then-girlfriend, Annette, and was sung by Anka's little brother, 10-year-old Andy Anka.

But the highlight of the show from Clark's perspective had to be the two songs performed by Duane Eddy, the popular guitarist who became a target during the hearings since virtually every aspect of his career had been controlled by Clark.

With a sort of thumb-in-your-eye bravado, Clark had Eddy play two songs from Clark's recently released movie, *Because They're Young*—the title song and "Shazam."

Eddy's recording of those songs turned out to be the best-selling single of his career.

CHAPTER 15

LANDING ON HIS FEET

Dick Clark wasn't the only disc jockey eager to put the payola issue behind him.

Many of the nation's deejays who had lost their high-profile radio jobs in the previous seven months had found employment in their chosen profession, albeit at many different venues—and salaries.

Tom Clay, one of payola's earliest casualties, resurfaced briefly at WBRB in Mt. Clemens, Mich., before returning to Detroit at WQTE. He wasn't there long before he walked out. Clay called it "our little misunderstanding," but station owner Ross Mullholland was more precise: "It was a question of who was going to run the radio station."[1]

Alan Freed, who quit his $40,000 a year job at WABC over the affidavit flap, moved west to Hollywood, Calif., where he landed a six-day-a-week job at KDAY that paid $25,000. Making the move with Freed were two of his co-workers from his days at WINS—program director Mel Leeds and librarian Bruce Wendell.

KDAY station manager Irving Phillips made it clear that Freed's contract included a clause that Freed would strictly adhere to FCC rules. KDAY, which had already banned rock & roll records,

---

1. *Billboard*, October 10, 1960.

did give Freed some leeway in what he played, encouraging him to find hits from the rhythm & blues genre, his forté.

Stations across the country continued to switch formats and some deejays made it clear that payola was no longer a factor in their decisions on what to play.

Tom Edwards, a Cleveland disc jockey who claimed to never have accepted as much as a cup of coffee from a song plugger, had left WERE during the payola probe for entrepreneurial reasons and resurfaced at WADC in Akron, Ohio, where he had a country & western show.

Edwards, whose insights were frequently found on the editorial pages of *Billboard* magazine, used the magazine to tell the song pluggers to leave him alone.

"I am tired of 'phony friendships' which last only as long as you are able to help out," Edwards wrote. "I don't need you and you got along without me for the past 10 months, so let's keep it that way."[2]

Clark, though ousted from the music business, maintained his position of influence in the TV world. *American Bandstand* was on 135 stations in mid-1960 and his *Saturday Night Show* was seen on 93 stations.

A survey by the Gilbert Youth Research Co. indicated that Clark's popularity wasn't hurt a bit by the payola scandal. While 68 percent of the teens surveyed claimed that payola was "very wrong" or "undesirable," 69 percent of them said Clark was justified in promoting songs from his own record company on his TV show.[3]

Clark was reluctant to talk publicly about payola in the weeks following the hearings, but he did grant *New York Herald Tribune* columnist Marie Torre an interview in early June 1960.

"[Payola's] a difficult thing to talk about," Clark told Torre. "I'd just as soon put the subject to rest. Forget it. . . . As for myself, I wasn't affected professionally. I never had any feelings of guilt, I never lost any sleep over it—except one night when a magazine reporter broke into my house."

Clark did confide that his career goals had been stifled by his leaving the music business.

"My greatest ambition is to have financial security," he said.[4]

---

2. *Billboard*, July 11, 1960.
3. *Philadelphia Inquirer*, August 19, 1960.
4. *New York Herald Tribune*, June 7, 1960.

Life magazine reporter Peter Bunzel wrote a lengthy article in May 1960, portraying Clark as a charismatic pitchman who had created an intensely dedicated national following, almost like a preacher with a devout flock of parishioners. But Clark took issue with the article's opening paragraph:

> Back in September 1958 a roly-poly Tulsa boy named Billy Jay Killion came home from high school and wanted to watch Dick Clark's television program, *American Bandstand*. His mother, who didn't particularly care for rock & roll music, was all set to watch a different program, so she told Billy 'No.' He seethed the whole night long. Then in the morning Billy took out a rifle and shot his mother dead.[5]

Thirty years later, Clark was still complaining about the article.

"They took thousands of pictures. It was a great story. But they ended [sic] with the story of the kid who killed his mother because she wouldn't let him watch the *Bandstand*. . . . What sort of a devious mind would do this to you? Suck you in, take pictures of your kids and follow you, run pictures and end with the story of a kid that killed his mother? . . . It didn't make a ripple of sense."[6]

The *Life* article notwithstanding, Clark's career seemed to be solidly back on track by mid-1960.

ABC continued to stand by Clark and at least one sponsor—Coppertone suntan products—took a very public stance in support of Clark by making him the public face of an ad campaign that spring, using his photo in ads touting him as "the idol of teenage America as well as millions of adults."

Clark signed a two-day deal to appear at the Steel Pier in Atlantic City in July, reportedly for $12,500 plus 50 percent of all gate receipts over $50,000.[7] The first night at the Pier was a remote telecast of the *Saturday Night Show* and both nights featured Bobby Rydell.

Even the apparent national trend away from rock & roll strengthened Clark's position in the entertainment marketplace. With fewer deejays allowed to create their own playlists, "*American*

---

5. *Life*, May 16, 1960.
6. *The Late Show With David Letterman*, 1990.
7. *Philadelphia Inquirer*, June 27, 1960.

Bandstand contributed to, and thrived in, this atmosphere of sameness."[8]

While things seemed to be going well for Clark, the same couldn't be said for many former associates in the music business he'd left behind.

Two weeks after the House hearings wrapped up, Philadelphia Collections Commissioner Mortin E. Rotman subpoenaed the books of four Philadelphia music publishing and record companies, including Jamie Records and Universal Distributing Co., in order to determine if the companies owed city taxes for payola payments to disc jockeys.

It was even worse in New York City, where Alan Freed was among eight people arrested for commercial bribery. In all, Freed faced 26 counts. Also arrested were popular deejays Peter Tripp of WMGM and Tommy "Dr. Jive" Smalls of WWRL. One of the counts against Tripp accused him of receiving a royalty of one-half cent per record on each copy sold of "16 Candles"

Philadelphia District Attorney Victor H. Blanc sent four investigators to Washington where they spent 10 days studying materials from the House hearings before returning with a filing cabinet's worth of documents and evidence. As a result, Blanc started his own Philadelphia investigation of 39 deejays, radio station employees and record company executives.

Chips Distributing and Jamie Record Co. were on Blanc's list, as were Harold B. Lipsius, Harry Finfer, Ed Barsky, David Rosen, Edward Cohn, Bernie Lowe, Harry Chipetz, Ed Hurst, Joe Grady, Hy Lit, Tony Mammarella, Joe Niagara, Lloyd "Fatman" Smith, Mitch Thomas, Kae Williams and Georgie Woods. Blanc made a point of saying that Dick Clark was not involved.

Furthermore, Blanc declared, Clark had agreed to head a disc jockey association that would enable radio and television artists to police themselves.[9]

But Clark wasn't simply relying on others to spread the word of his innocence. After his testimony in D.C., Clark started writing to friends and supporters, thanking them for standing by him in what he saw as unjust persecution. By the time he was done, Clark had written a treatise 3,643 words long. It ran in its entirety in the pages of the August 1960 issue of *TV & Radio Mirror*.

In "An Open Letter From Dick Clark," he wrote about the guy in a drug store who said a lot of children were going to church to

---

8. *The Nicest Kids In Town*, p. 147.
9. *Philadelphia Inquirer*, August 20, 1960.

light candles for him. He wrote about how the staff and crew of the *Saturday Night Show* wished him well as he headed to Washington. He also told of how "reporters were hounding everyone I ever knew in show business and each would call me afterward and say, 'Don't worry. We're with you.'"[10]

He also wrote about how the "cruel accusations were written by extremely prejudiced people" and were lies, but said he took it as a sign of respect that investigators repeatedly asked him for autographs and pictures.

He wrote about how the whole experience had changed him and his family.

"I began to give more attention to the intimate aspects of living and it served to remind me of our basic philosophy," Clark wrote. "Barbara and I have never stressed material things. . . . It has always been our idea to live the way we planned before I was fortunate. To live simply with Barbara as the penny-watcher and with me securing the future so we'll always have a roof over our heads and clothes and be able to educate our son."[11]

Clark also hinted at his future—time at the shore, make another movie, write another book.

"I am writing a book," Clark said. "I don't know that it will ever be published, but it's the story of a young man in the music business. It's a fictional story about the music world I've known. Some of the material is very funny and some very tragic. I'm writing it for my own amusement, but I hope someone will read it and want to publish it. In spite of all these activities, I don't really want to be a writer or an actor or a businessman.

"My first love, from the time I was twelve or thirteen, was radio and television. I'd like always to stay in television."[12]

The editors at *TV & Radio Mirror* didn't let Clark go unchallenged, however. It asked reporters at newspapers in 12 large cities to ask teenagers and their parents: How will the House hearings affect Dick Clark's popularity?

Janice Crabb, 18, of Minneapolis said, "I suppose that now he'll have an even greater following than he did before because he's made rather a martyr of himself and to his followers now he can do no wrong. But in this person's opinion, he's a poor example of a hero."

---

10. *TV & Radio Mirror*, August 1960.
11. Ibid.
12. Ibid.

Her dad, Robert M. Crabb, said: "I always thought there was something rancid about rock 'n' roll music. . . . What little I saw of Dick Clark and his afternoon television show seemed harmless, however, . . . But when he turned sociologist via a national teenage advice column, I thought he was being ridiculous."

Generally, though, the comments were positive. Frank Littlefield of Detroit, the father of teenager James Littlefield, said: "Clark is wholesome. None of this beatnik-beard kind of thing. He seems like the kind of person we'd like to have our boys grow up to be. It may sound trite, but he's the All-American Boy type. He's no showoff. He appeals to young and old alike. Just a plain, common, everyday sort of person, which, I think, is why people like him."[13]

* * *

As good as Clark was in his role as the amiable host and as relevant as the music he played was to his young audience, *American Bandstand* would have failed without the ebullient, energetic, teenage dancers that lit up the screen every weekday afternoon.

At its core, *Bandstand* was a unique visual experience. Not only could you listen to the music you enjoyed in the comfort of your own living room, but you could also see that you weren't the only one who got happy feet when Danny and the Juniors belted out "At the Hop."

Bandstand also benefited from being in Philadelphia, a city with rich dance history. That was especially true in the black community, many of whom had migrated from the juke joint south, bringing with them dances like the Monkey Glide, the Chicken Scratch and the Shimmy.

South Street and its black clubs were where you would go if you wanted to hucklebuck, kangaroo dip or bunny hug. Flash tappers like the Nicholas Brothers were national sensations, playing for two years at Harlem's Cotton Club and appearing in many Broadway shows and Hollywood movies. And women tap dancers like Edith "Baby Edwards" Hunt and Hortense Allen Jordan drew huge crowds wherever they appeared.

From its earliest days, *Bandstand* spread the gospel of dance. There was the Bunny Hop craze that broke out during the Bob

---

13. Ibid.

Horn years. When Clark took over just as rock & roll was coming into vogue, so, too, did the dances change.

It was the bop that inspired "At the Hop" and made Pat Molittieri an early *American Bandstand* star. There was a steady parade of dance contests on the show, seven in all during the Philadelphia years, each featuring a slightly different style of dancing. The show introduced at least two new popular dances to American teens before 1959—the stroll and the calypso.

For all of *American Bandstand*'s influence on teenage dance, it wasn't the only show to tap into youthful kinetic movements. Indeed, two of the more popular teen dances of early 1960 broke out elsewhere.

"(Do the) Mashed Potatoes" by Nat Kendrick & the Swans made a brief appearance on the pop charts but was a Top Ten rhythm & blues hit after breaking out in Miami.

An even bigger dance craze was the Madison, thanks to a recording by former Baltimore streetcar motorman, Al Brown. "The Madison" by Al Brown & the Tunetoppers was just the fifth release for the Amy label. Within 10 days, Brown's recording faced stiff competition from Philadelphia-born Ray Bryant's "Madison Time," which enjoyed the support of a major label, Columbia.

The Madison was a line dance with precise steps, unlike the stroll. The dance was intricate enough that Columbia included an instruction sheet with every 45 it sold. Both records enjoyed airplay, even on Baltimore's *Buddy Deane Show*, which heavily promoted the song. Columbia recruited two of Deane's regulars—Joan Darby and Joe Cash—to do a tour of teen dance shows in the east and midwest, demonstrating the Madison.

As Clark emerged after months mired in the fog of payola, a burst of dance energy was what *American Bandstand* needed to reassert its influence on pop teen culture. As he scoured the charts, Clark thought the answer might lie with a singer who'd built his career around a series of "dirty" R&B songs years earlier, Hank Ballard.

Ballard wasn't the type of singer you'd normally see on *American Bandstand*. His lyrics were sexually charged and chock full of black slang and his stage presence would be considered raunchy by just about every *Bandstand* standard.

But his Annie trilogy—"Work With Me Annie," "Sexy Ways" and "Annie Had a Baby"—had sold a lot of records and his latest offering, "Finger Poppin' Time, "had a catchy, danceable tune. The B-side of an earlier release also had promise—in the right hands.

LANDING ON HIS FEET

That B-side had been brought to Clark's attention months earlier, about the same time the payola scandal first broke although precisely how Dick Clark came to learn about "The Twist" is a matter of dispute.

According to Clark's version, he was shocked to see a black couple lewdly gyrating on *Bandstand* in the summer of 1960. He ordered the cameras to ignore the couple, but later questioned them about the dance. When told it was the Twist and that Ballard's song was all the rage, Clark called Bernie Lowe at Cameo and suggested that his label might have a winner if it came up with a more palatable version of Ballard's song that could be played on *Bandstand*.

Another version has Buddy Deane calling Clark after teens on his Baltimore show were demanding the song and telling Clark he might want to jump on the record. The third version also involves Deane but also involves Freddy Cannon, a Clark favorite whose career was made by Swan Records, a label once half-owned by Clark.

Although it's difficult to believe that Deane, a rival of Clark's whose show preempted *Bandstand* in Baltimore, would tip off the opposition about a hot record, the other two stories are plausible.

Cannon and Bernie Binnick had, indeed, made the trip to Deane's show in November 1959 to plug Cannon's latest Swan release, "Way Down Yonder in New Orleans." Hank Ballard & the Midnighters were performing at the Royal Theater in Baltimore at the same time and it's reasonable to assume that Deane would dust off some of Ballard's old tunes to play on his show while Ballard was going through his week-long stint at the Royal.

After seeing how the kids on Deane's show reacted to "The Twist," Binnick and Cannon brought a copy of the record back to Clark and played it for him.

"I can't play that, it's too black. Give it to Freddy here and we'll play it," Clark told Binnick.[14]

Binnick declined, since "Way Down Yonder" showed signs of being a breakout hit and commanded his attention. It would be another six months before Clark revisited the possibility of covering Ballard's song, and when Lowe agreed to tackle the project, Clark made a deal with King Records owner Syd Nathan that would ensure Ballard's financial future and establish Chubby Checker as Philadelphia's newest contribution to rock & roll.

---

14. *DISCoveries*, June 1994.

Nathan was one of the early rock era's more colorful figures. Originally in the business of selling radios, Nathan had stumbled into the music business when a customer paid off a debt with a truckload of records. He quickly learned that the big money in the music business went to publishers and label owners.

At 5'2" and 250 pounds, Nathan was a comical looking figure with his Coke-bottle glasses and ever-present cigar, but his promo men were among the more efficient in the business, beating the bushes in old jalopies full of records, sandwiches, and pints of whiskey.

Ballard's "Finger Poppin' Time" on Nathan's King label had enjoyed a decent run up the charts but was starting to slide when Clark approached Nathan. The song would be a good one for a dance contest on *American Bandstand*, Clark told Nathan, and, since the song was fairly tame by Ballard standards, we might even be able to work out an appearance on the show. Plus, if Hank can come up with a non-controversial follow-up, we'll give that a push, too. In exchange, we'd like to do a cover of "The Twist" by a local boy. Hank's version is just a little bit too raw for us.

The temptation of having Dick Clark get behind two of his songs and cover a third was too much for Nathan to ignore. He accepted Clark's proposition.[15]

True to his word, Clark started playing "Finger Poppin' Time" for his summer fast dance contest and invited Ballard on *American Bandstand*. "Finger Poppin' Time's" chart fortunes turned around immediately as it began a climb into the Top 10 that would result in a 26-week run on *Billboard's* Hot 100.

Meanwhile, Bernie Lowe took a good look at "The Twist" in order to "turn the song upside down or sideways or whatever and do it again," as per Clark's instructions.[16]

"There's no sense turning it upside down," Lowe reported back to Clark. "It's too simple."[17]

Lowe and arranger Dave Appell broke down Ballard's song, note for note, and wrote an arrangement for the Cameo house band, Appel's Applejacks. They recorded the instrumental in the fifth-floor Cameo studios then took the master a few blocks away to the Reco Art Studios where they added the vocals.

Since the Cameo version of the song was to be a virtual copy of Ballard's song, Lowe looked for a singer who could mimic Ballard's

---

15. "Ronny Elliott Remembers Dick Clark," ninebullets.net, April 3, 2012.
16. *Rock, Roll & Remember*, p. 100.
17. Ibid, p. 101.

voice. He decided to roll the dice on an 18-year-old South Philadelphian, Chubby Checker.

Checker had already recorded three records for Cameo's sister label, Parkway, and although the last two had been stiffs, the success of his first release pushed him to the top of the list. Young Checker, whose first big break came when he mimicked several rockers for the Clarks' Christmas card, further displayed his ability to copy other singers with his first Parkway release, "The Class."

It took just 35 minutes for Checker to add the vocal to the *Twist*, backed by another group of young Philadelphians, the Dreamlovers.

But, if Clark and Lowe thought they had "The Twist" all to themselves, they were mistaken. Although Nathan had agreed to let Clark push a cover version of the song on his television shows, Nathan had his own version that had already proven itself hit material.

Nathan re-released Ballard's version of "The Twist" on almost the same day Checker's version hit the shelves. Ballard's version took off first, but Checker's version broke into the Hot 100 in a big way, debuting at No. 49 on August 1. Five days later, Checker introduced his version of "The Twist" to a national audience for the first time on Clark's *Saturday Night Show*.

Watching a husky teenager dressed in black slacks and a checkered sports coat gyrating as if he were grinding out a cigarette with his feet while toweling off his rear end must have been quite a sight for Clark's audience that night. It was a sight that would become quite familiar for years to come as Americans took to the Twist much as they had taken to the hula hoop two years earlier.

Within seven weeks of its debut, Checker's "The Twist "was No. 1 on *Billboard's* Hot 100. Ballard's version also started a steady climb as did "Finger Poppin' Time."

With Clark's help, a third Ballard song, "Let's Go, Let's Go, Let's Go," also became a Top 10 hit in 1960. When "Let's Go" jumped to No. 49 on *Billboard's* Hot 100 on October 10, it marked the first time any singer had three songs in the top 50 at the same time, a big achievement for a singer that hadn't had a single song on the pop charts before aligning himself with Dick Clark.

For the summer of 1960, Clark decided (with the encouragement and blessing of Leonard Goldenson) to occasionally take his *Saturday Night Show* out of New York City.

On June 9, he began what he called an "On the Road" series by broadcasting from Pittsburgh, Pennsylvania. For five consecutive weeks, the *Saturday Night Show* originated from Hollywood (two shows), the Treasure Island Naval Base in San Francisco Bay and Chicago.

When in Hollywood, he crowned Miss California at Santa Monica Civic Auditorium and filmed a visit with Annette Funicello in her Encino, Calif., home for later viewing on *American Bandstand*.

Clark also took *Bandstand* on the road, but not nearly as far, In July, he did the show's first outdoor show since going network with a "Splash Party" theme from the Drexelbrook Swimming and Tennis Club and in September he did a western-themed show from Frontierland in Pennsville, Pennsylvania.

The summer ended on a down note for Clark, however, when it was announced that the *Saturday Night Show* would end after its Sept. 10 broadcast.

A major factor was the loss of Beech-Nut as a sponsor. Beech-Nut said it would move some of its sponsorship to *American Bandstand*, but the bulk of its ad money was moving to NBC-TV, where it had signed on to *The Shirley Temple Show* and a new show billed as "the network's answer to Dick Clark," *Saturday Prom*.

The final blow to *The Saturday Night Show*, ironically, came from one of Clark's earliest supporters, ABC television president Ollie Treyz. Treyz' concept of "bridging" was widely credited with the success of ABC-TV's recent prime time successes.

With bridging, an hour-long show started on the half-hour instead of the hour under the theory that if you hooked someone in that first 30 minutes they wouldn't switch away to another show at the top of the hour.

Treyz wanted to bridge the *Saturday Night Show*'s replacement, *The Roaring 20s*, in the 7:30–8:30 P.M. slot, which would necessitate moving Clark's show from its 7:30–8 P.M. slot. ABC officials suggested moving Clark 30 minutes earlier to a 7 P.M. slot, but not enough affiliates agreed so the show was canceled.

The loss of a prime time show had to sting, but Clark could find some solace in the knowledge that his goal of providing wholesome entertainment seemed to be working. Maybe payola had shaken the bad apples off the tree after all.

Hollywood seemed eager to latch on to wholesome young singers, many of whom built a following in Bandstandland. Connie Francis was in her first dramatic role in *Where the Boys Are* and Bobby Darin had a multi-picture deal with Paramount. Fabian,

Frankie Avalon, and Paul Anka were also in the motion picture business. Even Clark was ready for his second dramatic movie role in an adaptation of the novel, *The Young Doctors*, to be filmed in the fall in New York.

Bob Marcucci of Chancellor Records borrowed a page from Clark's playbook as he announced a "Win a Date with Avalon and Fabian" promotion tied to the release of their *Good Old Summertime* and *Summer Scene* albums.

Avalon was also following in the footsteps of Bandstandland alums Darin and Anka, studying under choreographer Nick Castle before making his night club debut at Washington's Casino Royal.

Avalon's South Philadelphia neighbor, 18-year-old Bobby Rydell, was also hitting the night club circuit, including a stint with George Burns at the Sahara in Las Vegas. Rydell was also signed for a Timex TV special with Red Skelton.

Clark's *Saturday Night Show* might be ending, but ABC hadn't given up on the primetime youth market. After *Coke Time* premiered on the network on June 27, 1960, *Billboard* called it "one of the best showcases for youthful recording talent ever presented on TV" and called emcee Pat Boone and Bobby Darin "The Perry Como and Frank Sinatra" of 1960.[18]

Payola watchers found themselves strung out all summer as politicians and lobbyists jockeyed for position, more interested in collecting votes in an election year than they were committed to the task of creating genuine reform in the music or broadcasting businesses.

In the end, they came up with a bill that made payola a criminal offense, prohibited quiz frauds and set fines up to $10,000 for broadcasters who "willfully or repeatedly" violate the Communications Statute or FCC rules. Pres. Eisenhower signed the bill into law in September.

But few in the business believed that Congress had actually killed payola.

Reporter June Bundy wrote in *Billboard* that payola stopped for a while, but had returned, albeit in a more discreet fashion. Some deejays sent their wives to pick up their payments; others met in secret at locations separate from broadcast facilities.

In Philadelphia, Bob Heller, who had been general sales and promotions manager at Chips Distributing when Clark was part owner, quit that job to start his own distributorship. In his new

---

18. *Billboard*, July 4, 1960.

business, Heller promised cocktail parties to introduce dealers and distributors to record company executives and "disk jockey contact which will personally introduce artists and execs."[19]

Clark had no need for Heller's services. He'd once again showed his hit-making power in the post-payola era with "The Twist." He'd lost the *Saturday Night Show*, but he had a financial interest (and non-starring role) in another movie with *The Young Doctors* and confided to friends that he was working on that novel about a young man in the music business.

"The moral is that he finds you can't live by bread alone," Clark said of the book.[20]

The print arm of the Annenberg media empire rallied to Clark's side when *TV Guide* published an article about Clark titled "Guilty Only of Success."

In the article, Clark claimed he was exonerated by the House hearings and that he was given a 10-minute standing ovation by the teen dancers upon his return to the *Bandstand* studio, where he compared the atmosphere to a drugstore.

"When I was a boy we used to hang around a drugstore back home," he explained. "It was very wholesome. You never get into trouble in a drugstore. . . . And that's the way it is on *Bandstand*. We have a wholesome atmosphere."[21]

There were a lot of small-town drugstore vibes rippling through Bandstandland that fall.

Former regulars Kenny Rossi and Tommy DeNoble dropped by to lip-sync to their latest records. Another ex-regular, Justine Carrelli, was prominently featured in print ads for Johnny Tillotson's latest release, "Poetry in Motion." Chubby Checker popped in to do "The Twist" and danced off with his gold record.

Frani Giordano took the top prize of a transistor radio in the *Bandstand* Halloween costume contest with her portrayal of Vampira, complete with flowing black gown and wig to match.

Clark made one of his cross-network appearances on October 23 when he appeared on *The Jack Benny Program* on CBS, portraying himself as Benny seeks advice on how to attract young viewers to his show.

Attracting young viewers—especially young female viewers— was still a great *American Bandstand* strength, as verified by a November 1960 study by the American Research Bureau that

---

19. *Billboard*, June 13, 1960.
20. Rick DuBrow, *United Press International*, 1960.
21. *TV Guide*, Sept. 10, 1960.

found that *Bandstand* drew some 6.5 million adult female viewers each week ages 13–29.

Bandstand could also take credit for show favorite Duane Eddy's slipping past Elvis into the top spot as the World's Outstanding Musical Personality in the Fall 1960 New Musical Express poll in Great Britain.

But there were also signs that Clark's grip on the teenage popular music scene might be loosening a bit.

In Philadelphia, NBC-owned WRCV claimed that its billings had increased by 20 percent since switching to big band music in January. Furthermore, its live remote broadcast of a "Dance In the Square" promotion drew a large crowd to the Levittown Shoparama and included Ed Hurst among the record spinners.

Look magazine, noting that Dick Stewart was looking very much like "the next Dick Clark," dispatched a reporter and photographer to San Francisco to document Stewart's rise at KPIX-TV.

NBC had made a full frontal assault on Clark's turf when it drew up plans for *Saturday Prom*. The show was slotted two hours earlier than Clark's *Saturday Night Show* but had signed Beech-Nut as a major sponsor. Beech-Nut's departure from Clark's show doubtless hastened the show's demise and it was long gone by the time *Saturday Prom* debuted on October 15.

Merv Griffin was the host for the show and the Si Zentner orchestra provided music for the young singers that appeared on stage. Conway Twitty was the first singing guest on the show that promised to honor a different high school group each week.

Producer Ed Pierce fired a shot across the *Bandstand* bow a month into the show when he invited Clark's rival from Baltimore, Buddy Deane, onto the show. Not only that, he invited Deane to bring along a few regular dancers from his show.

Deane was only too happy to oblige. That evening, four teen-aged couples from Baltimore introduced a national audience to a new dance, the Fish Walk.

The Fish Walk never made a splash on *American Bandstand* and *Saturday Prom* lasted less than six months, but Dick Clark knew he could take nothing for granted. That was made abundantly clear in a phone call he received from the wife of an old friend in the record business one morning.

"Are you aware of what's going on between my husband and your wife?" she asked.[22]

---

22. *Rock, Roll & Remember*, p. 226.

CHAPTER 16

FLYING SOLO

Dick Clark was shocked. Bobbie unfaithful? It can't be true. From the day he literally bumped into Barbara Mallery between classes at A.B. Davis High School in Mount Vernon, N.Y., 15 years earlier, he thought they were destined to be together the rest of their lives.

Even after Clark's family moved to Utica and Mallery moved to Maryland with her widowed mother, Clark often made the long drive in his aging, beat-up Ford to see her. After he'd persuaded her to finish her college at nearby Oswego State College, they vowed they would marry.

Bobbie wanted to finish school and Clark wanted to have some money in the bank before they wed, which they did on June 28, 1952, six weeks after he'd landed a radio job at WFIL in Philadelphia.

They'd settled into what Clark thought was an idyllic life. Bobbie taught school for two years while Clark climbed the ladder at WFIL, winning audition after audition for coveted TV commercial spots and earning a regular spot on the radio roster. After their son, Richard A. Clark II was born on January 9, 1957, Dick and Bobbie were just settling into their new roles as parents when the network latched onto *Bandstand*.

As Clark grew into his role as a national celebrity, Bobbie was right at his side. She was an occasional visitor to the *Bandstand* studio and, though she appeared shy in public, she always stood up for her husband and the wholesome values he promoted.

But she was also envious of her husband's hectic schedule, especially when compared to her domestic duties. So Clark started inviting her to meetings with sponsors, rehearsals and personal appearances, which she found to be boring.

Increasingly, Clark's business took him to New York, sometimes four or five times a week. To make the two-hour trip, Clark woke at 5:30 A.M. In New York, he would race from meeting to meeting before returning to Philadelphia by 2 P.M. in time for *Bandstand*.

In an article in *TV Radio Mirror* that was published before the public was aware of trouble in the Clark's marriage, Clark told of the anguish a friend felt as he went through a divorce.

Clark noted that the friend, a performer, had been on the road 45 weeks in the previous year. His wife didn't like show business, he said.

"Maybe this performer's wife didn't know what was ahead of them," Clark said. "Maybe they didn't sit down and talk about it ahead of time."

He added that he and his wife were different than his friend. They've discussed the problems and uncertainties of the show, he said.

"Bobbie is always ready for the unexpected,"[1] he said.

Clark said that he and Bobbie had discussed how filming *The Young Doctors* during the Christmas holiday of 1960 would interfere with the family's holiday plans, but they agreed that the sacrifice could be worth it if helped Clark develop a meaningful film career.

"You can't kid about the importance of a career to a man's ego," Clark said. "But above that—always—is being with people you love. Business must be secondary to people. Show business being what it is, husband and wife have to work a little harder to secure their happiness."[2]

Looking back, Clark conceded that he probably hadn't paid enough attention to his wife. Too many missed dinners, movie dates and anniversaries took their toll. But, before he confronted his wife about what he had been told, he hired a private detective who confirmed the affair.

---

1. *TV Radio Mirror*, January 1961.
2. Ibid.

"After much soul-searching, Bobbie and I decided to get a divorce,"[3] he said.

But, with Christmas approaching, the couple decided to keep the news to themselves for a while and didn't even tell their families. Clark threw his energies into *American Bandstand*, which remained as popular as ever.

Although times seemed to be changing rapidly in America, most of the changes seemed to point to a bright future for Clark and his show.

Sure, record sales were down a bit, but payola was in the past now and a corps of young comedians, led by the "buttoned-down" mind of young Bob Newhart, were leading a resurgence in sales. *Howdy Doody* and Clark's old friends, Arthur and Katherine Murray, were no longer on the air and Lucy and Desi had split up, but newlyweds Bobby Darin and Sandra Dee were the cutest couple ever and Barbie had a new boyfriend named Ken.

A young Senator from Massachusetts named John Kennedy had just been elected president, the census showed there were nearly 41 million people ages 10–24 in the U.S. and Pepsi Cola's new advertising slogan was "Those who think young."

There was a youth movement behind the scenes in the music business, too. The old a.&r. men who had dominated popular music before rock & roll were being replaced by younger men, many barely out of school. Rising a.&r. men Jerry Lieber & Mike Stoller, Snuff Garrett, Don Kirshner, Berry Gordy Jr., and Phil Spector were all in their 20s and all were younger than Dick Clark.

But Clark tried to do his part to support the American youth movement. The summer swim party broadcast from Drexelbrook was such a hit he returned for a skating party. In addition to the Halloween and Frontierland shows, there were other themed programs, like the Roaring Twenties and a Hong Kong party.

Although the regulars who made the show such a hit in the early years were mostly gone, he invited them back in August for "Old Regulars Day." Frani Giordano was still around in late 1960, breaking boys' hearts from coast to coast. So were the Jimenez sisters, Carmen and Ivette, and their distinctive blonde-streaked hair.

But the new regulars were popular, too—Arlene DiPietro, Mike Balara, Barbara Levick, Betty Romantini, Joe Fusco, Bunny Gibson, and Eddie Kelly.

---

3. *Rock, Roll & Remember*, p. 227.

Bandstand apparently had its haters as well, as two suspected bombs were sent to the WFIL-TV studios in a 10-day period around Thanksgiving.

The first consisted of some ominous looking tubing, connected by wires that ran to an apparent blasting cap, enclosed in a cigar box wrapped in plain brown kraft paper. After the device was removed to police headquarters at 55th and Pine, U.S. Army ordnance experts determined that the blasting cap was nothing more than tree bark and the entire device was harmless.

Similarly, the second suspicious package that arrived from Bloomfield, N.J., was removed to the athletic field of nearby Drexel University where it was found to contain a small stuffed dog.

Clark probably found the Christmas filming schedule of *The Young Doctors* to be more of a relief than the stress he initially thought it would place on his family. He and Bobbie were still sharing the house in Wallingford, but Clark spent little time at home.

Each day for two weeks, longtime friend Ed McAdam would drive Clark to New York for filming before returning him back to Philadelphia in time for *Bandstand*.

"To keep my mind off Bobbie and what had happened, I started drinking, a foolish answer to an emotional problem, but an answer nonetheless. I'd arrive on the set with a terrible hangover and do my scenes with a splitting headache. I was living on straight vodka; I came as close as I could ever come to being an alcoholic in those months."[4]

As far as *American Bandstand* went, Clark was running out of South Philadelphia teenagers to promote and those who had carried the show in its early network years had mostly moved on. But Chubby Checker was still around. So was "The Twist." Everybody, it seemed, was recording twist songs. That included Danny & the Juniors ("Twistin' USA") and Fabian ("Kissin' & Twistin'").

Checker actually tried to move on from "The Twist." He followed his mega-hit with another danceable tune, "The Hucklebuck," which cracked the top 20. His next dance record, "Pony Time," did even better, making it to the top of *Billboard's* Hot 100. Danny & the Juniors responded with "Pony Express" just as Checker's disc hit the top spot. Not to be outdone, Bernie Lowe rushed out a Checker LP, *It's Pony Time*, that covered a wide

---

4. Ibid, p. 228.

range of dances with "The Hully Gully," "The Mashed Potato," "The Shimmy," "The Watusi," "The Stroll" and "The Charleston."

In April 1961 Clark decided that the Pony would be the dance for his next contest. Curiously, though, he didn't pick Checker's No. 1 hit or Danny & the Juniors' song for the contest. He did, however, keep it in the Philadelphia family, picking Titus Turner's Jamie recording, "Pony Train," a song that never cracked the *Billboard* charts.

The pony contest drew the strong public response Clark expected from his dance contests. One viewer who occasionally visited *American Bandstand* in person, Rick Fisher, used his allowance to buy 100 postcards, which he dutifully filled out and mailed in support of his favorite dancer on the show, Carmen Jimenez.

Despite Fisher's effort, Jimenez and her partner, Frankie Vacca, finished third, trailing winners Frani Giordano and Mike Balara and runners-up Joyce Shafer and Norman Kerr.

While the pony enthusiasts were dancing up a storm, Bernie Lowe was touting yet another dance song by Checker in a full-page *Billboard* ad. The ad for "Dance the Mess Around" described Checker as "The Chart Wrecker," a hyperbolic boast for an artist whose lone song on the charts was on the decline.

It was perfectly logical that Lowe and his Cameo-Parkway franchise would be fueling a dance craze. Lowe's a.&r. director, Dave Appel, directed a strong cast of musicians capable of cranking out danceable tunes on short notice. His Applejacks had promoted dances from the earliest days of Cameo, including "Mexican Hat Rock" and "Rocka-Conga" in 1958 and a remake of the song that had been such a big hit in the Bob Horn *Bandstand* era, "The Bunny Hop," in 1959.

Although the Pony was the dance of choice in Bandstandland, the young dancers' parents had found a dance craze of their own. The pachanga and charanga, which have their roots in Cuba, became popular with older adults in nightclubs, particularly in New York City. Apparently, the popularity of the Cuban dances inspired some of those adults to move on to the Twist.

The New York Safety Council reported that for at least one week-long period in 1961, 90 percent of cases involving back trouble were attributed to too much twisting.

As summer approached, Clark and his wife were ready to go public with their pending divorce. Clark had moved out of the

FLYING SOLO

Wallingford house that spring, into the Parktown Apartments. On May 17 they let the world in on their sad secret in a news release from WFIL-TV:

> It is with deep regret that we confirm the report of our impending divorce. We have tried very hard to resolve our differences but have decided that it is best that we take this action. We have consulted our attorneys and the divorce papers will be filed in the near future.

Although it would take six months before the Clarks' divorce was final, within weeks of their public announcement, Bobbie Clark had moved to Youngstown, Ohio, with their son, Dickie. Clark took the separation so hard that when Bobby Vee wanted to lip sync his latest hit, "Please Don't Ask About Barbara," on *American Bandstand* he was told no, a full year after the couple had broken up.

In 1960, when the Congressional payola hearings threatened Clark's career, it was rumored that Leonard Goldenson was looking for a replacement in case the *American Bandstand* star crumbled under the pressure. The smart money in 1960 was on Bob Green, the affable host of a highly rated program at WINZ in Miami.

But one year later, Clark faced a more personal and even more unpredictable crisis as the dark clouds of divorce had driven him to depression and the bottle. If Goldenson was looking for a replacement in 1961, he'd have to look elsewhere. Green had married singer Anita Bryant in June 1960 and gave up his radio job to manage his wife's career.

There were several suitable replacements—Jim Lounsbury in Chicago, Buddy Deane in Baltimore and Milt Grant in Washington, D.C.

But there was another less obvious choice, should Goldenson deem it necessary to replace Clark. Clay Cole, a young Ohioan who was following a similar career path as Alan Freed and who was making quite a splash in New York City, where syndicated columnist Dorothy Kilgallen unabashedly reported that Cole was "being groomed as the next Dick Clark."

Born Albert Rucker Jr. on January 1, 1938, young Cole grew up in Hubbard, Ohio, a small town of about 7,000 near Youngstown. Rucker's passion for the theater led him to a spot on a local radio program in sixth grade. By high school, he was starring in school plays and writing for the *Hubbard News*. After lip-syncing with friends to the Modernaires' *Juke Box Saturday Night* for a polio benefit show in 1953, he and his friends became regular guests on a local variety television show that led to the creation of a Saturday night program for teens, *Rucker's Rumpus Room*.

In 1954, he landed his first radio job on WKBN, the same station where Freed had been a sports announcer 10 years earlier. By his senior year, *Rucker's Rumpus Room* had moved to NBC affiliate WFMJ-TV, where he persuaded station officials to start a teen dance program called *One O'Clock Jump*, patterned after Lounsbury's show in Chicago.

After *TV Radio Mirror* ran an article on *Rucker's Rumpus Room* and Steve Allen invited him on the *Tonight* show, Rucker headed to New York City.

He landed a $29 a week job as an NBC page and moved into an apartment with seven other pages. He took dance and voice lessons and briefly had a Saturday night show on WJAR in Providence, R.I., *Al Rucker and the Seven Teens*. The Providence connection led to a job offer from WNTA-TV in Newark, N.J., to host its weekday *Rate the Record Show*, a show previously hosted by Hy Lit who made a daily commute from Philadelphia. It was during his *Rate the Record* run that Al Rucker became Clay Cole, a name appropriated from a relative from Chicago.

At WNTA-TV, Cole shared a desk with news anchor Mike Wallace and became friends with Freed, who gave Cole use of an apartment and introduced him on stage at his 1959 Labor Day Concert at Brooklyn's Fox Fabian Theater as "the next big television star."[5]

Rate the Record soon morphed into *The Record Wagon*, whose format was much closer to *American Bandstand*'s, prompting Kilgallen's observation of Cole and a cover story in the January 1960 *Hit Parader*.

Cole was a presenter at the 1960 Grammy Awards and was mentioned in a *Mad* magazine satire about disc jockeys. A pair of 14-year-olds started a fan club called the Claymates.

From spring into fall, Cole broadcast six nights a week from the bandshell at Palisades Amusement Park. One of the highlights

---

5. *Sh-Boom*, p. 69.

of *The Clay Cole Summer Show* was the crowning each Sunday of a new finalist in the Miss America Teenager pageant, a Cole concoction. Fabian's appearance on the show was so successful that a helicopter had to be dispatched to rescue the teen heartthrob from adoring fans.

With friends, Cole recorded a song called "Here, There, Everywhere," which was released by Roulette. It became a *Billboard* "Best Bet" and Gloria Stavers created a feature for *16* magazine called "Here There Everywhere with Clay Cole." The column appeared for years and Stavers wrote every word.

In the fall of 1960, Cole's popularity—and exposure—was at an all-time high. He could be seen on three different WNTA-TV programs, seven days a week.

Cole spent a week in October 1960 emceeing shows at the Apollo Theater and over Christmas took over the holiday shows at the Brooklyn Paramount that Alan Freed had previously hosted, setting attendance records and earning an invitation back for the Easter 1961 shows.

Cole's appeal had spread to Europe where the Twist had sparked a dance revival, several months after it broke out in the states. The North German TV Network sent a crew to WNTA to film Cole and some of his regular dancers for a segment explaining the Twist and the Pony to its estimated audience of 20 million Germans.

But, before the Easter shows at the Brooklyn Paramount, WNTA-TV was sold, costing Cole all his TV jobs. Without a base to promote the show, he lost the Easter job, too, as he was replaced by Murray "The K" Kaufman. Cole auditioned to replace Dick Van Dyke (who had left to try his hand at television) in Broadway's *Bye Bye Birdie* but lost out to Gene Rayburn.

With his search to return to television going nowhere, Cole huddled with his agent Roz Ross of GAC. The Twist was having a major resurgence among adults in New York City. Maybe we could do something with that?

Cole was a regular at the Peppermint Lounge, which was known as a seedy sailor bar before *New York Journal-American* society columnist Cholly Knickerbocker described it as the "in" place for adult twisters. Although the tiny lounge had a listed capacity of just 200, that appeared to be more of a suggestion than the law.

The house band of Joey Dee and the Starliters was developing a following of its own and a bevy of attractive young female dancers offered the less-adventurous patrons a vicarious way of indulging their Twist fantasies.

Among those dancers were three teenage girls who were admitted when security mistook their beehive hairdos and shiny dresses for entertainers instead of patrons. The teens took full advantage of the situation, showing off their dance skills and landing a steady gig as The Dolly Sisters that paid each girl $10 a night. The girls—sisters Veronica and Estelle Bennett and their cousin, Nedra Talley—would later show singing skills, too, and had a long and successful recording career as The Ronettes.

Cole, who often claimed that Chubby Checker's first televised appearance of "The Twist" was on his show, persuaded Checker to do a week at the Apollo in June 1961 for $2,000. Cole provided eight dancers to back Checker in what proved to be a good week.

Stage shows helped Cole pay his bills while he continued his search for a suitable TV job. He accepted a job as teenage activities director of the newly opened Freedomland amusement park in New York, where he emceed shows from Freedomland's 3,000-seat coliseum.

For four weeks in the summer of 1961, Cole played Sammy Fong in the play *Flower Drum Song* at Long Island's Gateway Playhouse, commuting by seaplane from Freedomland in order to arrive in time for the opening curtain.

In Philadelphia, Clark was still trying to regain his footing. With Bobbie and Dickie in Youngstown, he had moved back into the house in Wallingford and immersed himself in *Bandstand* and whatever other activities he could cobble together.

He emceed a pre-game program at Connie Mack Stadium, handing out transistor radios to the oldest and youngest sets of twins who showed up for a benefit baseball game between the Phillies and Minnesota Twins.

More surprisingly, Clark filled in for the vacationing Dorothy Kilgallen as a guest columnist at the *New York Journal American* in early July. Kilgallen had carried on a running diatribe against *American Bandstand* and rock & roll for years.

Clark also revived the *Dick Clark Caravan of Stars*, a touring show that put him in touch with teenage fans at venues beyond the studio. He'd enjoyed emceeing stage shows and record hops in the past but with the distractions of the payola investigation, he'd put those outside ventures on hold.

Just as he was arranging Caravan shows for his usual August break from *Bandstand*, Clark received word from ABC that the network was cutting the show from 90 minutes a day to 50 minutes.

Before the Caravan, though, Clark planned a summer tour preview that would include a stop at one of his favorite venues, the Hollywood Bowl. His old rival, Alan Freed, also had his sights set on the Bowl.

Freed, who was still awaiting trial on commercial bribery charges in New York, had relocated in Los Angeles, where he had helped boost radio station KDAY from No. 22 in a 24-station market to No. 3. He had also signed a contract to host concerts in large venues. He was going to launch the bold enterprise on June 25 at the Hollywood Bowl with a concert headlined by Brenda Lee and Jerry Lee Lewis.

A week before the Bowl show, however, Freed quit KDAY after a dispute over Freed's promotion of the show. Freed had bought air time for a series of "teaser" ads that advised listeners to "save the date." He planned to announce details in the days immediately preceding the show. But KDAY officials allowed another promoter with a show on the same date to purchase air time, which Freed claimed created confusion about his show. Although the Hollywood Bowl show went off as planned, Freed was once again without a station to plug his shows and the concert plan fizzled.

Clark's first concerts were in Atlantic City where his two-night stand at the Steel Pier with Duane Eddy, Chubby Checker, Freddy Cannon, and the Shirelles on July 29–30 drew season-high crowds.

Clark made the most of his time in Los Angeles in the days preceding his August 11 Hollywood Bowl program, even giving the press an early peek at his new film, *The Young Doctors.* In an interview with Murray Schumach for *The New York Times*, Clark said he was still working on his novel about the music business and might consider getting involved in a Broadway musical, but not as an investor.

"Being a backer is not for me," he said. "I like being a putter-together and letting others put money into the things you assemble."[6]

Clark also spoke of his fascination with business.

"Business and business deals are fascinating," he said. "I get enormous pleasure and excitement sitting in on conferences with accountants, tax experts, and lawyers."[7]

---
6. *New York Times*, August 17, 1961.
7. Ibid.

Clark also told *Variety* that he had big plans for Dick Clark Productions.

Those plans included a state-of-the-art production facility in Philadelphia, a market research center and a publications center. He boasted that the production facility would rival anything in Hollywood and would be the future home of *American Bandstand*.

"We'll produce specials and lease our mobile and studio facilities to other companies, such as Desilu and Red Skelton are now doing in Hollywood," he said.[8]

Clark said he already had commitments for four hour-long fashion specials and was developing a half-hour TV series, *The Danny Striker Show*. He said he'd be partnered in other ventures with Robert Keeshan, better known as Captain Kangaroo.

After the Hollywood show, Clark's road show made stops in Wichita, Cincinnati, and Indianapolis before stopping in Detroit for what had become an annual stop, the Michigan State Fair over Labor Day.

In Detroit, Clark took time out to do something he hadn't done in more than 15 years: he asked someone for a date. That someone was Loretta Martin, a young secretary to singer JoAnn Campbell who was traveling with her boss. The occasion was an after-show party hosted by the Shirelles.

"Loretta and I went to the party, but wound up out in the dark by the motel pool, kissing, having a long talk, and generally getting to know each other," Clark said.[9]

After the Michigan shows wrapped up on Sept. 4, Clark returned to Philadelphia and Martin returned to New York City where she shared an apartment with Campbell. They reunited on Sept. 9 in Atlantic City for the finals of the 35th Miss America pageant at Boardwalk Hall, beginning what would be a whirlwind courtship.

The Canadian-born Martin, 24, had only been with Campbell for a few months, following short stints as Conway Twitty's secretary and then with Twitty's manager, Don Seat.

Since word of the Clarks' breakup, rumors swirled in the press about who might become the next Mrs. Clark. Clark, who still was legally married, was not pleased with the speculation, especially when Dorothy Kilgallen identified Connie Francis as the front-runner. After Ed Sullivan linked Clark to "a cute recording star," Clark met with Francis to clear the air.

---

8. *Variety*, August 16, 1961.
9. *Rock, Roll & Remember*, p. 247.

FLYING SOLO

Clark did little to conceal his relationship with Martin, though she was perfectly content to stay in the background. In Atlantic City, he teased her to smile for the ever-present photographers. The couple was spotted at the Copacabana in New York at a Steve Lawrence and Eydie Gorme concert, backstage at a show in Trenton, N.J., where Campbell was performing and at the Philadelphia Zoo, with young Dickie Clark in tow.

On one particularly nasty, rainy night in early October, Clark made the drive to New York for a birthday party at the Campbell-Martin apartment, taking time to shop for a special gift for Martin. Knowing of her fondness for silver, he was disappointed to find jewelry stores closed. He arrived at the party at 11:30 P.M. with the only silver item he could find—a compass from a hardware store. He later replaced the compass with a more appropriate gift—a silver charm bracelet.

Clark's divorce became final on November 21, 1961, just in time for his 32nd birthday party at the Wallingford house, with Martin as the hostess.

Clark's trips to New York to see Martin became more frequent, three or four times a week. People noticed, especially Clark's old friend Gloria Stavers, whose apartment was in the same building as Campbell and Martin's. But Stavers, like most of her many visitors, assumed it was Campbell that Clark was seeing so often.

Although Clark's personal life was centered on his growing romance with Martin for the last four months of 1961, he was just as focused on his professional life.

His second movie, *The Young Doctors*, was released in September and received mixed reviews overall, though Clark generally drew praise for his dramatic supporting role. For six weeks—from late September through mid-November—he was busy touring with *Dick Clark's Caravan of Stars*. There were 22 dates in all, headlined by Paul Anka, Chubby Checker, Duane Eddy, and Linda Scott.

And, of course, *American Bandstand* continued chugging along, as popular as ever, promoting every new dance that came along—the Fish, the Bristol Stomp, the Majestic, even the Fly, a silly dance that originated with *Bandstand* regulars after Flossie Harvey chased a fly in her home. Chubby Checker took "The Fly" straight to the Top 10 of *Billboard's* Hot 100.

For "Chart Wrecker" Checker, "The Fly" was merely a diversion from what had become his bread-and-butter, "The Twist."

While Checker was pushing the Hucklebuck, the Pony and the Mess Around, the rest of the dancing world seemed fixated on the Twist.

The song's originator, Hank Ballard, had also tried to capitalize on his Twist success by emphasizing other dances—"The Hoochi Coochi Coo," "The Continental Walk" and "The Switch-A-Roo"—but none caught on, prompting Syd Nathan of King Records (Ballard's label) to send a memo to the trade press, reminding people that it was Hank Ballard who started this crazy Twist stuff, not Chubby Checker.

By late 1961, the Twist had grown beyond a dance aimed at teenagers. It was a bona fide social movement.

Ed Sullivan invited Checker on his Sunday night show, where he was joined by 16 twisting dancers recruited from the Broadway musical, *Do Re Mi*. The TV networks did news reports on the phenomenon, even CBS, which banned the playing of rock & roll. Even Arthur Murray ran print ads for Twist lessons, conceding that even though it wasn't Murray's favorite dance "if you're young at heart, you just have to dance it these days."[10]

The Peppermint Twist Lounge in New York City was the epicenter for the Twist movement reprise. Roulette Records signed house band Joey Dee & the Starliters to a contract and the group's first single, "The Peppermint Twist," was racing up the charts. Roulette's owner Morris Levy couldn't pry Dee from the Peppermint Lounge, but he did institute an all-Twist policy at his East Side club, the Roundtable. Alan Freed, Dick Clark's former rival who was once managed by Levy, opened Alan Freed's East Side Twist Club.

Record labels scrambled to release Twist records. Many of them had nothing in common with Chubby Checker and Hank Ballard's hit. Count Basie and his orchestra had *The Basie Twist*. Atlantic took a bunch of uptempo Ray Charles songs and packaged them into an LP they marketed as *Do the Twist*. RCA Victor even got into the act with Elvis, plucking "Rock-a-Hula Baby" from his *Blue Hawaii* soundtrack LP and pitching it as a Twist record.

Record dealers in Boston, who months earlier were blaming live shows and the rise of bowling for a dip in record sales, were crediting the dance craze for a resurgence in disc sales in their area.

---

10. *Billboard*, October 30, 1961.

FLYING SOLO

Despite his role in igniting the whole Twist movement, it looked as if Dick Clark was being left behind as the dance entered its unexpectedly successful second act. Although his good friends at Cameo-Parkway continued to feed the dance craze machine with a string of popular songs whose artists were thrilled to appear on *Bandstand*, they were unable to deliver the biggest star in the Twist universe, Chubby Checker.

Checker's exploding popularity had catapulted him well beyond the orbit of Bandstandland. He proudly carried the title of King of the Twist into the Christmas shopping season of 1961.

When "Dance the Mess Around" stalled at No. 24 on the *Billboard* charts earlier in the year, Bernie Lowe, Kal Mann and Dave Appell wisely steered Checker back to the Twist, where he immediately registered a Top 10 hit with "Let's Twist Again," a song that would go on to win a Grammy as the Best Rock & Roll Record of 1961.

His follow-up, "The Fly," also reached the Top 10 and earned him a spot on *American Bandstand* on Sept. 27, which marked his last appearance on *Bandstand* for nearly 10 months.

"The Fly" proved to be just an interlude in Checker's remarkable Twist career, however. The Parkway brain trust already had another Checker twist tune, "Twistin' USA," pegged for a holiday release, but with the dance making a strong move to a new, older audience in the U.S. and just catching on in Europe, they made a bold decision: Why not re-release the original?

Why not, indeed.

On November 13, 1961, Checker's version of "The Twist" (with "Twistin' USA" on the flip side) reappeared on *Billboard's* Hot 100 at No. 55, beginning an improbable run to the top for a second time, the only song in U.S. rock & roll history to achieve that feat. For the next six months, there would be no one hotter in the music business than Chubby Checker.

At the time of "The Twist's" re-release, Checker had already released three Twist albums on Parkway with a fourth ready to go. He'd been booked for a 1962 European tour and had a June engagement at the Copacabana lined up. The cost of booking Checker into a club had risen from $500 a week to $2,500 and he'd already made one movie, the forgettable (and, perhaps, regrettable) *Teenage Millionaire*, a quickie that was primarily a way to get the photogenic Jimmy Clanton on the big screen and to let Superman's pal, Jimmy Olson (Jack Larson) take a turn at the mike, although Checker performed four songs.

Taking a page out of Clark's business book, Checker twisted his way into opportunities that extended well beyond record sales. Managers Kal Mann and Henry Colt joined forces with Henry Saperstein in Los Angeles to create Twist-related merchandise on Checker's behalf. Soon Checker had deals for black and red Twister shoes by Thom McCan, Twister neckties and a Twister kit, complete with fold-out, footprint guides to the dance. There was even a deal for a Twist commercial for Duncan Hines Fudge Mix.

Teenage Millionaire aside, it looked as if Checker would be following fellow South Philadelphians Frankie Avalon and Fabian as a motion picture star, too. At least three film producers were racing to be the first to get a Twist movie on screen, perhaps by the end of the year. Surprisingly, Dick Clark, who still owned a handful of companies he had created to produce TV shows and movies, was not one of them.

And all three of those would-be Twist movie makers wanted Checker.

The first of the Twist movies to capture Checker on film was, ironically, a British film with ties to Dick Clark and Alan Freed. Producer Milton Subotsky had been a co-writer on Clark's 1957 movie, *Jamboree*, and on Freed's *Rock, Rock, Rock* in 1956. In 1961, however, Subotsky was in England to make a low-budget film about the flourishing Dixieland jazz movement in that country.

The original intent was to film British pop stars, wrap them around a flimsy storyline and rush the movie into British theaters. To direct the film, which was titled *It's Trad, Dad*, Subotsky had hired an up-and-coming Brit, Richard Lester.

When Subotsky learned that Sam Katzman was planning to shoot a film about the Twist, he saw an opportunity to beat his old rival to the screen. *Trad* was already in the editing stage when Subotsky decided to add the Twist to his film. Checker was scheduled to arrive in the UK in early 1962, but Lester couldn't wait. He took a crew to America instead.

Lester, who within two years would be directing the Beatles in their first film, *A Hard Day's Night*, filmed Checker (doing "Lose Your Inhibitions Twist"), Gary U.S. Bonds and Gene McDaniel on his quick U.S. trip and rushed back so they could splice the Americans into their film.

Katzman, indeed, was planning a Twist movie. Katzman had a long track record of producing low-budget movies in short periods of time. Since earning his first producer credit in 1932, Katzman had tacked on 220 more. One of those, *Rock Around the Clock*, would provide the template for the new film, to be titled *Twist Around the Clock*. With a virtually identical storyline, the only difference in the two movies would be the music.

The entire production schedule was only 28 days, meaning a Christmas release was possible. When Columbia Pictures signed Checker to star in the film, it also claimed overseas rights to his recordings. Checker's co-star was the man Dorothy Kilgallen had labeled "the next Dick Clark," Clay Cole. Cole was placed in the role by his agent, Roz Ross of General Artists Corporation, the same woman who had booked the acts for Dick Clark's Caravan of Stars.

Katzman may not have known he was in a race with Subotsky to be the first to get the Twist on the big screen, but he was certainly aware that another studio, Paramount Pictures, had the same goal.

Paramount had turned to Harry Romm to produce *Hey, Let's Twist*. The 65-year-old Romm was less attuned to rock & roll than was Katzman, but he produced Frank Sinatra's first movie in 1946 and for 20 years had managed the Three Stooges. In recent years, he'd produced two movies that starred the musical odd couple of Louis Prima and Keely Smith.

Romm wanted Checker, too, but Checker's contract with Columbia sent Romm looking elsewhere. He came up with a winning combination when he landed Peppermint Lounge house band Joey Dee & the Starliters and Henry Glover as the film's music director.

While Dee and his band successfully transferred the energy of "the Pep" to the big screen, the addition of Glover to the crew was inspired. As a.&r. man for Syd Nathan at King Records, Glover had produced Ballard's Annie trilogy and "The Twist."

Glover had quit King around the time of the payola probe and moved to Roulette Records, which is where Romm found him. Glover and Dee teamed up to write the movie's signature song, "The Peppermint Twist." "The Peppermint Twist "would go on to be a huge hit record, displacing Chubby Checker's "The Twist" from its second trip to the top of *Billboard's* Hot 100 in January 1962.

Although Paramount Pictures was part of the ABC-Paramount conglomerate that also included the ABC-TV network that owned *American Bandstand*, there wasn't a spot for Dick Clark in *Hey, Let's Twist*.

Several scenes were filmed in the Peppermint Lounge, which was just a couple of blocks from the Little Theater where Clark produced his *Saturday Night Show*. Clark had been to "the Pep" at least once with girlfriend Loretta Martin and her boss, JoAnn Campbell.

Campbell was added to the cast, along with male lead Teddy Randazzo, a rock movie favorite since his days with the Three Chuckles in the mid-1950s. The movie also included an uncredited first-movie performance by Joe Pesci as one of the Peppermint dancers.

The final scenes for the movie were shot at a party at the Pep on December 5, 1961, and the frantic race to the screen began in earnest. For *Hey, Let's Twist*, the process took less than three weeks. It hit theaters, December 23 in Atlanta. *Twist Around the Clock* was just four days behind, December 27 in Los Angeles.

But both movies were beaten to the big screen by another low-budget quickie, *Twist All Night*. It was easily the weakest of the three U.S. twist movies, with Louis Prima in the male lead paired with buxom English bombshell, June Wilkinson. American International Pictures premiered the film in San Francisco on December 12.

It's Trad, Dad lagged well behind the others, with a March premiere in England and debuting in the States as *Ring-a-Ding Rhythm* in September.

Clark may have mostly missed out on the second Twist blitz, but *American Bandstand* was still riding high every weekday afternoon and he continued to recover from the one-two punch of payola and divorce. James Brown, Curtis Mayfield and the Impressions, Glen Campbell and Lou Rawls made their national television debuts on *Bandstand* during this time and old friends like Dion, Fats Domino and Freddy Cannon occasionally dropped by.

Teen Screen and *16* magazines continued to print articles on the *Bandstand* regulars. *Teen Screen* even added pages of color pictures to run with Myrna Horowitz's writings in several editions. *Bandstand*-friendly *TV Guide*, while acknowledging the national Twist wildfire, proclaimed that "If Chubby Checker is the King of the Twisters, then Dick Clark is their prime minister. He is the man who rates most of the credit—or blame—for making the Twist what it is today."[11]

Clark continued to pursue other opportunities, too. He was cast as a pilot and Mahalia Jackson was cast as a stewardess in a production for NBC-TV's *DuPont Show of the Week*. The show,

---

11. *TV Guide*, January 6, 1962.

titled *Wings of Flames*, was originally set for December 1961 but was pushed back to 1962 before being abandoned entirely.

Clark made investments outside show business, as well, investing in the south New Jersey franchise of Dr Pepper and picking up three East Coast franchises of the Philadelphia-based hamburger chain, Steer Inn. At the grand opening of his restaurant on Admiral Wilson Boulevard in Camden, N.J., in February 1962, traffic from teens was so heavy that roads had to be shut down and traffic diverted to other routes.

Jerry Blavat and Loretta Martin were also on hand at that grand opening, as were many regulars from *American Bandstand*. Clark's romance with Martin was going strong entering 1962. In February, they traveled to Las Vegas where Clark was best man for Duane Eddy's February 4 wedding to Miriam Johnson.

The Twist was still *the dance* in the first two months of 1962, though it was starting to fade. Chubby Checker and Joey Dee were still running strong and Gary U.S. Bonds ("Dear Lady Twist"), Sam Cooke ("Twistin' the Night Away") and Billy Joe & the Checkmates ("Percolator Twist") were making strong moves up the charts.

But Checker's "Slow Twistin'" gave a hint of the transition that was to come. A young Philadelphia teenager named Florence LaRue temporarily set aside her gospel music to provide the uncredited companion vocal on Checker's newest release.

Within a month, LaRue (now known as Dee Dee Sharp) had her own record, "Mashed Potato Time," a Cameo release that was destined to be a Top 10 hit and spark a dance craze all its own. Never mind that James Brown had been doing the dance for years, now that it had found a home in Bandstandland, its popularity was virtually guaranteed.

As Dick Clark prepared to offer up steady helpings of the song in the 1962 *American Bandstand* dance contest, he was also preparing for something much more important.

On April 25, 1962, Clark and Loretta Martin were married by Rev. Luther H. Kettels at Calvary Methodist Church in Philadelphia and immediately took off on a three-week honeymoon to Acapulco.

CHAPTER 17

FAREWELL TO BANDSTANDLAND

Dick Clark faced a particularly uncertain future as he and wife Loretta returned from their Mexican honeymoon. Earlier that spring, as rumors started to circulate that *American Bandstand* would be cut further, from 50 minutes a day to 30 minutes a day, Clark started to circulate some rumors of his own.

A teen dance show like *American Bandstand* can't be done in 30 minutes, Clark let it be known. Furthermore, even though he had nearly three years to go on his contract with ABC-TV, he'd probably ask for a release from that obligation should the show be trimmed again.

But ABC-TV executives also seemed determined to "upgrade" the network's afternoon offerings. They had started the transition a few months earlier when they lopped *American Bandstand* to 50 minutes, giving the 10 minutes immediately after Dick Clark's show to *American Newsstand*, a public affairs program aimed at teens, complete with its own youthful anchorman, 26-year-old Roger Sharp.

In the wings, ABC had another educational program aimed at young teens, *Discovery*, a science/culture/history show produced by the same team that had produced NBC-TV's *Mr. Wizard*. If *Discovery* was added to the ABC afternoon schedule, *American Bandstand* would, indeed, be pared to 30 minutes.

For the time being, though, *American Bandstand* offered something that *American Newsstand* and *Discovery* didn't—rocking & rolling teens dancing to the latest dance craze. But that scene was losing steam, too.

Through the first half of 1962, the Twist showed amazing staying power, despite being banned in many communities and by Catholic dioceses. There was also the widely played news story of popular Twist singer Danny Peppermint's near-electrocution while recording a live album at the Thunderbird Lounge in Las Vegas.

Roulette Records was still reporting strong sales of Joey Dee's "Peppermint Twist" after having the best November-December sales period in the label's history. Things were going well at Cameo Records, too, where they had Chubby Checker record several of his more popular Twist tunes in Italian, French and German for distribution to a hungry European market.

After slumping sales from 1957 to 1959, Cameo enjoyed such a rebound after a string of hits by Bobby Rydell and Checker in 1960 and 1961, that it announced it was going public, with stock in the label to be available on the American Stock Exchange by late summer.

Dick Clark's tour booker, Roz Ross, stayed on the Twist bandwagon, too, despite her move from GAC to the William Morris Agency in early 1962. Making the move with her was a slew of rock stars—and Clay Cole.

Ross and Cole had created *Clay Cole's Twist-a-Rama*, a touring show that included the Capris and the Ronettes. Ross booked *Twist-a-Rama* into the Camelot Supper Club in New York, "a tourist trap with a hefty cover charge, watered whiskey and a convenient midtown meeting place for the mob."[1] *Billboard* reviewer Sam Chase was impressed with Cole's show, calling it swift-paced and compared Cole to the versatile Ray Bolger.

Chubby Checker was having success on the road, too. His "Twist Party" review set an attendance record of 15,500 at the Cow Palace in San Francisco in February, with another 6,000 turned away.

---
1. Sh-Boom, p. 183.

But by May, the Twist was all but dead. Checker's Twist tour drew increasingly disappointing crowds and Joey Dee's followup Twist movie was retitled *Two Tickets to Paris* from *Viva the Twist*, removing Twist from the title altogether.

Musical tastes were shifting—and the changes were not good for *American Bandstand*.

Bluesman Ray Charles had rekindled interest in country music with a couple of successful albums—on ABC-Paramount, no less. Cameo-Parkway boss Bernie Lowe, who now had shareholders to satisfy, did his best to respond to the shifting marketplace, signing TV cowboy Clint Eastwood to a recording contract. Lowe also recorded albums by newsman Chet Huntley and professional bowler Don Carter as he attempted to cover all the bases. Bob Marcucci at Chancellor Records entered the country market, hiring Jimmy Bowen to head up the label's new country western department in Los Angeles.

Thankfully for Clark, Cameo continued to serve the *Bandstand* dance scene, primarily through Chubby Checker and his protégé, Dee Dee Sharp, but also through another Philadelphia group, the Orlons, who struck gold with "Wah Watusi" in the summer of 1962.

Cameo could have had another major hit that summer, but Bernie Lowe passed on a Carole King-Gerry Goffin demo they had recorded with their baby sitter. When Lowe rejected the song—"The Loco-Motion" by Little Eva—King-Goffin publishers Don Kirshner and Al Nevins used it as the first release for their new Dimension Records.

Facing such an uncertain television future, Clark took a serious look at his options. If he wanted to maintain his position as a power broker on the teen music scene, he was going to have to do it himself. ABC seemed determined to limit his air time and who knew how long *American Bandstand* could hold on.

The answer was surprisingly simple: He'd take what he'd learned in Philadelphia and put it to work in his first love—radio. His bosses at ABC gave him the OK to put together a nationally syndicated radio program. Within days, Clark had signed up with Mars Broadcasting of Stamford, Conn., to put together a network of radio stations by year's end. In the meantime, Clark called on a media ally to take public his fight to keep *American Bandstand* from being slashed yet again.

Cartoonist Josh King created a campaign in support of *Bandstand* in his wildly popular *Betty Goes to Bandstand* strip in *16* magazine. For three issues, the strip repeated the rumors that *Bandstand* was being cut to 30 minutes. King rallied the troops to write ABC in protest.

In early fall, after the network had confirmed that the show would be cut to 30 minutes on October 1, Dick Clark used the pages of the magazine (and King's strip) to assure readers that since ABC had made "certain concessions," America's Oldest Teenager would be staying on in Bandstandland for the foreseeable future.

Bandstand fans were doubtless pleased with the news, but Clark's career path continued to diverge from that which seemed so clear in the pre-payola days.

United Press TV columnist Rick DuBrow carried on a running one-sided feud with Clark. After Clark was presented a gold key to Willow Grove Park in Philadelphia for "what you have done for the youth of America," DuBrow responded, "I would like to know just exactly what it is that Dick Clark has done for the youth of America.

"So far as I can see, his *American Bandstand* show can take credit for a consistent and vast contribution to the formation of bad taste among a large segment of the young generation.

"Each day he offers his viewers a steady diet of music that is primitive, animalistic, guttural, moronic, almost always forgettable and at times bordering on the suggestive.

"And through it all, he smiles boyishly and benignly as his juvenile admirers comfort themselves in a sort of unfeeling trance, frequently assuming dance positions that can only be described as ugly."[2]

Clark's attempt at making amends with Jerry Lee Lewis also didn't go so well.

Lewis made his first *Bandstand* appearance since the backlash over his marriage to his young cousin four years earlier when he popped into the WFIL studios to lip-sync to his version of Chuck Berry's "Sweet Little Sixteen" on August 23, 1962. Lewis followed that appearance the next night as a headliner for a series of shows Clark was emceeing at Atlantic City's Steel Pier.

Apparently annoyed at Clark's suggested playlist, Lewis appeared on stage with a pair of panties on his head and proceeded to play a set of seldom-heard songs, driving the crowd into a

---

2. *United Press*, "TV In Review," July 11, 1962.

frenzy. Clark immediately imposed a new ban on future Lewis *Bandstand* appearances, a ban that would last two years.

The next month, the FBI was called in when Clark received an anonymous death threat in a letter postmarked White Bear Lake, Minn. "You better get off television soon or else I will kill you. I have a rifle and I will use it," went the threat.[3]

Despite the threat, Clark didn't miss a beat. Although he was spending much of his time developing his new radio show, he went through the motions of hosting *American Bandstand*.

The Bug, the Liftoff and the Waddle went nowhere as dance crazes and Cameo-Parkway was pressing its luck with songs like "South Pacific Twist" by the Rocky Fellers, "Bristol Twistin' Annie" by the Dovells and "The Popeye Waddl*e*" by Don Covay, although the Covay record was on the right track.

The Popeye was a popular dance that had been sparked by Huey "Piano" Smith & the Clowns in New Orleans earlier in the year, but by the time Bernie Lowe greenlit Chubby Checker's "Popeye, the Hitchhiker," the dance was pretty much passé.

Disc jockeys in Pittsburgh and Baltimore quickly figured that out, flipping to Checker's B-side, "The Limbo Rock." After Cameo's marketing team shipped limbo poles to selected deejays, the song—and yet another Cameo-sparked dance craze—took off.

It was just in time for Checker's 21st birthday, which he celebrated in style, buying a $75,000 house for his parents and throwing a lavish party where he received the keys to two cars—a 1963 Buick Riviera Coupe and a Cadillac Eldorado—from his co-managers Henry Colt and Kal Mann.

The celebration probably helped ease the sting of a lawsuit filed by Harry Lipsius alleging that Checker and his associates at Cameo-Parkway had lifted the tune from Gary U.S. Bond's mega-hit "Quarter to Three" and repurposed it as Checker's "Dancin' Party."

Another insult came when shoemaker Thom McAn dropped its line of Twistin' shoes and replaced it with bossa nova shoes, a more current dance popular among adults.

The music business was in disarray as the holiday season of 1962 approached. The best-selling record in America had nothing to do with a popular dance. In fact, it had nothing to do with music at all. Comedian Vaughn Meader had assembled a talented

---

3. FBI documents, Sept. 18, 1962.

cast to perform a series of skits he'd written about America's most popular family, the Kennedys.

Since John F. Kennedy had become president in January 1961, there was an insatiable interest in Kennedy and his photogenic family. Meader perfectly meshed the Kennedys' idiosyncrasies with the mood of the country in a satirical album, *The First Family*.

The LP was easily the star of the holiday season, outselling every single on the market on its way to total sales of a staggering 7.5 million records. Of course, it had a lousy beat and was impossible to dance to, so the hottest record of the season never made it onto *American Bandstand*.

It was apparently of little concern to Dick Clark, however, since he was busy putting the final touches on his syndicated radio show that was about to debut.

For Clark, re-entry to radio was a calculated risk. His goal was to achieve through syndication what had once been the norm in network radio—a national audience. There hadn't been a successful national radio deejay in at least a decade.

For Clark, though, it made good business sense. With a radio show widely available in major markets across the country, he would have the hit-making clout he had enjoyed in the glory days of *American Bandstand*. Promotion men should welcome the opportunity to address a national audience with a single plug.

Clark knew, though, that for his show to be successful, it would have to offer the intimacy of one-on-one communication, a principle he had learned from observing Arthur Godfrey as a youngster.

"I loved [Godfrey] . . . because he had the ability to communicate to one person who was listening or watching," Clark said. "Godfrey knew there was only one person listening at a time."[4]

To achieve that feeling, Clark and Mars came up with an intricate series of drop-ins that would give the two-hour taped show a local feel. In addition, several of the 25 songs played during each day's program would come from local record charts. Similarly, some of the 18 commercials would be for local businesses.

Clark also offered exclusive artist interviews, something only a person of his stature could do. Clark recorded many interviews in advance. For those that were done by phone, Mars came up with an ingenious technique to make them sound as if they were

---

4. Archive of American Television interview, 1999.

live. While doing the interview, each party recorded their end of the conversation on tape. The tapes were then spliced together to give the interview a "live" sound.

The syndication process itself created some interesting scenarios. Since the program was marketed for a 4–6 P.M. slot, at one point it appeared as if Clark's radio show might be aired on WIP in Philadelphia at the same time *American Bandstand* was on WFIL-TV. That clash was avoided, however, when WIP executives found the Clark show format incompatible with its middle-of-the-road format.

One of the stations signing on for Clark's show was WOLF in Syracuse, an early stop in his radio career. Prior to the show's launch, Clark took part in WOLF's "Cavalcade of Disk Jockeys," a sort of homecoming for former WOLF on-air personalities.

Mars was aiming for a 100-station network but had yet to land a spot in the New York market when it began advertising in trade publications.

In one ad, Mars asked prospective buyers to do a simple test: randomly call local phone numbers and ask them if they recognize names from a list of local radio personalities. Then ask them if they recognize the name "Dick Clark." In Mars' own tests in three markets, only 12 percent of competitors' names were recognized while 87 percent knew who Clark was.

Despite his widespread name recognition, Clark wasn't the only deejay pursuing radio syndication. George "Hound Dog" Lorenz was pitching a similar two-hour show in many of the same markets Clark sought. Many other big-name jocks were apparently skipping on national syndication.

Milt Grant seemed content with a small network of stations in the Washington, D.C., area and Jim Lounsbury was similarly positioned in the Chicago area. Buddy Deane was sticking with his TV dance show in Baltimore, though he was considering returning to his radio roots at WITH in that city

Alan Freed, the best-known disc jockey in the country before Clark came along, was continuing in his downward post-payola spiral. After KDAY in Los Angeles, Freed jumped to WQAM in Miami, where he was let go after three months for emceeing a stage show.

Freed finally stood trial on payola bribery charges in New York in December 1962. After being found guilty on two counts, he received a six-month suspended sentence and a $300 fine. Freed retreated to his home in Palm Springs, Calif., and took a job as an a.&r. man for an old friend, Bobby Shad of Time Records.

Before Clark launched his Mars show, he landed an additional radio job—a nightly 5-minute capsule of commentary and features on the ABC radio network called *Dick Clark Reports*.

The Mars syndication began on January 1, 1963, with 15 stations. One of those stations, WHK in Cleveland, banked the first 12 days of programs to air a 24-hour "spectacular" on January 12–13.

With *Bandstand* taking less of his time, the radio show had become Clark's primary focus. Others in the entertainment business were less-focused on *Bandstand*—and Philadelphia—too.

ABC-TV, which had granted Clark the opportunity to expand his exposure on other networks as one of its concessions when *Bandstand* was trimmed to a half-hour, no longer saw Clark as vital to its prime-time musical offerings.

Nighttime programming chief Dan Melnick had already arranged for a new Saturday night show, *Hootenanny*, devoted to the increasingly popular genre of folk music. All the new program—which would originate from a different college campus each week—needed was a sponsor, which it would find before its April 6 debut.

Also planned was a Thursday night variety show starring country star Jimmy Dean, whose "Big Bad John" had edged out "The Twist" as the top tune on the nation's jukeboxes in 1961.

Folk music wasn't the only music trending highly with young Americans. The rolling, reverberated sounds of what was called surf music were sweeping in from the California coast. As guitarist Dick Dale was regularly drawing turn-away crowds at the Harmony Park Ballroom in Anaheim, bleached-blond California teens were picking up guitars or sitting down to drum kits to emulate the sound.

Three of those teens were brothers who joined with a cousin and neighbor kid to form a group known as the Beach Boys, whose tight harmonies and simple lyrics had drawn the attention of a major West Coast label, Capitol Records (Dick Dale ended up on Capitol, too) and resulted in hugely popular national surf-themed hits.

Dale's success led him to be cast in a lead role in American International Pictures' surf movie, *Beach Party*, which would co-star one-time Clark favorite Frankie Avalon and every teenage boys' favorite, Annette Funicello.

It was good news for Avalon, whose movie career was already established, but not such good news for his manager, Chancellor Records owner Bob Marcucci. Avalon was still cutting records, but he hadn't had a Top 20 hit since *Why* in 1959.

Avalon's stablemate and one-time top-selling artist at Chancellor, Fabian, had left the label and Marcucci in a bitter dispute. Marcucci was working hard at diversifying Chancellor's catalog, but hadn't given up the dream of creating another teen idol. In late 1962, he'd signed Rod Lauren (at 24, a rock & roll veteran) and 16-year-old South Philadelphian Frankie Pescatore, promptly renaming him Dean Randolph.

Marcucci also planned to enter the movie business. With Avalon, he formed Astra Productions and had a screenplay written for a movie titled *You're Only Young Once*. The film's title came from a song recorded by Fabian a couple of years earlier and Avalon and Lauren were picked to co-star. The movie plan would fizzle, but the stage was set for Marcucci to relocate to California.

In yet another sign that Philadelphia's position as the center of the rock & roll world was slipping, *Billboard*'s new column to cover the rock scene was written by Nick Biro, a reporter who worked from a home base in Chicago.

To Dick Clark, it no longer made sense to be tethered to a daily television program that was netting him a measly 30 minutes of airtime each day. A better arrangement, he determined, was to record a week's worth of shows at a single time. He settled on Saturday as the perfect time to tape the five programs for the next week.

While the move killed any sense of immediacy that a live daily show allowed, the change did have its benefits. To the kids attending, it meant they could catch more stars in the studio with a single admission. They were encouraged to bring a change of clothes for the different shows, but that only added to the excitement for some. Clark immediately spread the word to promo men: Have your stars ready to go on Saturday and only on Saturday.

The biggest benefit to Clark was that he had more free time to concentrate on other projects, especially on dramatic television. After talks with ABC, the network allowed him to shoot a pilot show for a possible fall series. In the show, tentatively titled *Kincaid*, Clark would portray a policeman named Sgt. Andy Kincaid working with juvenile delinquents in a youth center. The pilot was filmed and aired as an episode of the *Stoney Burke* series in April but was not picked up for a series.

FAREWELL TO BANDSTANDLAND

Clark was also interested in exploring television game shows. He planned a trip to England to take part in two shows—*Thank Your Lucky Stars* and *Juke Box Jury*—but had to cancel since the trip was too close to wife Loretta's due date for their first child.

Instead, Clark made a trip to Chicago for the National Association of Broadcasters convention, where he pitched his radio show, which was now on 19 stations in the U.S. and looking at opportunities in Canada. After the convention, Clark made a promotional tour around his syndication circuit. The effort proved worthwhile. By June 1963, he was on 39 stations, including two in Canada.

Clark's novel about the music business was apparently put on hold as he instead published another advice book for teens in the summer of 1963, *To Goof Or Not To Goof.* In the book Clark dishes tips on table manners, phone etiquette, curfews, driving and how to handle a girlfriend: "Treat your girl as if she was a gorgeous but not very strong creature who should be protected from the ugly realities of life, such as how dinners are bought or where theater tickets are from."[5]

Much of the advice was at best dated and at worst sexist, but Clark did share a few revealing personal vignettes. Like the time he and some friends were caught trying to sneak into a movie theater. Or the time he overextended himself while buying a car and was forced to pay the consequences. He even reflected on his first marriage, saying it had been a "young marriage entered much too early" and "a starry-eyed mistake."[6]

Many *American Bandstand* regulars spent much of their summers at the New Jersey shore and the summer of 1963 was no different. Ed Hurst, the deejay whose radio show had spawned the original *Bandstand* was out of radio and in the insurance business, but for the fourth straight year was presenting *Summertime on the Pier,* a live two-hour telecast from the Steel Pier in Atlantic City every Saturday and Sunday afternoon.

In New York City, Clay Cole had a similar show from Freedomland's Moon Bowl every Saturday night. In the Philadelphia area, Hy Lit and Jerry Blavat were drawing nice crowds with rock shows on the roofs of refreshment centers at drive-in theaters.

But for Dick Clark, summer meant hitting the road.

---

5. *To Goof Or Not To Goof*, p. 82.
6. Ibid, p. 188.

Touring promised to be a lucrative enterprise for Clark in 1963. Working with Roz Ross at William Morris, he planned two tours for the year—one in the summer, another in the fall. Attendance had been falling off for rock tours in recent years, but Clark's Caravans of Stars were the exception.

The summer tour covered 21 dates between July 15 and August 6 and grossed $250,000, a respectable number for the times. Huge crowds were reported for Montreal and Cincinnati and some 3,000 fans were turned away in Huntington, W. Va. Clark was with the tour most nights, only returning to Philadelphia for the weekend *American Bandstand* tapings.

Clark enjoyed travel on his Caravans, occasionally taking a turn behind the wheel of one of the two buses usually used. Longtime associate Ed McAdam often drove one of the buses and took care of business along the route. Bus travel could be grueling, with empty soda cans and bottles rattling across the floor while sweaty, tired performers tried to catch some rest.

After one of the Caravan buses was mistaken for Freedom Riders and briefly terrorized in the south, Clark "took pity on us," said Dee Dee Phelps of the singing duo Dick and Dee Dee. "he decided to throw a huge party for us after the show. . . . [he] had us secretly draw names of the other performers on our tour from a hat. We were to get up on a makeshift stage with the band backing us and perform at the party as if we were that person whose name we drew (some males drew females, and vice versa.)"

"Everyone created costumes, fashioned from bath towels and whatever garb could be borrowed, like women's wigs and heels."[7]

American Bandstand barely had time to celebrate its sixth anniversary before it was cut yet again. Effective Sept. 7, 1963, *Bandstand* became a weekly show on ABC-TV, occupying the 1:30–2:30 P.M. slot each Saturday. Taking the weekday slot once occupied by rock stars and dancing teens would be reruns of *Wagon Train*, renamed *Major Adams, Trailmaster*.

And, just as teen America was getting used to surf music, Dick Dale and the Beach Boys were steering young ears toward the drag strip with songs about hot rods and car clubs. If American rock & roll wasn't your thing, you could look across the Atlantic, where a curious musical phenomenon was taking root in the blue-collar seaport of Liverpool, England.

---

7. *Vinyl Highway*, pp. 178–79.

FAREWELL TO BANDSTANDLAND

A shaggy-haired quartet of British youngsters known as The Beatles, whose musical tastes were cast out of the bluesy roots of the earliest U.S. rockers who found their way into the UK nearly a decade earlier, was taking England by storm with catchy tunes, clever lyrics, and an infectiously buoyant on-stage presence.

But the Beatles found themselves entangled in a maze of agreements that had no fewer than four U.S. record labels planning to issue records by the mop-tops. One of those labels was Swan, which issued "She Loves You"/"I'll Get You" in mid-September 1963.

Smelling hit potential, Tony Mammarella suggested to Clark that maybe he would want to get behind this record. Bernie Binnick dropped by the *Bandstand* office to play it for Clark. Clark was not impressed but offered to give "She Loves You" a spin on the Rate-a-Record segment of the show.

The song got a lukewarm response, an average of 71. A picture of the group drew snickers from the raters. Dick Clark did not get behind the record.

As teen America was adjusting to *Bandstand's* new weekly format, Clark was doing some adjusting of his own.

"I knew I had to get out of Philadelphia and move to either New York or Los Angeles if I wanted to continue in the entertainment business," Clark said.[8]

Although Clark had grown up dreaming of being a big radio star in New York, it was obvious that California was the place he needed to be. Many of the people whose careers he had helped launch were already there—Fabian, Frankie Avalon, Bobby Darin, *Saturday Night Show* producer Deke Heyward, Chancellor's Bob Marcucci. RCA Victor was building new offices and a studio on Sunset Boulevard and Vee Jay Records was relocating to Los Angeles after nine years in Chicago.

Before he started his fall Caravan in New Jersey on November 8, Clark checked things out on the west coast. While there, he taped what amounted to a preview of what a Los Angeles-based show might look like. Since 1961, Clark had enjoyed a strong business relationship with Dr Pepper.

The Dallas-based company threw much of its advertising budget to *American Bandstand* when it began national distribution in 1961. It was known for its zany promotional giveaways, awarding

---

8. *Rock, Roll and Remember*, p. 252.

such items as a diamond doorknob, solid gold dinosaur, even an island in the Bahamas.

Clark formalized his relationship with the company in 1962 when he formed the Dick Clark Bottling Corporation to handle distribution of Dr Pepper in Philadelphia and southern New Jersey. Dr Pepper had recently signed 16-year-old Donna Loren to be the soda's national spokesperson and wanted to introduce her via a TV special.

In late October, Loren and Clark co-hosted a taping of *Dick Clark's Dr Pepper Celebrity Party,* a program that would air right after Thanksgiving as a prime-time special on ABC-TV. The program was taped at the Sunset Strip home of Bob Marcucci, a pink Spanish villa that had previously been owned by Laurence Olivier and Anne Baxter.

The program primarily consisted of Clark chatting with a wide range of people in the entertainment business, the kind of people that would be available to a popular West Coast TV host just about any day of the week, although Loren did lip-sync a couple of numbers.

John Ashley and Deborah Walley were there. So were Dick & Dee Dee, Connie Francis, Johnny Crawford, and Paul Peterson. Frankie Avalon and Annette Funicello were there, as were Trini Lopez, Connie Stevens, and Nick Adams. Miss Teenage America (Judy Doll) dropped by. Heck, even neighbor Johnny Mathis, who was on his way to the store to buy some guava jelly, stopped to see what the ruckus was all about.

One other duty Clark performed before hitting the Caravan road was to do the narration for a holiday special by Podrecca's Piccoli Theater, a marionette act that was extremely popular on Ed Sullivan's show. The Podrecca program was produced by WFIL-TV and was pitched nationally as a syndicated show.

Clark and his wife Loretta both accompanied Dick Clark's Fall Caravan of Stars tour. As usual, Clark had put together a strong cast of popular singers, including Bobby Vee, Little Eva, the Ronettes, Brian Hyland, the Dovells, Jimmy Clanton, Linda Scott, and Paul & Paula. Clark had also hired Billy Cook, a former *American Bandstand* regular, to assist him while on the road.

The 31-day tour, which was to run through December 8, got off to a fast start, setting box office records in Utica, N.Y., and Hartford, Conn. Despite a tight schedule, Clark treated the entourage to one of his catered parties in Elkhart, Ind., on November 17.

Within a week, the tour had a major disruption after shows in Madison, Wis.; Davenport and Sioux City, Iowa and Wichita, Kansas. The entourage made the overnight trip from Wichita to Dallas, Texas, in time to check into the Sheraton Hotel for a little rest before that evening's show at the Dallas Memorial Auditorium.

When they learned that President Kennedy and his wife would soon be passing the hotel in a motorcade en route to a luncheon engagement, many of the entourage, including Clark, stood on the hotel steps and waved to the motorcade as it slowly passed.

Grace Broussard (of the Dale and Grace singing duo) then went back inside the hotel and made an appointment to get her hair done. As she waited for her appointment, news came on television that President Kennedy had been shot, just blocks from the hotel. The news got worse when it was announced the President was dead.

"Once that happened, I decided there was no need to get my hair done," Broussard later said. "I knew that night's show would be canceled."[9]

Dick Clark had retreated to his hotel room and was napping as news of the shooting spread. He was awakened by a phone call from an ABC-TV programming executive. Rubbing the sleep from his eyes, Clark switched on the TV and received the grim news.

Although it was not known at the time, suspected JFK assassin Lee Harvey Oswald had apparently planned to attend the Clark Caravan that night in Dallas.

At 7:30 A.M. that day, Oswald bought a ticket to the Caravan from J.W. "Dub" Stark of the Top Ten Record Shop in suburban Oak Cliff. Oswald returned a short time later and bought a second ticket to the show, Stark said.[10]

That evening's show was, indeed, canceled, as was a Saturday night show in Oklahoma City. The tour resumed on November 24 at Kiel Auditorium in St. Louis.

By the time the tour wrapped up two weeks later, the nation was in a somber mood. That was especially true of the teenagers in Philadelphia who were just about to lose altogether their fading status as the stars at the center of American rock & roll. Even *16* magazine, the longtime advocate for Dick Clark and *American Bandstand*, appeared to be throwing in the towel.

---

9. *Albany Herald*, November 21, 2013.
10. *Assassination Research* "The JFK Assassination Chronology," compiled by Ira David Wood III, p. 3.

Its popular *Bandstand* specials—*Secret Bandstand Album* and *Regulars' Fun Time*—which sold like crazy at a buck a piece just months earlier were being unloaded at the fire sale price of two for $1.

As Clark went about the business of preparing his final *American Bandstand* shows in Philadelphia, ABC aired one of the quirkiest episodes of the show's first 6½ years. The January 4, 1964, show featured the Trashmen and their Top Ten hit, "Surfin' Bird."

The Trashmen were a garage band out of the Twin Cities in Minnesota and "Surfin' Bird" was a mashup of two earlier hits by the Rivingtons—"Papa-Oom-Mow-Mow" and "The Bird Is the Word" (the similarities would later be sorted out in court).

When Clark informed the band that he'd only spring for one ticket to Philadelphia, the band selected Steve Wahrer, the band's drummer and lead singer. Thus, *Bandstand* viewers were treated to just one Trashman, Wahrer, hopping around and lip-syncing to one of the strangest songs of that period.

One week later, Clark taped the final three episodes of *American Bandstand*'s Philadelphia run. The last episode—featuring Johnny Tillotson ("Talk Back Trembling Lips") and Linda Scott ("Who's Been Sleeping In My Bed") was broadcast on February 1, 1964.

Two days after the final taping, WFIL moved to its brand new Triangle Broadcast Center at 4100 City Line Avenue, a building that included a shiny new studio that was intended to be the future home of *American Bandstand* when construction began in 1962.

Although *American Bandstand* was leaving Philadelphia, the music world kept spinning. The governor of Indiana created a stir when he asked his state's broadcasters to stop playing "Louie Louie" by the Kingsmen because of its dirty lyrics. Cameo's Bernie Lowe seemed to be taking a swipe at Tony Mammarella's Swan Records when he released a record, "The Boy With the Beatle Hair," by an anonymous group called "The Swans."

The future of Clark's syndicated radio show was put in doubt when Pepper Sound Studios bought out Mars Broadcasting and announced it was moving into the radio soap opera field.

And, although Clark would no longer be able to pluck young Italian singers out of South Philadelphia, Californians proudly pointed out that singers Jan and Dean and Dick and Dee Dee and record producers Kim Fowley and Bruce Johnston were all recent products of University High School in Los Angeles.

Clark had an entourage of valued friends and employees that were to accompany him to Los Angeles, where he'd be setting up shop in the Capitol Records Tower at Hollywood and Vine. That included longtime aide Ed McAdam, secretary Chris Betlejeski and announcer Charlie O'Donnell.

They filled up a moving van and still didn't have enough room for everything. They rented a U-Haul trailer and stuffed it with the familiar *American Bandstand* lectern, Clark's personal collection of *Life* magazines, boxes of records and leftover files.

As Dick Clark was leaving Philadelphia, the Beatles were arriving in America. It was a significant transition. The British Invasion was on and Bandstandland was dead.

EPILOGUE

Dick Clark's first Los Angeles show on February 8, 1964, featured Jackie DeShannon and Dick and Dee Dee. The next week, he did a tribute show to the Beatles. For the next 25 years, *American Bandstand* would still be available to American viewers, making it one of the longest-running shows in TV history.

It wasn't easy. *American Bandstand* was no longer must-watch TV for America's teenagers. Many former *Bandstand* watchers were drawn instead to the show's prime-time progeny, like *Hullabaloo* and *Shindig*, which, although they didn't feature dancing kids from the neighborhood, did have high energy professional dancers that visually complemented the show's main attraction, the top recording artists of the day.

By 1972, *Bandstand* was no longer the top-rated dance program on television. That distinction went to *Soul Train*, a syndicated program geared to black artists and dancers hosted by Don Cornelius.

Cornelius was raised on Chicago's south side and had served in the Marines before returning to his hometown and work as a car and insurance salesman while holding down a part-time position at radio station WVON. It was there that he developed the idea for a dance show featuring black soul music. A small independent UHF station gave Cornelius the time to pursue the

EPILOGUE

idea and by 1971 *Soul Train* had grown into a syndicated program available in eight markets.

Viewers liked Cornelius, with his cool demeanor, deep bass voice, and bell-bottom slacks. They also liked watching the *Soul Train* dancers, whom Stu Bykofsky of the *Philadelphia Daily News* called "the sexiest women on TV."[1]

By 1972, *Soul Train* was on 90 stations, drawing more viewers than *American Bandstand* with its thumping soul music and Cornelius as the pitchman for black-oriented products such as Afro Sheen and Ultra Sheen.

ABC-TV executives took notice. With *American Bandstand* slipping in the ratings, it might make sense to rotate another dance show into *Bandstand's* Saturday afternoon slot on alternate weeks. *Soul Train* was the logical choice. When Clark got wind of the possible change, he was angered.

"It's my time slot," he tersely responded. "If ABC wants a black *Bandstand*, I'll do it."[2]

And he did. In the summer of 1973, the Clark-produced *Soul Unlimited* began its run on ABC, appearing on alternate Saturdays in the *American Bandstand* time slot. *Soul Unlimited*, which had hip black deejay Buster Jones as its host, never caught on and was gone in a few weeks.

Clark did his best to keep *American Bandstand* afloat in his California years, even though it represented less and less of his business as Dick Clark Productions grew in many different directions.

Clark, who had three children of his own, sometimes referred to *American Bandstand* as his "fourth kid."

"I'm sure a psychologist would have a lot of fun with this," he once confessed to Bykofsky. "I'm in love with [*American Bandstand*]. I protect it. I want it to have a happy birthday. I want it to be around. I've thrown my arms around it on a lot of occasions—it changed my whole life."[3]

Clark rarely missed an opportunity to present a prime time *Bandstand* reunion show—on the 25th, 30th and 40th anniversaries (even one on the 33 1/3 anniversary). He'd invite a few former regulars, some of the old Philadelphia singers and some then-current stars as if offering proof that the show was still relevant. Clark even recorded a few shows back in Philadelphia.

---

1. *Philadelphia Daily News,* November 21, 1995.
2. *Rock 'n' Roll Is Here to Pay,* p. 247.
3. *Philadelphia Daily News,* October 30, 1981.

As the show's 30th anniversary approached, Clark had his PR firm send out letters to the nation's governors and to the mayors of cities that carried *American Bandstand*, asking that October 30, 1981, be officially declared "Dick Clark's American Bandstand Day." Nineteen governors and 33 mayors complied.

One staple of the reunion shows was *Bandstand* footage Clark had squirreled away. He once tried to buy the old film and kinescopes from ABC, but the network said they weren't for sale. When the tapes finally were available, Clark snatched them up and deposited them in the Dick Clark Media Archives. Archive director of acquisitions Don Barrett estimated that 70 percent of *American Bandstands* survive.[4]

Though Clark was stingy in releasing *Bandstand* footage from the Philadelphia years, he offered snippets in film loops that appeared on vintage TVs in a string of Bandstand Grille restaurants he opened in the 1990s. Ironically, the *Best of Bandstand* videotape Clark marketed in the 1980s didn't include a single performance from *American Bandstand*. Instead, he used clips from the *Saturday Night Show* (except for one Buddy Holly clip that came from *Arthur Murray Dance Party*).

Clark also used *Bandstand* clips in many of his stage shows, prompting reviewer Jack Lloyd of the *Philadelphia Inquirer* to write: "Rarely has any one single vehicle been so exploited, so beaten into the ground so long after its day had come and gone."[5]

The Bandstand Grilles (there were about a half dozen at one point in the short-lived chain) were also decorated with thousands of artifacts from Clark's personal collection. An avid collector of pop music memorabilia, Clark had more than 20,000 items cataloged and stored in a Los Angeles warehouse.

The Beatles never appeared on *American Bandstand*, but the group's hairbrushes did. Clark had arranged with the manager of the Beatles' first U.S. tour to box up anything of value that the Fab Four had touched or thrown away. Included were four hairbrushes that Clark had John, Paul, George, and Ringo autograph before offering them on an *American Bandstand* giveaway. The contest drew 900,000 entries.

The British Invasion was just one of the many shifts in musical taste that Clark and *American Bandstand* would ride out during the show's California run. With each shift in music came

---

4. *Goldmine*, March 2, 1984.
5. *Philadelphia Inquirer*, October 1, 1975.

EPILOGUE

changes in the way kids appeared on the show. As psychedelic, heavy metal, disco and rap music swept over the show, so did bell bottom pants, Afro-style hair and freestyle dancing that probably would have seemed other-worldly to the kids back in Philadelphia a few years earlier.

Clark may have loosened the dress code, but he was still cautious about what he allowed on the air. In 1978, *Bandstand* banned the song *Disco Inferno* by the Trampps because it contained the offensive line "burn the mother down." In 1985, it banned Sheena Easton's *Sugar Walls* because it was "suggestive pornography."[6]

But *American Bandstand* was running on fumes in the mid-1980s. For Clark, the final indignity came when ABC said it was trimming the weekly show to a mere 30 minutes effective in the fall of 1987. Rather than accept the cut, Clark pulled the plug himself and took the program into syndication.

That move cost *Bandstand* its 35-year ties to the Philadelphia station that had given birth to the show in 1952. Instead of appearing on Channel 6 in Philadelphia (now WPVI), *American Bandstand* was seen on Channel 3 when it debuted as a syndicated show on Sept. 19, 1987.

Syndication didn't work out so well. In March 1989, Clark announced that he was taking the show to the USA cable network and that 26-year-old David Hirsch, a network TV novice from Detroit, would be replacing him as host.

On October 7, 1989, *American Bandstand* aired its final show, providing trivia fans the answer to the question: Who was the last musical act to appear on *American Bandstand*? (A: The Cover Girls).

By the time the show folded, Clark was probably relieved. As far as return on investment goes, it was a loser. Still, Clark continued to speak fondly of the show that had provided such a solid platform for a career that netted him riches far beyond what he had imagined as a young boy, listening intently to Arthur Godfrey in his bedroom.

One regret Clark often expressed was that he hadn't hung on a little longer, stretching the show into the 1990s—what would have been its fifth decade.

While most of Clark's activities after leaving Philadelphia were centered on the West Coast, he continued to travel extensively. He said in the 1980s that his airline miles topped 4 million.

---

6. *Anti-Rock*, p. 258.

Shortly after setting up shop in Los Angeles, Clark was commuting from California to New York every Sunday night to tape five *Missing Links* programs over two days so he could be home in time for dinner on Tuesday.

Although *American Bandstand* no longer had the star-making potential and devoted audience that marked its Philadelphia years, Clark sought to capitalize on the California youth music culture in other ways.

When CBS was looking for a summer replacement for its popular Jackie Gleason series in 1965, Clark prepared a pilot show that paired music of the day with some California icons. Half of the pilot was shot at a ski lodge at Big Bear; the other half was shot at a Southern California surfing beach. To show how cool the show was, Clark's team took the popular slang expression "That's where it's at" and transformed it into *Where the Action Is*.

The show never replaced Gleason, but ABC gave it a shot and *Action* was a successful program for nearly two years with much of the action filmed at various Southern California locales and rejuvenating the career of Freddy Cannon, who sang the title song to the show. It also introduced America to Paul Revere & the Raiders, who went on to have a solid string of Top 40 hits.

After *Action* was canceled in 1967, Clark followed up with a string of other teen music shows—*Happening '68, It's Happening, Get It Together* (with Sam Riddle as host) and *Shebang* (with Kasey Kasem as host)—but none achieved the success of *Bandstand* or *Action*.

Clark also continued his Caravan tours from his California base. He hired away Roz Ross from William Morris to organize the tours, which had as many as three separate units on the road at one time.

When Michigan broadcaster Victor Lundberg had a surprise hit in 1967 with his conservative essay "An Open Letter to My Teenage Son," Clark felt compelled to respond.

Clark's response, "Open Letter to the Older Generation," urged older people to show a greater understanding for the youth of America. One year later, Clark showed just how much he understood the youth of America by producing two films that exploited the emerging psychedelic hippie culture.

The first film, *Psych-Out*, is notable primarily for presenting Jack Nicholson and Bruce Dern early in their acting careers. Nicholson wrote the original script for the film, but the final screenplay bore little resemblance to Nicholson's work. The trite storyline was utterly predictable but the film was shot in San Francisco's Haight-Ashbury neighborhood when the hippie movement was flourishing and is a more-or-less accurate portrayal of what things looked like at that time.

Clark and his *Psych-Out* director Richard Rush teamed up for another 1968 production, *The Savage Seven*. Though the film includes music by Cream and the Iron Butterfly and marks the acting debut of Penny Marshall, there is little to distinguish this story of bikers gone amok on an Indian reservation.

Clark also had a cameo role as a newsman in Samuel Z. Arkoff's *Wild In the Streets*, another absurdity that had a rock star being elected president and lowering the voting age to 15 while ordering pensioners into retirement homes where they were force-fed LSD.

As if to redeem himself, Clark also had a serious role as a criminal in *Killers Three*. During the filming in North Carolina, Clark narrowly escaped serious injury when a fight scene with a stuntman called for them to fall through a plate glass window. Clark fell through the breakaway glass prop, but the stuntman tumbled through an adjacent pane of real glass, suffering numerous cuts and lacerations.

Although Clark had a handful of dramatic roles on television, his true love was in television production.

"If he's got 10 minutes, he produces a show," said longtime friend Ed McMahon. "Between phone calls, he produces a show."[7]

Clark's big break as a producer came in 1973 when ABC lost its contract to televise the Grammys. Can you come up with something similar, network executives asked Clark? The result was *The American Music Awards*. It ran just 30 minutes in its first broadcast, but Clark's format of using public opinion polling to pick winners proved popular (the concept was copied a year later by the *Peoples Choice Awards*).

That same year, Clark launched another show that was an immediate hit, *The $10,000 Pyramid*. *Pyramid* took full advantage of Clark's hosting skills, which he also used in hosting *New Year's Rockin' Eve*. Both shows were popular for decades.

In 1981, Clark debuted another show that would prove to have staying power. Originally put together as a special, *TV's Censored*

---

7. *Los Angeles Daily News*, December 27, 2000.

Bloopers became a staple on NBC after beating blockbuster rival *Dallas* on its premiere.

Clark had hit on a winning formula with his TV production company—give customers what they want and do it cheaply. That lesson was reinforced by his experience with *Psych-Out*, where he barely broke even. With a TV movie, he knew upfront what networks would pay. If a show was a ratings hit, he'd do even better with the next one.

He wasn't above exploiting a profitable idea, either. For instance, *TV's Censored Bloopers* spun off six similar shows.

"We squeezed out of the towel every drop of potential," said Clark's chief operating officer Fran LaMainia.[8] "[We give] value for price. It may not be creative, but it makes a lot of sense."

One area where Clark enjoyed particular success was with awards shows. In 1996, Dick Clark Productions produced 14 of them. NBC president Brandon Tartikoff said Clark's productions are the "McDonald's of television . . . you consume them and then you don't remember much about them."[9]

Clark's success in television made him a rich man. At the time of his death in 2012, it was estimated he was worth $200–250 million. He sold Dick Clark Productions to Washington Redskins owner Dan Snyder in 2007 for $175 million. It was sold again in 2012 for $350 million.

Although Clark never flaunted his wealth, he clearly enjoyed it.

Even after moving from Philadelphia to California, Clark was very much bi-coastal. In the early years, he flew to New York weekly. Although the frequency of his long-distance commutes tapered off over the years, he never gave up his East Coast ties. He maintained residences in Los Angeles and in New York.

When he first moved to California, Clark bought a big house in Encino that included a pool suitable for his two young kids (soon to be three). He later moved to Malibu where he owned multiple properties over the years. One of his Malibu homes had a living room waterfall, log cabin bedroom and garage full of rare cars. Another was fashioned out of rock and stones and resembled a house from the Flintstones TV series on 23 acres atop bluffs overlooking the Pacific Ocean.

In New York, he had a 39th floor Trump Plaza art deco penthouse decorated in silver and pink before moving to a fifth-floor

---

8. *Philadelphia Magazine*, December 1996.
9. Ibid.

EPILOGUE

Manhattan apartment dominated by black and white leather that overlooked the East River. Each of his residences included a jukebox stocked with songs made popular on *American Bandstand*.

Clark remained a workaholic over the years and wore a gold watch with two faces—one for Eastern time, the other for Pacific time. He never lost his affinity for Philadelphia and the show that launched his show business career.

Twice a year he stocked his California freezer with vermicelli, spaghetti, linguini and manicotti from Talluto's in South Philadelphia. He often spoke of Philadelphia as a city that, despite its size, always seemed like a small town to him. "Philadelphia changed my whole life," he said. "I'm not a native son, but when people say are you a Philadelphian, I say, 'Yeah, you bet your ass I'm a Philadelphian.'"[10]

When cable channel VH1 came calling with a plan for an *American Bandstand* marathon in the mid-1990s, Clark was happy to comply. He made several attempts at making a *Bandstand* movie over the years but was never able to come up the right script.

While Clark may have waxed nostalgic about *American Bandstand* at times, he never strayed far from his hard-core business roots.

In 1996, Candace Rich, a longtime *American Bandstand* fan from Florida, put a tribute page to the show and the kids who danced on it on her website, The Fifties Web. The page proved popular. For nearly two years, Rich offered *Bandstand* fans a site where they could read Rich's musings on their shared experience of growing up in the 1950s.

Unfortunately, Rich got caught up in the litigious side of Dick Clark Productions when she received a "cease and desist" letter from Clark's attorneys, who sent similar letters to a dozen or so other sites they thought were attempting to cash in on Clark's likeness or *American Bandstand*'s enduring popularity.

In their letter, Clark's lawyers claimed trademark protection for the terms *Bandstand, American Bandstand,* and even "Oldest Living Teenager." Rich, whose site offered nothing for sale, was puzzled by the ham-fisted threat of a lawsuit.

"I don't get it. I just don't get it," Rich responded to the attorneys in a letter posted on her website. "Why would anyone want to curtail a fan site? What element of the free publicity poses a threat?"

---

10. *Philadelphia Daily News*, October 30, 1981.

Acquiescing to Clark's demands, Rich altered her website—putting bold-face Xs over the word *Bandstand*, changing references to the show to "You Know What" and references to Clark to "You Know Who." The absurdity of the situation was apparently recognized by Clark's lawyers, who offered an apology. Within a few weeks, Rich was up and running again.

The cool demeanor that Clark exhibited in public was much different than his behavior in private.

"Pretty much what you saw," Clark said, "was Dick Clark according to the mores of the time. I was cast as an All-American boy, and although I smoked and drank and swore and all of that in private life, that was not presentable for television. That was the myth that was built up."[11]

Clark, of course, was instrumental in perpetuating that myth. "It was 150 percent deliberate and well thought out," he told Henry Schipper of *Rolling Stone*. "In order to perpetuate my career, first and foremost, and secondly the music."[12]

When he took over *Bandstand*, he said, "you had to be as pure as the driven snow. It was the Eisenhower era. That was the only way people would accept you."[13]

Admitting that he had "no discernible talent," Clark credited his success to his ability to "throw the spotlight on other people."[14] Furthermore, he found the magic formula of how to deal with teens: "I didn't emulate them. I didn't dress like they did. I didn't talk like they did. But I thought like they did."[15]

When not before the camera though, Clark was a different man. His temper was legendary, especially in the early days of *Bandstand*, when he was known to erupt in screaming fits.

Singer Kenny Dino was witness to one of Clark's rants in 1961 when he arrived for a *Bandstand* appearance. When Dino's manager, Al Dankoff, learned that Dino was expected to sign back his appearance check to Clark, he protested. As Dankoff was registering his objection, "Clark entered the office and yelled, 'That fucking kid will never be on this fucking show again'!"[16]

Clark's third wife, Kari (he divorced Loretta Martin in 1972), described him as moody and unpredictable, "an extremist. There is no gray to him, in any sense. Everything is black and white."[17]

---

11. *Rolling Stone*, August 17, 1973.
12. *Rolling Stone*, April 19, 1990.
13. *Philadelphia Inquirer*, November 18, 1984.
14. *Up Close*, TV interview with Patsy Smullin, 2001.
15. Ibid.
16. *Goldmine*, May 15, 1992.
17. *Philadelphia Inquirer*, November 18, 1984.

EPILOGUE

His attention span was so short, Kari said, that Clark couldn't sit through an entire album at home and only played 45s. Insiders knew that in order to pitch a project to Clark, it was wise to run it past Kari first.

Clark conceded that he could be ruthless in his business dealings. "I'll turn the (other) cheek once; the second time I take the guy's eye out!"[18]

Clark never denied that he was more interested in the business end of *American Bandstand* than the music part.

"I see no sin in being commercial," Clark said. "There can't be anything *wrong* with that, as long as this is a capitalistic country."[19]

Early in his career (but well after he'd earned his first million dollars), Clark claimed that he was driven to provide security for his sunset years. "I don't want people feeling sorry for me when I'm old," he said.[20]

"Clark was a hungry entrepreneur, working every angle to build a small empire of music concerns," *Rolling Stone* writer Henry Schipper wrote in 1990. Fred Goodman wrote that "Clark had so many angles he was round."[21]

Clark's self-assessment was even blunter: "I am an absolutely pure, unadulterated whore. I will do anything for a buck."[22]

Even as Clark's net worth was approaching $200 million, he was still bitter that the payola investigation forced him out of the music business, a move that he said cost him between $8 and $12 million. Especially grating was the fact that Clark was never charged with a crime, nor did he think he had done anything even slightly shady.

"I never took any money to play records," Clark said in a 1999 Archive of American Television interview. "I made money other ways. Horizontally, vertically, every which way you can think of, I made money from that show."

Still, Clark said, "I lived like a fugitive for seven months, sneaking into New York for my weekend show hidden in the back seat of a car to avoid the district attorney."[23]

Oren Harris' House committee didn't show him the proper respect, Clark said.

---

18. *Chicago Tribune*, July 21, 1981.
19. *TV Guide*, February 14, 1970.
20. *Philadelphia Daily News*, December 15, 1965.
21. *New York Times*, October 26, 1997.
22. *New York Journal-American*, Jack O'Brian column, February 9, 1977.
23. *Associated Press*, December 26, 1976.

"They thought people came in with carloads and bag loads of cash and put it in my office," Clark said. "It was offensive to me, they thought I was that ignorant."[24]

"The end result of the investigation," said Clark, "was the Chairman, Oren Harris, said something about the fact that you're a bright, young man and I hope we haven't inconvenienced you. '*Inconvenienced?*' Hell, they took my right testicle and almost my left!"[25]

In early 1977, while promoting his autobiography, *Rock, Roll & Remember*, Clark spoke about his payola experience at the New School for Social Research in New York City, allowing that he "probably gave a John Mitchell-Watergate laundering of the payola scene" in the book, adding "At Christmas time they'd back a truck up to my house and bring in 17 stereo sets and four televisions and silverware and goodies."[26]

Payola was clearly a subject Clark was only willing to discuss under his terms. Clark often said that the overriding lesson he learned from payola was "to protect your ass at all times." More often than not, he'd respond to payola inquiries with a wave of his hands and a terse "Next question." Sometimes he'd advise a reporter to "Go check your clips."

Before payola, Clark was a media darling. The teen press hung on his every word and the mainstream press, which was mostly controlled by white men who grew up in the big band era, generally treated him as a white knight rising against the dark forces of rock & roll, music they found either perplexing or sinister.

After payola, though, the questions got tougher and Clark became defensive, controlling the narrative as best he could. He started his own "blacklist," a file of those reporters who he felt had written negatively about him. Just as he had done with the young teens who wanted to dance on *Bandstand*, he created rules for those who wanted to interview him.

Appointments were made through assistants who screened reporters carefully. If photos were to be taken, they had to be posed to Clark's satisfaction. Absolutely no candid shots allowed. Nor were photos allowed of Clark with anyone his age. If Clark didn't like a reporter's questions, he'd simply sidestep them. If there was a pattern of impertinent questions, a handler would step in and whisk the questioner away.

---

24. *Rolling Stone*, August 17, 1973.
25. Ibid.
26. *New York Journal-American*, Jack O'Brian column, February 9, 1977.

EPILOGUE

Clark still managed to be charming in most of his on-camera interviews, although he almost always went "off the record" with his most honest and candid responses. But, when it came to his disdain for the media, Clark spoke out loud and clear.

In his interview for the Archive of American Television with James Moll, Clark told the story of how one writer wrote a glowing review but ended it with: "And how could something this good be connected to a guy like Dick Clark?"

"No wonder you're a peon at a broken-down manual typewriter somewhere working your brains out for bupkus," Clark said. "He must think I was stupid or unimaginative. He had the wrong impression. That offended me. I never called him, never wrote him, you don't do anything with those people."[27]

When *Philadelphia Magazine* reporter Pat Jordan pointed out that *Washington Post* TV writer Tom Shales had called Clark an "exploiter, albeit a benign one," Clark retorted:

> Exploiter!" snaps Clark. He flicks his fingers off his chin to dismiss Shales. "Listen, if the world turned to polkas, we'd play polkas. Anyone with five cents of brains can be a critic. It's fashionable to make fun of me and guys like Lawrence Welk. But if you could spend 40 or 50 years in a career you love with a devoted audience that makes you a millionaire, what gives someone the right to be critical." Then he adds, "If journalists had any real talent, they'd be writing scripts or novels.[28]

Critics were a favorite Clark target. Even Gail Shister of the *Philadelphia Inquirer* wasn't immune from Clark's wrath. When she pointed out "the less-than-glorious critical reception to *Bloopers*" in an interview, Clark went off.

"Do you think we care about you people (critics)?" Clark snapped. "Do you think anybody in television cares what you write about television? . . . That's an extraordinary show. It's in the Top 20 in the ratings every week. Do you think I care whether you or your colleagues don't like it? I care whether the people like it."[29]

Although Clark won a handful of Emmys over the years, little of his work drew praise from the critics. It was of little concern to Clark.

---

27. *Archive of American Television* interview, July 29, 1999.
28. *Philadelphia Magazine*, December 1996.
29. *Philadelphia Inquirer*, November 18, 1984.

"Not everyone enjoys filet," Clark said. "They often prefer hot dogs."[30]

"I've always dealt with light, frivolous things that didn't really count; I'm not ashamed of that," he said. "There's no redeeming cultural value whatsoever to 'Bloopers,' but it's been on for 20 years. It's a piece of fluff. I've been a fluffmeister for a long time."[31]

Clark often said: "I don't make culture. I sell it. I'm the storekeeper. The shelves are empty. I put the stock on. I make no comment, pro or con."[32] But, when it came to *American Bandstand*, Clark was particularly sensitive to criticism that the show's emphasis on "teen idol" music had somehow emasculated rock & roll.

From author Rick Coleman: "Clark captured America's young like an ice cream man, feeding them mostly soft serve vanilla with sprinkles of rock 'n' roll."[33]

From author Wes Smith: "Pepsodent pop stuff that was being hyped on Dick Clark's *American Bandstand* . . . [was] turning rock-'n'-roll into white teenage nursery rhymes."[34]

Author Richard Goldstein called Clark the "Master of Mediocrity."[35]

In *Rock 'N' Roll Is Here to Pay*, authors Steve Chapple and Reebee Garofalo write that rock & roll slipped from 1958 through 1964 and that *American Bandstand* and its "watered-down 'Philly sound'" was largely responsible. They call music from that period "Philadelphia Schlock."

Dick Clark took strong exception to those claims.

"I've taken a lot of lumps over the years from people who say I've homogenized the music and only presented people from Philadelphia, and that's all bullshit," Clark said. "What I *play* is what's asked for. . . . We stock the store with what the public wants."[36]

"[Critics] always speak disparagingly of teen idols, forgetting that Elvis Presley was a teen idol, the Beatles were teen idols, Bing Crosby and Frank Sinatra had been teen idols. It's a stupid journalistic thing to be critical of artists who are appreciated by the young."[37]

---

30. *TV Guide*, February 14. 1970
31. *Archive of American Television* interview, July 29, 1999.
32. *History of American Bandstand*, p. 16.
33. *Blue Monday: Fats Domino and the Lost Dawn of Rock 'n' Roll*, p. 164.
34. *The Pied Pipers of Rock 'n' Roll*, p. 2.
35. *Goldstein's Greatest Hits*, p. 201.
36. *Rolling Stone*, April 19, 1990.
37. *Goldmine*, December 28, 1990.

EPILOGUE

Clark never backed off in his defense of *American Bandstand* and for more than 30 years he controlled the narrative about the show. But, starting with John Jackson's 1997 book, *American Bandstand: Dick Clark and the Making of a Rock 'n' Roll Empire*, the conversation shifted. There was more to the story that Clark had been telling, and much of that story was wrong.

For decades Clark had been telling reporters and writers about his bold move to integrate *American Bandstand* at a time when America was fraught with racial tension. While Clark was right about the tension, his claims of integration were well off the mark.

Philadelphia had a rich black culture long before Dick Clark took over *American Bandstand*. The city had the largest free black population of any northern U.S. city in the late 18th and 19th centuries. By the 1850s, Philadelphia was seen as an intellectual and cultural mecca for blacks. The underground railway ran through Quaker Samuel Johnson's house at Germantown Avenue and Washington Lane and black migration from the south intensified after the Civil War. The city had more than 63,000 black residents by 1900.

The urbanization of the early 20th century rapidly raised the city's black population, with many of the new arrivals settling in West Philadelphia's "Black Bottom" neighborhood, just east of the eventual site of WFIL's studios. By the time the studios opened in 1952, the neighborhoods around the station were mostly integrated.

Black enrollment at West Philadelphia High School—just six blocks from the *Bandstand* studio—had tripled between 1945 and 1951, from 10 percent to 30 percent. For the most part, black and white teens at the school got along. Pictures from school yearbooks in the mid-1950s show kids of both races dancing at the school's prom or gathering at Joe's Snack Bar across the street from the school. They often got together for dances, too, in the basements of the row houses that lined the area's streets.

But such open-mindedness wasn't the Philadelphia norm.

During *Bandstand's* early years, there was a pitched battle over housing, especially in West Philadelphia where the Angora Civic Association worked tirelessly to mobilize white residents to keep blacks out of the area. The national movement toward school desegregation was also taking root in Philadelphia whose schools exhibited signs of de facto segregation. Even the city's roller rinks were segregated, drawing the ire of the ACLU, NAACP and Philadelphia's Commission on Human Relations.

As Clark told it, he recognized the injustice of denying black teens the same rights as white teens and did his best to rectify the situation by admitting teens of all races to the *American Bandstand* studio.

"When I was involved in the show in '56 we began to integrate with a greater purpose in mind because it was obvious that was going to happen," Clark said. "It was just too painfully obvious that rock 'n' roll—and by extension *Bandstand*—owed its very existence to black people, their culture and their music. "It would have been ridiculous, embarrassing *not* to integrate the show."[38]

In 1997, Clark wrote: "There was one important change that Tony [Mammarella] and I made in 1957. Up until that time, the dancers on *Bandstand* had one thing in common—they were all white.... So in 1957, we were charting new territory. I don't think of myself as a hero or civil rights activist for integrating the show; it was simply the right thing to do."...

"When Tony and I made the decision to bring in black dancers, no one told us we had to, and we didn't make a big deal out of it. We found some black teenagers who wanted to dance on the show and invited them into the studio."[39]

On NBC's *Today* show in the spring of 1997, Clark was asked whose decision it was to integrate *American Bandstand*.

"It was mine and a fellow named Tony Mammarella," Clark replied. "In those days . . . it was still segregated, we didn't socialize together. We said, in those days we called people Negroes, we've got to get some Negroes involved in this show, so we began to bring them in gradually and the lovely thing about it was, nothing happened. Nobody got hurt, no sponsors rebelled."

He expanded on that in a 1999 interview with James Moll for the Archive of American Television.

"There was no rule that they shouldn't come, no formal station policy or anything, but if you were black in those days you just didn't do that," Clark said. "And occasionally you would get one or two strays in . . . [in 1957 or '58] and with no instructions whatsoever we [Tony Mammarella and Clark] said we'd better bring some black kids in here because things are changing and if we don't, there's going to be problems. Probably protests, so we began to filter in a few. . . .

---
38. *Goldmine*, December 28, 1990.
39. *Dick Clark's American Bandstand*, pp. 19–20.

EPILOGUE

"We didn't do it because we were do-gooders or liberals. . . . It was none of that. It was just, eh, it's probably a thing we ought to do. It was naive. But it worked. If the whole world could have done it that way, wouldn't it have been great? That was probably the show's greatest contribution, to bring blacks and whites together in a social atmosphere."[40]

Once Clark started telling the story about *Bandstand's* substantial role in the civil rights movement, it took hold. Curiously, Clark didn't tell the story when the civil rights movement was flowering in the 1960s. It wasn't until the mid-1970s—when Don Cornelius' *Soul Train* was a true contender for the Saturday afternoon teen dance show crown—that Clark started touting his bona fides as a longtime force for racial equality.

In 1976, Clark laid the gauntlet down on page 82 of his autobiography, *Rock, Roll & Remember*: "*Bandstand* was a segregated show for years. It became integrated in 1957 because I elected to make it so."

Despite Clark's grandiloquence, the historical record shows his claims to be untrue. The record also shows no evidence that Clark's failure to integrate *American Bandstand* while in Philadelphia was because of any racial prejudice on his part. It's more likely that his reluctance to act was purely a business decision and his "false memories" were a projection of how he had wished things had turned out.

But the truth is that *Bandstand* was a segregated show when Dick Clark took it over in 1956 and it was still a segregated show when he left Philadelphia in February 1964. Furthermore, keeping blacks out of the *Bandstand* studio was a deliberate act calculated to make the show more appealing to its mostly white audience.

In his unpublished memoir, *Bandstand Off My Back*, Tony Mammarella devoted an entire chapter to the subject entitled "No Blacks Allowed."

Mammarella minced no words in explaining how the practice of racial segregation began under Bob Horn and continued well after Dick Clark took over the show and took it nationally on ABC-TV.

Mammarella wrote how the first *Bandstand* program drew strictly a white audience but how blacks soon started showing

---

40. *Archive of American Television* interview, July 29, 1999.

up in increasing numbers. Horn hired a black "tough" to keep the blacks in line and established an all-white Committee to oversee on-air decorum. But the number of blacks attending continued to grow, and some of the black teens started intimidating their white counterparts.

Horn doubled the size of the Committee to 40 members and gave them membership cards with special admission privileges. He also divided the kids who showed up outside the studio each day into two lines—one for boys and one for girls. Since there were more black boys than black girls (Mammarella concluded that black males must have dropped out of school at a higher rate than black females) in the lines, the black males that were admitted didn't have dance partners, so they sat in the stands.

Finally, they published a set of rules that applied to everyone, regardless of race color or creed. But, Mammarella wrote, "Black kids were poor kids, so you hit where they can't fight back. You . . . just make rules that only white kids can follow."

For one thing, every boy was required to wear a suit jacket, shirt, and necktie. Mammarella estimated that this rule alone eliminated 95 percent of all the black boys since they didn't own a suit jacket.

Another rule required teens to check coats, hats, pocketbooks and school books upon entering. Since it was assumed black boys would not check their coats and hats and black girls would not check their pocketbooks, this rule also proved effective.

Mammarella claimed that 98 percent of the black males stopped coming within one week and all blacks were gone within two weeks. Mammarella also claimed that "the 'whites only' policy had the blessing and encouragement of every top official at WFIL-TV and the parent company, *The Philadelphia Inquirer*. That includes Roger W. Clipp, George Koehler, Lew Klein, Walter Annenberg, Bob Horn, Dick Clark, and me."[41]

Walter DeLegall, who was a black student at West Philadelphia High School in *Bandstand's* early days, believes Mammarella's claims to be true.

"Every day after school, we would head for the TV studio which was near my high school—West Philly High. Black kids from Overbrook High would come also. For the most part, the white kids from West Catholic, etc., were intimidated when we

---

41. *Bandstand Off My Back*, unpublished manuscript by Tony Mammarella.

EPILOGUE

got on the floor. They wouldn't get up unless the bunny hop was playing. Then my crowd all sat down."

"After a while, the producers decided that they wanted to change the image of the show, so they created a new policy. To get in the studio, boys must be wearing a suit jacket and tie. Since no black students went to school dressed like that, we couldn't get in anymore. The white kids had no problem with the new dress code. We stopped going and so did the black girls, for the most part."[42]

As John Jackson pointed out in his book, of about 75 photographs published in *The History of American Bandstand* only one showed any blacks. No blacks were visible in the dozens of photos in the 1955 *Bandstand* yearbook and "a check of 16 pictures showing the *Bandstand* audience [in Clark's 1976 autobiography], showed 340 racially identifiable faces, none of them black."[43]

Rick Fisher, a semi-regular during *Bandstand's* final years in Philadelphia said: "I don't ever remember seeing any African-Americans on *Bandstand*."

Charles Amann, a life-long fan of the show, had begun a project to document the stories of the regulars who appeared on *Bandstand* in Philadelphia before his death in 2013. As part of his project, Amann recorded a series of video interviews with some of the better-known regulars and released them on YouTube under the *Bandstand's Best* title. Here are excerpts from some of those interviews:

> Carmen Jimenez: "I was aware of segregation on *American Bandstand* because I would see when the cameras were positioned near the black [dancer], Dick would say move the camera."
>
> Eddie Kelly: "I never saw a black person dance with a white person. Never. And I remember only seeing two black couples dancing and they weren't dancing every song."
>
> Joyce Shafer: "Integration that Dick Clark speaks of, did not take place. We never saw any black people dancing with the white people. We were told by Dick Clark we were not allowed to associate with them."

---

42. *TotalTheater.com*, "The Real Hairspray Story," By Steve Cohen, December 2002.
43. *Anti-Rock*, p. 107.

Ronnie Caldora was a popular regular who was profiled in 1961 in *Movie Teen Screen* as "Regular of the Month." He was also one of the more rebellious regulars.

"There had been a scandal over some of the kids getting paid for touring with [*Bandstand*] sock hops across the country," Caldora said. "I was part of that group but I didn't get caught. We'd take limousines to places like Wilkes-Barre and get $500 for dancing at these things."[44]

In the studio, though, Clark was harder to deceive.

"Dick had this studio mike that would call you out. 'Hall—get back.' You couldn't dance too close. You couldn't bump and grind. And you certainly couldn't dance with someone who wasn't your color. One time I danced with this beautiful black girl, and I don't know if it was Dick or Bob the Cop who said, 'Do that again and you're off the show for two weeks'."[45]

Although the "whites only" rules went into effect on Bob Horn's watch, Dick Clark continued the practice when he took over. When they went national, ABC insisted that the rules remain in place—"Just keep the show white, you're gonna be alright" (according to Mammarella in *Bandstand Off My Back*).

All of the major TV networks were leery of putting black faces before their cameras in the 1950s. Outside of *Amos & Andy*, black roles were few and far between. Bob Lewine, who held executive positions at all three networks during his lengthy television career, said: "At ABC we hired Sammy Davis, Jr. to do a pilot. It was based on Andy Hardy and had Sammy singing, dancing, and playing the drums. I remember Sammy saying, "We're gonna have an all-black cast." I said fine. We showed it to [ad agency Young & Rubicam] and they walked out in the middle of it, so we gave up."[46]

Joe Cates, an ABC producer/director around the same time, said: "On a show celebrating the Fourth of July, Tom Moore, the former head of broadcasting at ABC, said, "What are you doing with the niggers? Cut the niggers out."[47]

With *American Bandstand*, ABC officials had more specific concerns. They had pulled the plug on Alan Freed's network show just a week before *Bandstand* premiered following the uproar that ensued after black singer Frankie Lymon was spotted on camera dancing with a white girl.

---

44. *Philadelphia City Paper*, April 3, 1997.
45. Ibid.
46. *The Box: An Oral History of Television 1920–61*, p. 517.
47. Ibid.

EPILOGUE

While Clark and Mammarella understood the network's position, they were uncomfortable with it.

"From the beginning, we knew the "white only" policy was morally wrong, but we trained our collective conscience to justify our position," Mammarella wrote. "All this rationalization was sandwiched in between being successful. We didn't dwell on the racial aspect of the show."[48]

American Bandstand was a cultural island of whiteness in a neighborhood full of black faces, yet Rick Fisher notes: "I didn't know any black people that even wanted to go to that show."

Weldon McDougal, a black student at West Philadelphia High School who said he had no trouble getting into *Bandstand* in 1952–53 before the strict rules went into effect, claims that black kids weren't that crazy about *Bandstand* because Bob Horn played "corny music."[49]

But try to get in they did.

In the early days of *Bandstand*, Horn indiscriminately used the term "Committee." Horn used the term at first to describe the volunteer committee he had created to maintain decorum on the show. However, he also used the term to describe what was basically a ticketing system to the show.

These secondary committee members received membership cards, mostly distributed at the end of each day's show, that allowed the bearer into the studio on specific future days. In a January 16, 1953, story in the *Philadelphia Bulletin*, Horn told reporter Harry Harris that about 5,000 high school kids had been given these membership cards.

When Moe Booker learned that Horn was issuing tickets to the show through committee memberships and that committee members were allowed to recommend friends for memberships, he and some of his black friends decided to test the system.

"We took a very, very, very, very, very, very fair black girl. She went, walked in, was given the membership card just like that," Booker said.

The girl came out, showed off her card and went back into the WFIL studios with her black friends. When she recommended her friends for membership, they were refused on the grounds that they had to be recommended by a committee member.

---
48. *Bandstand Off My Back*, unpublished manuscript by Tony Mammarella.
49. *The Nicest Kids in Town*, p. 43.

Booker said they pointed to their card-carrying friend and asked, who recommended her?

"At which point they closed the door and didn't talk to us anymore."[50]

Walter Palmer, a black student at West Philadelphia High School, tried a different tactic. He had several of his friends mail in membership applications using Irish, Italian and Polish sounding surnames. Although the tactic worked, it had a less than desirable outcome.

The memberships did get Palmer and his friends into the studio, but he said they were often greeted with violence from their white counterparts. Some of the fights degenerated into "all-out race riots outside the studio," Palmer said.[51]

Shortly after Dick Clark took *American Bandstand* national, a group of black South Philadelphia teens made plans to attend the show to watch another South Philadelphian, singer Bobby Brookes. Although they wrote for tickets a week ahead of Brookes' appearance, they received no reply so they showed up at the studio anyway.

They arrived early but were ignored as the WFIL doorman allowed white teens into the building. They were greeted by racial slurs when they complained but were finally admitted after a reporter from the *Philadelphia Tribune* showed up and asked for an explanation from the station manager.[52]

The *Tribune*, Philadelphia's biggest black newspaper, was a consistent advocate for black teens who wanted to attend *Bandstand*. It ran its first front page story about the issue shortly after Clark took over hosting duties.

The story—headlined "No Negroes on Bandstand Show, TV Boss Says They're Welcome"—reported on the many complaints the paper had received about racial segregation on the show and WFIL program manager Jim Felix's defense of what he called the show's "first come, first served" policy.

During the Philadelphia years of *American Bandstand*, the *Tribune* printed at least seven editorials or letters to the editor about the barring of black teens from the show. One of the *Tribune's* columnists, Masco Young, once criticized Clark for "emceeing one of the most famous Jim Crowed shows on TV."[53]

---

50. *From Hucklebuck to Hip-Hop: Social Dance in the African American Community*, p. 36.
51. *The Nicest Kids in Town*, p. 45.
52. *The Nicest Kids in Town*, p. 183.
53. *Philadelphia Tribune*, February 20, 1960.

EPILOGUE

Besides confronting *Bandstand's* segregationist policies, the *Tribune* got behind the music that appealed to its teen readers. The paper ran articles on popular local black groups like the Dreamers, the Opals, and Ronald Jones & the Classmates and featured a popular column called "Teen Talk." Popular disc jockey Georgie Woods also had a weekly column entitled "Rock and Roll with Georgie Woods."

Woods started organizing stage shows in Philadelphia in 1955 and was soon billing himself as the "King of Rock 'N' Roll." Woods, who would go on to be a good friend and trusted advisor to Dick Clark, was also committed to fighting juvenile delinquency and promoting civil rights.

Philadelphia's black teens were well served musically by Woods and several other popular black deejays, most notably Jocko Henderson and Kae Williams, but if they wanted to dance on TV in the 1950s they had just one choice, *The Mitch Thomas Show*.

Thomas was a Florida native who was raised in New Jersey, served in the U.S. Army in World War II and became the first black disc jockey in Wilmington, Delaware, in 1949. By the 1950s, he found himself working with Woods and Henderson at WDAS.

When given the opportunity to host a dance show on WPFH-TV in Wilmington, he jumped at the chance. *The Mitch Thomas Show* debuted on August 13, 1955, as part of a plan by WIBG owner Paul F. Harron to bring the Philadelphia area its first successful independent television station.

Harron had bought the station (then known as WDEL, Channel 12) earlier that year and promptly changed its call letters to conform to his initials. The popular music that had been such a big part of WIBG's radio success also played a big part as Harron's team assembled programming for its television operation.

Although located 25 miles southwest of Philadelphia, Harron persuaded Al Grady and Ed Hurst to drop their weekly TV dance show at WPTZ and start a daily weekday show at WPFH that would compete head-to-head with Bob Horn's *Bandstand*. They, too, jumped at the chance, though their show wouldn't launch until seven weeks after *The Mitch Thomas Show*, a Saturday program that was aimed at the underserved black teen audience.

Thomas, who was Kae Williams' cousin, was affectionately known as MT. *The Mitch Thomas Show*, which mimicked the format of *Bandstand*, proved successful from the start and became known to many as "the black *Bandstand*."

Among Thomas' musical guests were Ray Charles, Little Richard, and the Moonglows. As did *Bandstand*, Thomas had a committee of regulars. Having a dedicated core of dancers was even more important to Thomas' show, given the remote location of the studio. When Grady and Hurst started their show, they arranged with a Wilmington bus service to deliver kids to WPFH daily to ensure a suitable number of teens to put before the camera. In case of inclement weather or another unforeseen disaster, they began recording shows so they'd have something to air if there weren't any kids available.

The dancers on *The Mitch Thomas Show* were every bit as popular locally as were the dancers on *Bandstand*. George Gray, the originator of the Walk, was known to fans of the show as Walkin' George. Rosalie Milton was known as Ponytail. Charlestene Lewis was known as Miss Cha Cha. But the most popular dancers on the show were undoubtedly Vera and Otis.

Otis Givens attended Ben Franklin High School in South Philadelphia when *The Mitch Thomas Show* first hit the air. Givens was a dance stylist, taking popular dances like the Philly bop and adding his own personal moves. He had taken those moves to *Bandstand* a few times in the Bob Horn era, thanks to an acquaintance who sometimes worked the door at WFIL.

For a year after Thomas began his Wilmington show, Givens watched every weekend from his home. After finally making the trip to the WPFH studio, he and partner Vera Boyer headed to the dance floor.

"The things we were doing made everyone back away," Givens recalled.[54]

Jack Fisher, an *American Bandstand* semi-regular, who danced on Grady and Hurst's show during the week and watched Mitch Thomas on Saturdays, noticed Givens.

"He was fantastic," Fisher said. "Ed Hurst used to call me Otis. That was his nickname for me because, everything Otis did, I tried."

Watching Otis and Vera wasn't the only reason Fisher watched the Thomas show.

"That's where we got all those dance steps," he said. "We stole them from the black kids. They were great."

But, just as Jimmy Peatross and Joan Buck were reluctant to say on-air that they had learned the strand from black dancers, *The Mitch Thomas Show*'s influence on Philadelphia's teenage

---

54. *South Philly Review*, January 13, 2005.

EPILOGUE

dancing scene was mostly overlooked. For example, many Thomas viewers claim that the Stroll actually originated in Wilmington, not Philadelphia.

Despite its success and influence, *The Mitch Thomas Show* lasted just three years and was gone by the summer of 1958, a victim of low ratings and a lack of sponsorship, according to station owners.

In retrospect, *American Bandstand*'s segregationist policies seem to have been effective.

The *Philadelphia Inquirer* had an advisor on Negro affairs who occasionally raised issues like how to address blacks or to ask (and get) a ban on all Stephen Foster songs, but, according to Tony Mammarella, the advisor never raised the issue of allowing black dancers on the show. Philadelphia Mayor Richardson Dilworth did occasionally question the absence of blacks on the show, but never in a forceful way.

In the spring of 1956, though, Dilworth did ask George Koehler to admit a group of 30 Negro boys and girls to the show. Mammarella described the situation:

> They were extremely well dressed. All were college students and all were light in complexion. They were not your everyday run of the mill teenagers, white or black.
>
> They entered the studio and immediately took seats in the stands. It almost seemed rehearsed. They smiled politely when the other kids were admitted to the studio. They sat through the first fifteen or twenty minutes of music. Then, two couples left the stands, entered the dance area, made one full sweep around the dance floor and returned to their seats in the stands. Five minutes later, they all got up and quietly walked out of the studio. They never came back and we never received another request like that again.[55]

After *American Bandstand* made the move to California, it truly did become an integrated program. By 1965, it had its first black regular—Famous Hooks.

* * *

Outside of longtime aide Ed McAdam, secretary Chris Betlejeski and announcer Charlie O'Donnell, the only other member of

---

55. *Bandstand Off My Back*, unpublished manuscript by Tony Mammarella.

Clark's Philadelphia team to make the move to California was director Ed Yates.

But Yates didn't make the trip with the others. It took several months of California shows before Clark realized that only Yates could direct the show to Clark's satisfaction. Yates had been with the show from the beginning, rising through the ranks from flipping cue cards to camera pusher to boom operator to cameraman before getting a shot at the directors' chair.

His day at WFIL started at 6 A.M. and typically involved three or four shows before wrapping up with *Bandstand*. Although his California workload was lighter, he missed the camaraderie of the Philadelphia crew. By 1969, he was through.

"I had had enough of *Bandstand* and Dick Clark and everybody," Yates said as he explained his decision to return to the Delaware Valley and a job as director of security at Independence Hall. He retired in 1974 and died on June 2, 2006.

Tony Mammarella continued as president and general manager of Swan Records through 1968. He presented the Beatles with their first gold record for *She Loves You* in 1965. From 1968 through 1975 he was Director of Public Relations for the Pennsylvania Turnpike Commission and worked as a freelance public relations specialist until his death at age 53 on November 27, 1977. He was still working on his book, *Bandstand Off My Back*, at the time of his death.

Bob Horn had a successful career with his own advertising agency, Bob Adams Advertising, in Houston in the early 1960s where he was credited with creating Houston's first Midnight Madness sale. He moved his family to a seven-acre spread just outside Houston where he raised quarter horses. He also opened a bar with his wife in Bellaire called the Town and Country Lounge.

Horn died at age 50 of a heart attack brought on by a heat stroke on July 31, 1966, while mowing his lawn. He is buried at the Forest Park Cemetery in Houston, Texas, with the simple epitaph, "Bandstand."

Former *Bandstand* regular Ron Joseph sought to produce a film about Horn entitled "We Have Company" in the 1990s, but the project was abandoned when potential investors balked because Horn didn't have strong national name recognition.

EPILOGUE

Alan Freed lived out his final years in his home in Palm Springs, Calif. In his final weeks, he sent old friend Morris Levy a handwritten letter, pleading poverty and begging for a loan. His wife, Inga, had taken a job at a Palm Springs hotel and he feared the gas and electricity to his home would soon be turned off if he didn't pay his bills.

Clark, who said "I was the last friend Alan had,"[56] claimed he was solicited by Freed around the same time. "He was groveling around and I tried to get him a job, and two days before he died I was called to contribute to keep him in the hospital."[57]

Freed's son, Lance, said he didn't remember Clark being around for his dad as he lay dying in a Palm Springs hospital, though he did concede the two had a cordial relationship *before* the payola hearings.

Freed was still facing tax evasion charges when he died of uremic poisoning at the age of 43 on January 20, 1965, the same day Lyndon B. Johnson was inaugurated as President of the United States.

Clay Cole, "the next Dick Clark," never quite achieved that title. A marijuana bust of his entourage in Newfoundland in 1962 pretty much derailed his career. He developed a drinking problem, tried to kill himself by swallowing a bottle of aspirin and briefly left show business altogether, taking a counter job at a New York City coffee shop and compiling best-selling record lists for *Billboard* magazine.

He started to bounce back in 1963, though, and was a steady TV presence with *The Clay Cole Show* through 1968, when he abandoned regular TV work to become a freelance television producer, working only when he wanted or when he needed the money. He died of a heart attack at age 72 on December 18, 2010.

Buddy Deane, whose Baltimore TV dance show eerily paralleled *American Bandstand*'s Philadelphia run, experienced firsthand the racial backlash Dick Clark feared.

The Buddy Deane Show started one month after *American Bandstand*'s debut and wrapped up operations one month before Clark headed west to California. Like *Bandstand*, Deane had a committee of regulars, featured the top artists of the day and had

---
56. *Rolling Stone*, August 17, 1973.
57. Ibid.

a devoted audience that tuned in every afternoon to check out the latest hits and hottest fashions. Unlike *Bandstand*, Deane took on the race issue head-on, allowing black kids into the WJZ-TV studio one Monday every month.

Officially known as "Special Guest Day," it was known as "Black Monday" among the area's black teens. It was a popular feature at first but as the civil rights movement took hold in the 1960s an increasing number of progressive teens found the concept of "Black Monday" to be offensive.

In 1962, a group of black and white students from Morgan State University picketed the station in an effort to keep that day's guest, Ray Charles, from appearing on Deane's show. The picketing was ineffective since Charles' appearance had been taped days earlier.

A more successful bid for integration occurred a year later, on August 17, 1963.

That date was a "Black Monday" and a local group—Baltimore Youth Opportunities Unlimited (BAYOU)—had secured tickets for that day's show. What program officials didn't realize was that BAYOU was the Baltimore branch of the Northern Student Movement—an integrated civil rights group.

A horde of black BAYOU members presented their tickets at the studio doors, quickly followed by several carloads of white teenagers who pressed into the studio behind them. Soon blacks and whites crowded the dance floor, dancing together.

Technicians lowered the lights so only silhouettes were visible while producers tried frantically to distort the image, dissolving it into squiggles and squares as they tried to sabotage their own broadcast.

But the damage was done. After the show, WJZ received bomb threats, arson threats and hundreds of complaints, mostly from angry white parents. The kids didn't seem to mind, but WJZ officials didn't know how to handle the situation. Finally, they just tore up Deane's contract[58].

On January 4, 1964, Deane dropped the needle on "The Party's Over" and the set faded to black as the record played. Deane high-tailed it back to his native Arkansas where he resumed his radio career. He died after a stroke at age 78 on July 16, 2003.

His days at *16* magazine were just a stepping stone for Steve Brandt, who went on to be a well-known gossip columnist for

---

58. *The Washington Post*, Sept. 17, 2003

EPILOGUE

Photoplay magazine, working out of Southern California. Brandt was assimilated into the jet set culture of Los Angeles in the late 1960s and was good friends with actress Sharon Tate, even standing up at her wedding to Roman Polanski.

After Tate and three other Brandt acquaintances were among the five people murdered in suburban Benedict Canyon on August 9, 1969, Brandt feared that he would be next. That November, he attempted suicide by swallowing a bottle of Tylenol but was rescued after he made a phone call from his West Hollywood apartment to the secretary of a good friend, singer Eddie Fisher, who was performing in Las Vegas.

Brandt was hospitalized in "very critical" condition but recovered.

Later that month, Brandt attended a Rolling Stones Concert at Madison Square Garden in New York City with some friends in the Andy Warhol cohort. He split from the group and retired early to his room at the Chelsea Hotel. When a concerned friend, actress Ultra Violet, called to check on him, Brandt said he had taken a bunch of sleeping pills. By the time help arrived, he was dead.

* * *

Despite being kicked off *American Bandstand* because they cut a record, neither Bob Clayton nor Justine Carrelli became recording stars.

Clayton, who married twice (neither time to Carrelli) went into business, managing a string of shoe stores and owning a couple of gift boutiques in his hometown of Wilmington, Delaware. He died on November 6, 2016.

After graduating from high school, Carrelli spent six months as a Marine Corps steno typist but really wanted a career in show business. She worked as a model, took voice lessons and got a job singing with Paul Dino's band. After marrying Dino, she gave up show business to raise a family and start a career in real estate.

After divorcing Dino, she married another musician, Woody Neel Bosco, and wrote a screenplay based on her experiences called *It Wasn't All Dancing*. She eventually settled in Las Vegas where she lives with her third husband.

Kenny Rossi and Arlene Sullivan took very different paths following their *Bandstand* experience.

For Rossi, that meant pursuing a recording career for a few years. He recorded for Adelphia, Roulette, and Mercury before entering the waterproofing business. He made four appearances on *American Bandstand* as a singer.

Sullivan, on the other hand, had a variety of jobs over the years, including as a blackjack dealer in Atlantic City. She continued a lifelong friendship with Annette Funicello following her *Bandstand* years and briefly pursued a modeling career. She is a co-author of *Bandstand Diaries*, a book that includes excerpts from her personal diaries.

Bunny Gibson was one of the few *Bandstand* regulars to actually have a show business career. Although she married and started a family at a young age, she divorced at age 24 and went to work supporting herself and two young daughters. She studied acting and landed spots in several commercials, including for Minute Rice ("My rice came out kinda drippy!") and Charmin.

She later moved to Los Angeles where, as Kathleen Klein, she landed a recurring role on *General Hospital*. Over the years she's appeared in dozens of plays, TV shows, and movies and has volunteered in programs to help the homeless and to promote dance among children.

Her *Bandstand* dancing partner, Eddie Kelly, was never really comfortable with his star status, saying "I don't have any talent." Nor was he close to Dick Clark, who barred him from the show twice, but their relationship mellowed over the years.

After *Bandstand*, Kelly worked in the music publishing business with MGM and 20th Century Fox before taking a job as job as records manager and office manager for a law firm in the New York City area. He relocated from New Jersey to Southern California in 2014.

Pat Molittieri, perhaps the best female dancer on *American Bandstand* during the Philadelphia era, spent a couple years in California pursuing her show business dream.

Despite voice lessons, her recording career never took off though she did go out with a musical revue at one time. She did a few commercials and was an extra in the movie *Where the Boys Are* but returned to Philadelphia where she worked as a receptionist at Women's Hospital and hoped for a career as an airline stewardess.

She married, had two children, and died in her mid-30s.

EPILOGUE

Two well-known regulars went on to have successful broadcasting careers—Jerry Blavat and Ron Joseph.

Blavat started his lengthy broadcast career in Camden, N.J., while *American Bandstand* was still in Philadelphia. He was just as well known over the years for the many record hops he conducted in the Philadelphia area as he was for his various radio duties. He once managed Danny & the Juniors, was the owner of the Memories nightclub in Margate, N.J., and published a book about his life, *You Only Rock Once*, in 2011.

Joseph also began his radio career while Dick Clark was still in Philadelphia. When he landed his first television program in 1962—*Spotlight on America* on WPCA-TV—Clark was his first guest. Joseph has hosted a number of rock-oriented radio and television shows ever since and was a pioneer in the field of low-powered television in the Philadelphia area.

Frank Brancaccio, who quit high school so he could concentrate on his *American Bandstand* celebrity, ultimately realized his dream of becoming an actor. He moved to New York where he was in several off-Broadway plays and had minor roles in the films *Godfather II* and *Serpico*. For a time he was an editor of a gay-oriented magazine and wrote a book titled *Ephemeral Nights*, which draws on his rough South Philadelphia upbringing to tell a story "about co-dependency, obsession, and self-destruction."

In the years since Dick Clark pulled *American Bandstand* out of Philadelphia, there have been numerous reunion shows and other opportunities for former regulars to get together, reminisce and, of course, dance. With the advent of the Internet in the 1990s, it became easier for ex-Bandstanders and fans of the show to connect and keep in touch.

But for the first 30 years following the move from Philadelphia, the best way to stay informed about *American Bandstand* was to stay in touch with Davey Frees.

Frees, who never danced on the show, was perhaps the show's biggest fan. He joined a fan club for the Jimenez sisters in 1960 as a 13-year-old and soon was running fan clubs for many of the Philadelphia regulars and collecting *Bandstand* memorabilia. The collecting was interrupted in 1967 when he was drafted into the Army.

After breaking a leg in Vietnam, he was sent to Philadelphia to recuperate. Following his release from the hospital, he discovered that his *Bandstand* collection had been destroyed by water from a leaky roof. He began writing to fan clubs and former regulars, trying to rebuild his collection.

In 1970 he consolidated all his fan clubs into the *American Bandstand Fan Club* and began publishing a newsletter, *Bandstand Boogie*. He soon had 400 members, a number that would double over the next 15 years.

At the time of this writing, Frees remains the go-to source for all things *Bandstand*, though art historian Charles W. Amann III made a strong bid for that title starting around 2005.

Like Frees, Amann never appeared on *Bandstand*, though he did dance on a similar show as a teenager in northern New Jersey. It was Amann's "strong kinship" to the music that led him to begin work on a book about the regulars of *American Bandstand*.

Amann titled his book project *The Princes and Princesses of Dance* and began interviewing regulars and acquiring *Bandstand*-related memorabilia. He authored a blog with the same name as the book and produced a series of videos related to his project.

He was the driving force behind an *American Bandstand* mural that was unveiled in the old WFIL-TV *Bandstand* studio to mark the 50th anniversary of the show on August 2, 2007, and produced a Broadway revue, *The Radio Hits of 1958*, that included several regulars at its premiere on June 30, 2008.

Amann died in December 2013 before he could finish his *Bandstand* project.

Around the time that John Jackson's book about Dick Clark and *American Bandstand* was released in the late 1990s, two other books in defense of Bob Horn were also released. The common thread in both of the pro-Horn books was Stan Blitz.

Blitz is listed as the author (as told to John Pritchard) of *Bandstand: The Untold Story*, which he self-published in 1997. In his book, Blitz paints Horn as the victim of an unspecified plot to remove him from *Bandstand*. Blitz claims Horn "was figuratively tarred, feathered and run out of Philadelphia—to be forgotten—a man with a ruined career."

Blitz was listed as a research assistant in another self-published book, *Musical Chairs: Bandstand Exposed* by Pete Christensen. The 1996 book has the same theme as *Untold Story*—Bob

EPILOGUE

Horn was railroaded by a powerful conspiracy—but this time as a work of fiction, though the author writes in his preface that "there was a Bob Horn and these incidents did happen to him."

Dick Clark and *American Bandstand* came under scrutiny in a 2008 documentary, *The Wages of Spin*. In the film produced and directed by Shawn Swords for Character Driven Productions, many of Clark's former business associates, as well as others associated with *Bandstand* and the Philadelphia music scene, spoke out on subjects ranging from payola to songwriting credits as they related to Clark's "empire building." The film spawned at least two sequels.

Dick Clark did, indeed, stay in the entertainment business as he told Gail Shister of the *Philadelphia Inquirer* "until they cart me away."

His on-screen presence was limited to New Year's Eve in his later years, as the host of his annual *New Year's Rockin' Eve* shows on ABC.

"The joke always was," Clark said, "that when Guy Lombardo died, God rest his soul, he'd take New Year's Eve with him. But he left it behind, and I got it."[59]

Clark suffered a serious stroke in December 2004, but returned to the New Year's Eve show the next year and was an annual fixture from that point until his death caused by a heart attack on April 18, 2012. He was 82.

When Shister mentioned to Clark that no matter what else he accomplished in his professional career, he'd probably always be remembered as "the smiling, antiseptic host of *American Bandstand*," he said that was fine with him.

"That image will be with me, hopefully, until I'm taken away," he said. "It's always the same thing: 'Dick Clark? He's the guy with the kids and the records.' It's terrific. What else could you ask out of life?"[60]

---

59. *Knight-Ridder News Service*, December 31, 1992.
60. *Philadelphia Inquirer*, November 18, 1994.

BIBLIOGRAPHY

BOOKS

Altschuler, Glenn C. *All Shook Up: How Rock 'n' Roll Changed America*. New York: Oxford University Press, 2003.
Barlow, William. *Voice Over: The Making of Black Radio*. Philadelphia: Temple University Press, 1999.
Bego, Mark. *The Rock & Roll Almanac*. New York: Macmillan, 1996.
———. *TV Rock*. New York: PaperJacks Ltd., 1988.
Berry, Chuck. *Chuck Berry: The Autobiography*. New York: Harmony Books, 1987.
Binzen, Peter. *Nearly Everybody Read It: Snapshots of the Philadelphia Bulletin*. Philadelphia: Camino Books, 1998.
Blavat, Jerry (as told to Steve Oskie). *You Only Rock Once*. Philadelphia: Running Press, 2011.
Blitz, Stanley J. *Bandstand: The Untold Story*. Phoenix, Ariz.: Cornucopia Publications, 1997.
Boris, Alan. *Philadelphia Radio*. Charleston, S.C.: Arcadia Publishing, 2011.
Brooks, Tim and Earle Marsh. *The Complete Directory to Prime Time Network TV Shows*. New York: Ballantine Books, 1979.
Broven, John. *Record Makers and Breakers*. Urbana, Ill.: University of Illinois Press, 2009.
Brown, James (with Bruce Tucker). *James Brown: The Godfather of Soul*. New York: Macmillan Publishing Company, 1986.
Castleman, Harry and Walter J. Podrazik. *Watching TV: Four Decades of American Television*. New York: McGraw-Hill Book Company, 1982.
Chapple, Steve and Reebee Garofalo. *Rock 'N' Roll Is Here to Pay*. Chicago: Nelson-Hall, 1977.
Christensen, Pete. *Musical Chairs: Bandstand Exposed*. 1996.
Clark, Dick with Fred Bronson. *Dick Clark's American Bandstand*. New York: Collins Publishers, 1997.
Clark, Dick with Paul Francis. *Murder on Tour*. New York: The Mysterious Press, 1989.
Clark, Dick. *To Goof or Not to Goof*. New York: Crest Books, 1963.
———, Dick. *Your Happiest Years*. New York: Rosho Corporation, 1959.
Cohodas, Nadine. *Spinning Blues Into Gold: The Chess Brothers and the Legendary Chess Records*. St. Martin's Press, 2000.
Cole, Clay. *Sh-Boom!: The Explosion of Rock 'n' Roll (1953–1968)*, New York: Morgan James Publishing, 2009.

BIBLIOGRAPHY

Coleman, Rick. *Blue Monday: Fats Domino and the Lost Dawn of Rock 'n' Roll*. Boston: Da Capo Press, 2006.

Cowen, Tyler. *In Praise of Commercial Culture*. Cambridge, Mass.: Harvard University Press, 2000.

Dannen, Fredric. *Hit Men: Power Brokers and Fast Money Inside the Music Business*. New York: Times Books, 1990.

Davis, Francis. *Like Young: Jazz, Pop, Youth, and Middle Age*. Cambridge, Mass.: Da Capo Press, 2002.

Dawson, Jim. *The Twist*. Winchester, Mass.: Faber and Faber, Inc., 1995.

Delmont, Matthew F. *The Nicest Kids in Town*. Berkeley, Calif.: University of California Press, 2012.

Du Noyer, Paul. *The Story of Rock 'N' Roll*. Spain: Carlton Books Limited, 1995.

Eliot, Marc. *Rockonomics: The Money Behind the Music*. New York: Franklin Watts, 1989.

Ennis, Philip H. *The Seventh Stream: The Emergence of Rocknroll in American Popular Music*. Hanover, N.H.: Wesleyan University Press, 1992.

Escott, Colin with Martin Hawkins. *Good Rockin' Tonight*. New York: St. Martin's Press, 1991.

Fong-Torres, Ben. *The Hits Just Keep On Coming: The History of Top 40 Radio*. San Francisco: Backbeat Books, 1998.

Forman, Murray. *One Night on TV Is Worth Weeks at the Paramount: Popular Music on Early Television*. Durham, N.C.: Duke University Press, 2012.

Francis, Connie. *Who's Sorry Now?* New York: St. Martin's Press, 1984.

Goldenson, Leonard H. *Beating the Odds*. New York: Charles Scribner's Sons, 1991.

Goldstein, Richard. *Goldstein's Greatest Hits*. Englewood Cliffs, N.J.: Prentice-Hall, Inc., 1970.

Gorman, Paul and Charles Shaar Murray, *In Their Own Write: Adventures in the Music Press*. London: Sanctuary Publishing, 2001.

Greenfield, Robert. *The Last Sultan: The Life and Times of Ahmet Ertegun*. New York: Simon & Schuster Paperbacks, 2011.

Harrington, Joe S. *Sonic Cool: The Death of Rock 'n' Roll*. Milwaukee, Wis.: Joe Leonard Corp., 2002.

Harris, Jay S. *TV Guide: The First 25 Years*. New York: Simon and Schuster, 1978.

Hopkins, Jerry. *The Rock Story*. New York: Signet, 1970.

Jackson, John A. *American Bandstand: Dick Clark and the Making of a Rock 'n' Roll Empire*. New York: Oxford University Press, 1997.

———. *Big Beat Heat: Alan Freed and the Early Years of Rock & Roll*. New York: Schirmer Books, 1991.

Johnson Jr., John and Joel Selvin. *Peppermint Twist*. Thomas Dunne Books: New York, 2012.

Kisseloff, Jeff. *The Box: An Oral History of Television 1920–1961*. New York: Penguin Books, 1995.

Lawson, Steven F. *Civil Rights Crossroads: Nation, Community, and the Black Freedom Struggle*. Lexington, Ky.: University Press of Kentucky, 2003.

Lewis, Myra with Murray Silver, *Great Balls of Fire: The Uncensored Story of Jerry Lee Lewis*. New York: Penguin Books, 1982.

Mammarella, Tony. *Bandstand Off My Back* (unpublished)

Marsh, Dave and James Bernard. *The New Book of Rock Lists*. New York: Fireside, 1994.

Martin, Linda and Kerry Segrave. *Anti-Rock: The Opposition to Rock 'n' Roll*. Hamden, Conn.: Archon Books, 1988.

Miller, Douglas T. and Marion Novak. *The Fifties: The Way We Really Were*. New York: Doubleday, 1977.

Nite, Norm N. *Rock On: The Illustrated Encyclopedia of Rock n' Roll*. New York: Thomas Y. Crowell Co., 1974.

Hugent, Stephen and Charlie Gillett (editors). *Rock Almanac*. New York: Anchor Books, 1978.

Oakley, J. Ronald. *God's Country: America in the Fifties*. New York: Dembner Books, 1986.

Phelps, Dee Dee. *Vinyl Highway*. Los Angeles: Altergate Publishing, 2007.

Picardie, Justine and Dorothy Wade. *Music Man*. New York: W.W. Norton & Co., Inc. 1990.

Pollock, Bruce. *When Rock Was Young*. New York: Holt, Rinehart and Winston, 1981.

Ray, William B. *FCC: The Ups and Downs of Radio-TV Regulation*. Ames, Iowa: Iowa State University Press, 1990.

Reisfeld, Randi and Danny Fields. *Who's Your Fave Rave?* New York: Boulevard Books, 1997.

Roberts, John W. *From Hucklebuck to Hip-Hop: Social Dance In The African American Community in Philadelphia*. Philadelphia: Odunde, Inc., 1995.

Rosin, James. *Philly Pop, Rock, Rhythm & Blues*, Philadelphia: The Autumn Road Company, 2013.

Sagolla, Lisa Jo. *Rock 'n' Roll Dances of the 1950s*. Santa Barbara, California: Greenwood, an imprint of ABC-CLIO, LLC, 2011.

Sann, Paul. *Fads, Follies, and Delusions of the American People*. New York: Crown Publishers, Inc., 1967.

Shaw, Arnold. *The Rockin' 50s*. New York: Hawthorn Books, Inc., 1974.

Shore, Michael with Dick Clark. *The History of American Bandstand*. New York: Ballantine Books, 1985.

Sklar, Rick. *Rocking America: How the All-Hit Radio Stations Took Over*. St. Martin's Press: New York, 1984.

Smith, Carlton. *Reckless: Millionaire Record Producer Phil Spector and the Violent Death of Lana Clarkson*. New York: St. Martin's Press, 2004.

Smith, Joe. Edited by Mitchell Fink. *Off the Record: An Oral History of Popular Music*. New York: Warner Books, Inc., 1988.

Smith, Ronald L. *Johnny Carson: An Unauthorized Biography*. New York: St. Martin's Press, 1987.

Smith, Wes. *The Pied Pipers of Rock 'n' Roll*. Marietta, Ga.: Longstreet Press, Inc., 1989.

Stein, Marc. City of Sisterly and Brotherly Loves. Philadelphia: Temple University Press, 2004

Sterling, Christopher H. (editor). *The Concise Encyclopedia of American Radio*. New York: Routledge, 2010.

Sutherland, Jon. T*he Bunny Hop: The Harvey Sheldon Story and the Bandstand Years*. Bloomington, Ind.: AuthorHouse, 2006.

BIBLIOGRAPHY

Szatmary, David. *Rockin' in Time: A Social History of Rock and Roll.* Englewood Cliffs, N.J.: Prentice-Hall, Inc., 1987.
Tobler, John. *This Day in Rock.* New York: Carroll & Graf Publishers, Inc.: 1993.
Tosches, Nick. *Hellfire: The Jerry Lee Lewis Story.* New York: Delacorte Press, 1982.
Walley, David G. *The Ernie Kovacs Phile. New York:* Bolder Books, 1975.
Ward, Brian. *Just My Soul Responding: Rhythm and Blues, Black Consciousness and Race Relations.* London: University College London Press, 1998.
Ward, Ed, Geoffrey Stokes and Ken Tucker. *Rock of Ages: The Rolling Stone History of Rock & Roll.* New York: Summit Books, 1986.
Warner, Jay. *American Singing Groups.* New York: Billboard Books, 1992.
Whitcomb, Ian. *After the Ball: Pop Music from Rag to Rock.* New York: Simon and Schuster, 1972.
Zak, Albin J. III. *I Don't Sound Like Nobody: Remaking Music in 1950s America.* Ann Arbor, Mic.: University of Michigan Press, 2010.
———. *Dick Clark Annual Yearbook.* 1958.
———. *Philadelphia: A Photographic Celebration,* China: Running Press, 2000.
———. *Radio & Television yearbook (1957)*
———. *TV Guide Roundup.* New York: Popular Library, 1961.

FILMS
Airplay: The Rise and Fall of Rock Radio, TOPICS Entertainment Inc., 2012.
Archive of American Television, Dick Clark interview, July 29,1999
Bandstand Days, documentary, Teleduction, 1997.
The Twist, A film by Ron Mann, 1992.
The Wage$ of Spin, Character Driven Productions, 2008.
Wildwood Days, Travisty Productions, 2004.

INTERVIEWS BY AUTHOR
Duane Adler, February 27, 2015
Bruce Aydelotte, June 3, 1999
Mary Ann (Colella) Baker, April 10, 2003, and April 22, 2003
Pamela Beasley, March 26, 2002
Walter Beaulieu, April 14, 2000
Stan Blitz, March 4, 1999
Dorothy (Bradley) Boring, April 23, 2003
Frank Brancaccio, December 9, 2015
Pamela (Brinker) Lester, December 11, 2015
Marvin Brooks, February 11, 2000
John Butterworth, April 29, 2002
John Carlton, March 2, 2000
Peter DeFeo, November 10, 2015
Ralph DiCocco, April 18, 2000
Earle Drake, February 10, 2000
Eleanor Faragalli, April 2, 2002

Jack Fisher, April 16, 2002
Rick Fisher, June 23, 2002
Tom Foley, April 29, 2002
Charlie Gracie, April 15, 2002
Shelly Gross, March 5, 2002
Charlie Heffernan, June 27, 1999
Matt Helreich, April 15, 2002
Ed Hurst, May 9, 2002
Ron Joseph, January 21, 2015
Al Kelly, June 7, 1999
Ed Kelly, June 23, 2017
George Koehler. April 1, 2002
Hank Latven, April 1, 2002
Marshall Lytle, April 20, 2002
Stan Marks, June 22, 2002
Robert Nash, April 19, 2003
Ray Otto, June 23, 2002
Marie K. Pantarelli, March 11, 2002
Sol Rabinowitz, March 26, 2002
Bill Russell, April 10, 2000, and April 18, 2000
Kathryn Sacchetti, November 20, 2015
Max E. Solomon, March 12, 2002
Allen Stone, March 18, 2002
Bob Tharp, March 25, 2003
Les Waas, April 2, 2002
Bill Webber, April 24, 2001
Marge Weiting, March 14, 2002
Barbara Marcen Wilston, Sept. 29, 1999
Ed Yates, March 25, 2001

MAGAZINES
Architectural Record
Billboard
DISCoveries
Dig
Goldmine
Life
Look
Modern Screen
Modern Teen, Publishers of Dig.
Movieland and TV Time
Music Business
Newsweek
Philadelphia Magazine
Rock
Rolling Stone
Saturday Evening Post
Sh-Boom
16, The Girl Friend-The Boy Friend Corp., New York, N.Y.

BIBLIOGRAPHY

Teen, 'Teen Publications, Hollywood, Calif.
Teen Magazine Presents My Bandstand Buddies, 1959.
Teen World, Reese Publishing Co., Inc., New York, N.Y.
Television Magazine
This Week
Time
TV & Radio Mirror
TV Guide
Vanity Fair

NEWSPAPERS
Albany Herald
The Associated Press
Chicago Tribune
Des Moines Register
Knight-Ridder News Service
Los Angeles Daily News
Main Line Today
New York Herald Tribune
New York Journal-American
New York Post
New York Times
The Panama American
Philadelphia Evening Bulletin
Philadelphia City Paper
Philadelphia Daily News
Philadelphia Inquirer
San Mateo Times
The Sandpiper
South Philly Review
United Press
Variety
West New York Reporter
Winnipeg Free Press

TELEVISION
Black Philadelphia Memories, documentary, WHYY-TV, Philadelphia, 1999.
The Late Show With David Letterman, 1990
Up Close with Patsy Smullin, California Oregon Broadcasting Inc., 2001
More Things That Aren't There Anymore, documentary, WHYY-TV, Philadelphia, 1994.
South Philly: Italian Style, documentary, WHYY-TV, Philadelphia, 1997.

MISCELLANEOUS
Assassination Research, "The JFK Assassination Chronology," compiled by Ira David Wood III
Charles Amann Blog, "The Princes and Princesses of Dance"
CQ Press, a publication of the Congressional Quarterly

FBI documents, Dick Clark death threat, Sept. 18, 1962
Freberg Music Corp. (ASCAP), 1959
Plaque on *Bandstand* set
Pulse of New York survey, Dr. Sydney Rostow, 1944
TotalTheater.com, "The Real Hairspray Story," By Steve Cohen, December 2002.
U.S. Government Printing Office, 1960.

Plus, people who shared stories and information through casual conversations or via email or other means: Marsha Bryan Bittle, Steven M. Bob of The Enterprise Center, Marian Driscoll, Davey Frees, Bunny Gibson, Rob Graham, Paul W. Herrmannsfeldt of Architectural Record, Peter Horn, Myrna Horowitz, Pam Mammarella, Jimmy Mullen, Pearl Polto, Norm Spilleth, Shawn Swrods, Joe Terry, Bobby Vee and Linda Zimmerman.

ABOUT THE AUTHOR

Larry Lehmer was a newspaper reporter and editor for 40 years, including 24 years at the *Des Moines Register*. During his time as a senior editor at *The Register*, the paper was named one of the country's top 10 newspapers by *Time* magazine.

During his newspaper career, Lehmer was a member of the Society of Professional Journalists and Investigative Reporters & Editors. He is a graduate of the American Press Institute in Washington, D.C., and a former member of the Association of Personal Historians.

Lehmer is also the author of *The Day the Music Died: The Last Tour of Buddy Holly, the Big Bopper and Ritchie Valens*, which was nominated for the 1997 Gleason Music Book Award. As a result of that book's success, Lehmer worked with the E! cable television network in producing an episode of its *Mysteries and Scandals* series, was a contributor to a VH1 documentary on Buddy Holly and was a featured subject on the ID-Discovery Channel's *The Will: Family Secrets Revealed* program on Ritchie Valens.

He lives in Urbandale, Iowa, with his wife, Linda.

CPSIA information can be obtained
at www.ICGtesting.com
Printed in the USA
BVHW031831070719
552807BV00001B/3/P